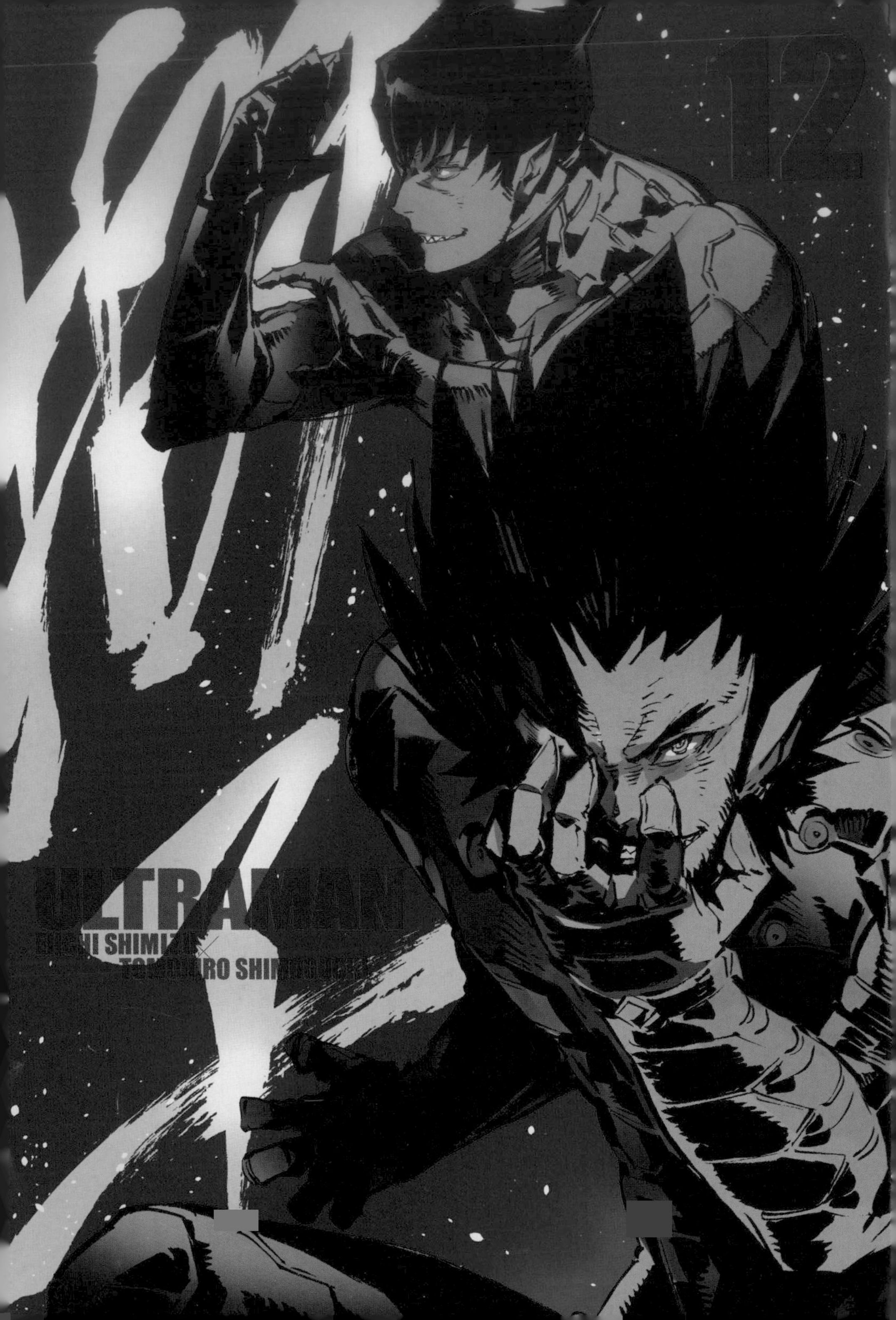
12
ULTRAMAN

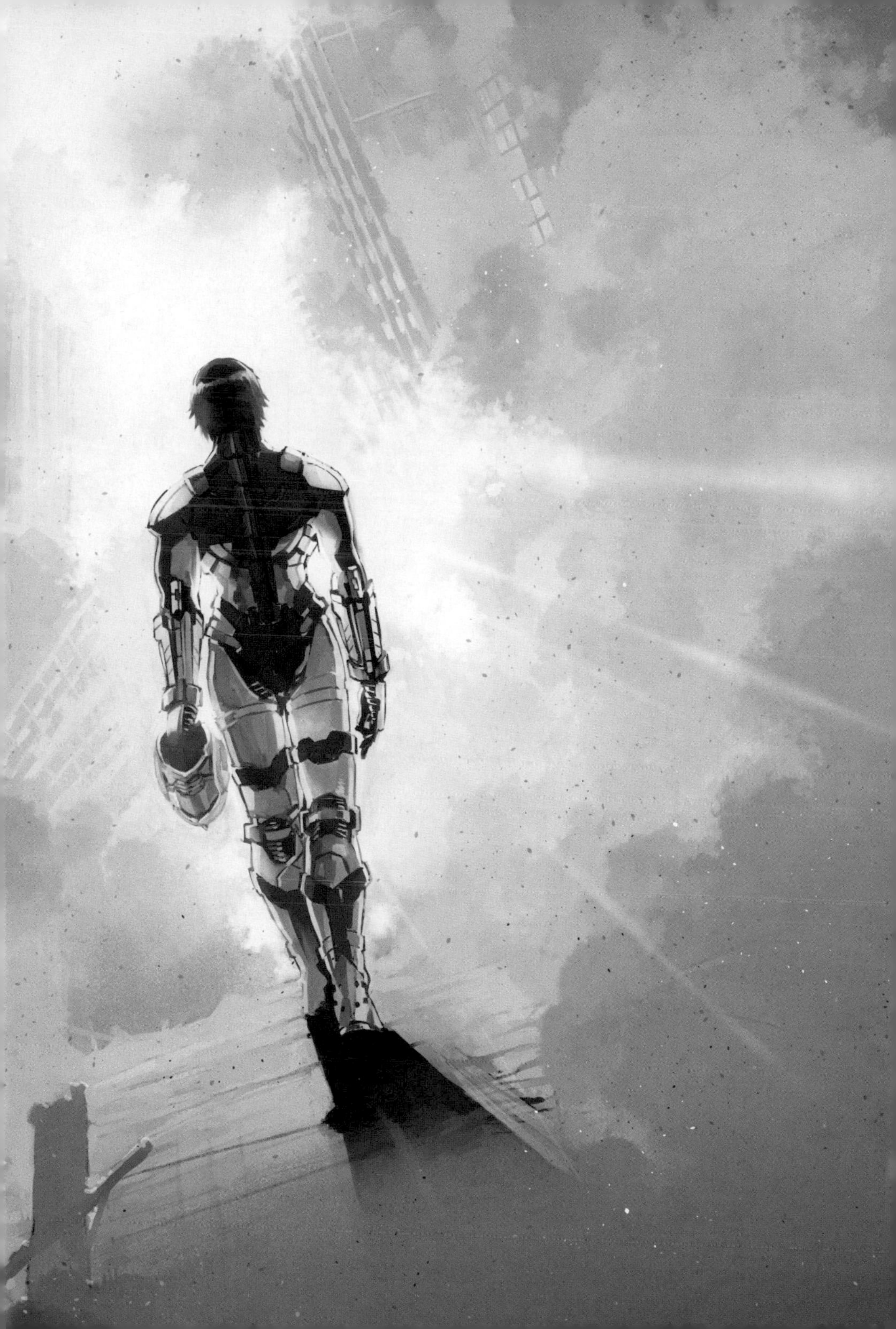

THIS IS THE BEGINNING OF A NEW AGE.

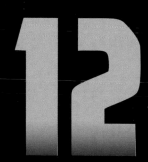

CONTENTS

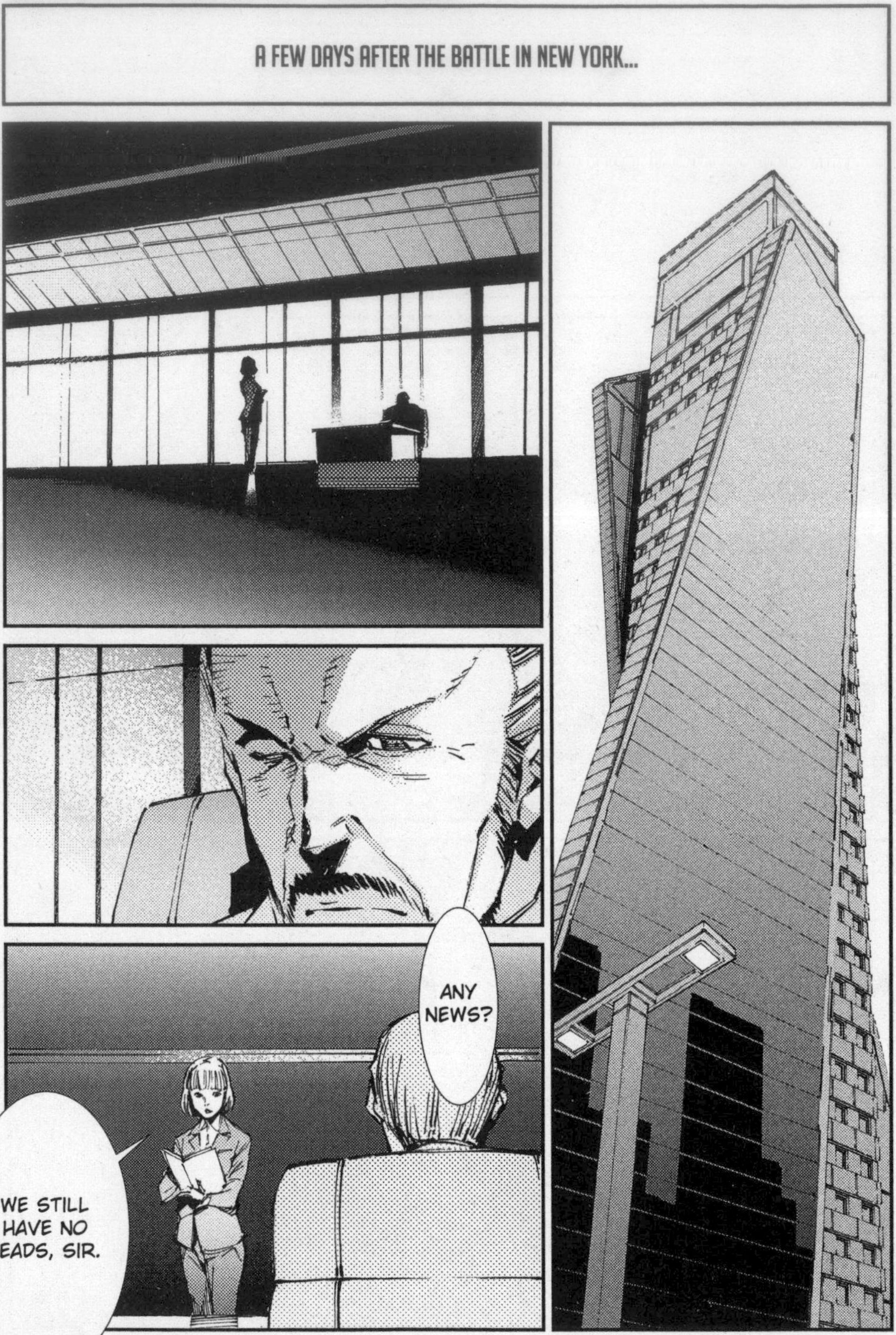
A FEW DAYS AFTER THE BATTLE IN NEW YORK...
ANY NEWS?
WE STILL HAVE NO LEADS, SIR.

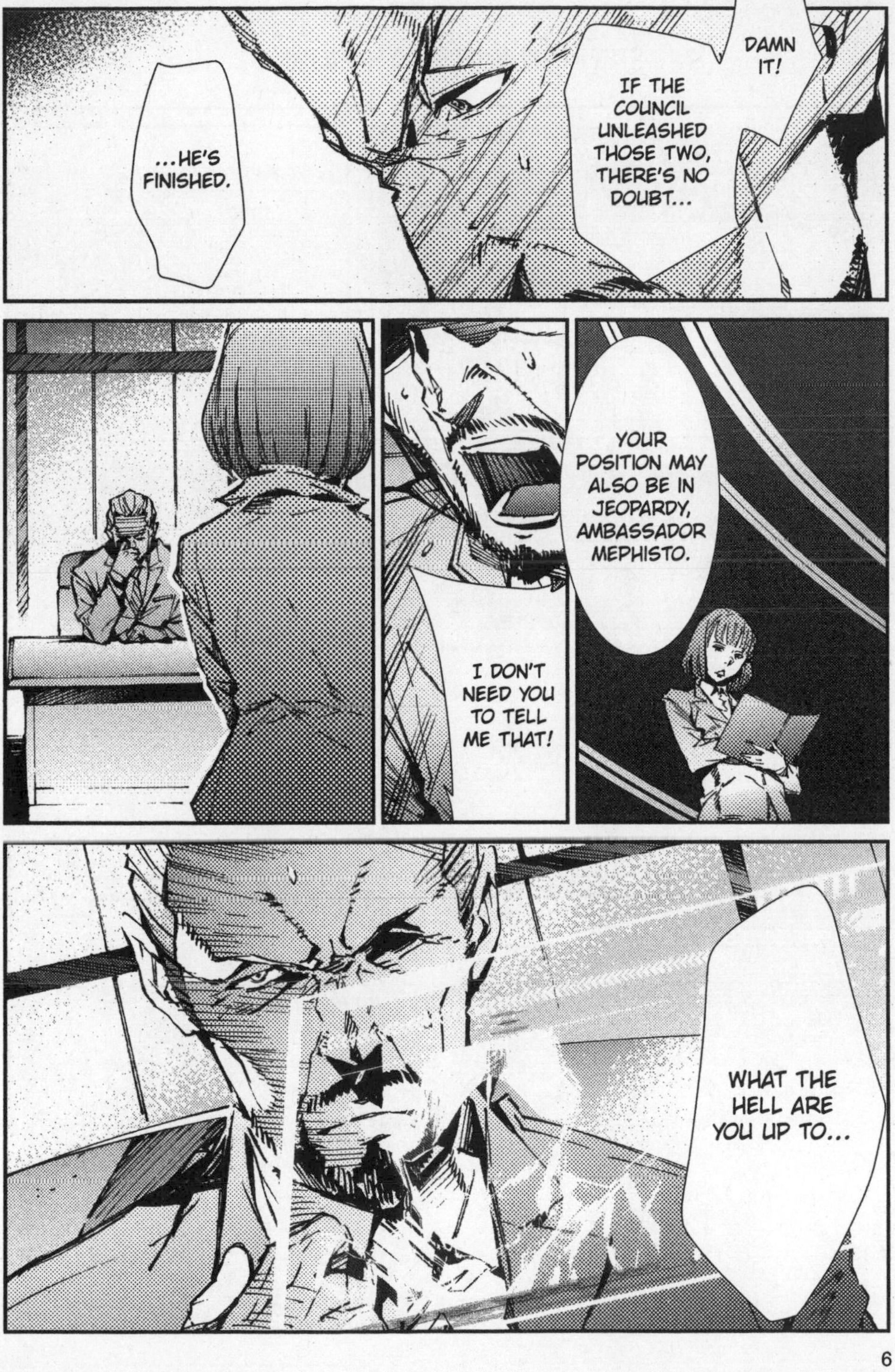
DAMN IT!
IF THE COUNCIL UNLEASHED THOSE TWO, THERE'S NO DOUBT...
...HE'S FINISHED.
YOUR POSITION MAY ALSO BE IN JEOPARDY, AMBASSADOR MEPHISTO.
I DON'T NEED YOU TO TELL ME THAT!
WHAT THE HELL ARE YOU UP TO...

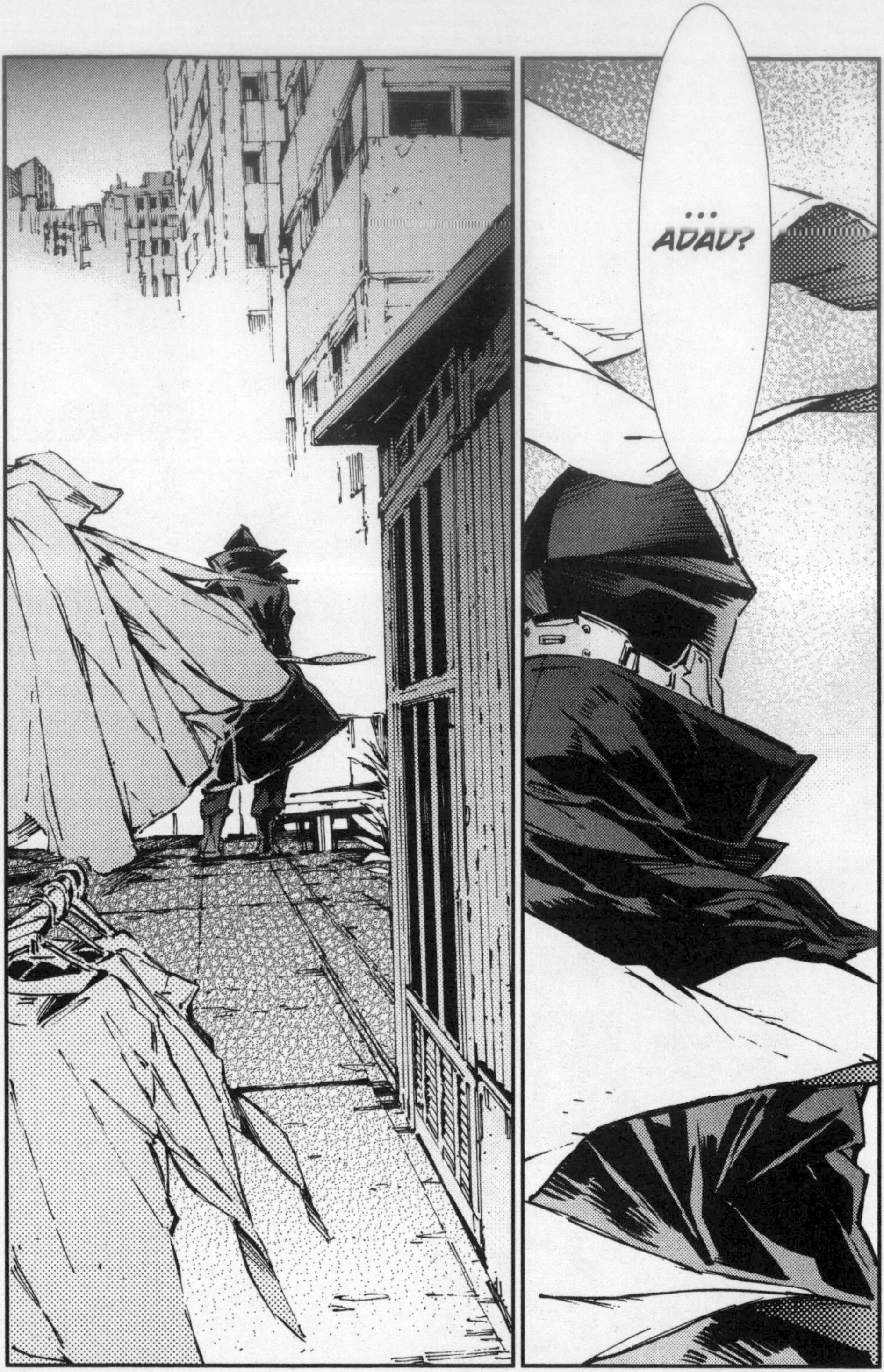
...
ADAD?

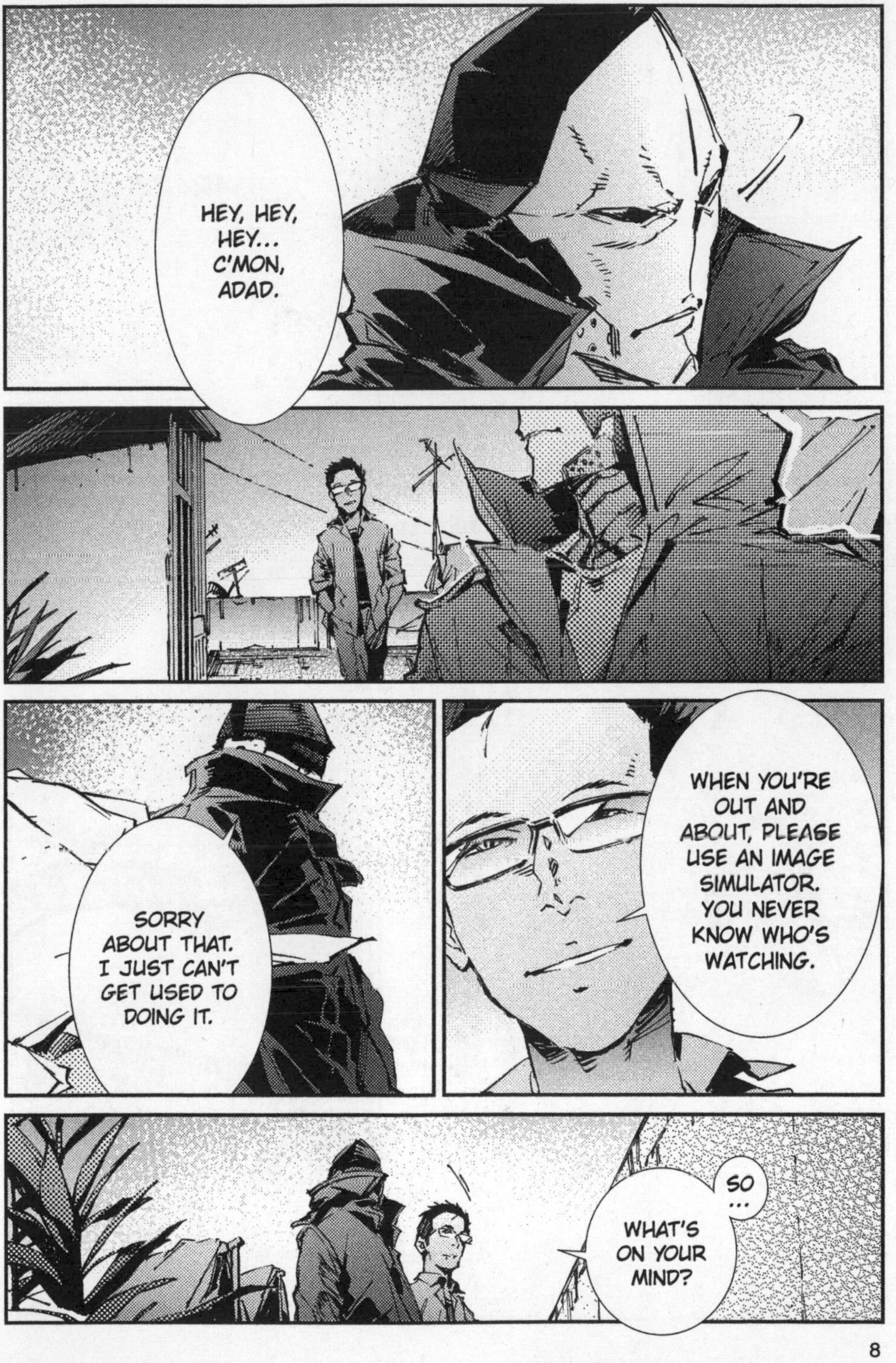
HEY, HEY, HEY... C'MON, ADAD.
WHEN YOU'RE OUT AND ABOUT, PLEASE USE AN IMAGE SIMULATOR. YOU NEVER KNOW WHO'S WATCHING.
SORRY ABOUT THAT. I JUST CAN'T GET USED TO DOING IT.
SO ...
WHAT'S ON YOUR MIND?

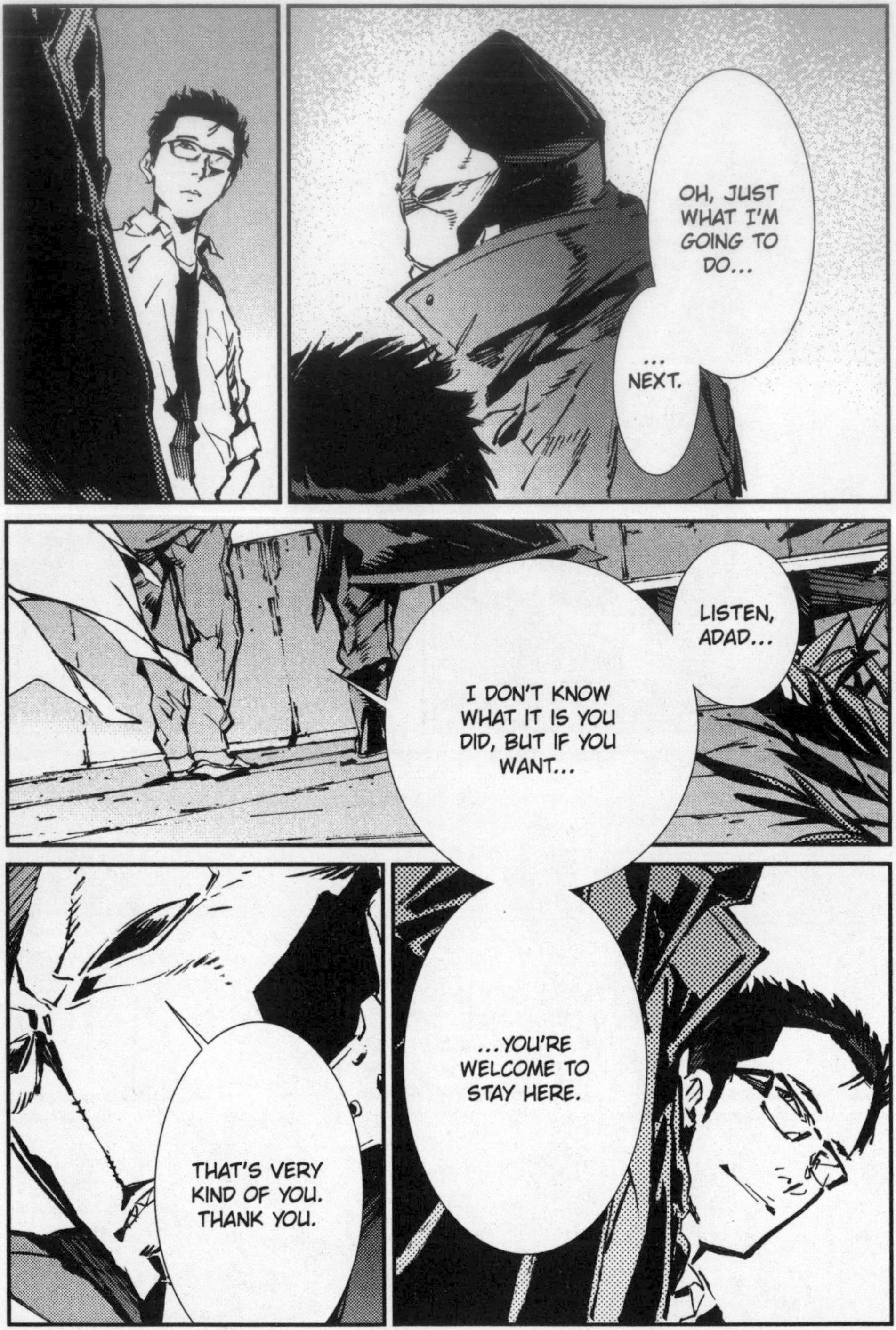
OH, JUST WHAT I'M GOING TO DO...
...NEXT.
LISTEN, ADAD...
I DON'T KNOW WHAT IT IS YOU DID, BUT IF YOU WANT...
...YOU'RE WELCOME TO STAY HERE.
THAT'S VERY KIND OF YOU. THANK YOU.

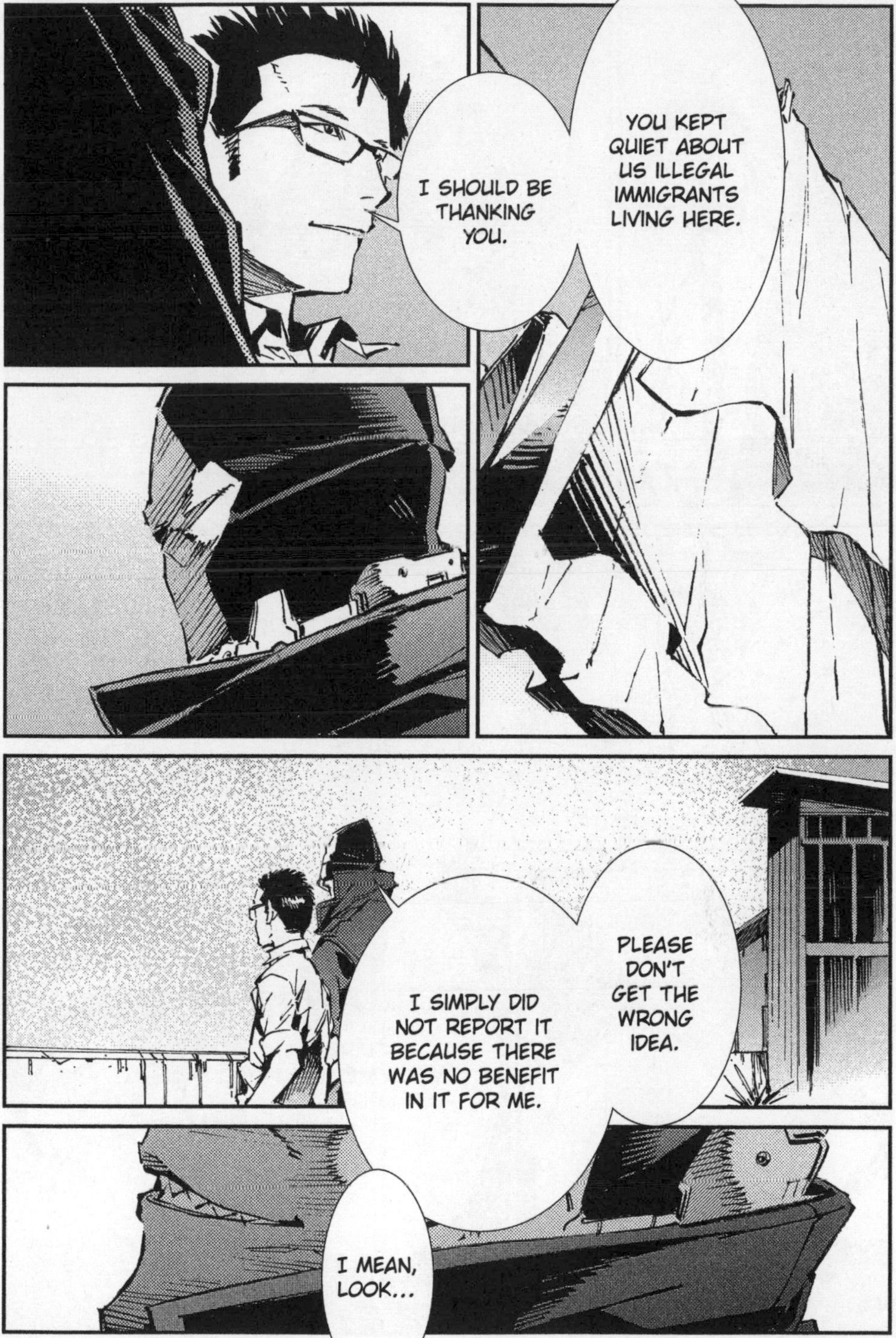
YOU KEPT QUIET ABOUT US ILLEGAL IMMIGRANTS LIVING HERE.
I SHOULD BE THANKING YOU.
PLEASE DON'T GET THE WRONG IDEA.
I SIMPLY DID NOT REPORT IT BECAUSE THERE WAS NO BENEFIT IN IT FOR ME.
I MEAN, LOOK...

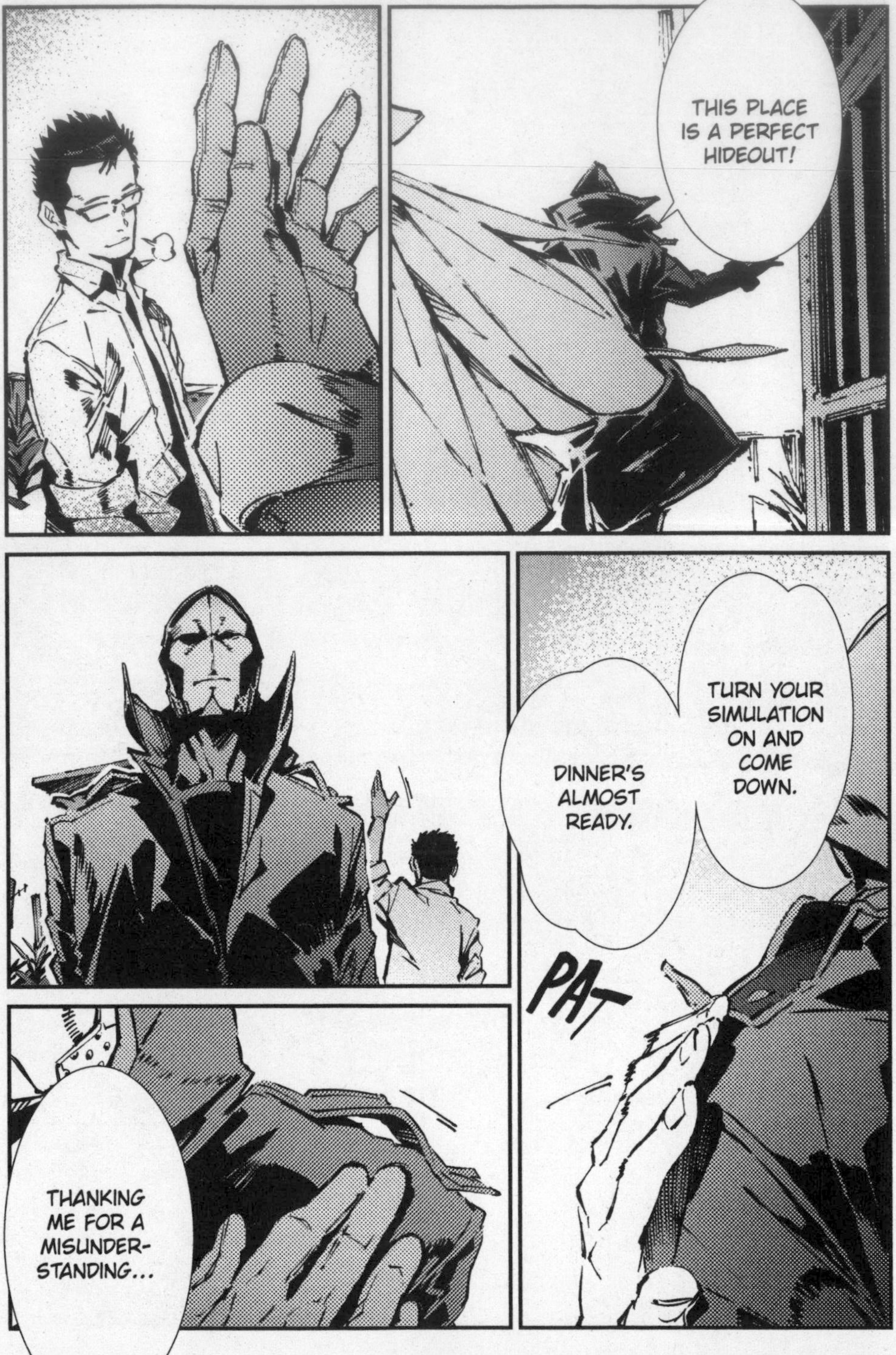
THIS PLACE IS A PERFECT HIDEOUT!
TURN YOUR SIMULATION ON AND COME DOWN.
DINNER'S ALMOST READY.
PAT
THANKING ME FOR A MISUNDER-STANDING...

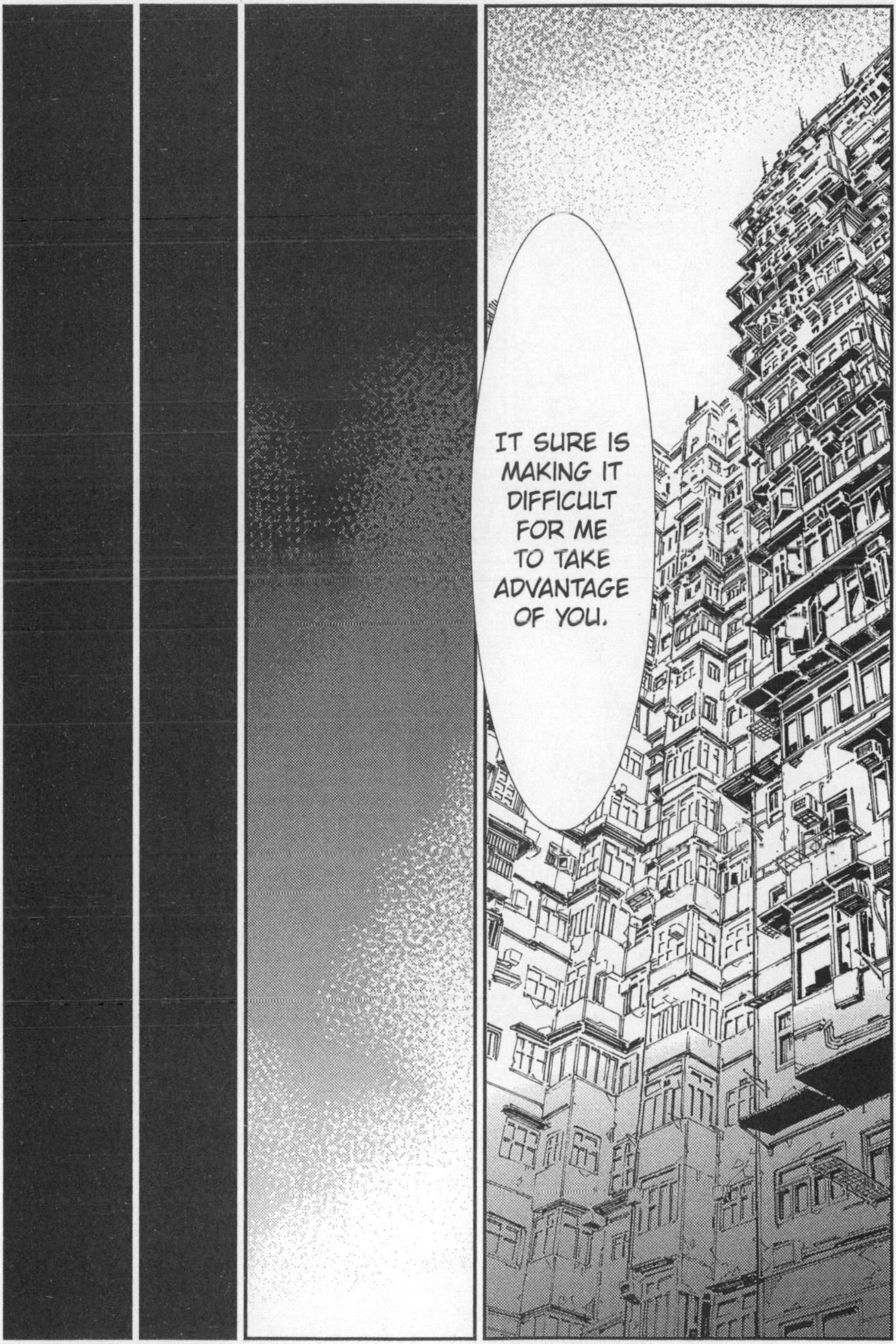
IT SURE IS MAKING IT DIFFICULT FOR ME TO TAKE ADVANTAGE OF YOU.

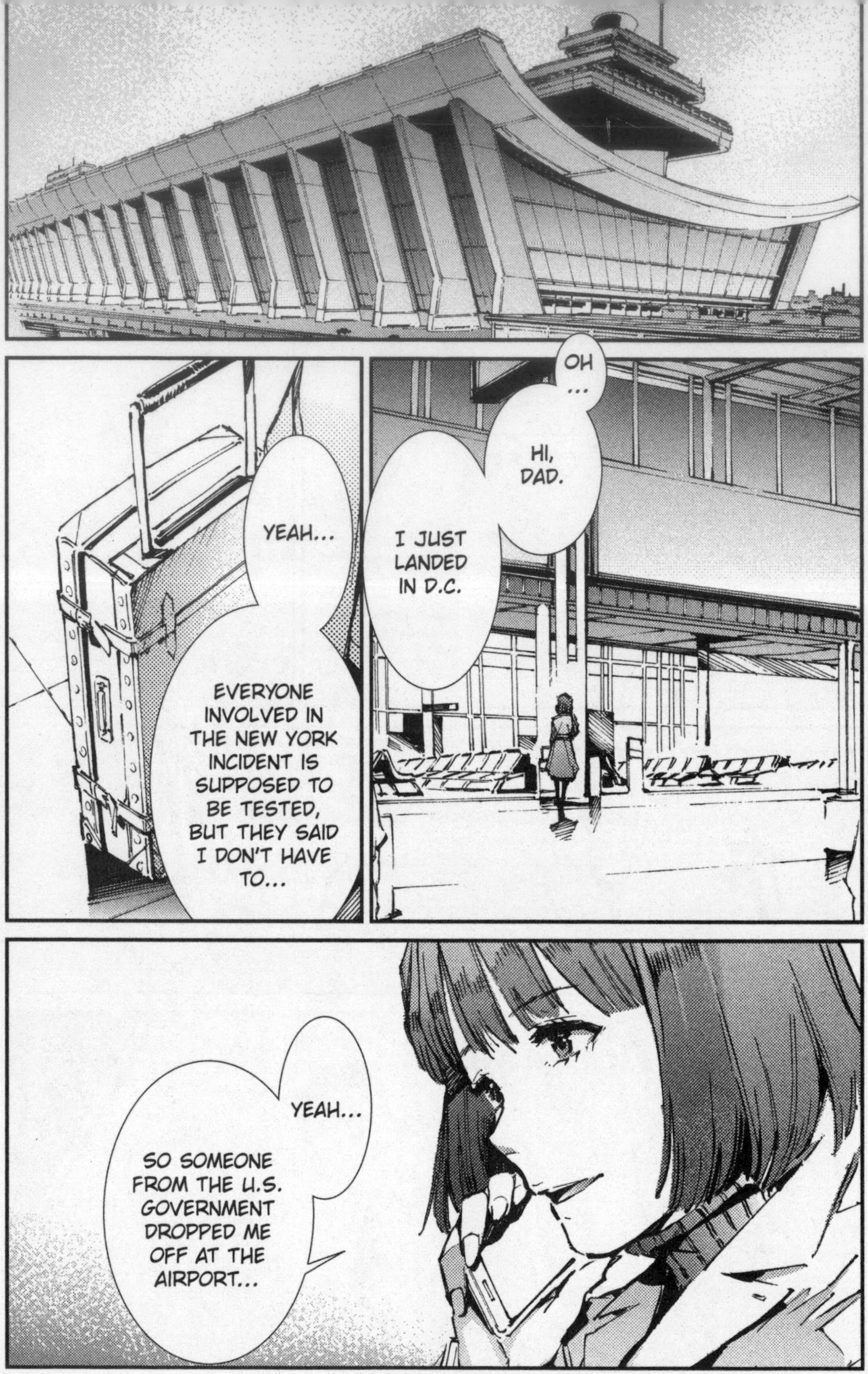
OH ...
HI, DAD.
I JUST LANDED IN D.C.
YEAH...
EVERYONE INVOLVED IN THE NEW YORK INCIDENT IS SUPPOSED TO BE TESTED, BUT THEY SAID I DON'T HAVE TO...
YEAH...
SO SOMEONE FROM THE U.S. GOVERNMENT DROPPED ME OFF AT THE AIRPORT...

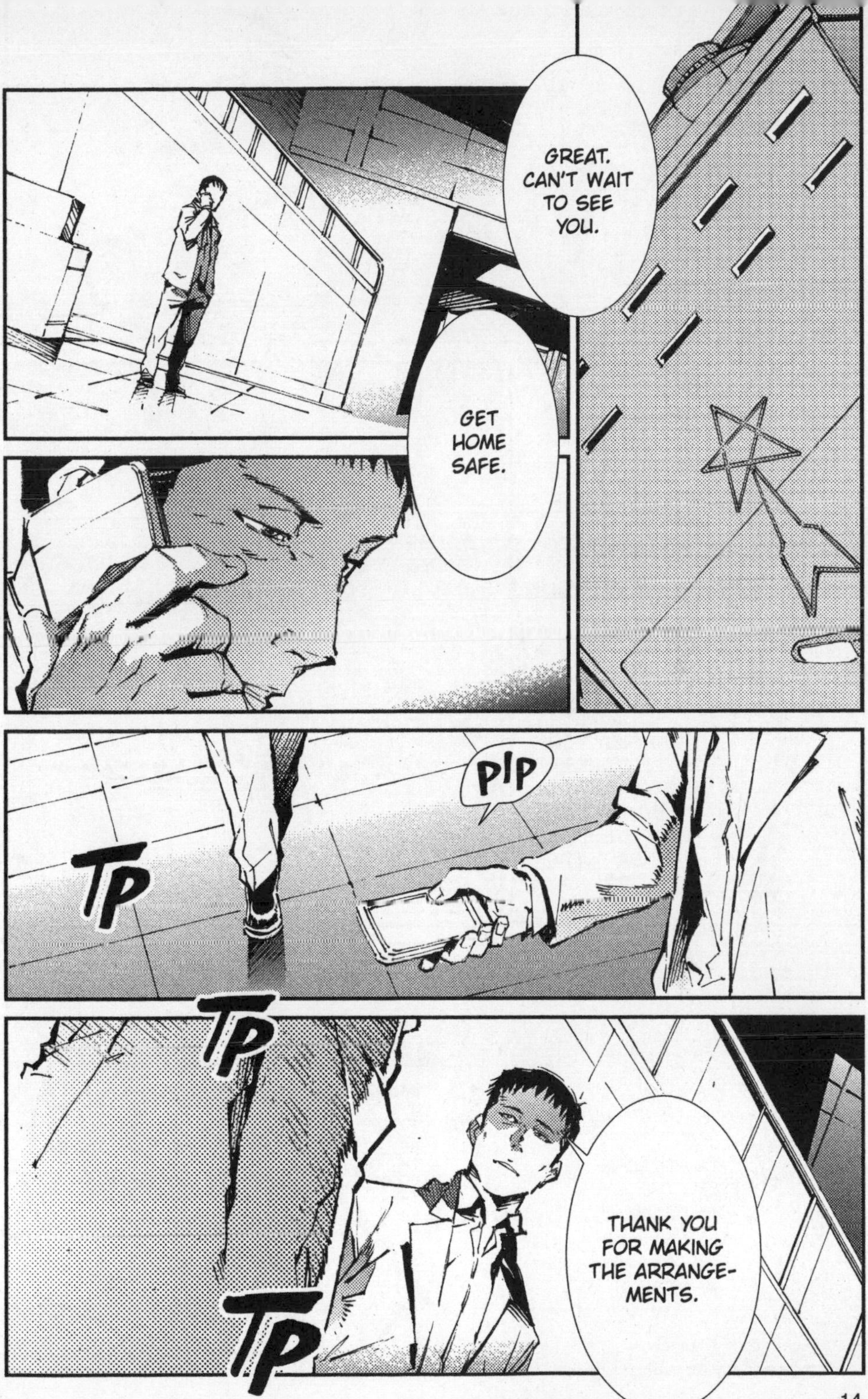
GREAT. CAN'T WAIT TO SEE YOU.
GET HOME SAFE.
PIP
TP
TP
THANK YOU FOR MAKING THE ARRANGE-MENTS.
TP

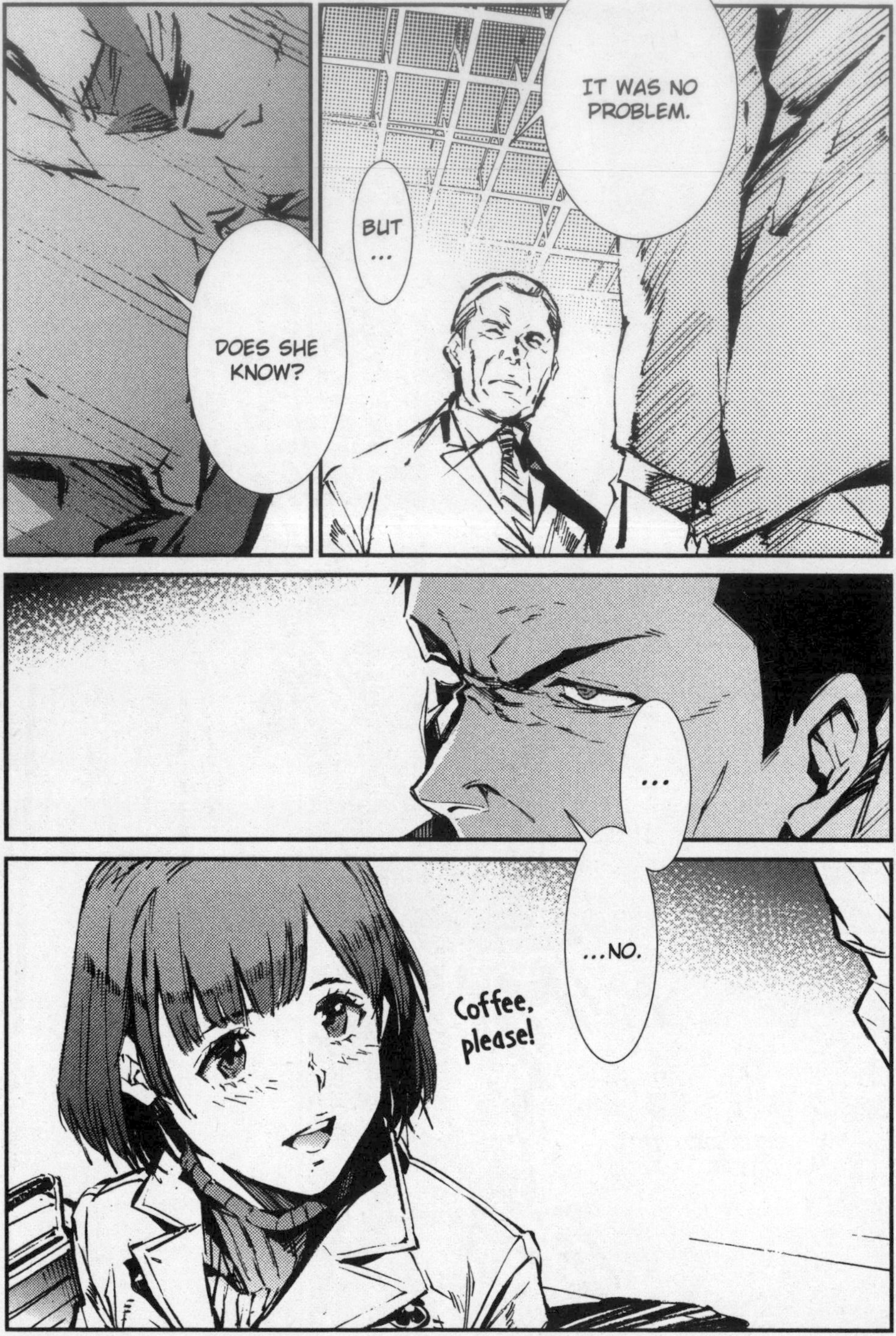
IT WAS NO PROBLEM.
BUT ...
DOES SHE KNOW?
...
...NO.
Coffee, please!

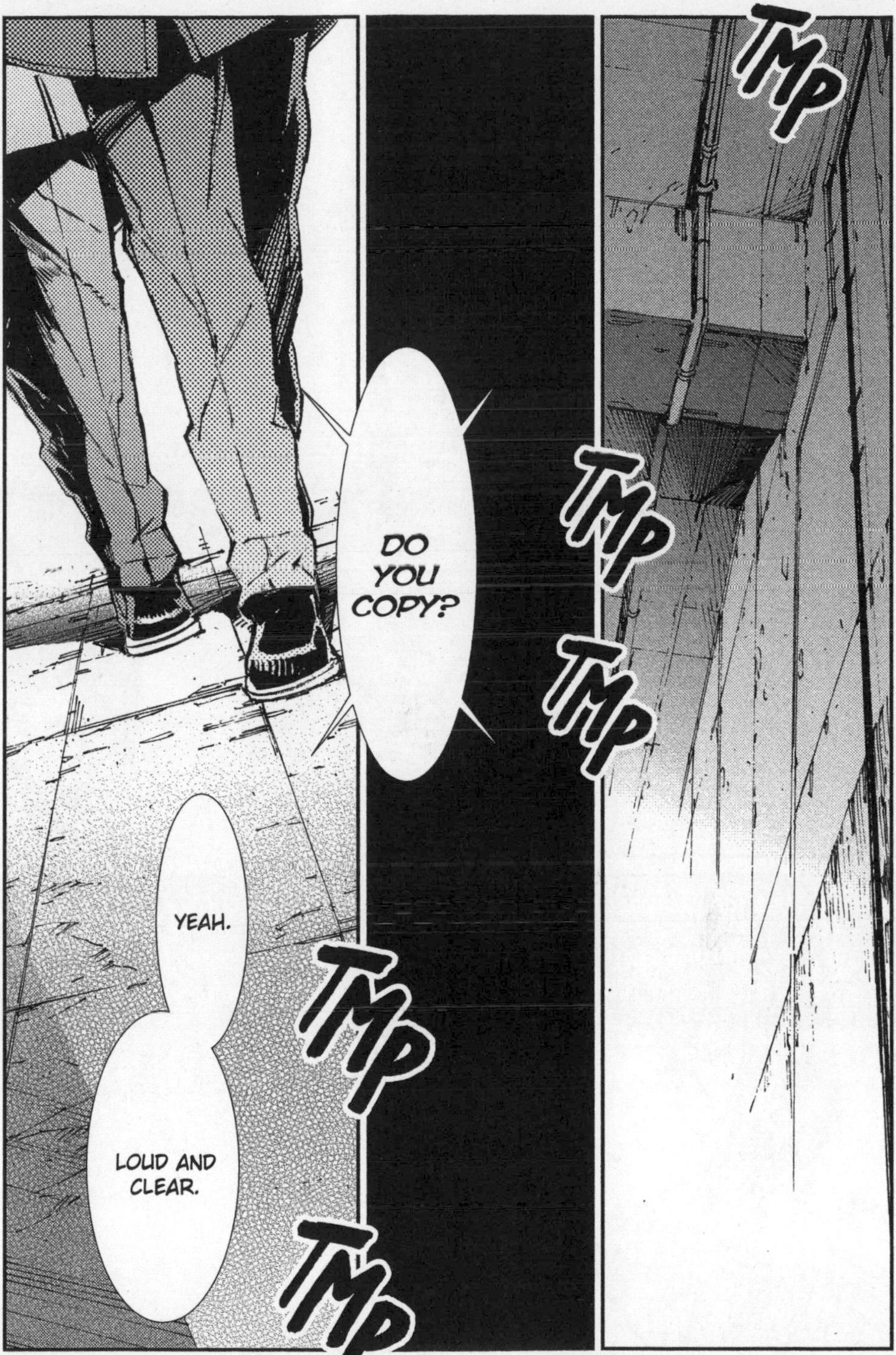
TMP
TMP
TMP
DO YOU COPY?
TMP
TMP
YEAH.
LOUD AND CLEAR.

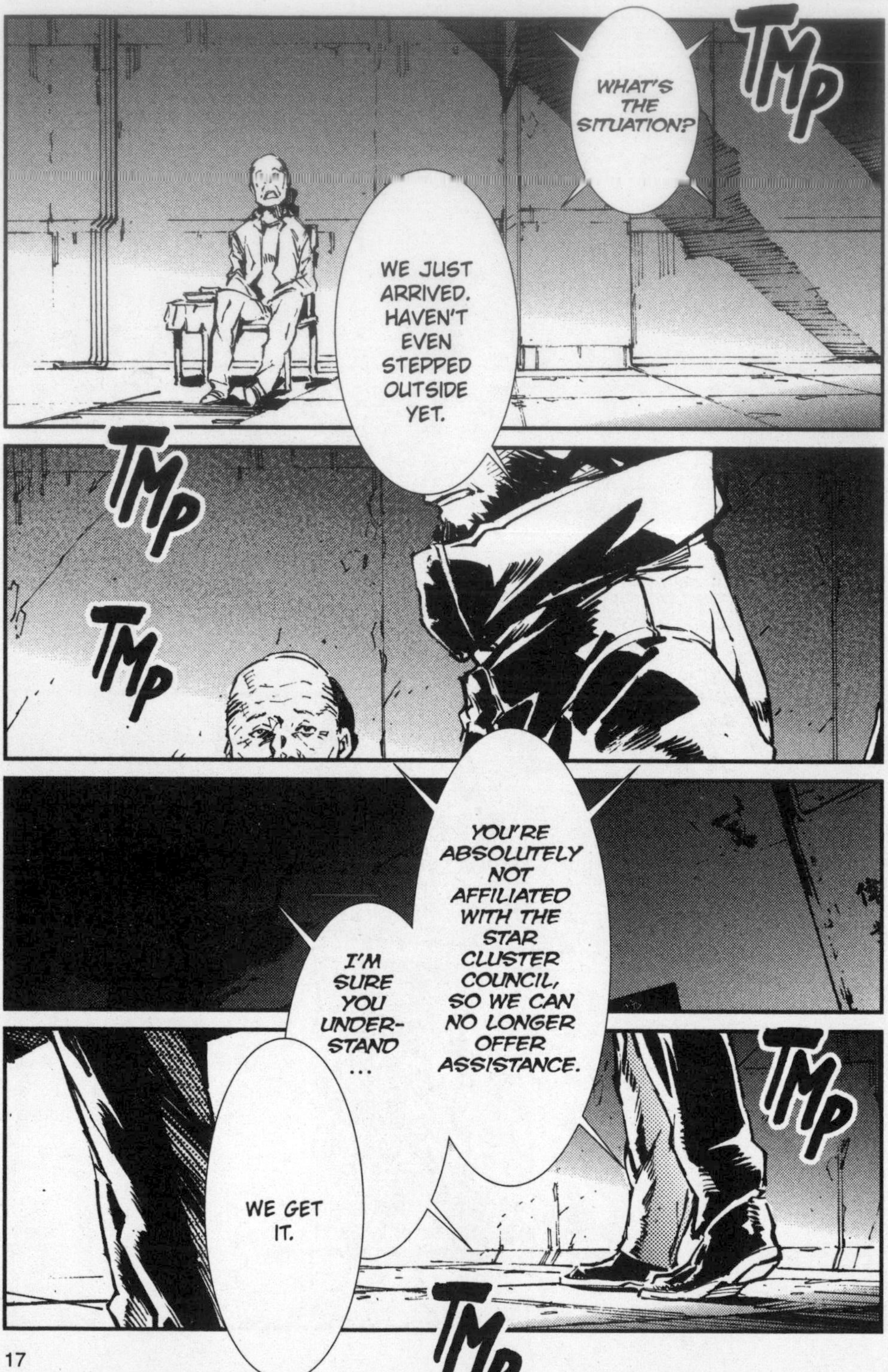
TMP
WHAT'S THE SITUATION?
WE JUST ARRIVED. HAVEN'T EVEN STEPPED OUTSIDE YET.
TMP
TMP
YOU'RE ABSOLUTELY NOT AFFILIATED WITH THE STAR CLUSTER COUNCIL, SO WE CAN NO LONGER OFFER ASSISTANCE.
I'M SURE YOU UNDER-STAND ...
TMP
WE GET IT.
TMP

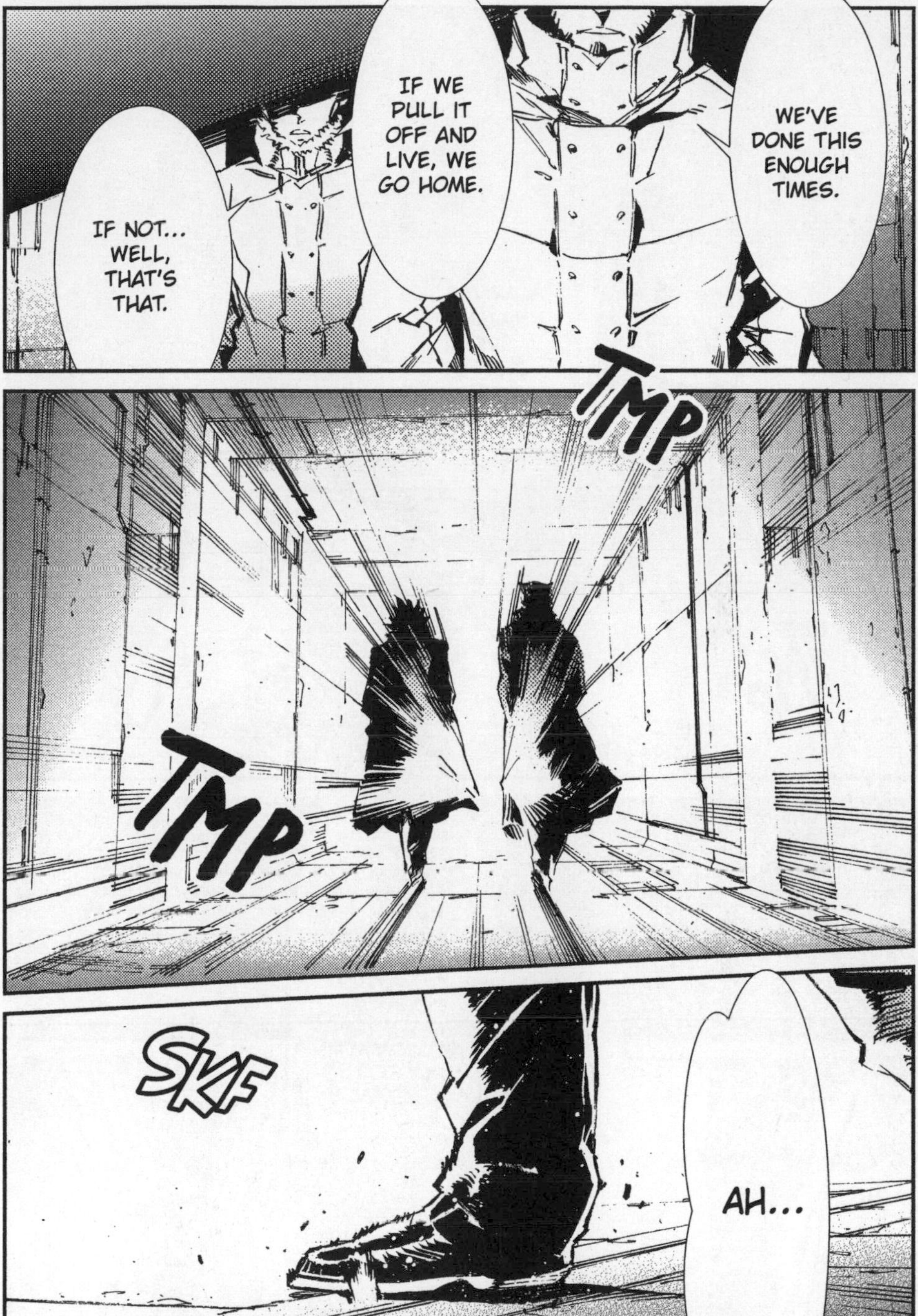

WE'VE DONE THIS ENOUGH TIMES.
IF WE PULL IT OFF AND LIVE, WE GO HOME.
IF NOT... WELL, THAT'S THAT.
TMP
TMP
AH...
SKF

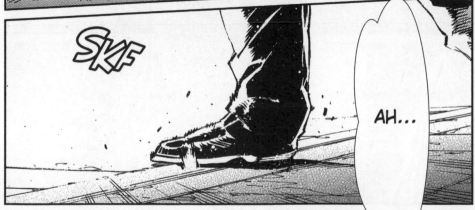

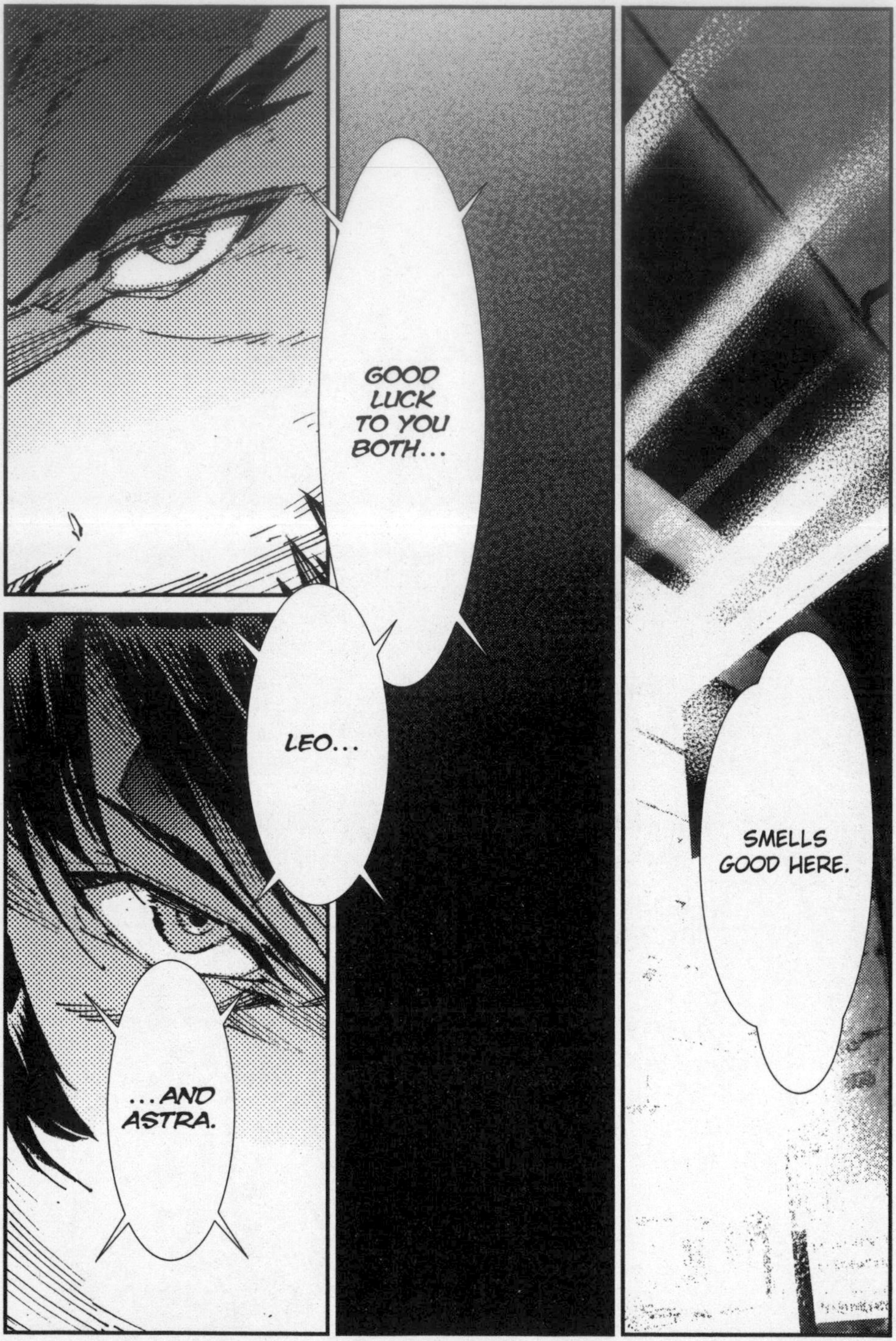
SMELLS GOOD HERE.
GOOD LUCK TO YOU BOTH...
LEO...
...AND ASTRA.

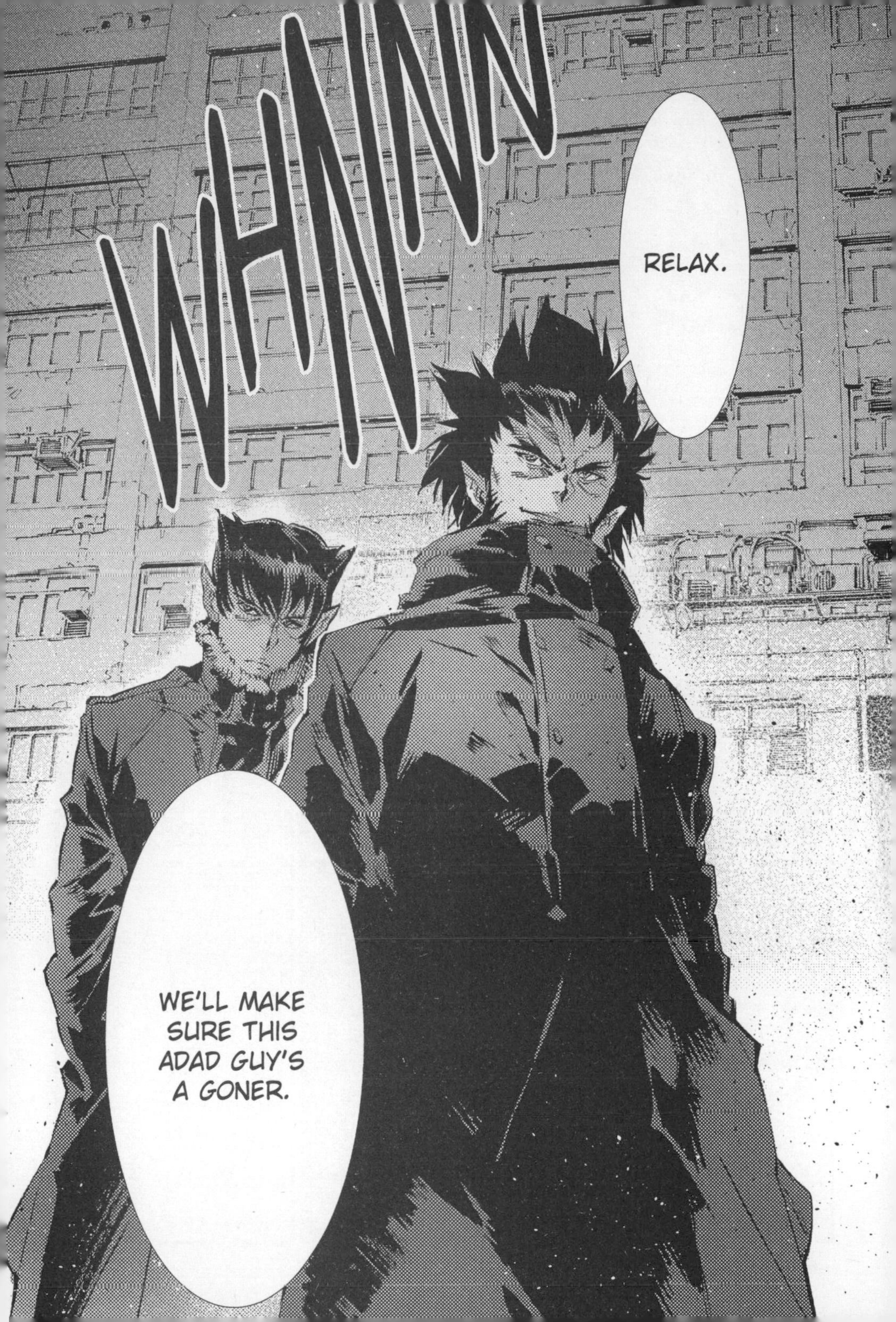
WHNNN
RELAX.
WE'LL MAKE SURE THIS ADAD GUY'S A GONER.

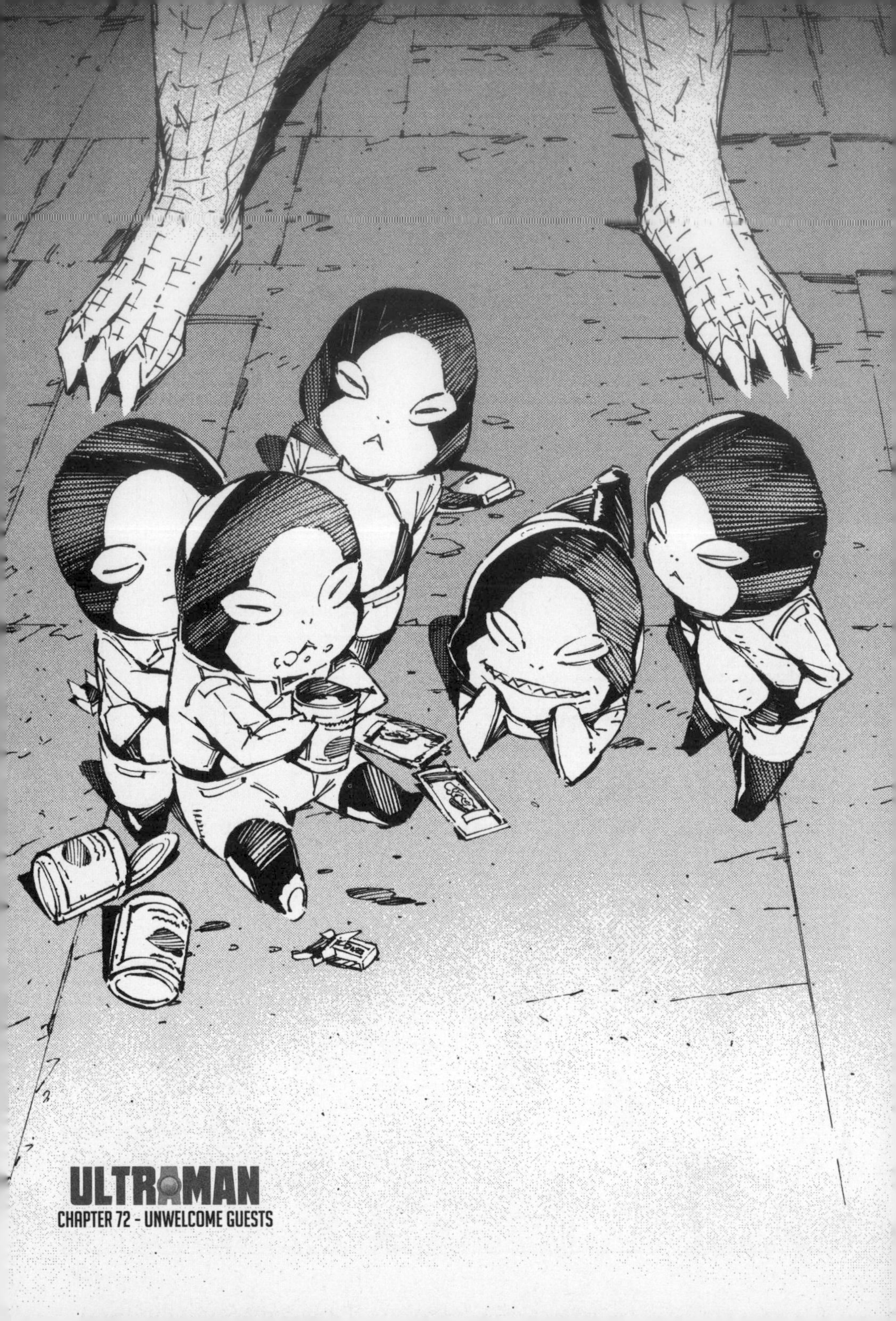

ULTRAMAN
CHAPTER 72 - UNWELCOME GUESTS

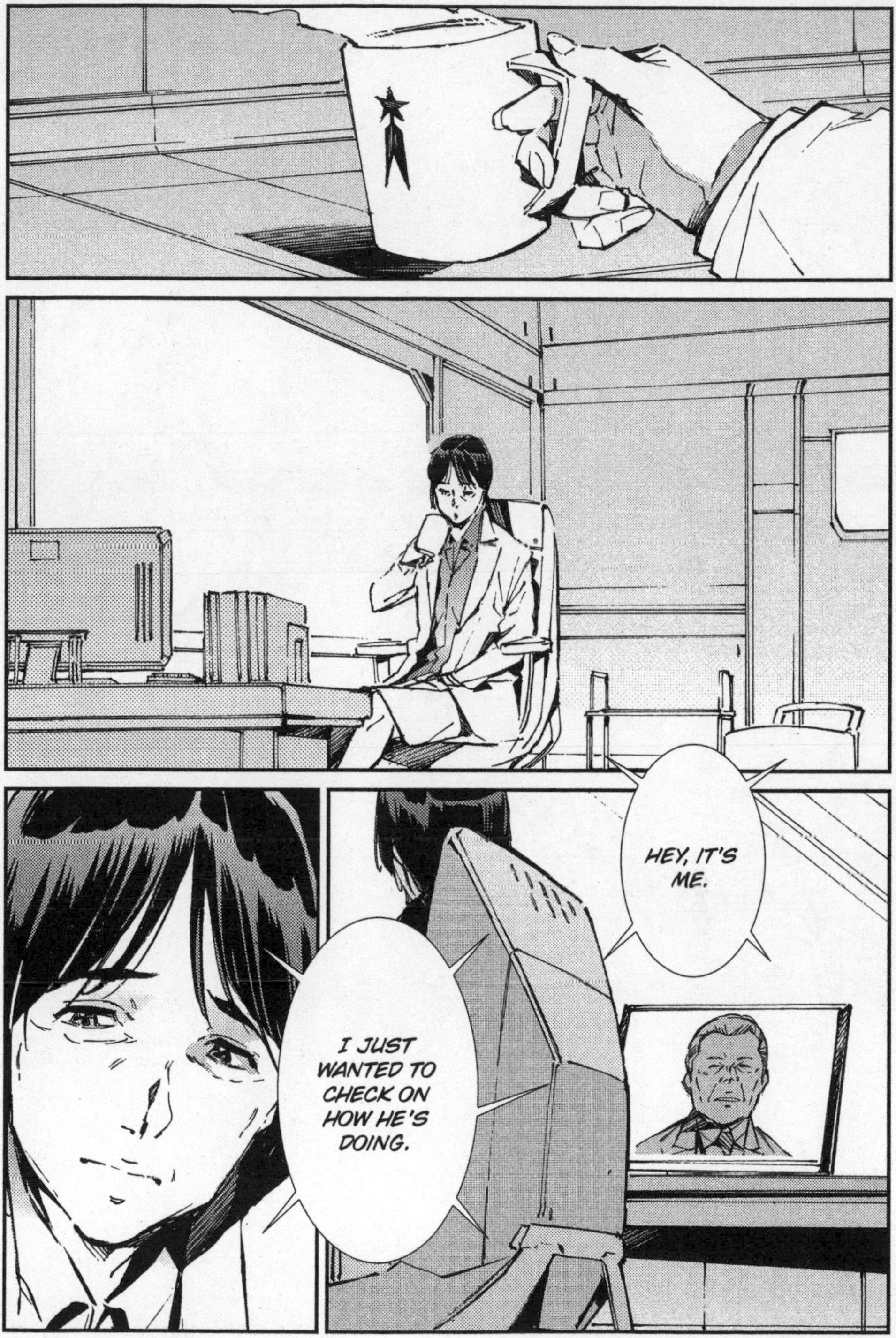
HEY, IT'S ME.
I JUST WANTED TO CHECK ON HOW HE'S DOING.

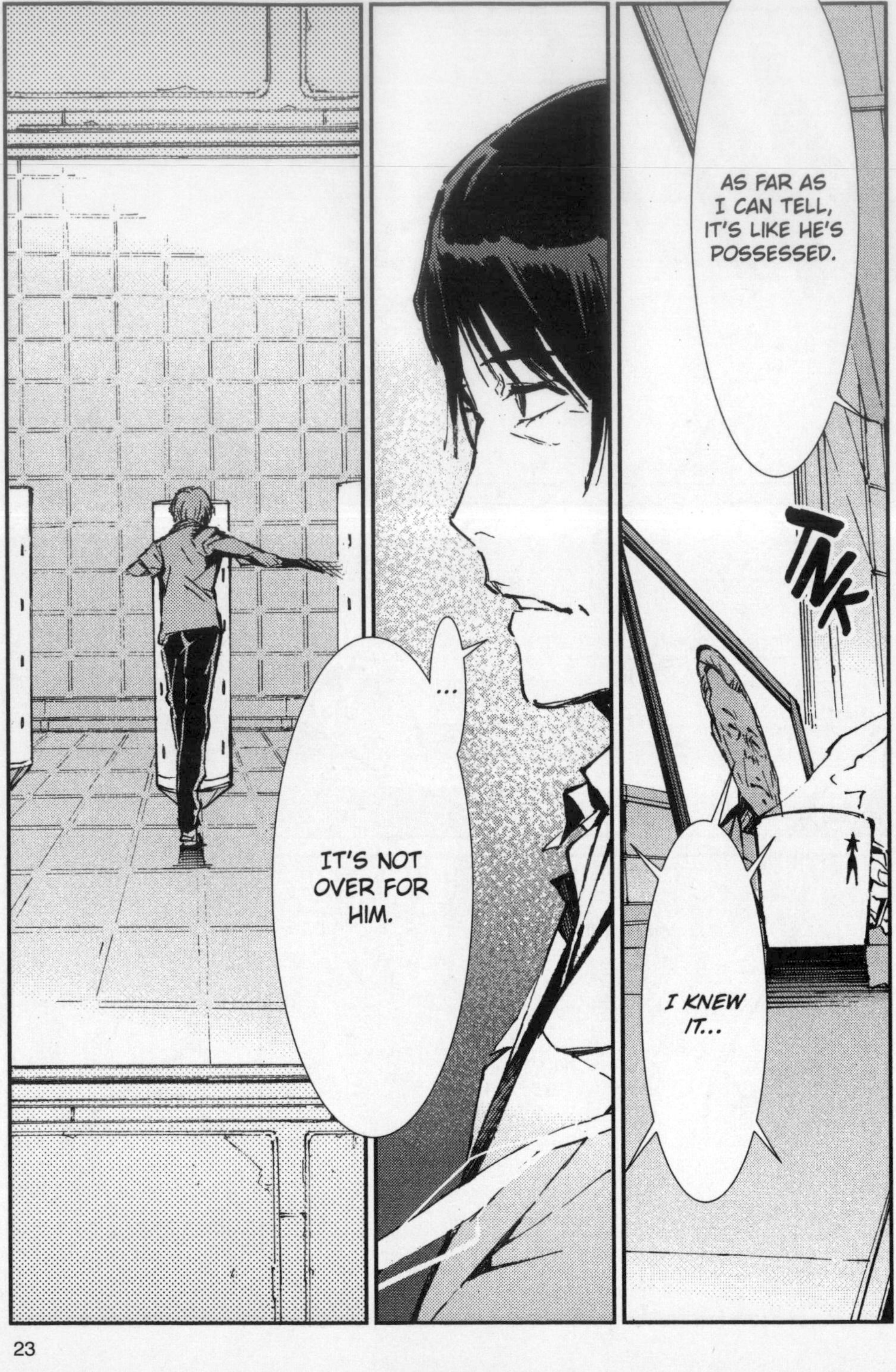
AS FAR AS I CAN TELL, IT'S LIKE HE'S POSSESSED.
TNK
I KNEW IT...
...
IT'S NOT OVER FOR HIM.

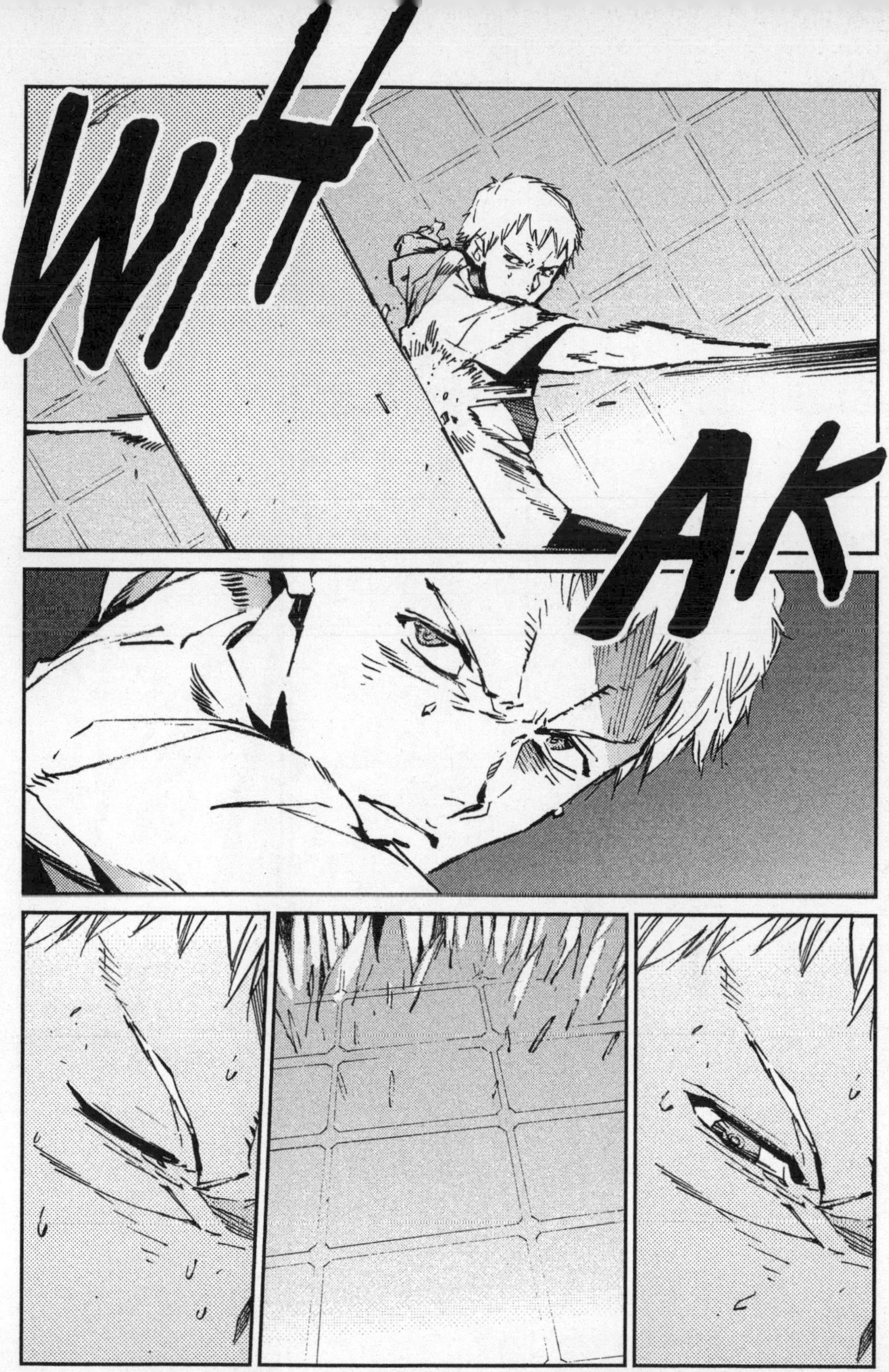
WH
AK

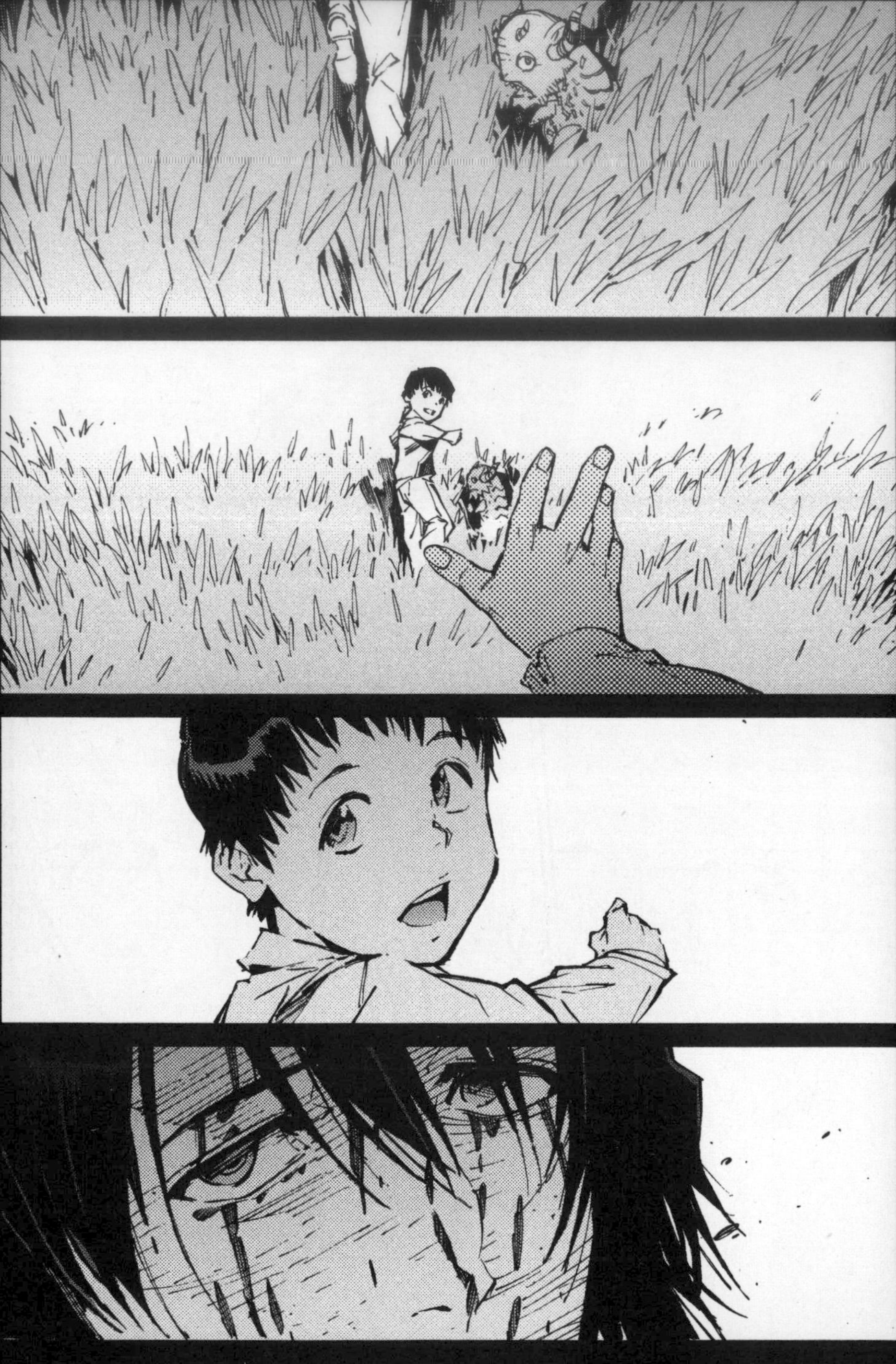

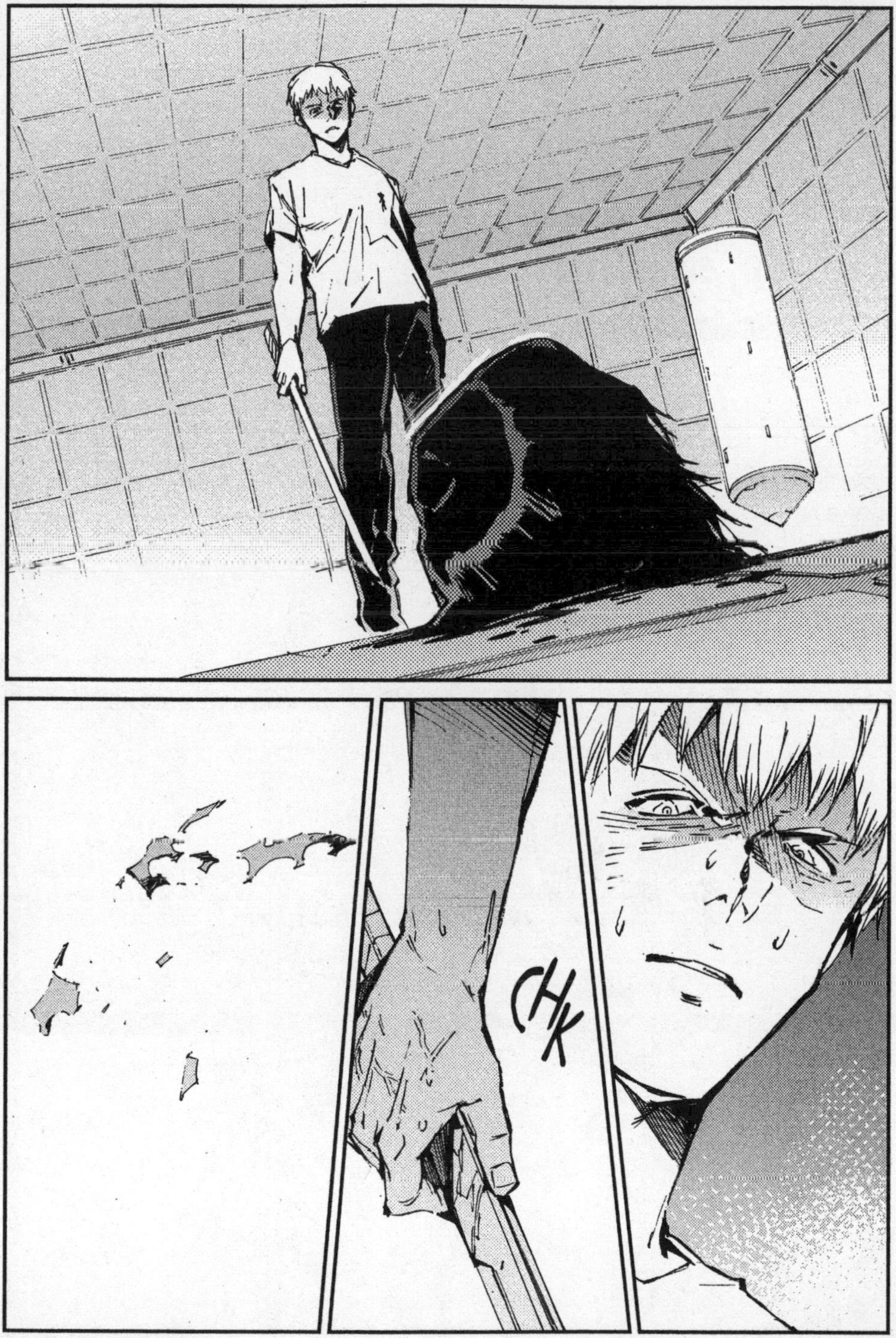
CHK

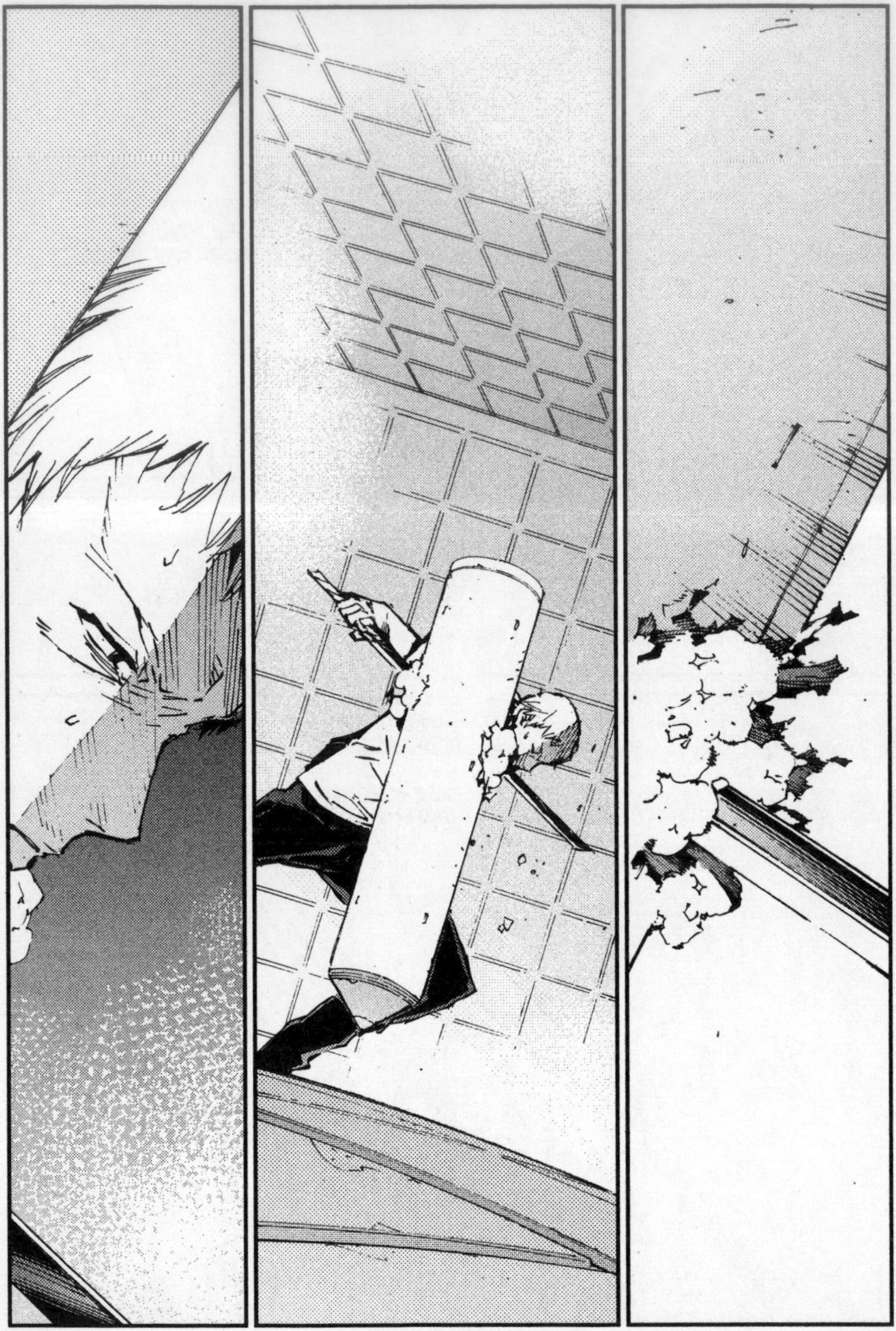

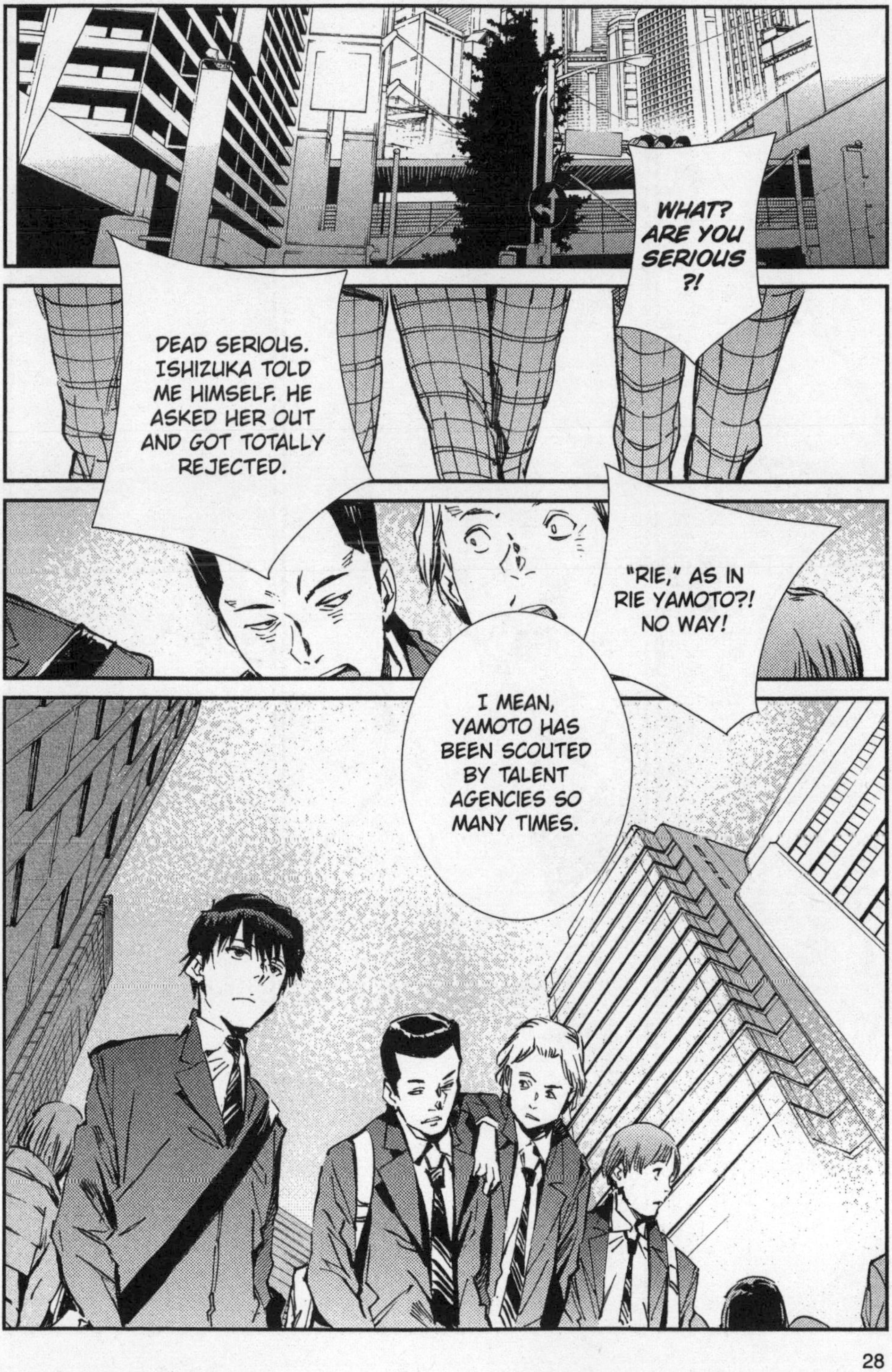
WHAT? ARE YOU SERIOUS?!
DEAD SERIOUS. ISHIZUKA TOLD ME HIMSELF. HE ASKED HER OUT AND GOT TOTALLY REJECTED.
"RIE," AS IN RIE YAMOTO?! NO WAY!
I MEAN, YAMOTO HAS BEEN SCOUTED BY TALENT AGENCIES SO MANY TIMES.

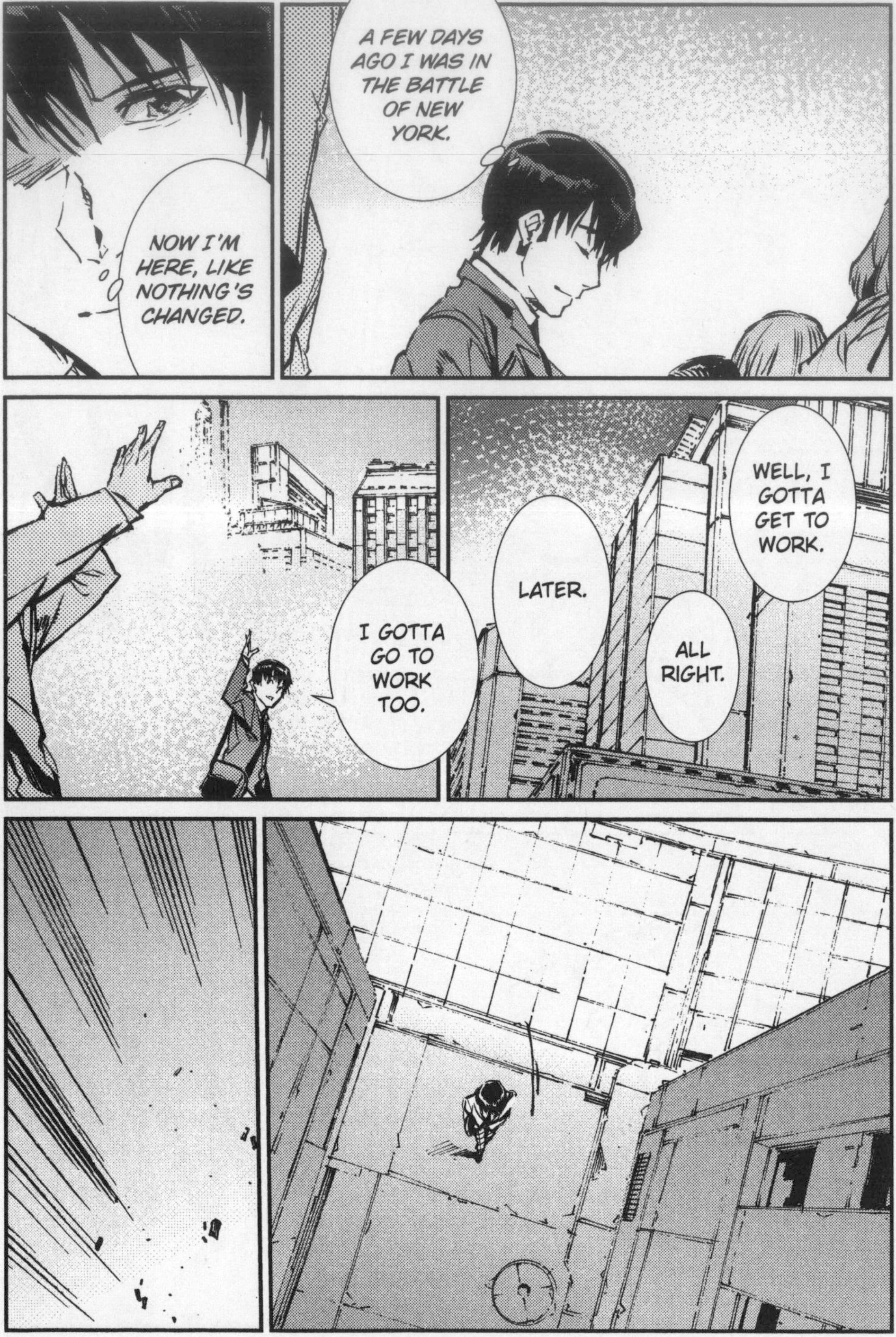
A FEW DAYS AGO I WAS IN THE BATTLE OF NEW YORK.
NOW I'M HERE, LIKE NOTHING'S CHANGED.
WELL, I GOTTA GET TO WORK.
ALL RIGHT.
LATER.
I GOTTA GO TO WORK TOO.

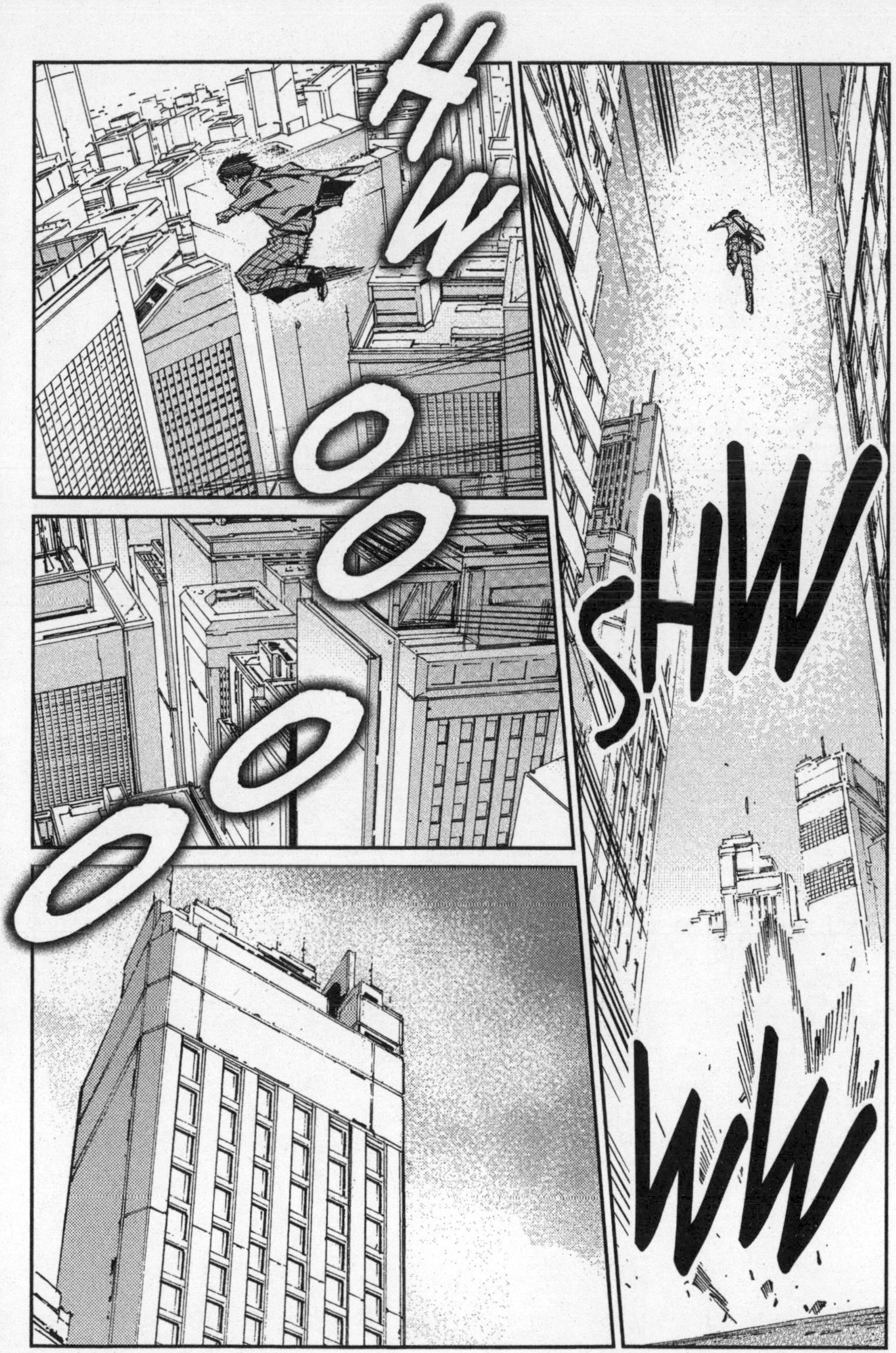
SHW
WW
HWOOOO

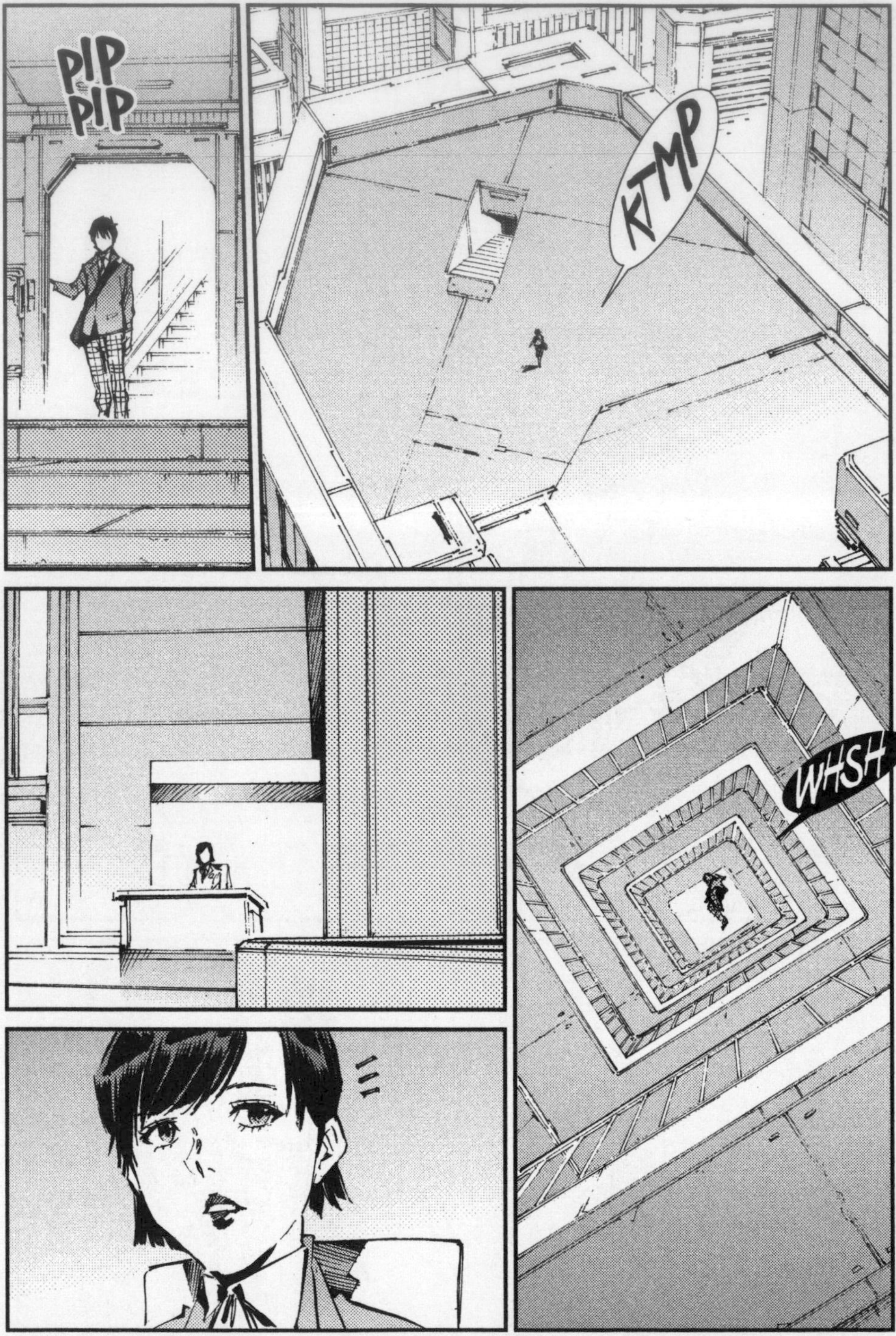
KTMP
PIP PIP
WHSH

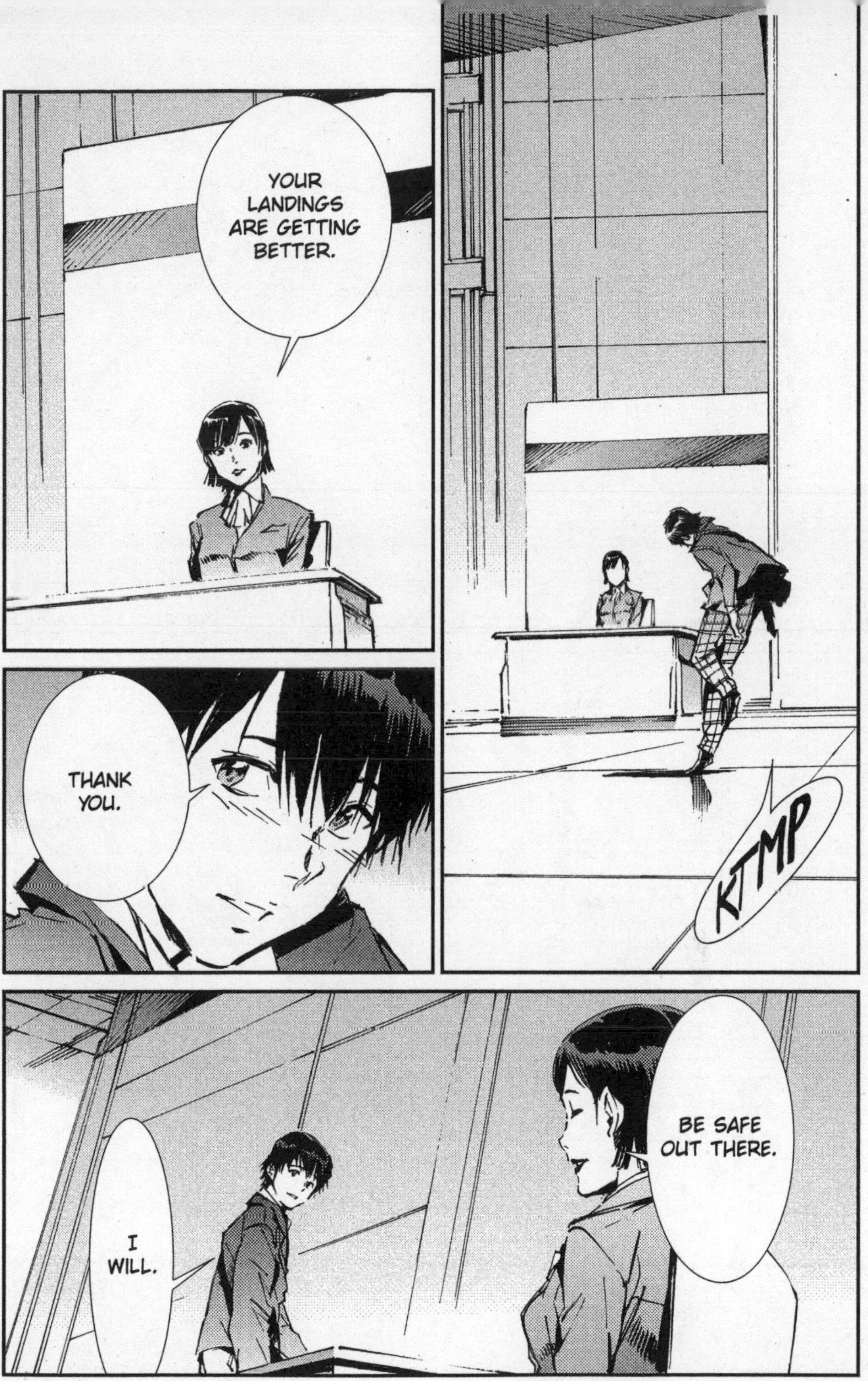
KTMP
YOUR LANDINGS ARE GETTING BETTER.
THANK YOU.
BE SAFE OUT THERE.
I WILL.

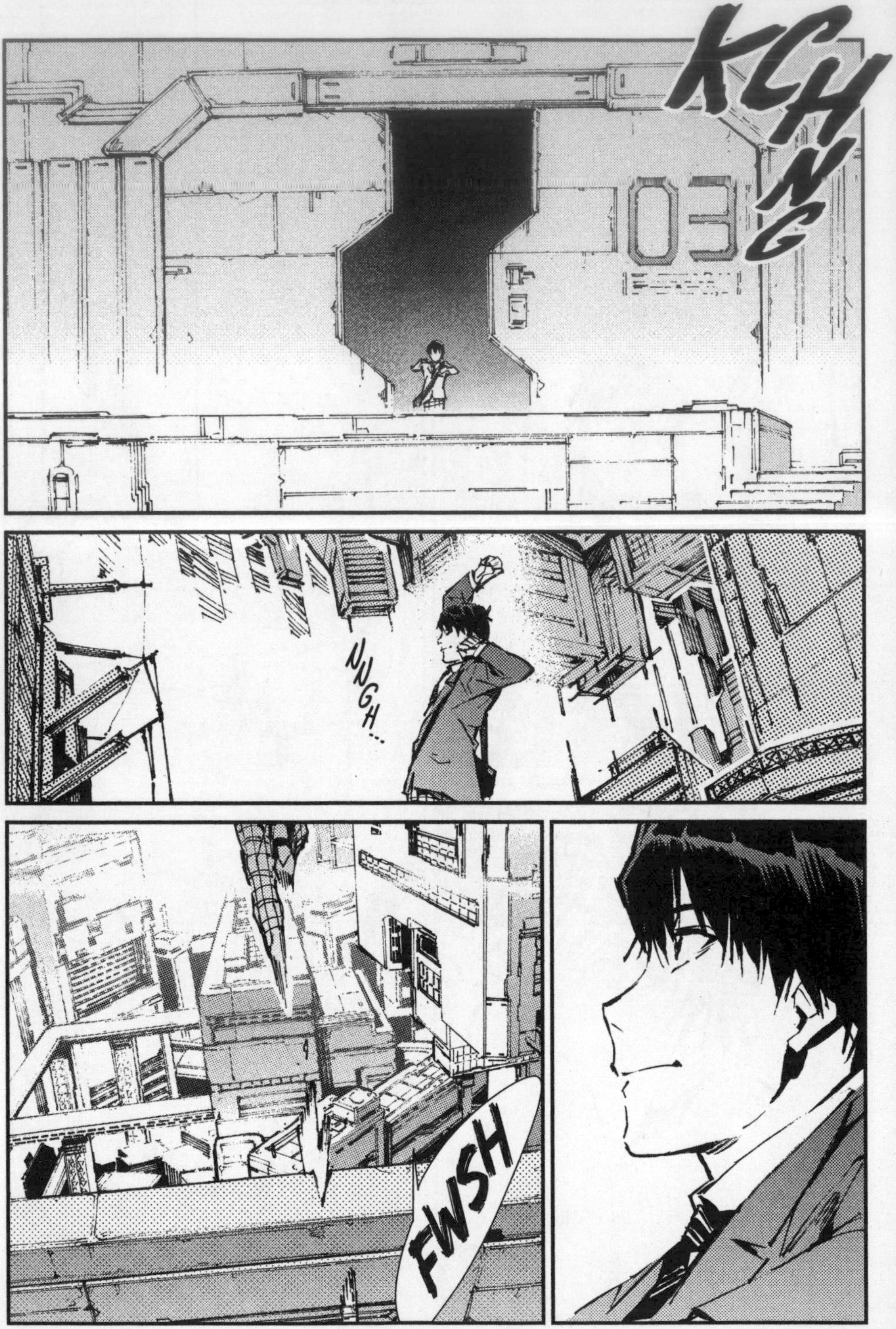
KCHNG
NNGH...
FWSH

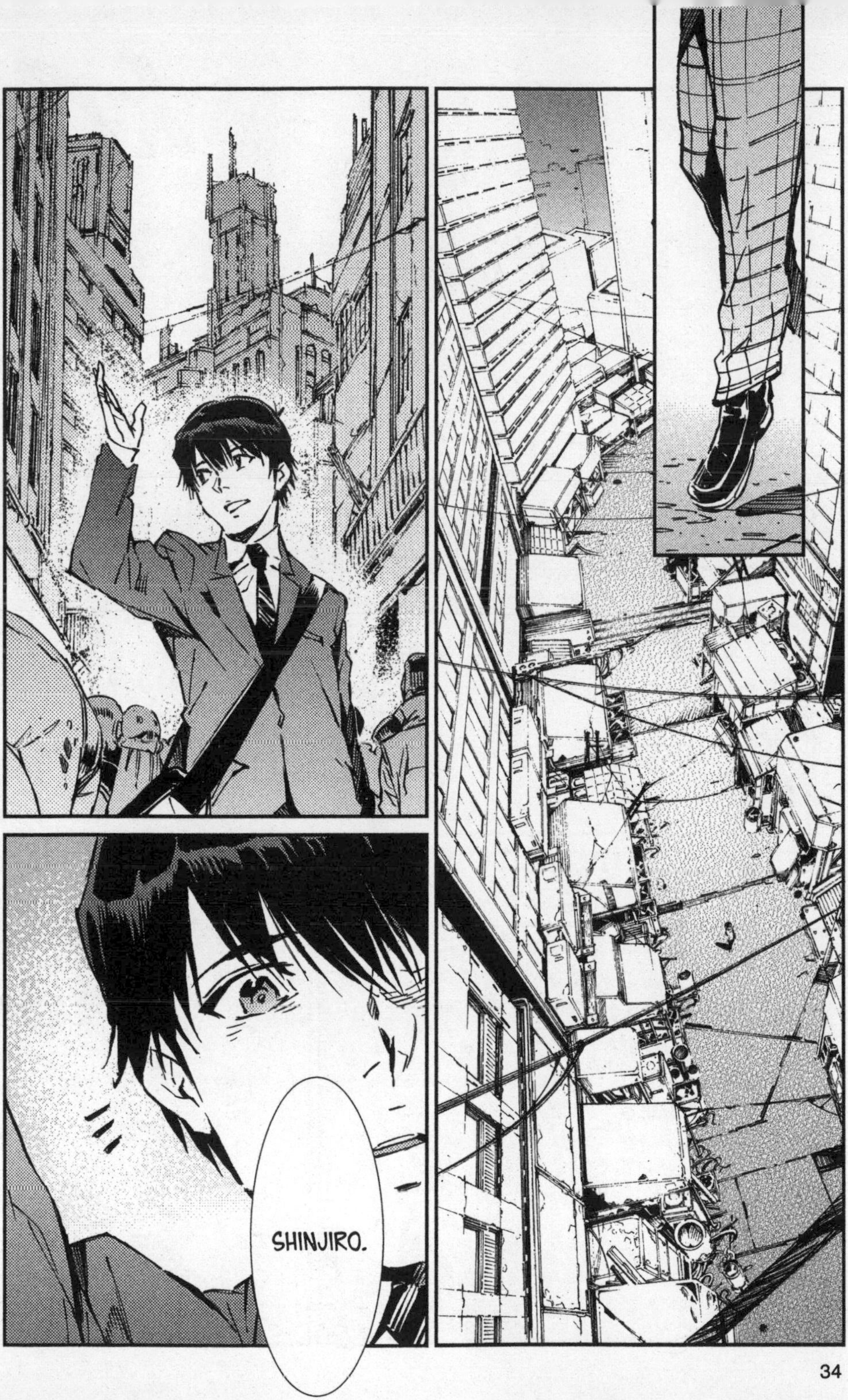
SHINJIRO.

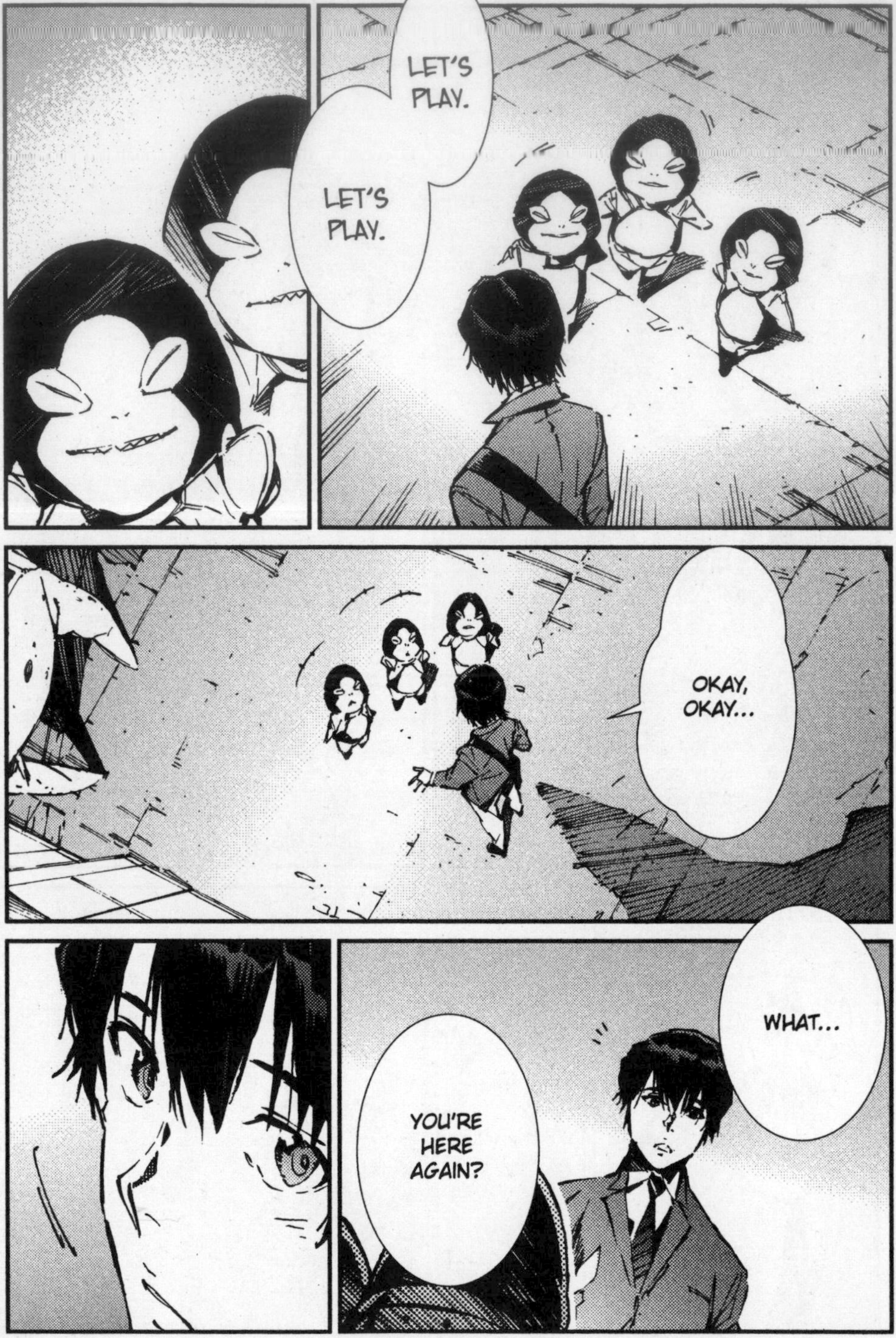
LET'S PLAY.
LET'S PLAY.
OKAY, OKAY...
WHAT...
YOU'RE HERE AGAIN?

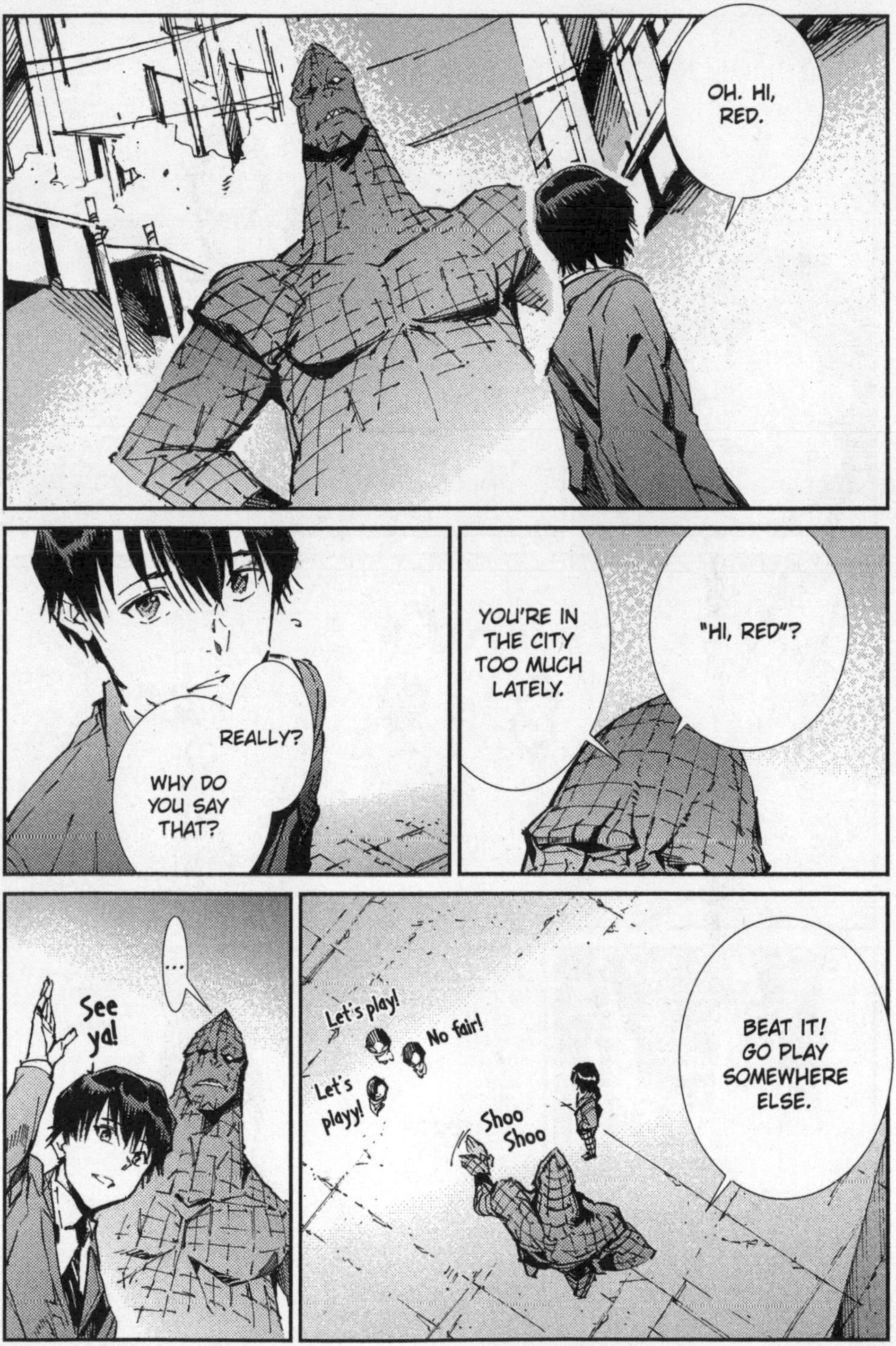
OH. HI, RED.
"HI, RED"?
YOU'RE IN THE CITY TOO MUCH LATELY.
REALLY?
WHY DO YOU SAY THAT?
BEAT IT! GO PLAY SOMEWHERE ELSE.
Shoo Shoo
No fair!
Let's play!
Let's playy!
...
See ya!

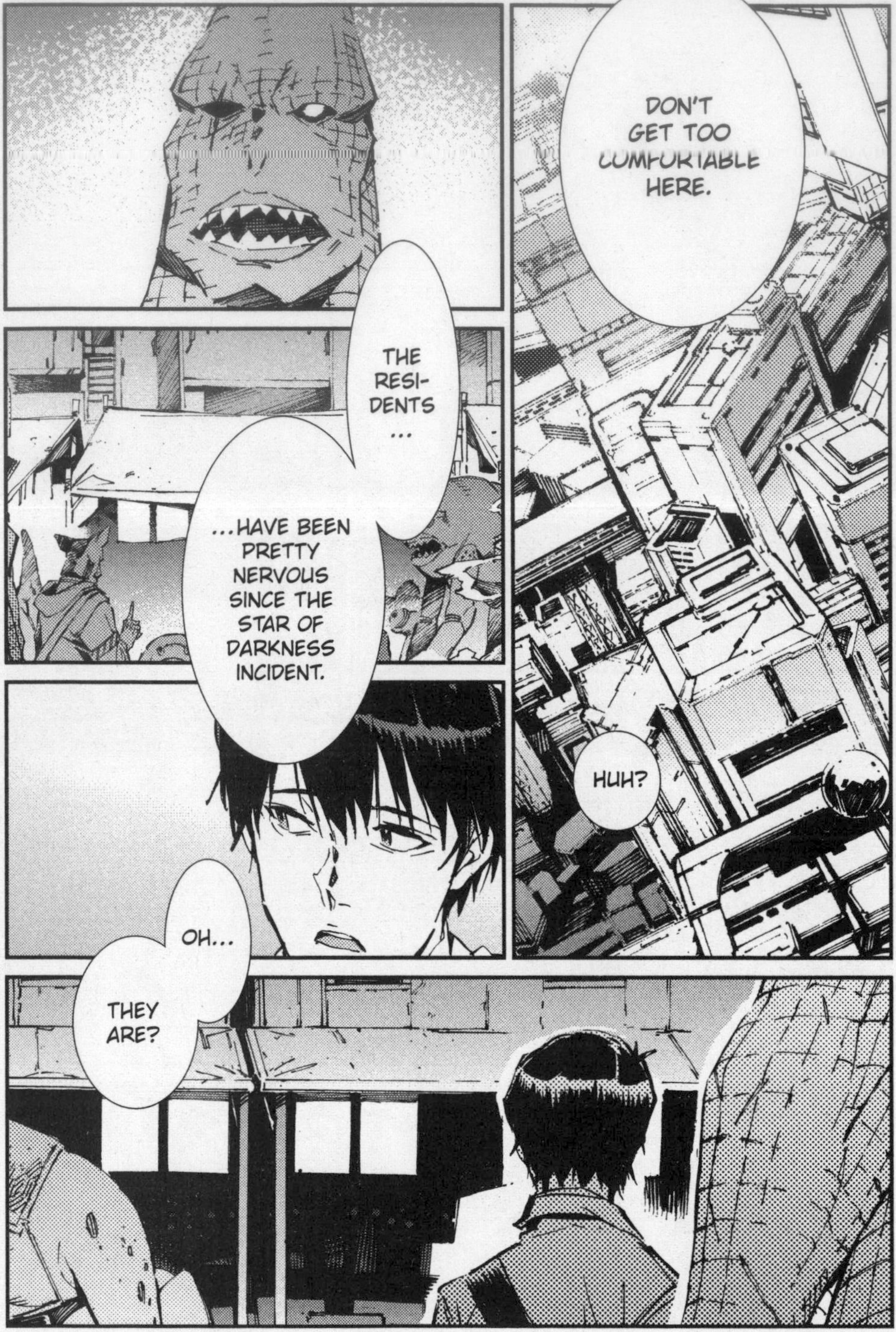
DON'T GET TOO COMFORTABLE HERE.
HUH?
THE RESI-DENTS ...
...HAVE BEEN PRETTY NERVOUS SINCE THE STAR OF DARKNESS INCIDENT.
OH...
THEY ARE?

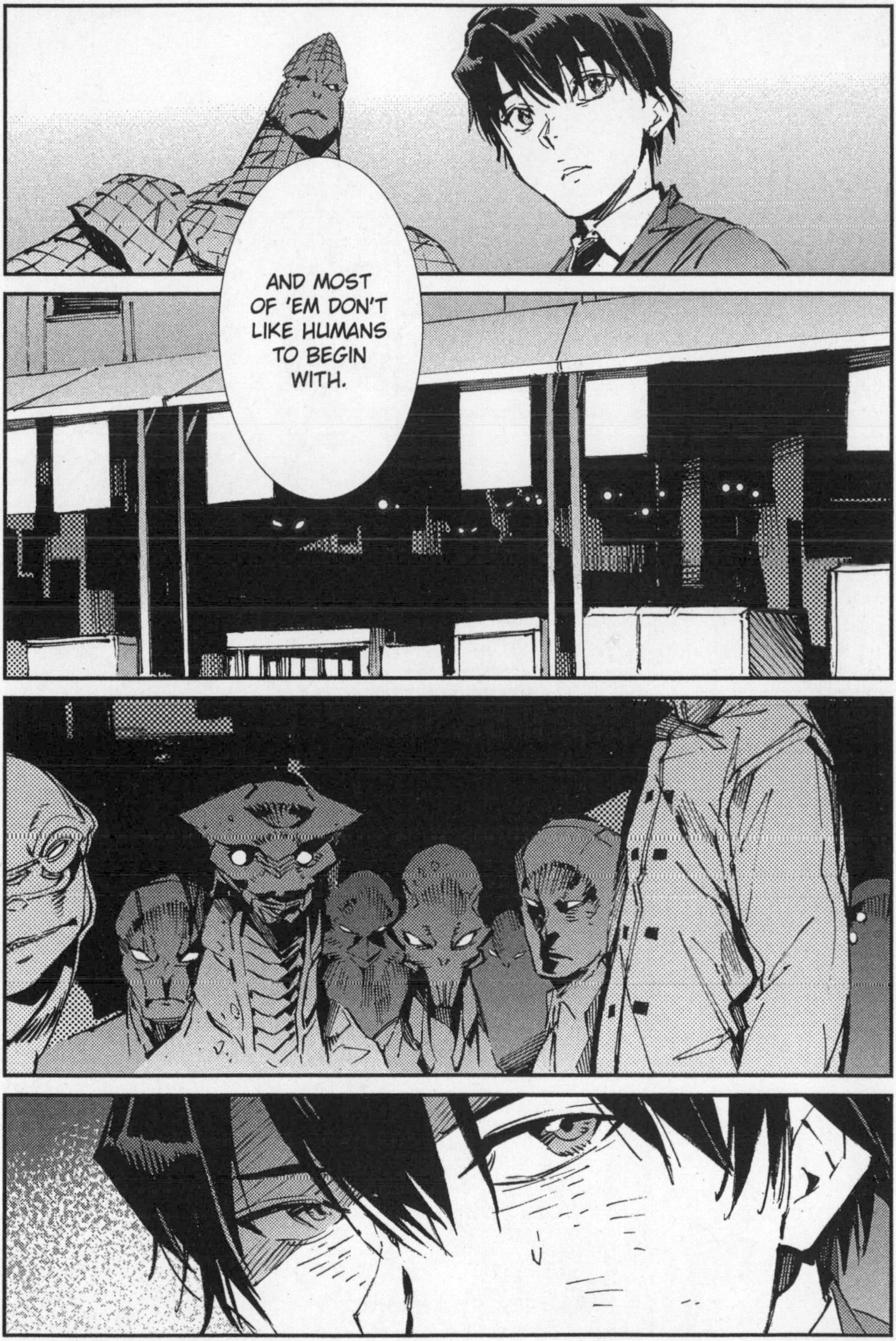
AND MOST OF 'EM DON'T LIKE HUMANS TO BEGIN WITH.

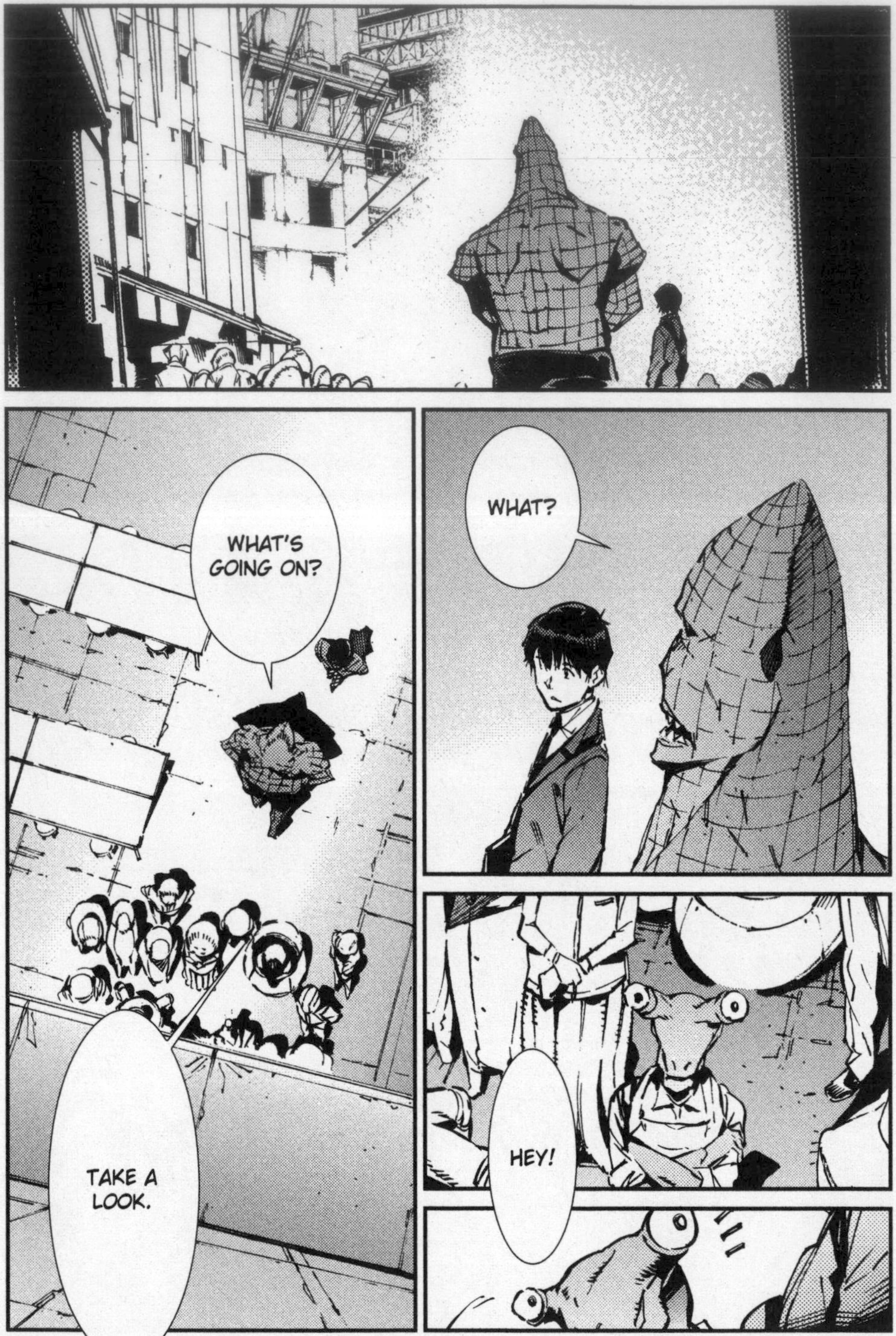
WHAT?
HEY!
WHAT'S GOING ON?
TAKE A LOOK.

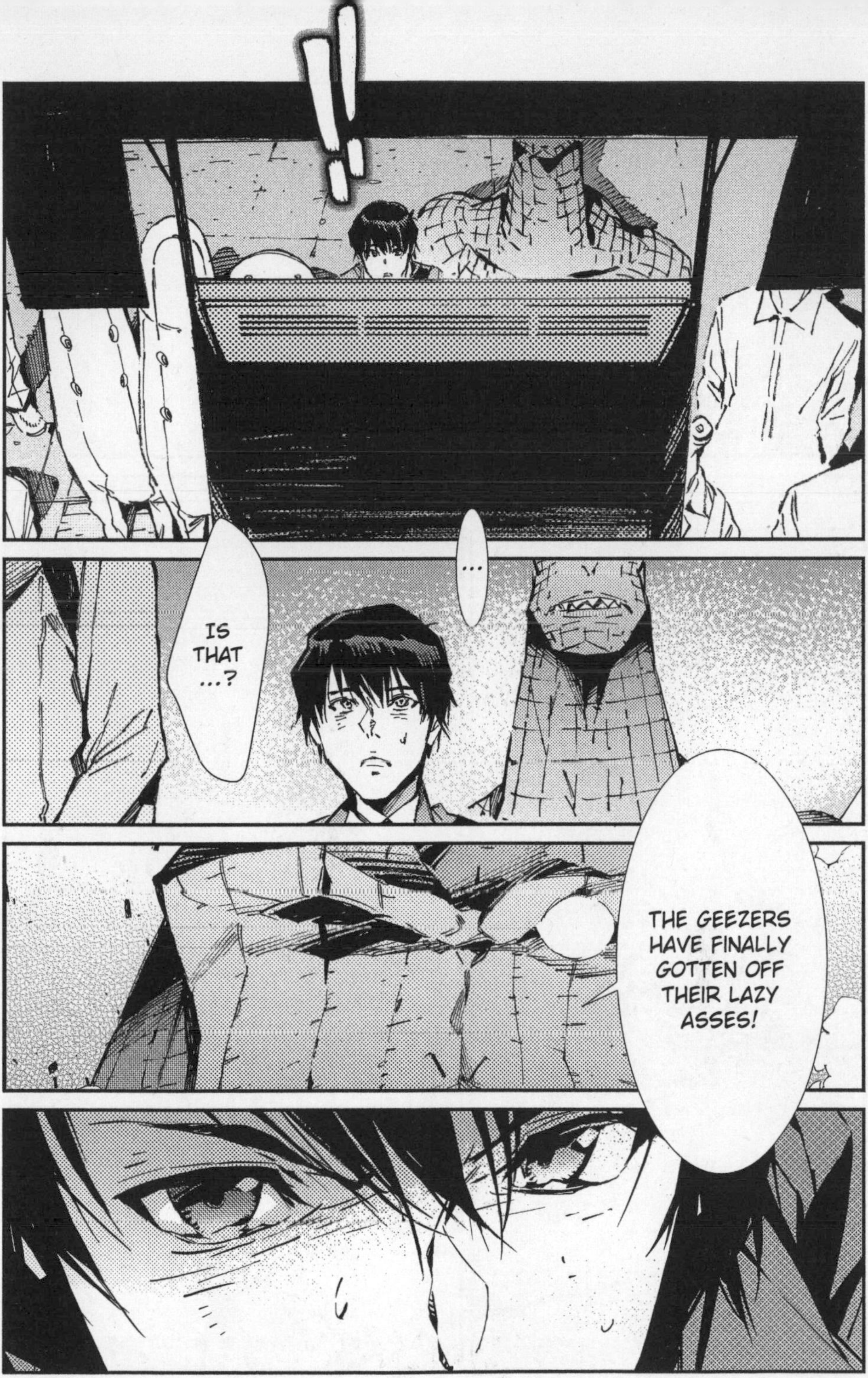
!!
...
IS THAT ...?
THE GEEZERS HAVE FINALLY GOTTEN OFF THEIR LAZY ASSES!

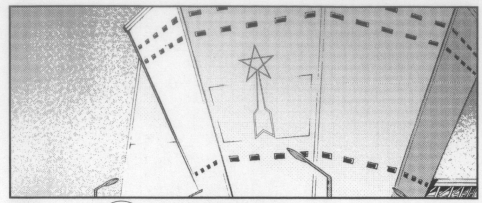

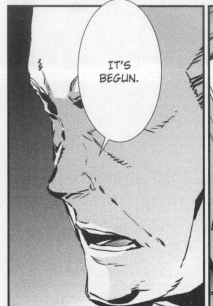

IT'S BEGUN.

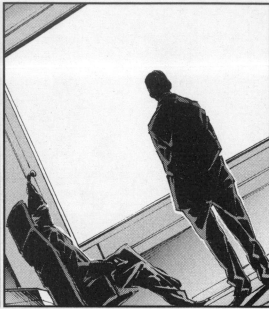

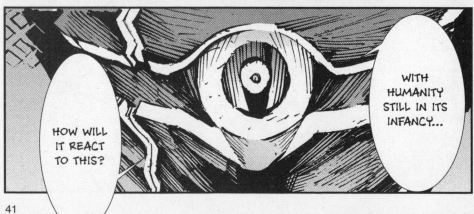

WITH HUMANITY STILL IN ITS INFANCY...

HOW WILL IT REACT TO THIS?

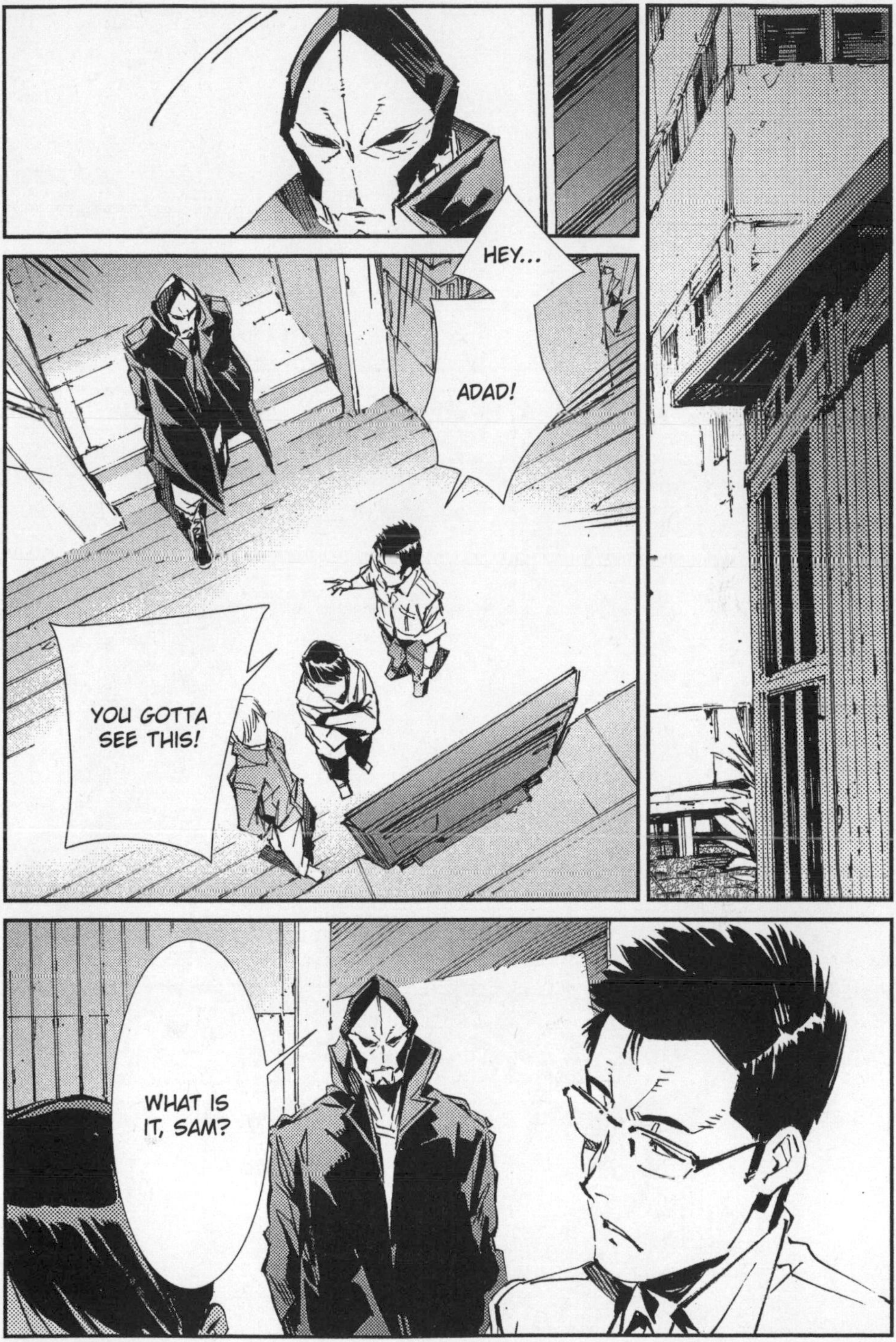
HEY...
ADAD!
YOU GOTTA SEE THIS!
WHAT IS IT, SAM?

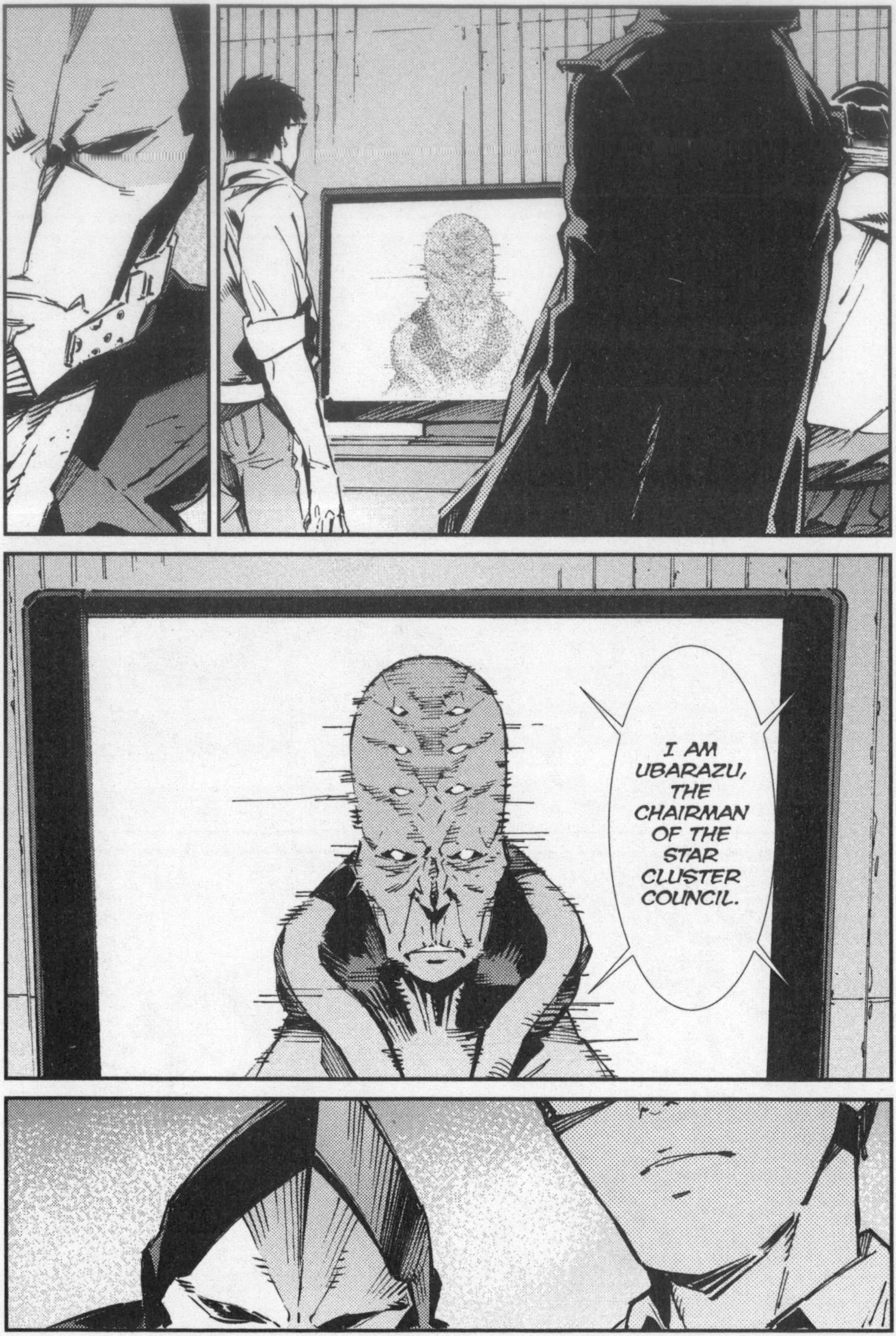
I AM UBARAZU, THE CHAIRMAN OF THE STAR CLUSTER COUNCIL.

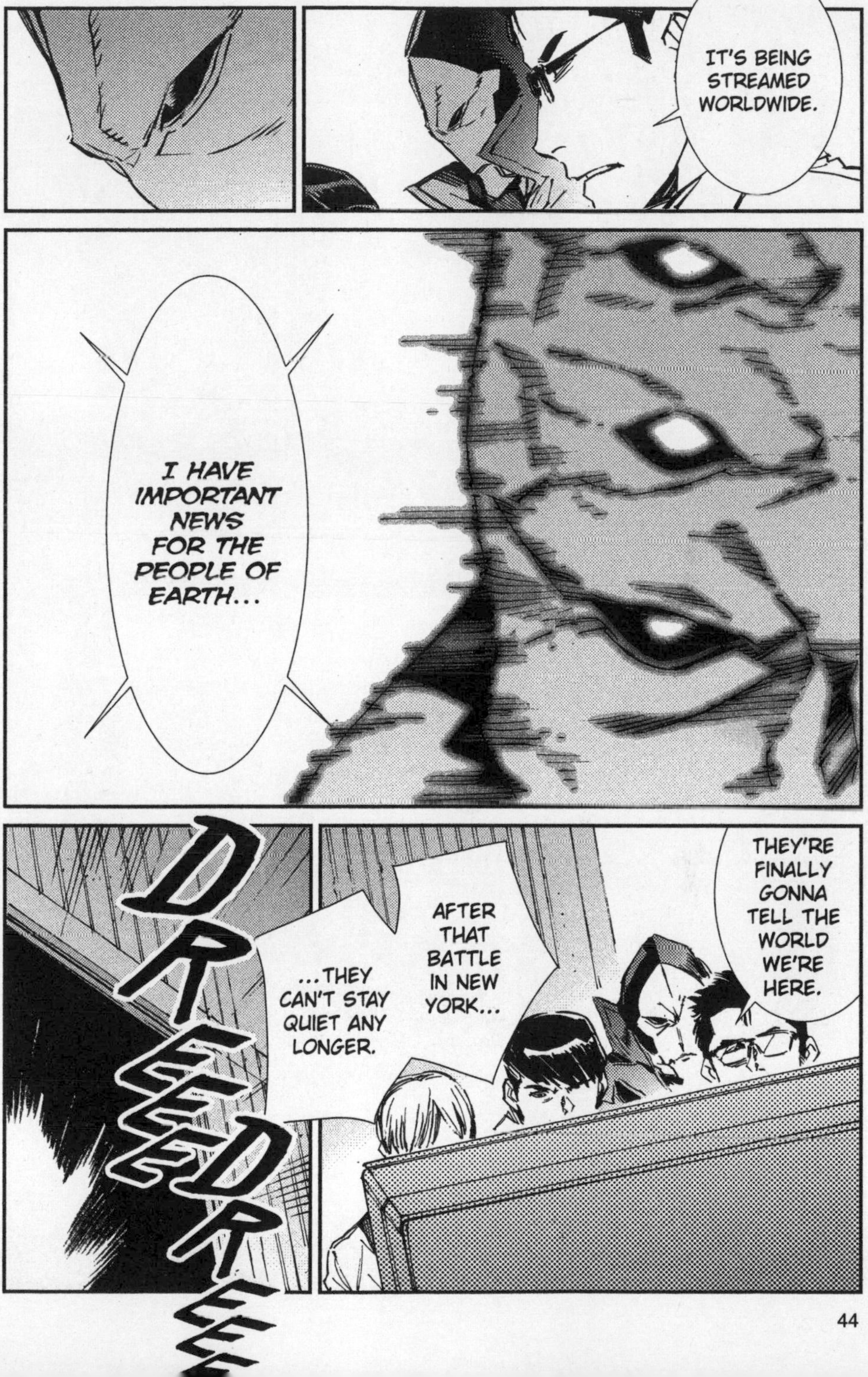
IT'S BEING STREAMED WORLDWIDE.
I HAVE IMPORTANT NEWS FOR THE PEOPLE OF EARTH...
THEY'RE FINALLY GONNA TELL THE WORLD WE'RE HERE.
AFTER THAT BATTLE IN NEW YORK...
...THEY CAN'T STAY QUIET ANY LONGER.
DREEEDREEE

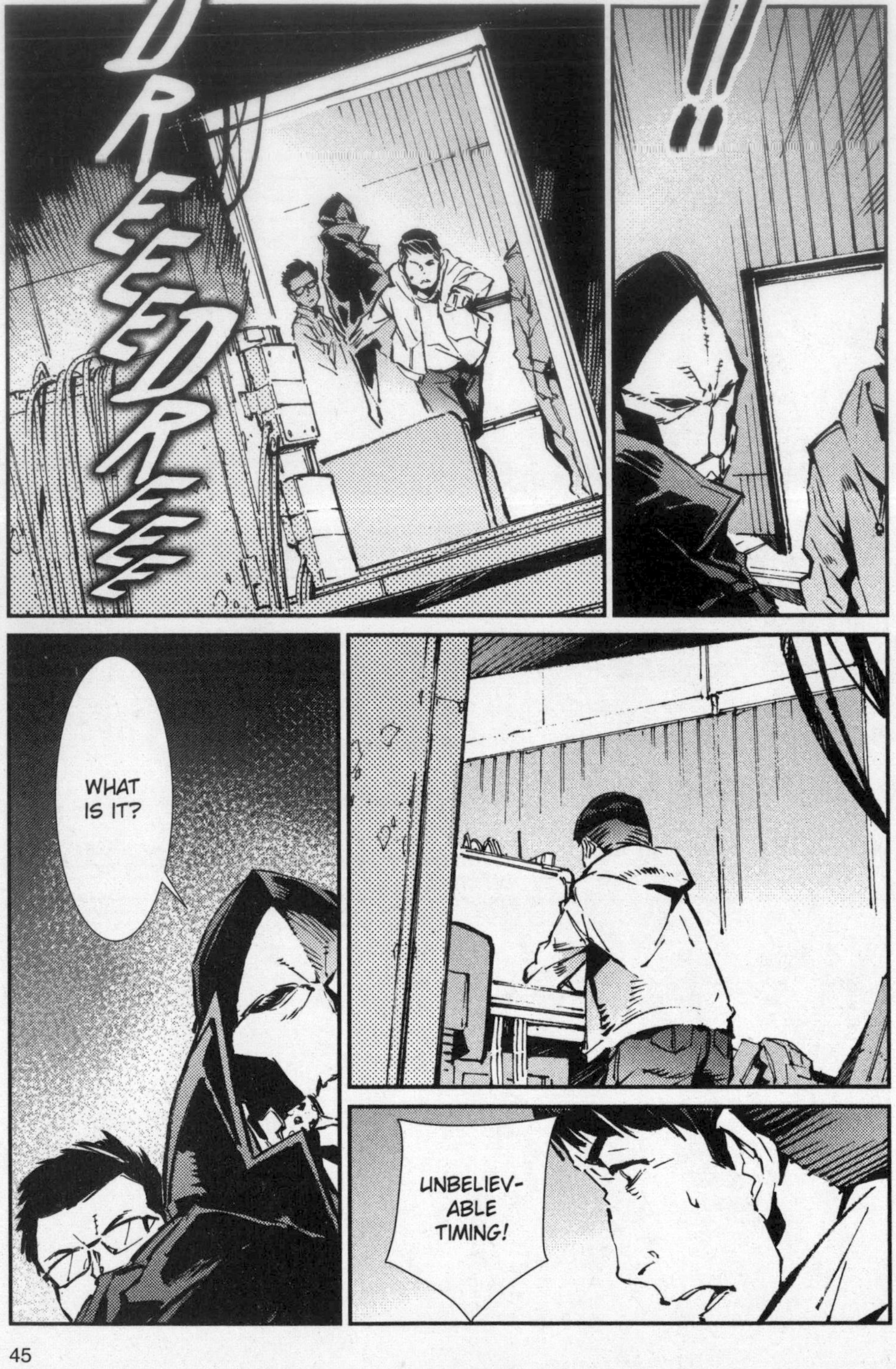
!!
DREEEDREEE
UNBELIEV-ABLE TIMING!
WHAT IS IT?

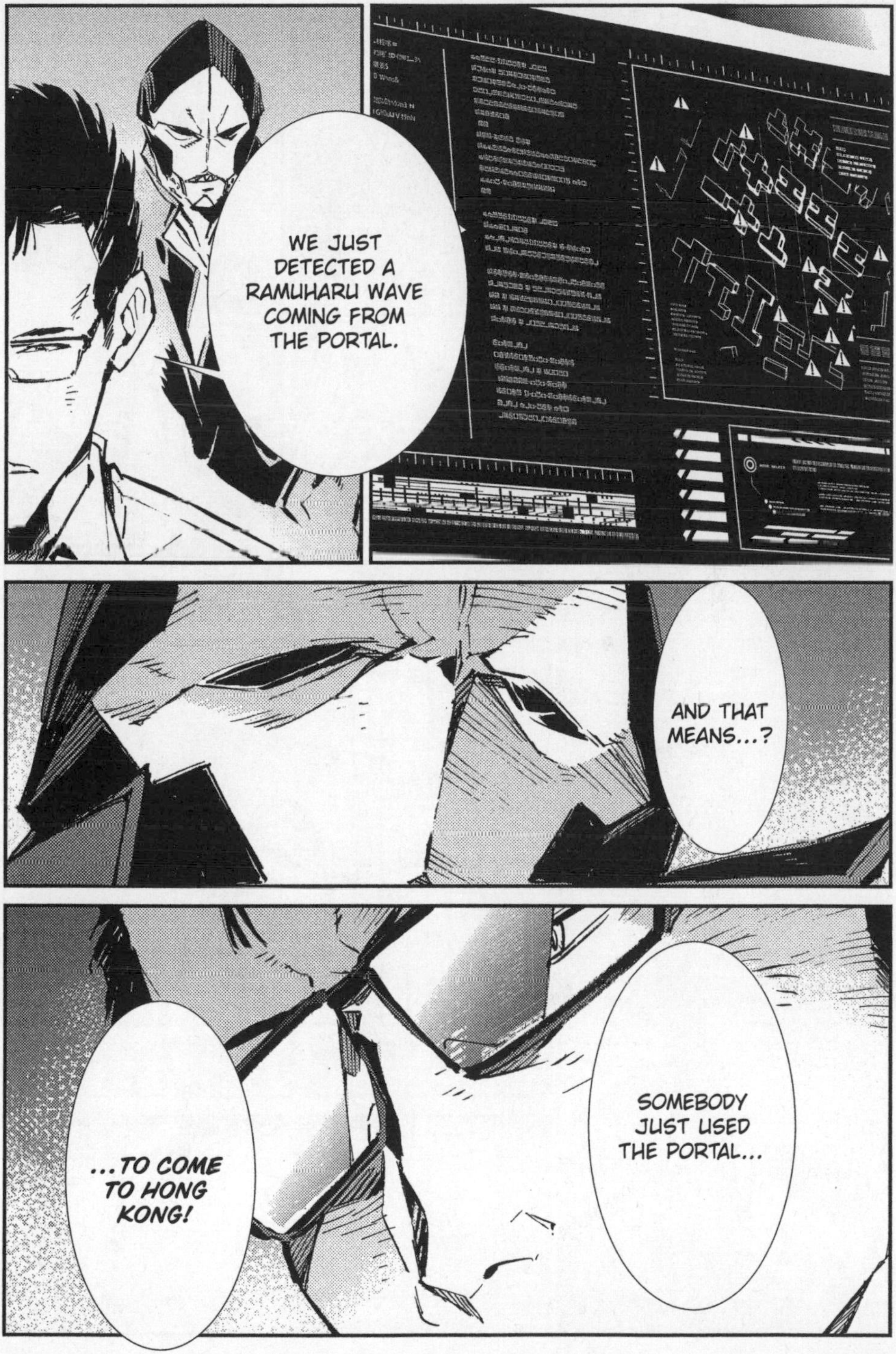
WE JUST DETECTED A RAMUHARU WAVE COMING FROM THE PORTAL.
AND THAT MEANS...?
SOMEBODY JUST USED THE PORTAL...
...TO COME TO HONG KONG!

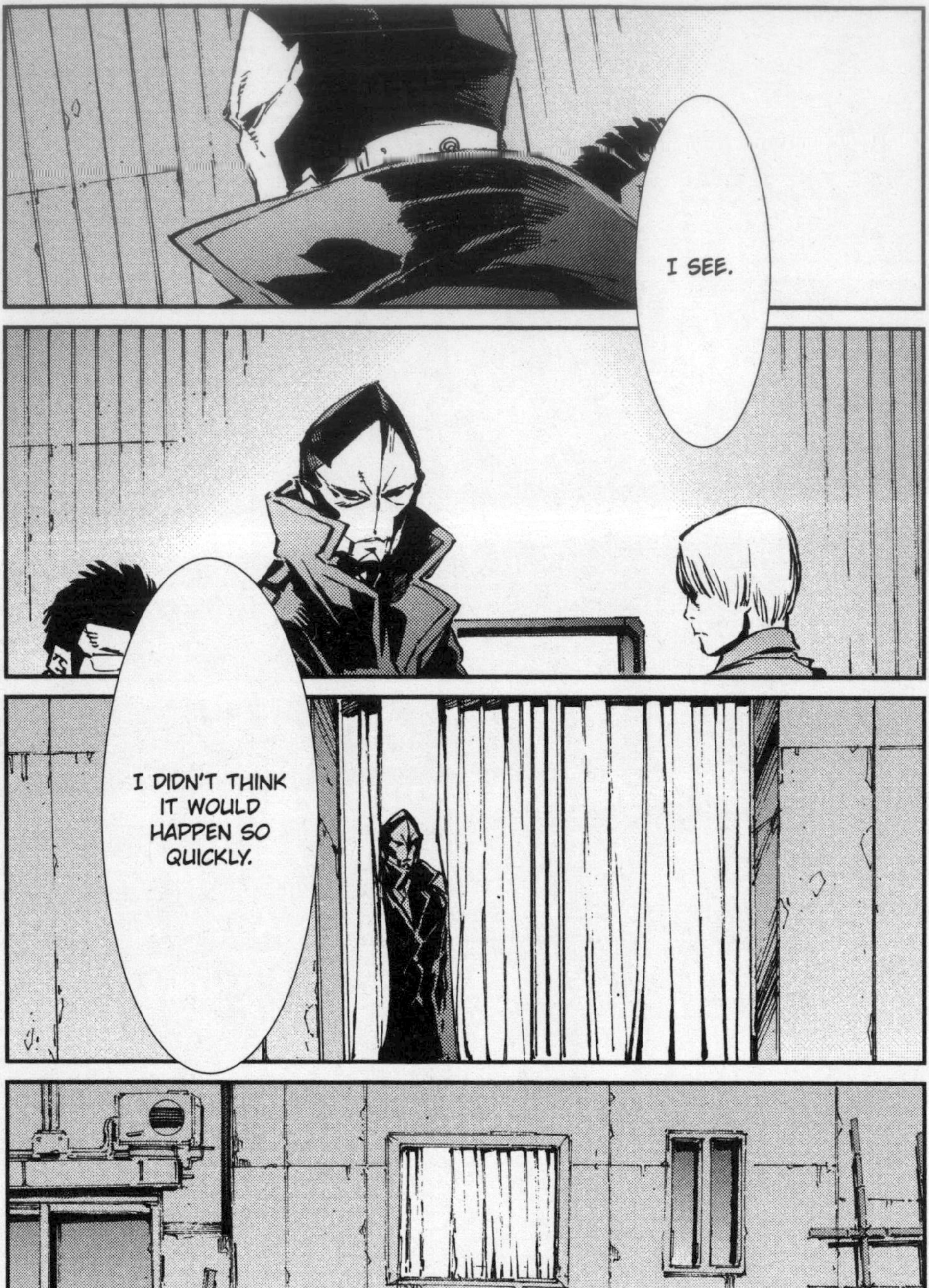
I SEE.
I DIDN'T THINK IT WOULD HAPPEN SO QUICKLY.

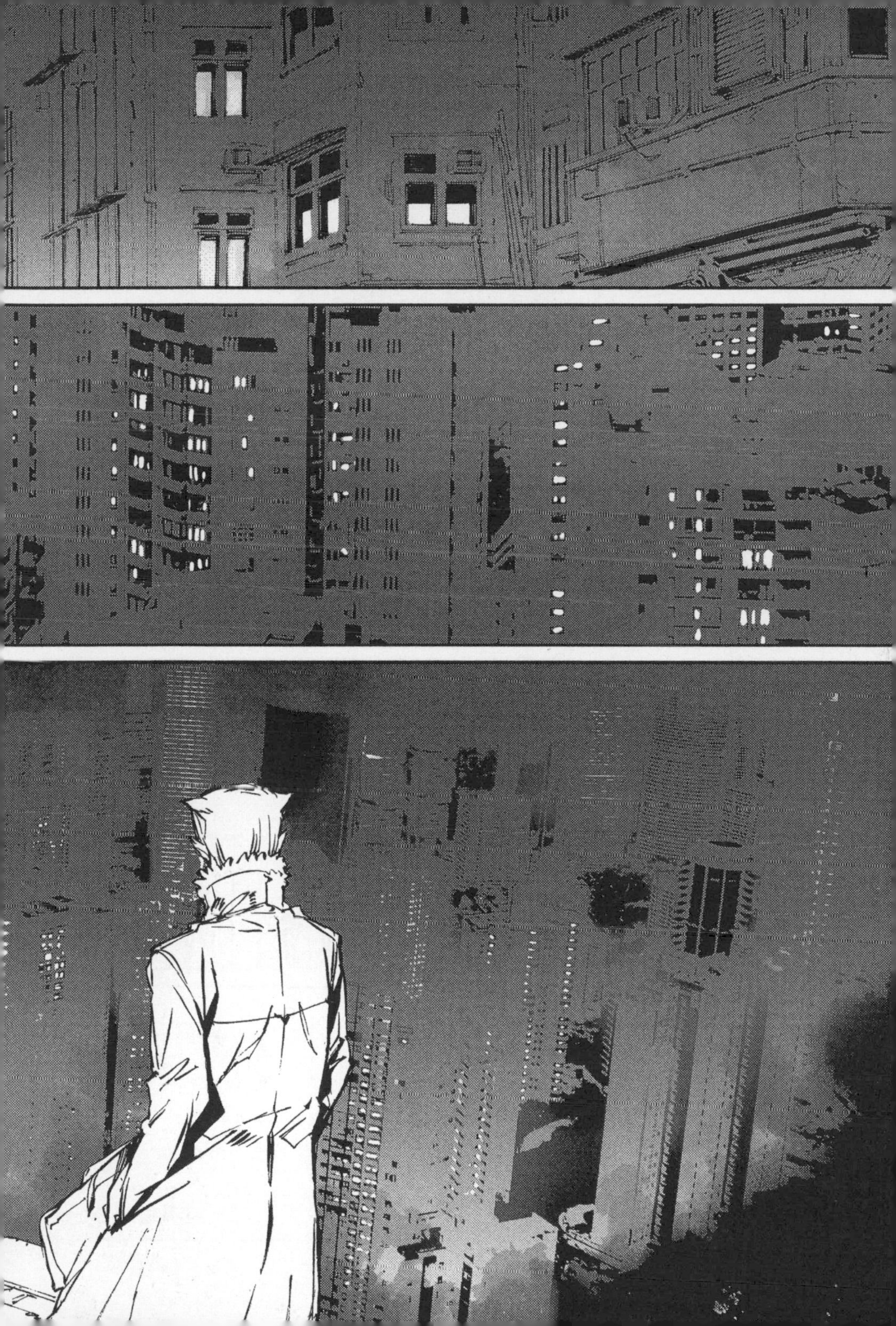

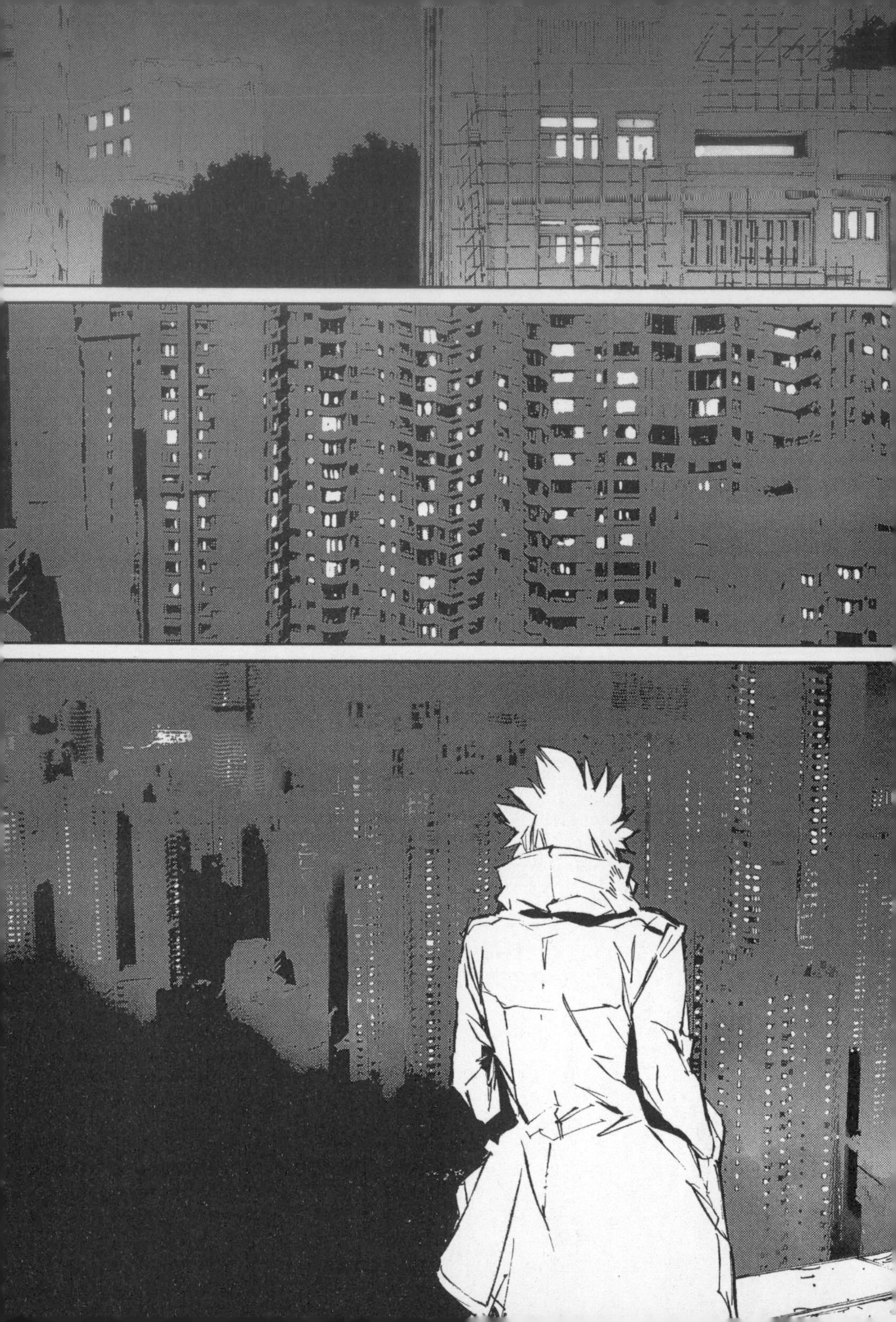

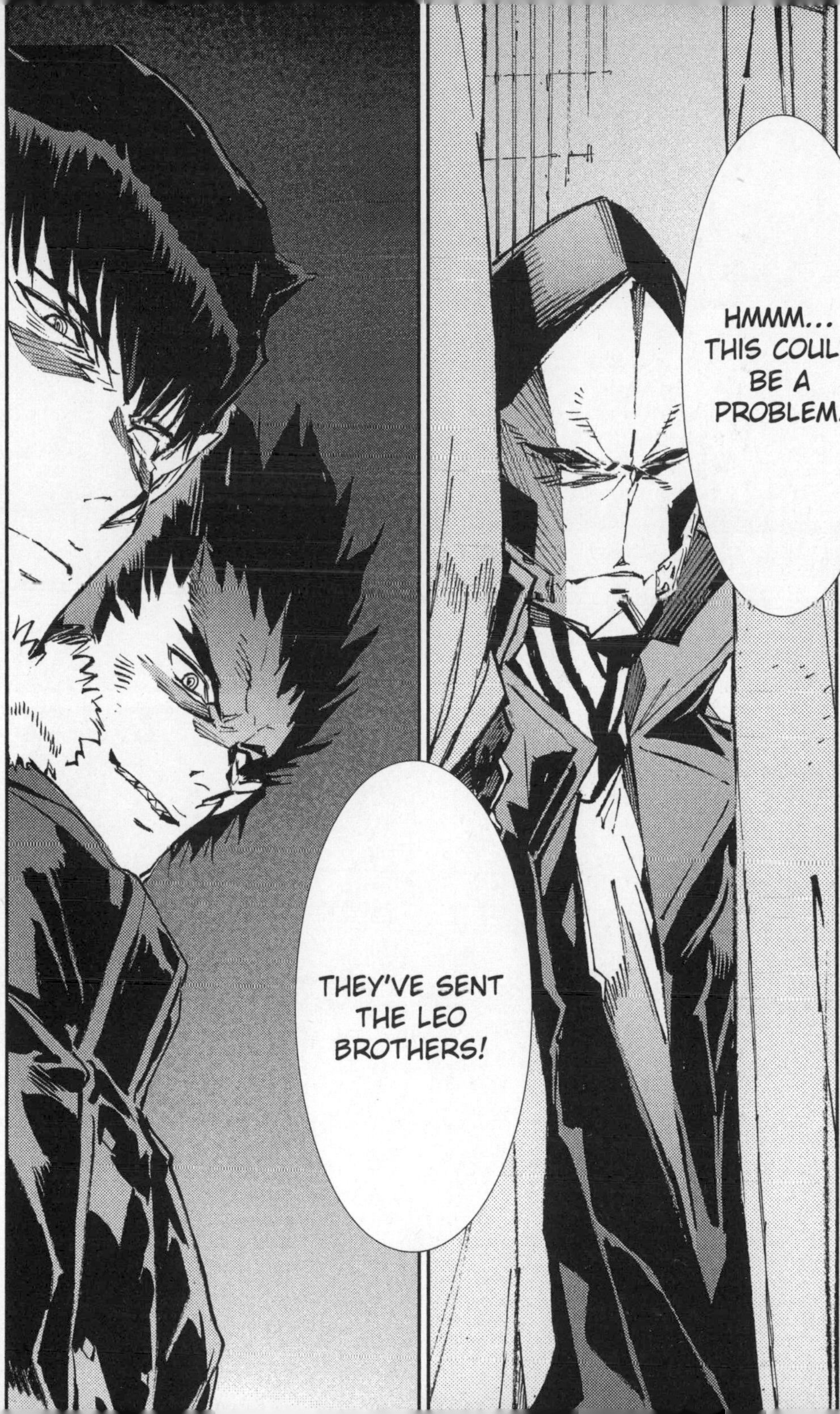
HMMM... THIS COULD BE A PROBLEM.
THEY'VE SENT THE LEO BROTHERS!

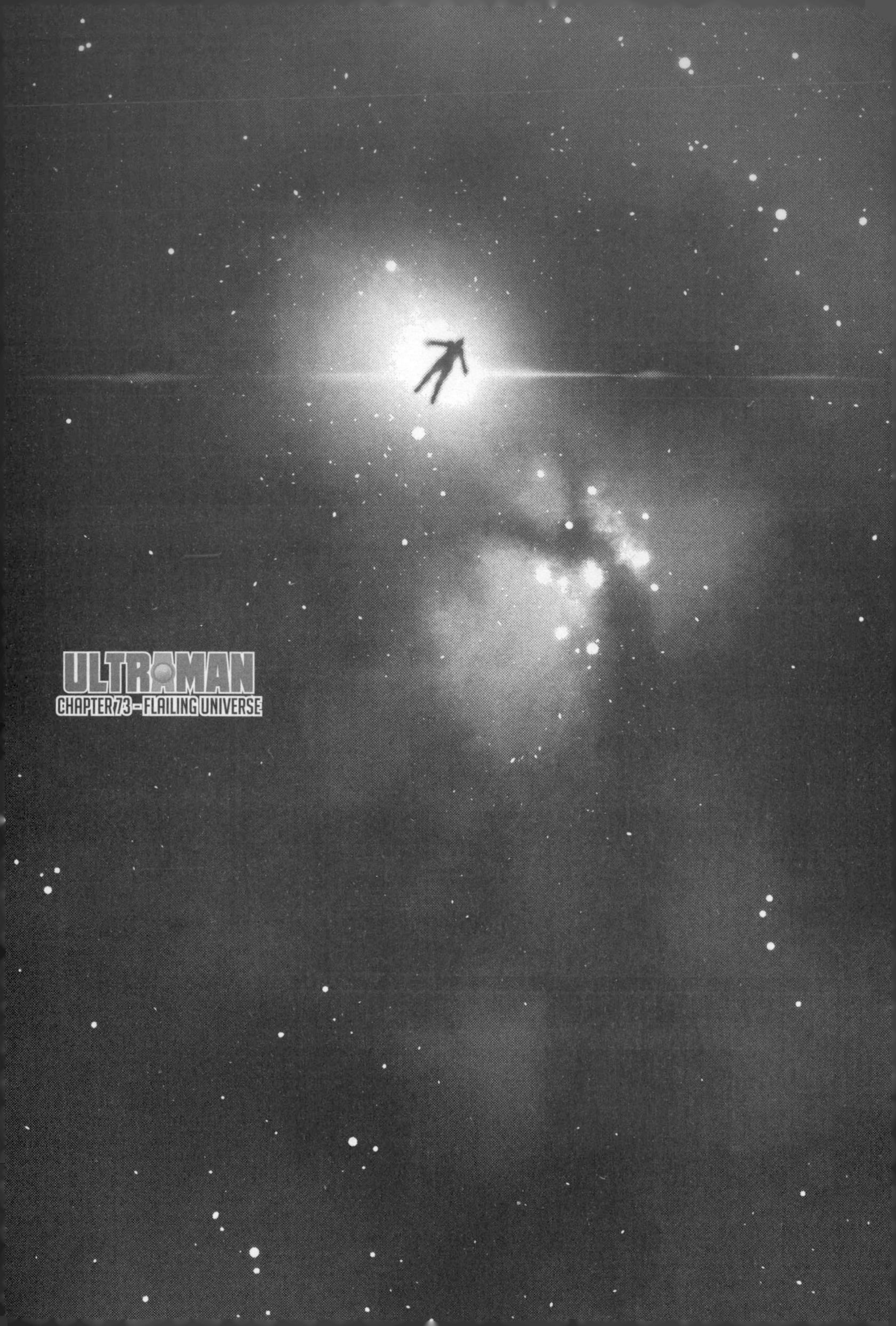
ULTRAMAN
CHAPTER 73 - FLAILING UNIVERSE

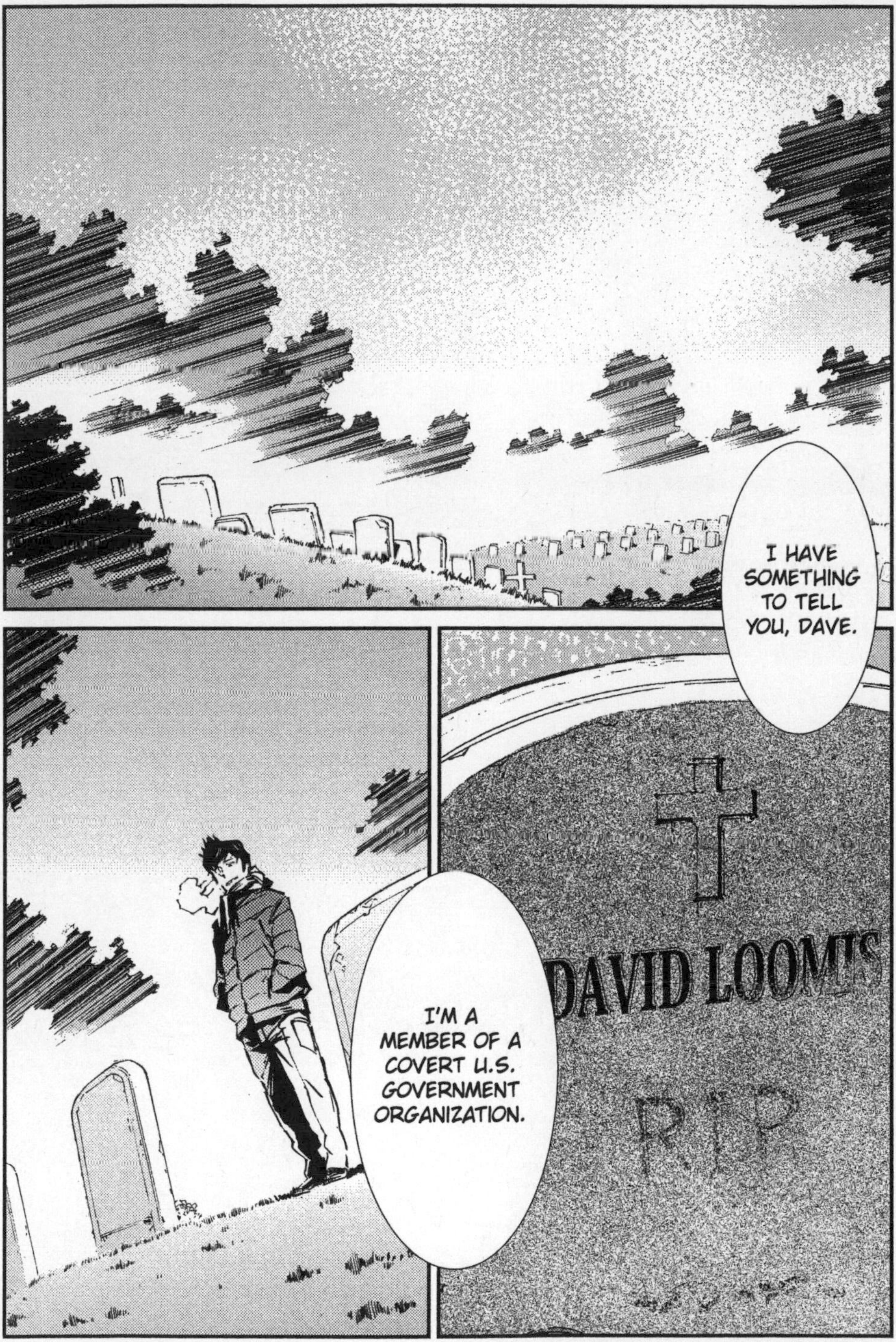
I HAVE SOMETHING TO TELL YOU, DAVE.
DAVID LOOMIS
RIP
I'M A MEMBER OF A COVERT U.S. GOVERNMENT ORGANIZATION.

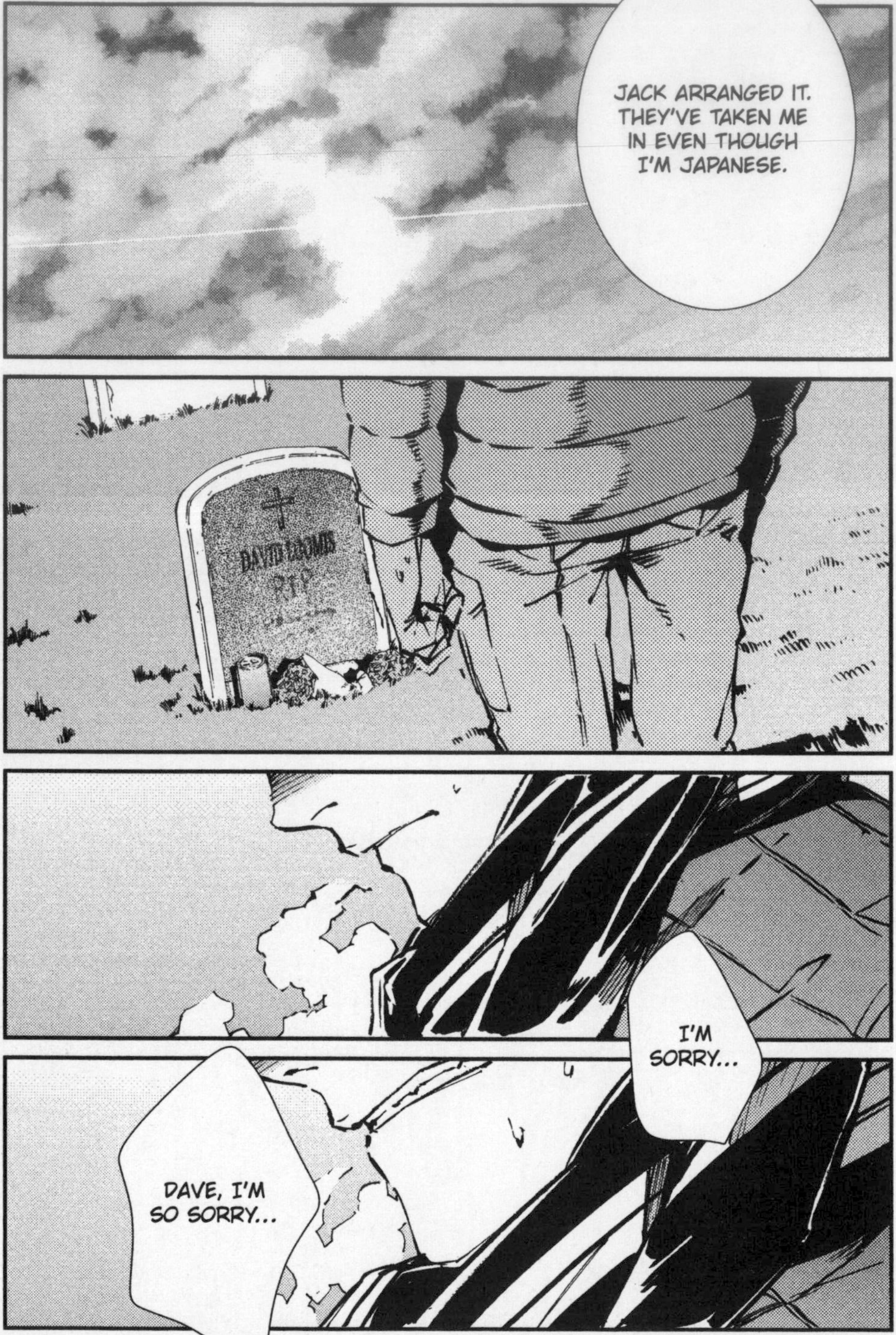
JACK ARRANGED IT. THEY'VE TAKEN ME IN EVEN THOUGH I'M JAPANESE.
I'M SORRY...
DAVE, I'M SO SORRY...

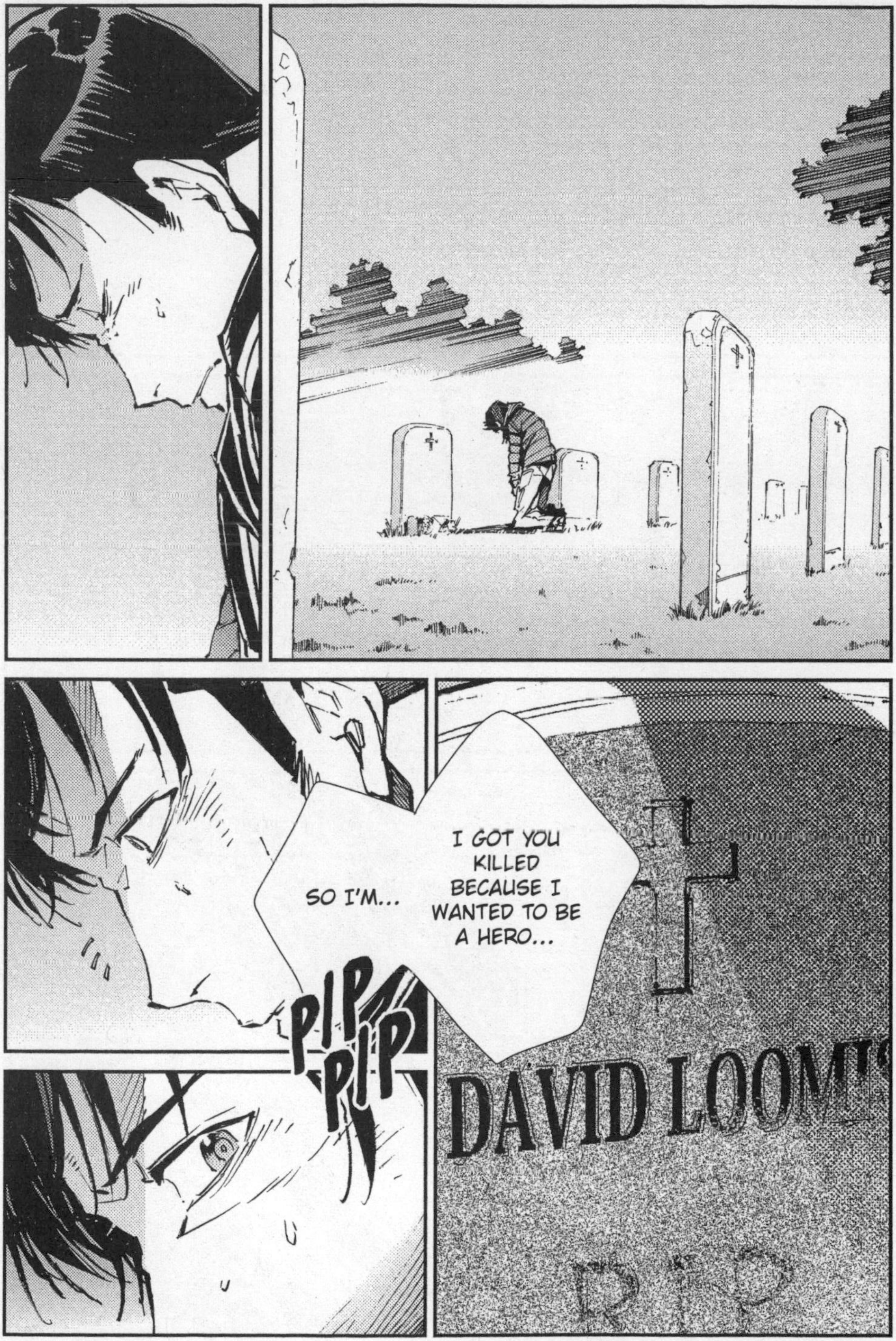
I GOT YOU KILLED BECAUSE I WANTED TO BE A HERO...
SO I'M...
PIP PIP
DAVID LOOMIS
RIP

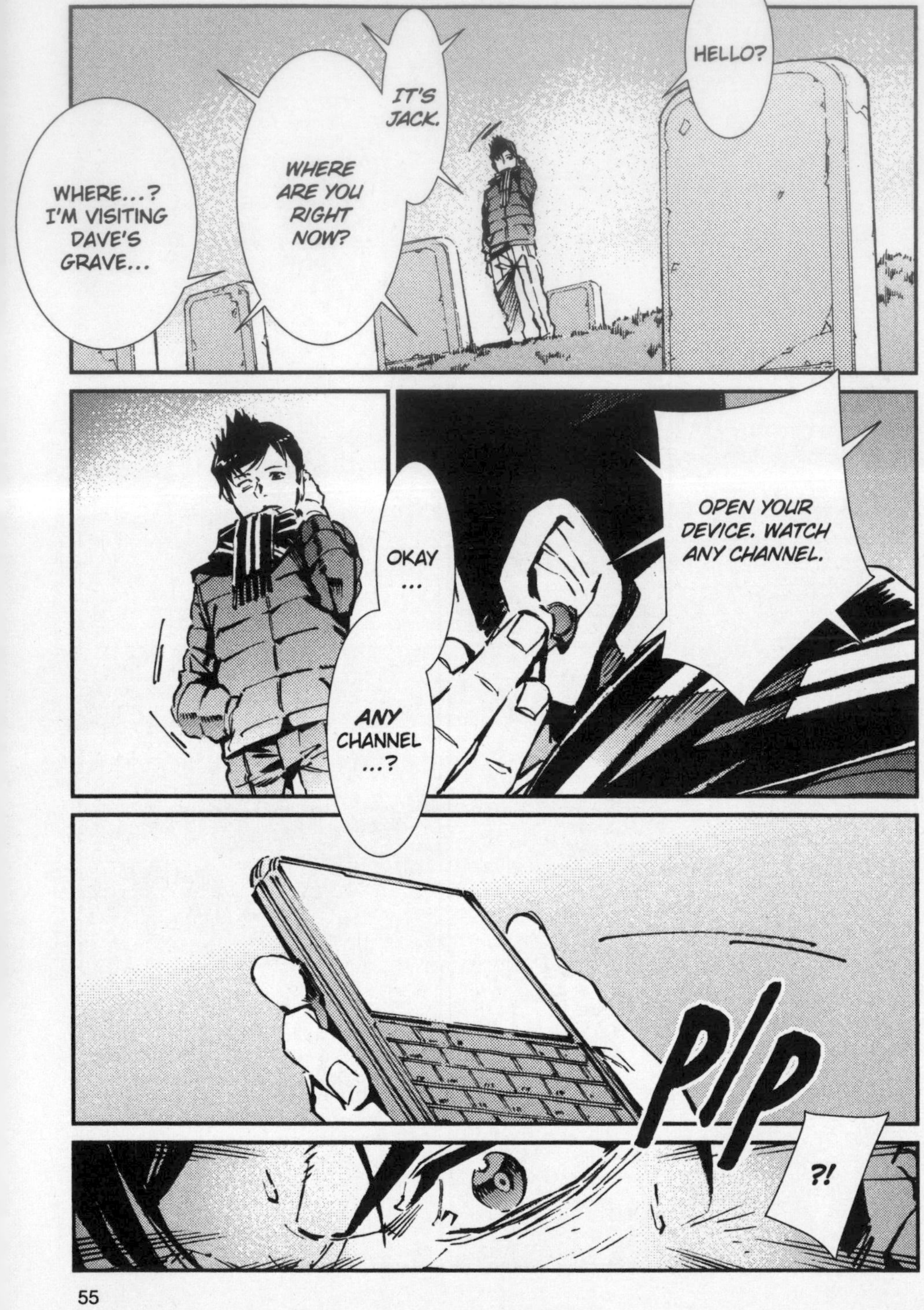
HELLO?
IT'S JACK.
WHERE ARE YOU RIGHT NOW?
WHERE...? I'M VISITING DAVE'S GRAVE...
OPEN YOUR DEVICE. WATCH ANY CHANNEL.
OKAY ...
ANY CHANNEL ...?
PIP
?!

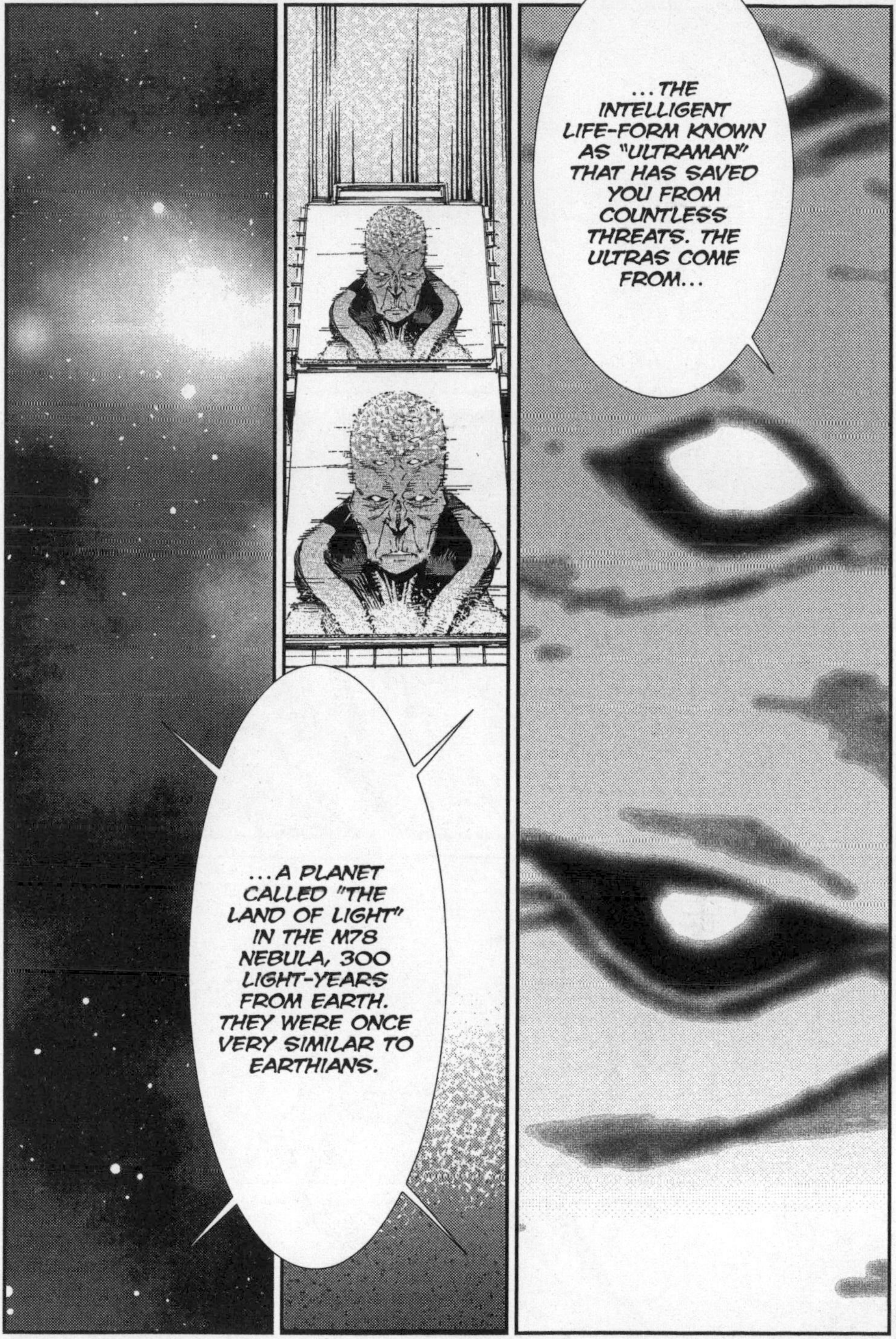
...THE INTELLIGENT LIFE-FORM KNOWN AS "ULTRAMAN" THAT HAS SAVED YOU FROM COUNTLESS THREATS. THE ULTRAS COME FROM...
...A PLANET CALLED "THE LAND OF LIGHT" IN THE M78 NEBULA, 300 LIGHT-YEARS FROM EARTH. THEY WERE ONCE VERY SIMILAR TO EARTHIANS.

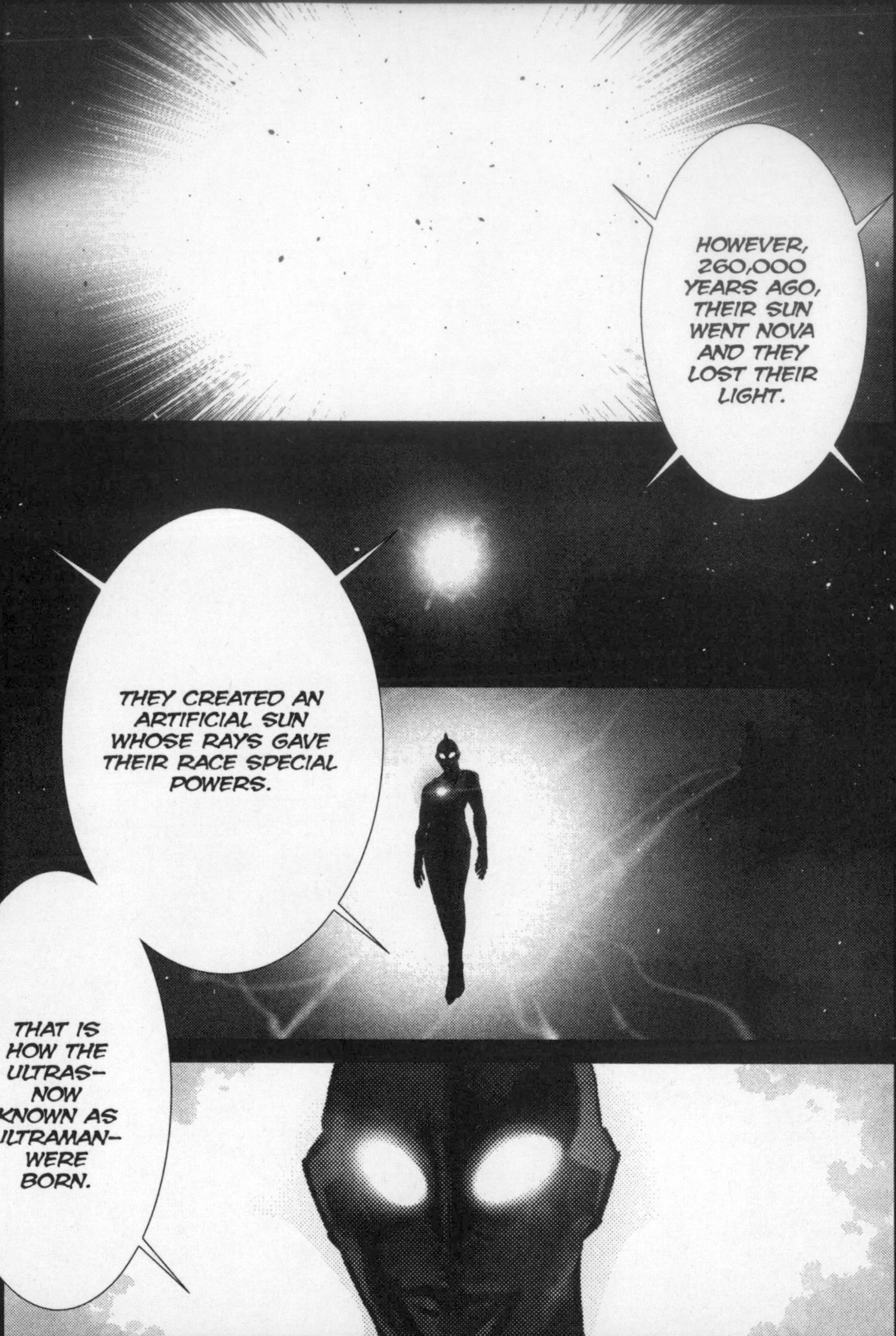
HOWEVER, 260,000 YEARS AGO, THEIR SUN WENT NOVA AND THEY LOST THEIR LIGHT.
THEY CREATED AN ARTIFICIAL SUN WHOSE RAYS GAVE THEIR RACE SPECIAL POWERS.
THAT IS HOW THE ULTRAS-NOW KNOWN AS ULTRAMAN-WERE BORN.

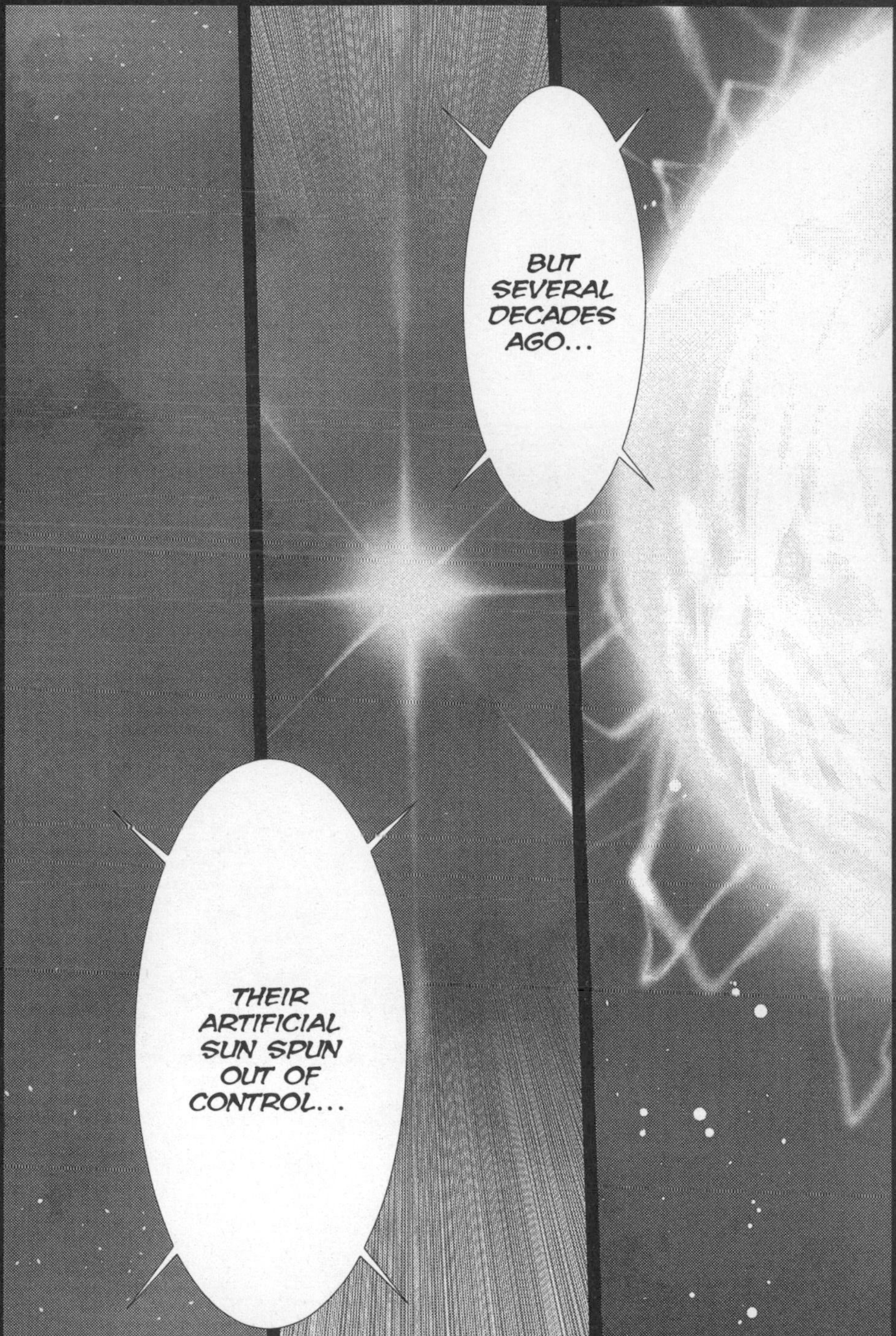
BUT SEVERAL DECADES AGO...
THEIR ARTIFICIAL SUN SPUN OUT OF CONTROL...

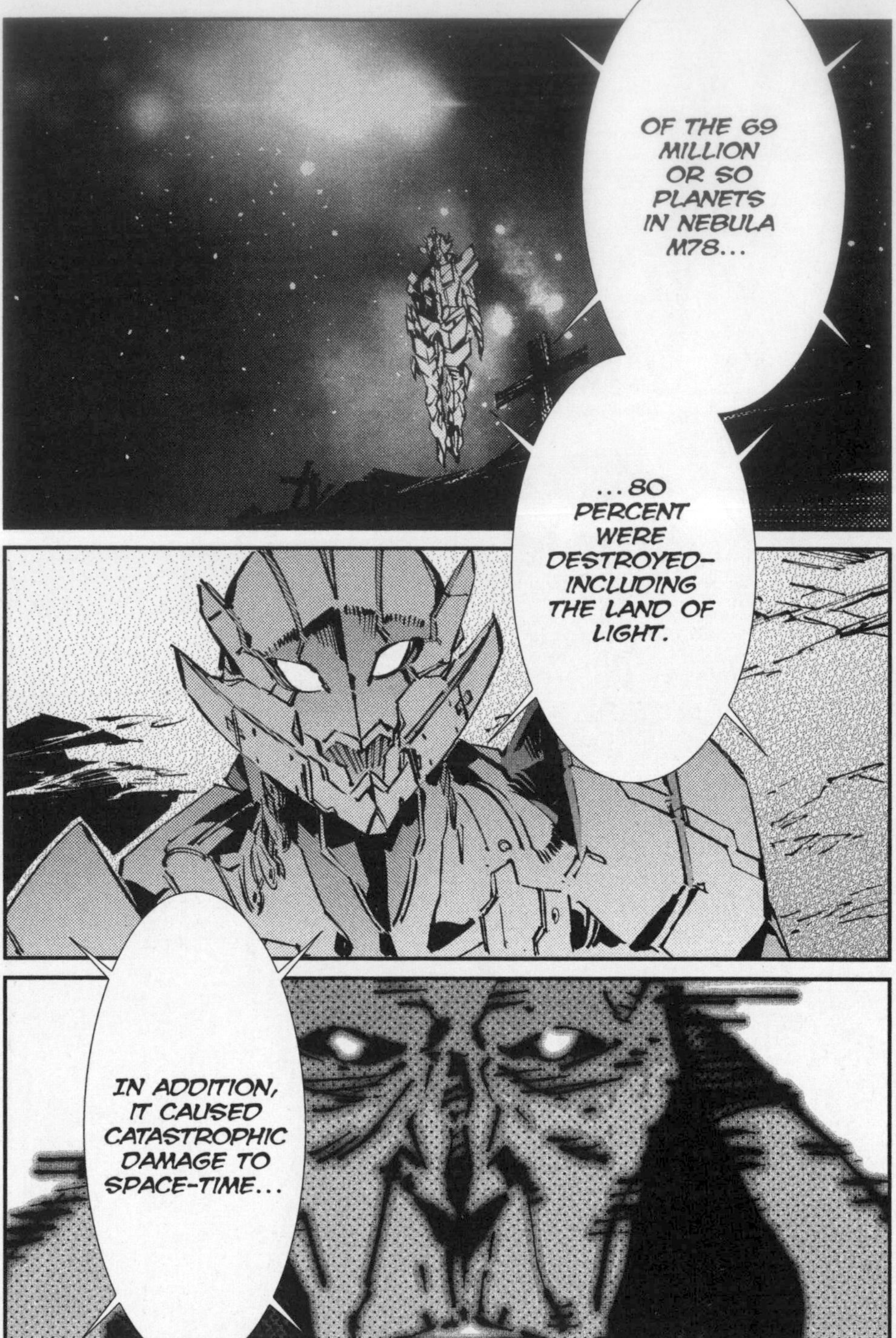
OF THE 69 MILLION OR SO PLANETS IN NEBULA M78...
...80 PERCENT WERE DESTROYED-INCLUDING THE LAND OF LIGHT.
IN ADDITION, IT CAUSED CATASTROPHIC DAMAGE TO SPACE-TIME...

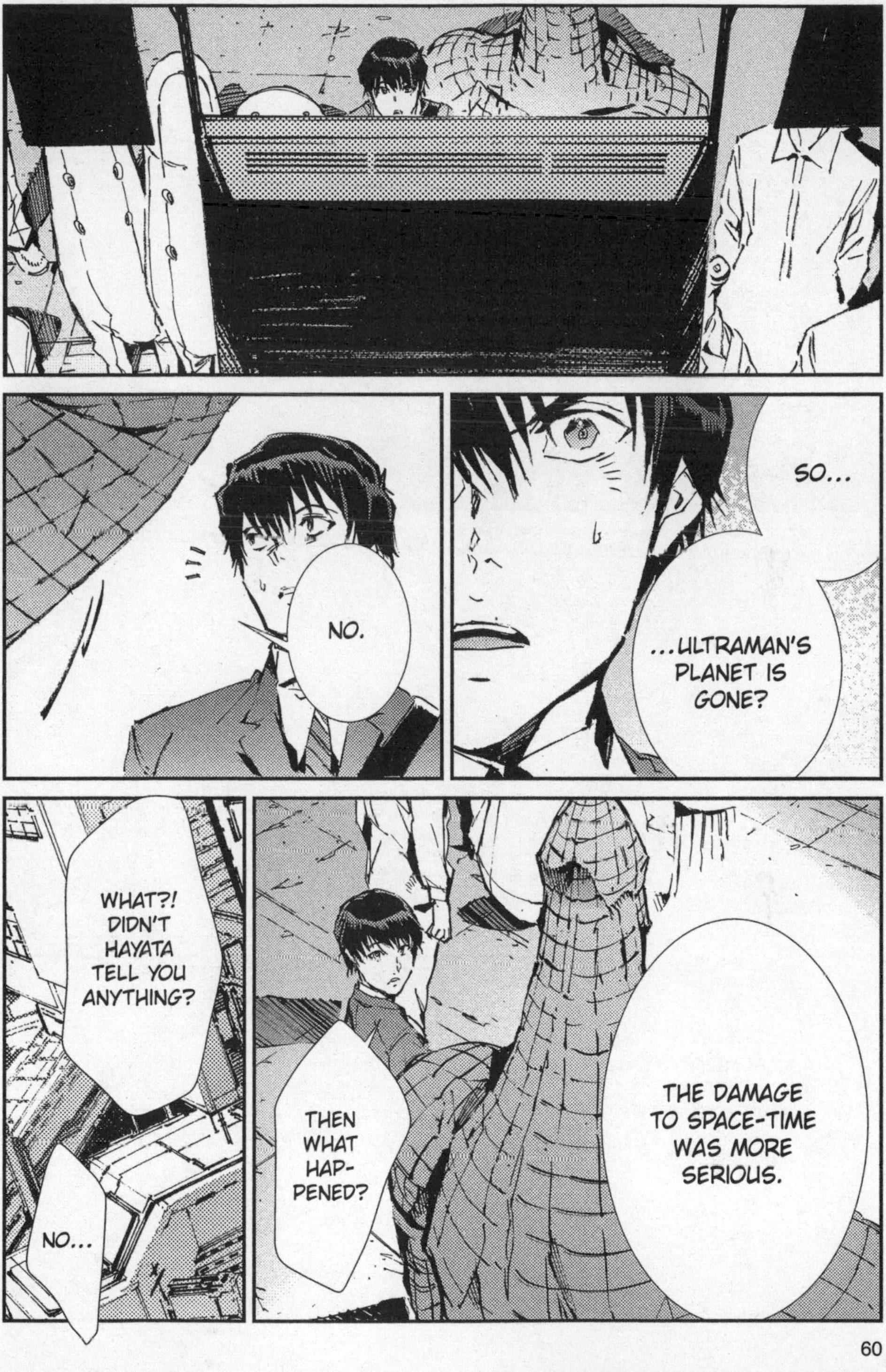
SO...
...ULTRAMAN'S PLANET IS GONE?
NO.
THE DAMAGE TO SPACE-TIME WAS MORE SERIOUS.
THEN WHAT HAP-PENED?
WHAT?! DIDN'T HAYATA TELL YOU ANYTHING?
NO...

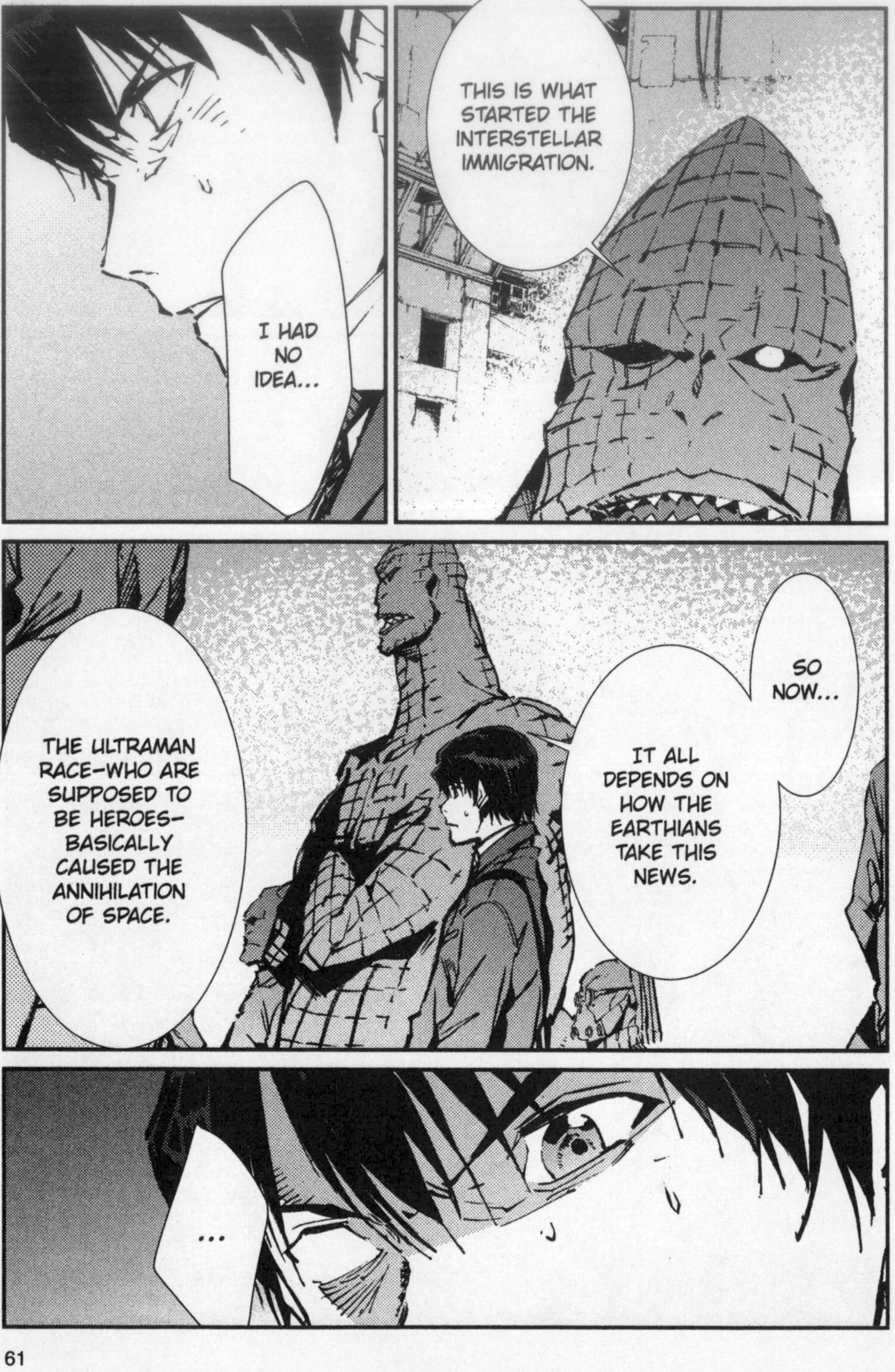
THIS IS WHAT STARTED THE INTERSTELLAR IMMIGRATION.
I HAD NO IDEA...
SO NOW...
IT ALL DEPENDS ON HOW THE EARTHIANS TAKE THIS NEWS.
THE ULTRAMAN RACE—WHO ARE SUPPOSED TO BE HEROES—BASICALLY CAUSED THE ANNIHILATION OF SPACE.
...

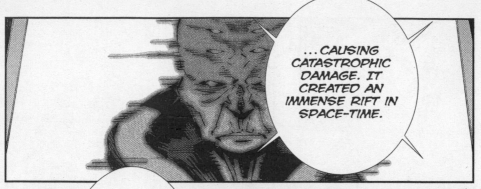

...CAUSING CATASTROPHIC DAMAGE. IT CREATED AN IMMENSE RIFT IN SPACE-TIME.

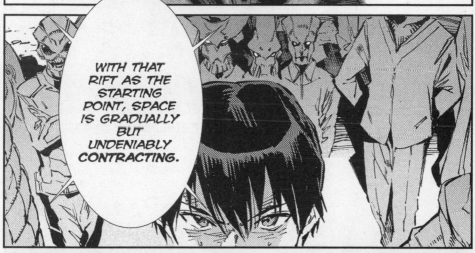

WITH THAT RIFT AS THE STARTING POINT, SPACE IS GRADUALLY BUT UNDENIABLY CONTRACTING.

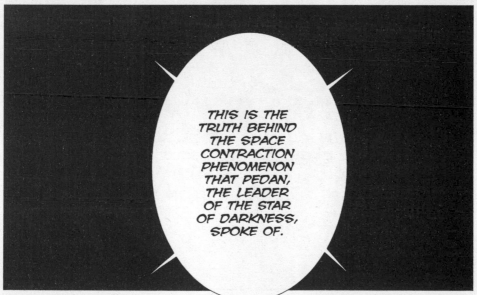

THIS IS THE TRUTH BEHIND THE SPACE CONTRACTION PHENOMENON THAT PEDAN, THE LEADER OF THE STAR OF DARKNESS, SPOKE OF.

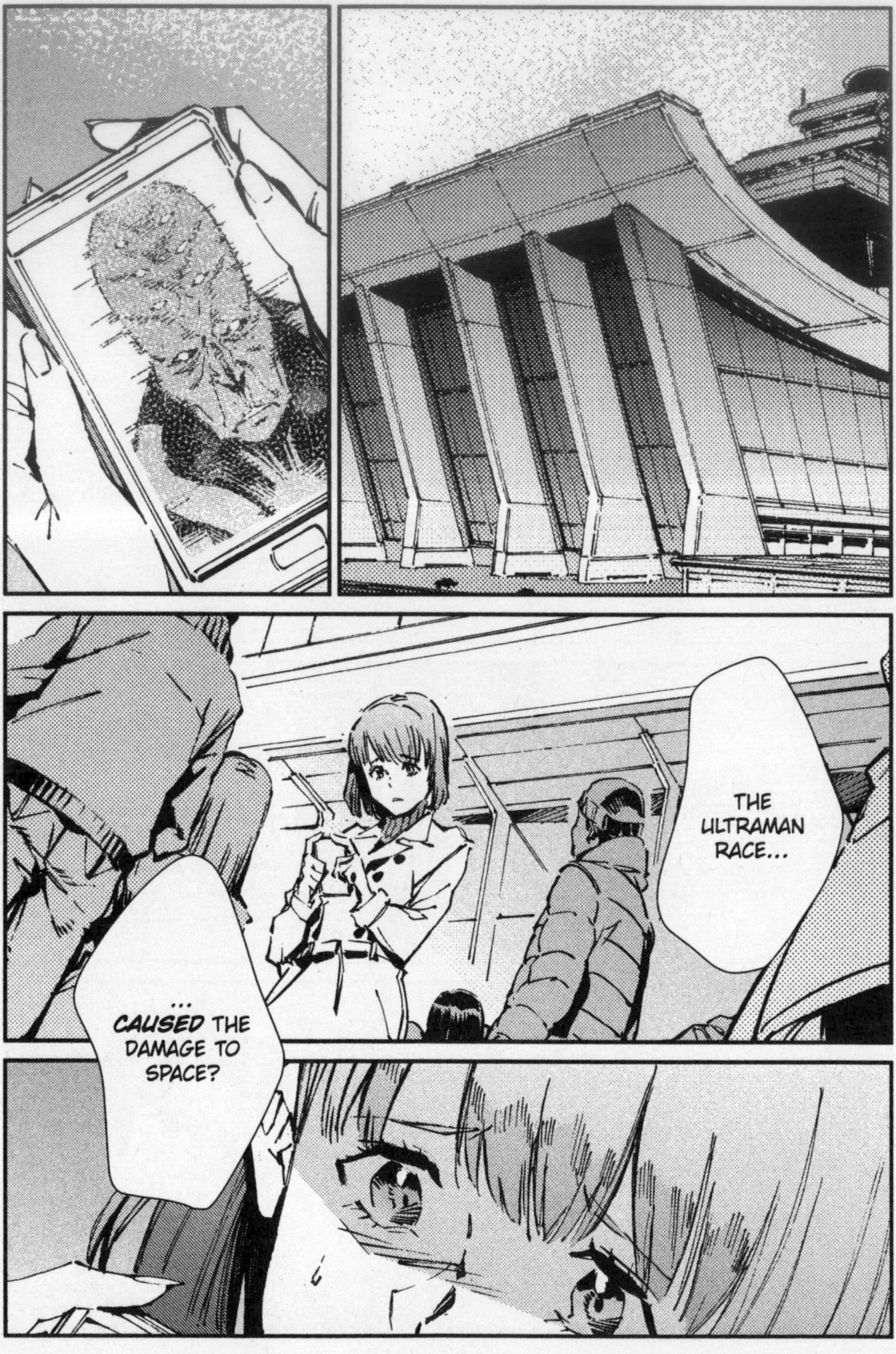
THE ULTRAMAN RACE...
... CAUSED THE DAMAGE TO SPACE?

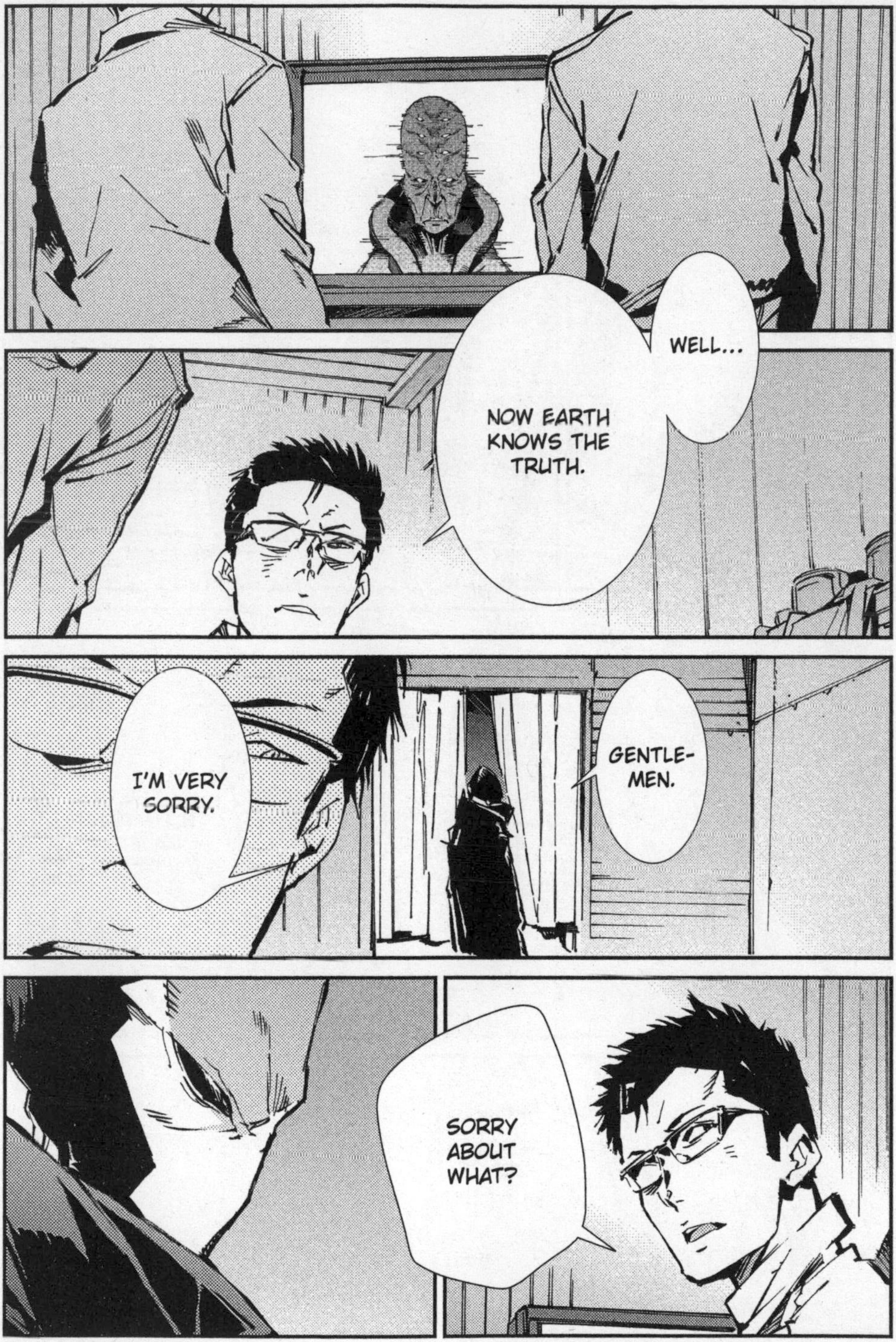
WELL...
NOW EARTH KNOWS THE TRUTH.
GENTLE-MEN.
I'M VERY SORRY.
SORRY ABOUT WHAT?

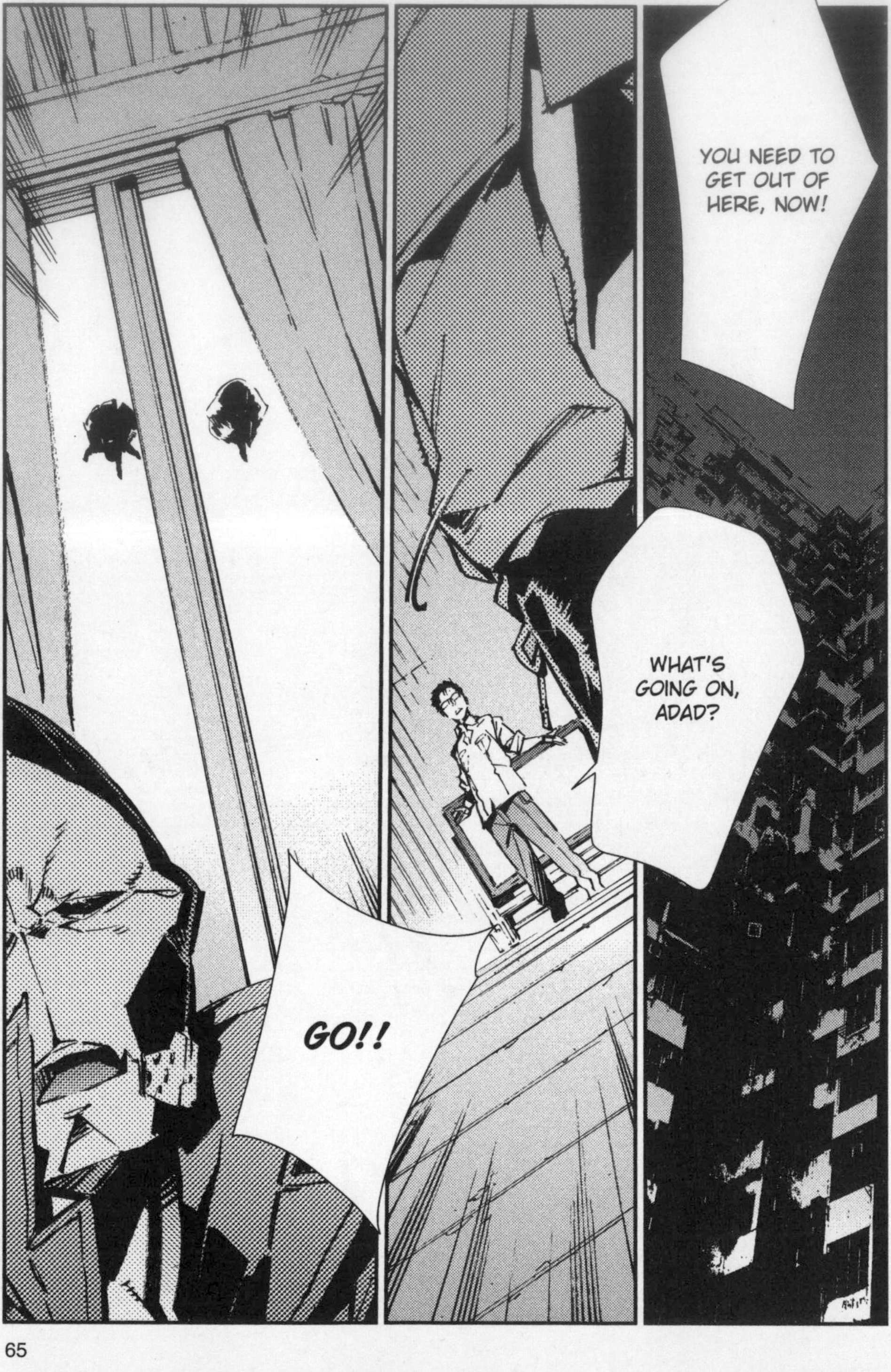
YOU NEED TO GET OUT OF HERE, NOW!
WHAT'S GOING ON, ADAD?
GO!!

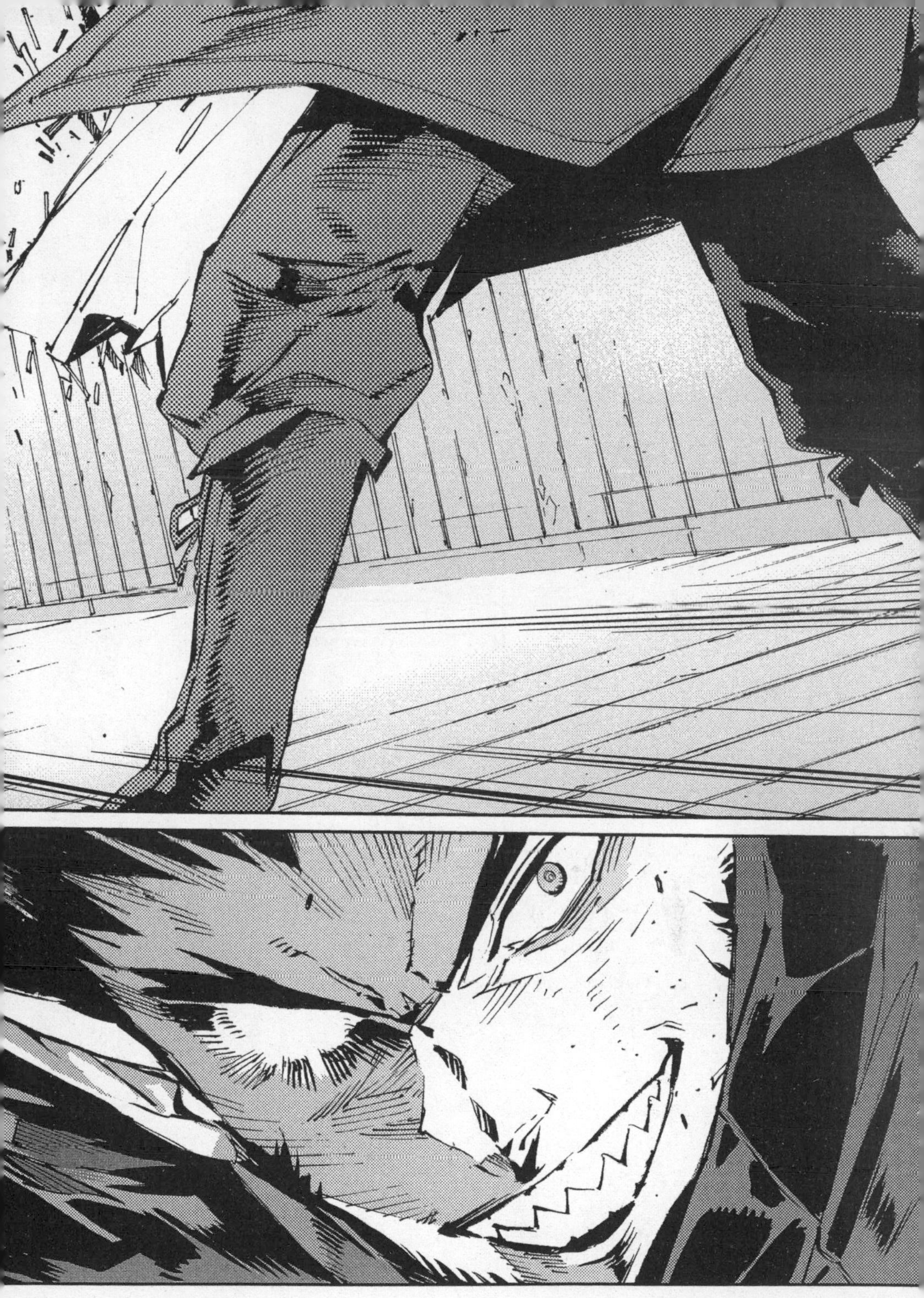

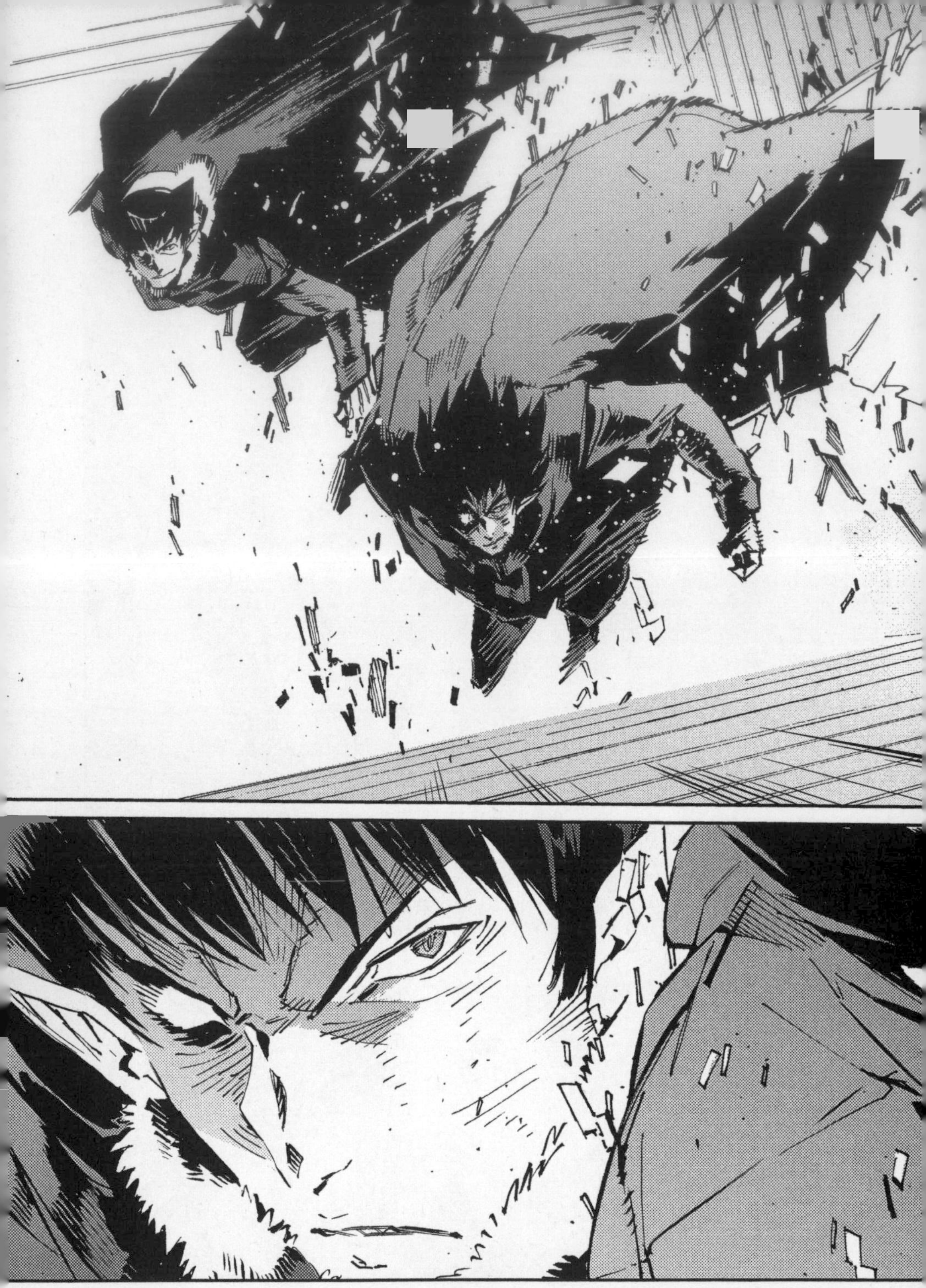

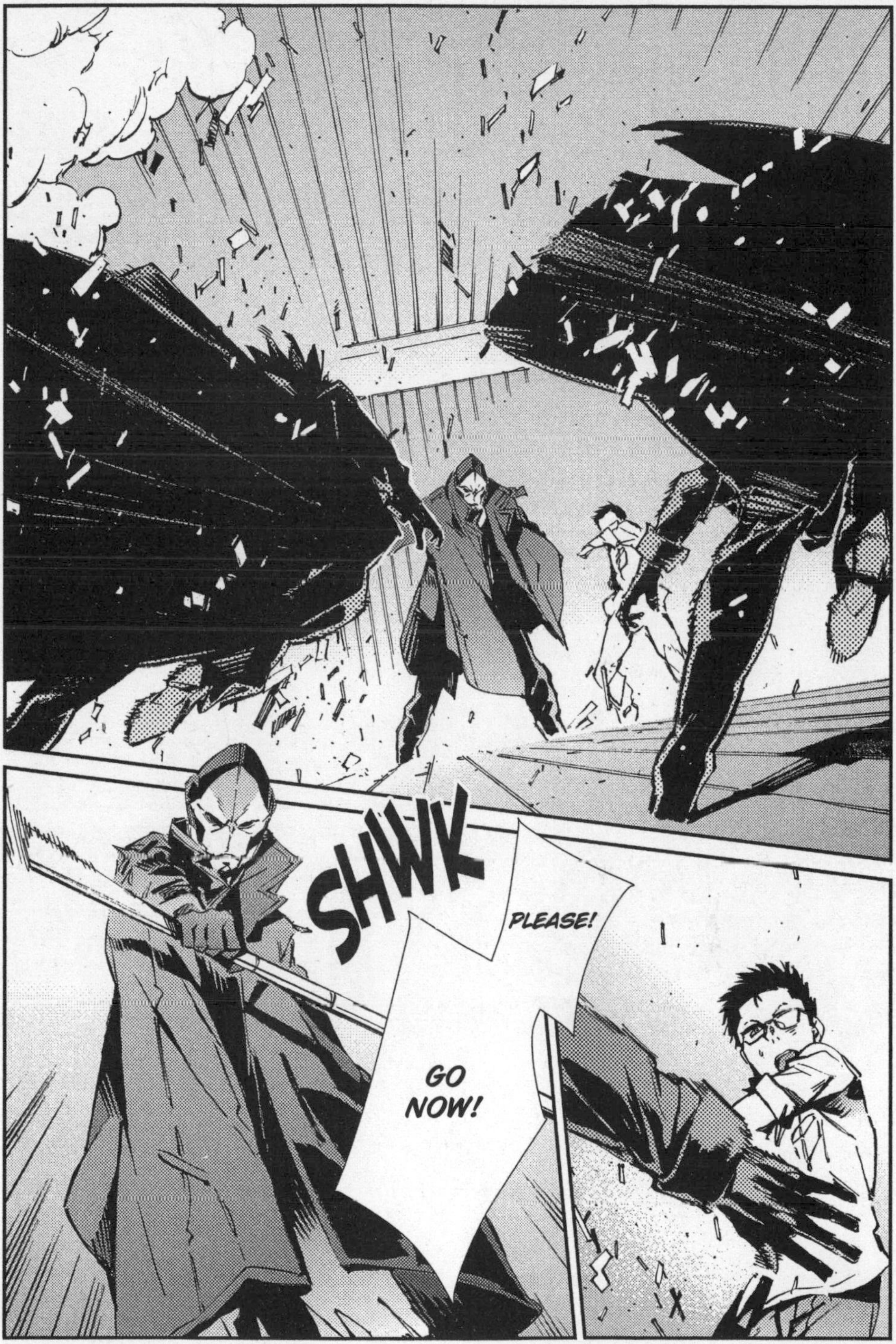
PLEASE!
SHWK
GO NOW!

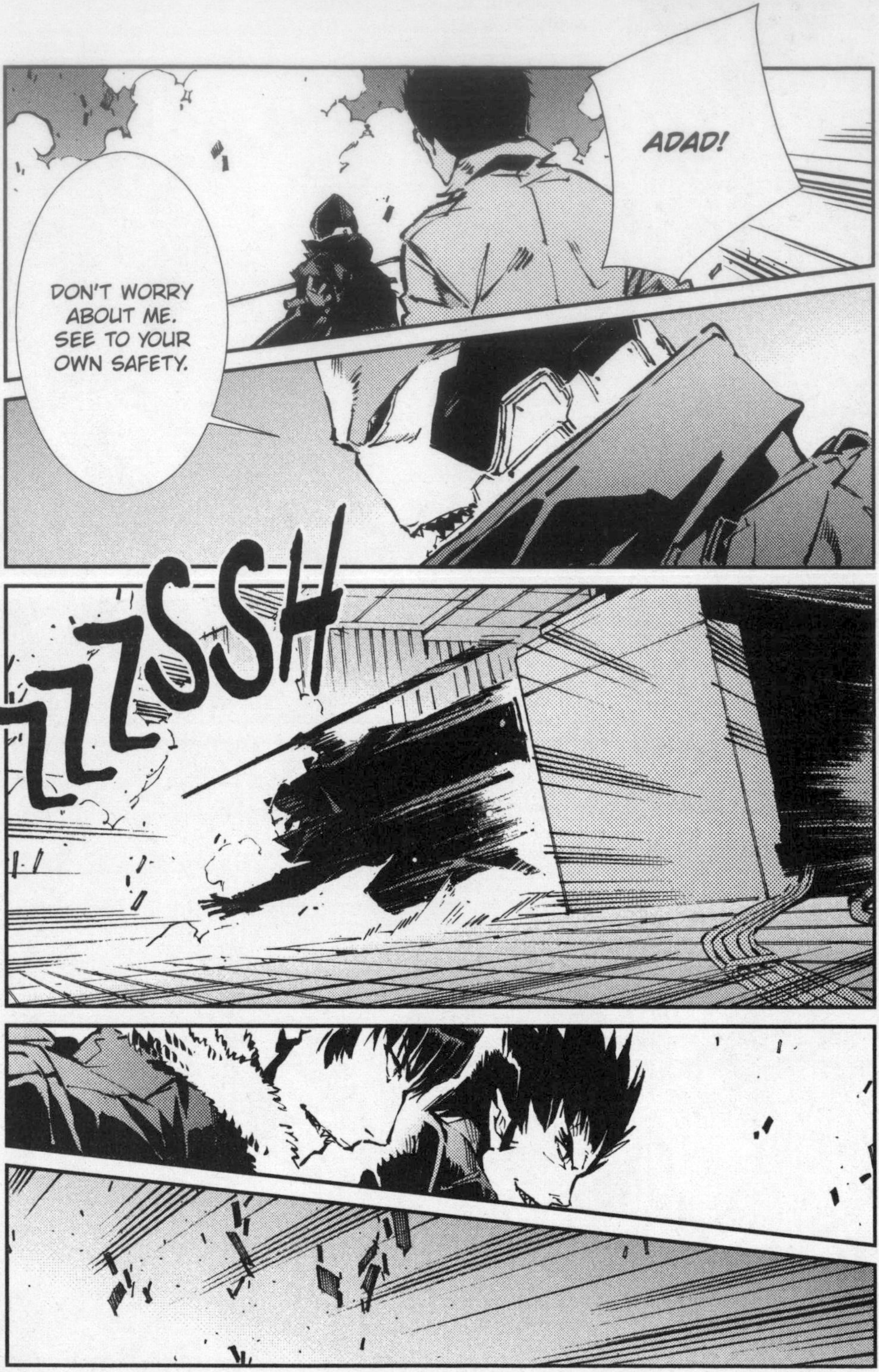
ADAD!
DON'T WORRY ABOUT ME. SEE TO YOUR OWN SAFETY.
ZZZSSH

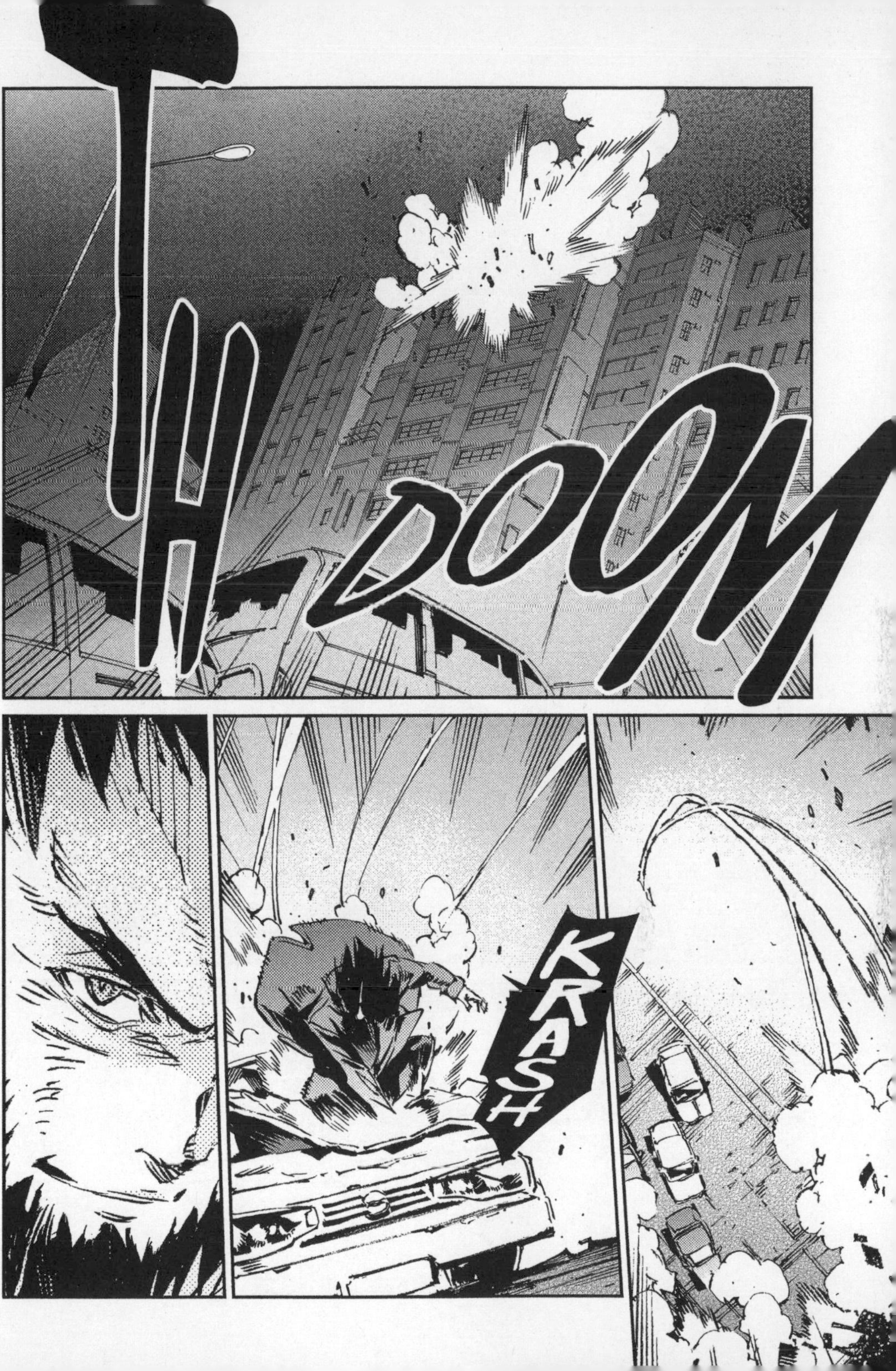
THDOOM
KRASH

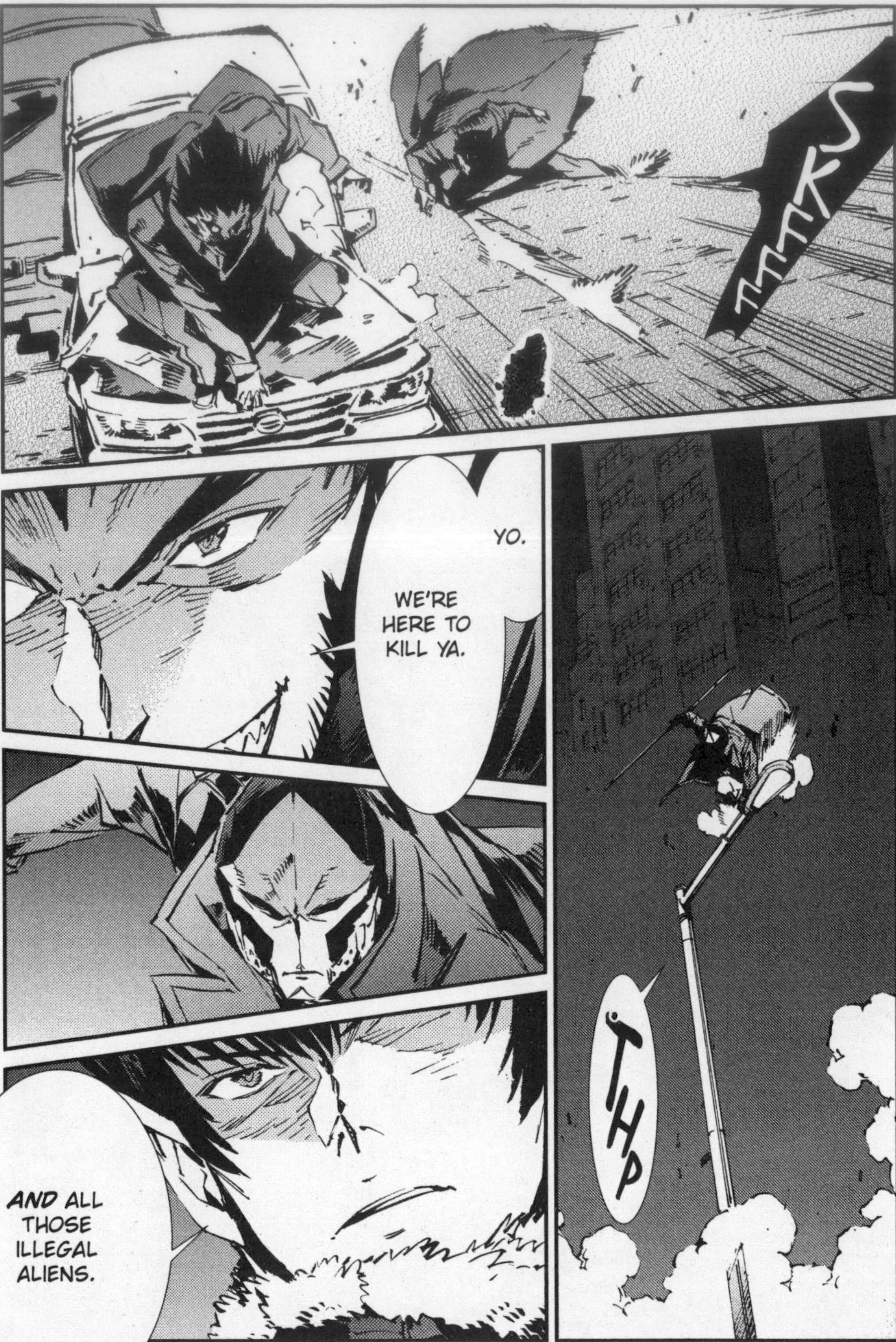
SKTTTT
THP
YO.
WE'RE HERE TO KILL YA.
AND ALL THOSE ILLEGAL ALIENS.

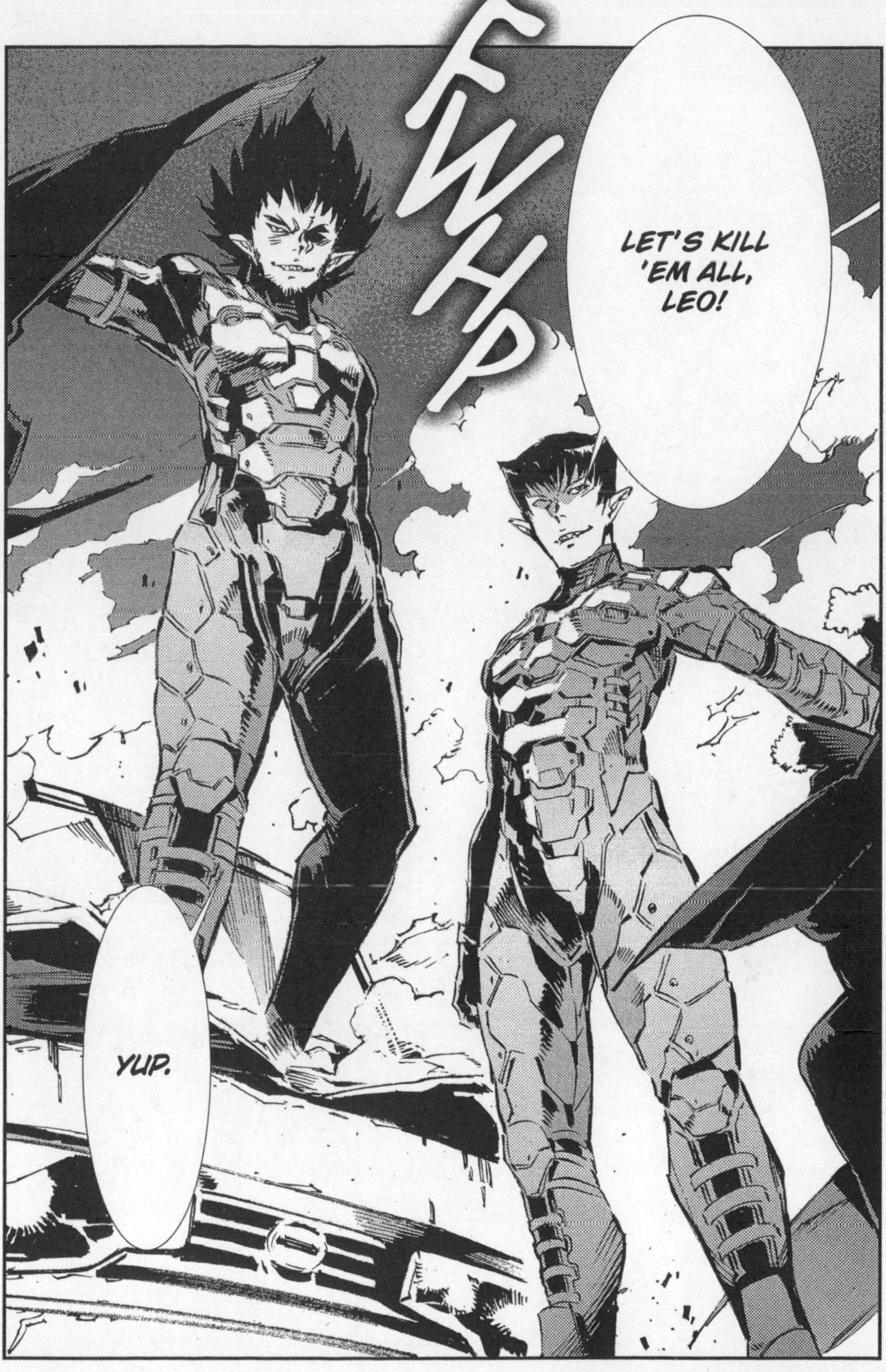
LET'S KILL 'EM ALL, LEO!
FWHP
YUP.

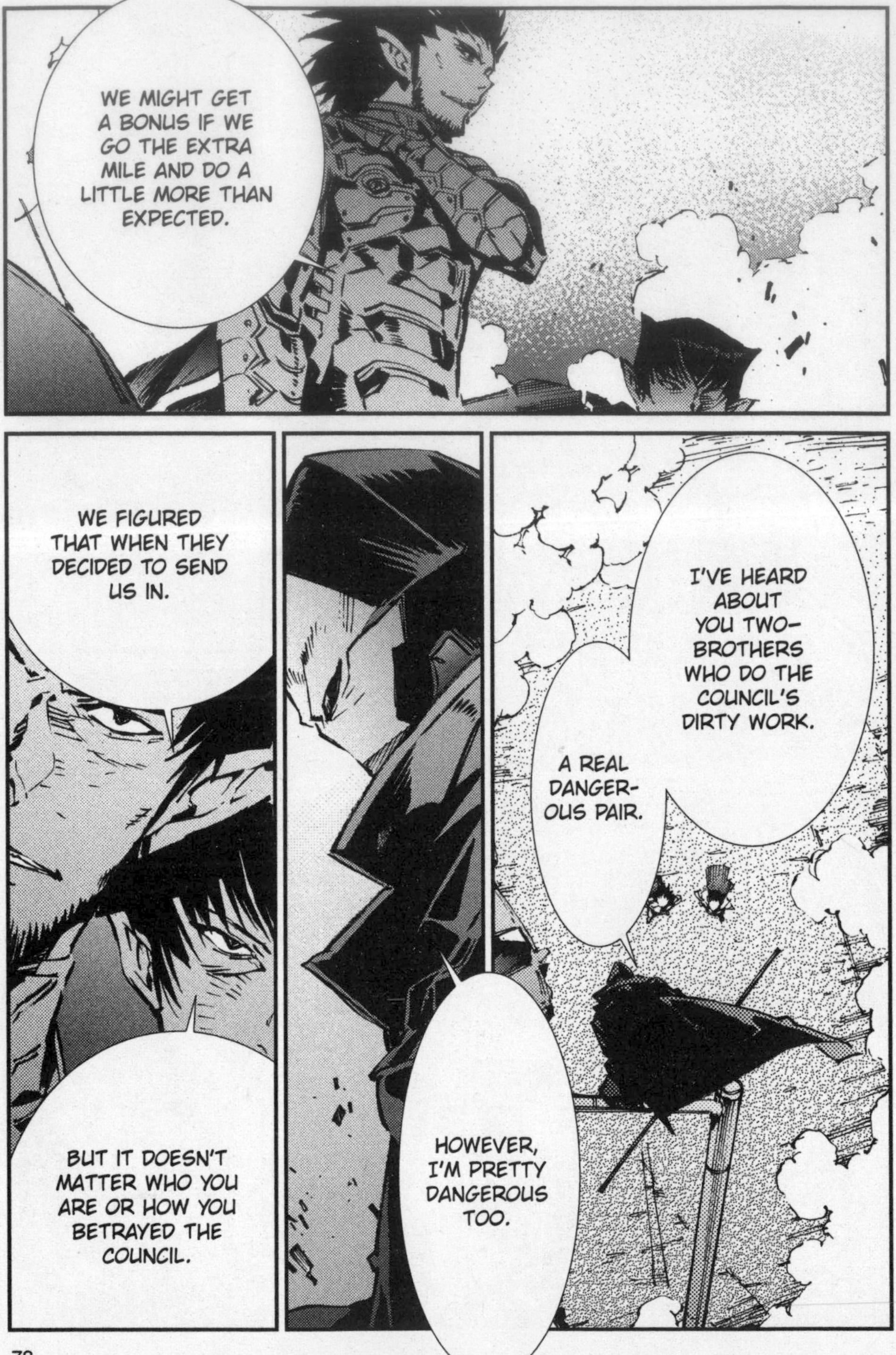
WE MIGHT GET A BONUS IF WE GO THE EXTRA MILE AND DO A LITTLE MORE THAN EXPECTED.
I'VE HEARD ABOUT YOU TWO— BROTHERS WHO DO THE COUNCIL'S DIRTY WORK.
A REAL DANGER-OUS PAIR.
HOWEVER, I'M PRETTY DANGEROUS TOO.
WE FIGURED THAT WHEN THEY DECIDED TO SEND US IN.
BUT IT DOESN'T MATTER WHO YOU ARE OR HOW YOU BETRAYED THE COUNCIL.

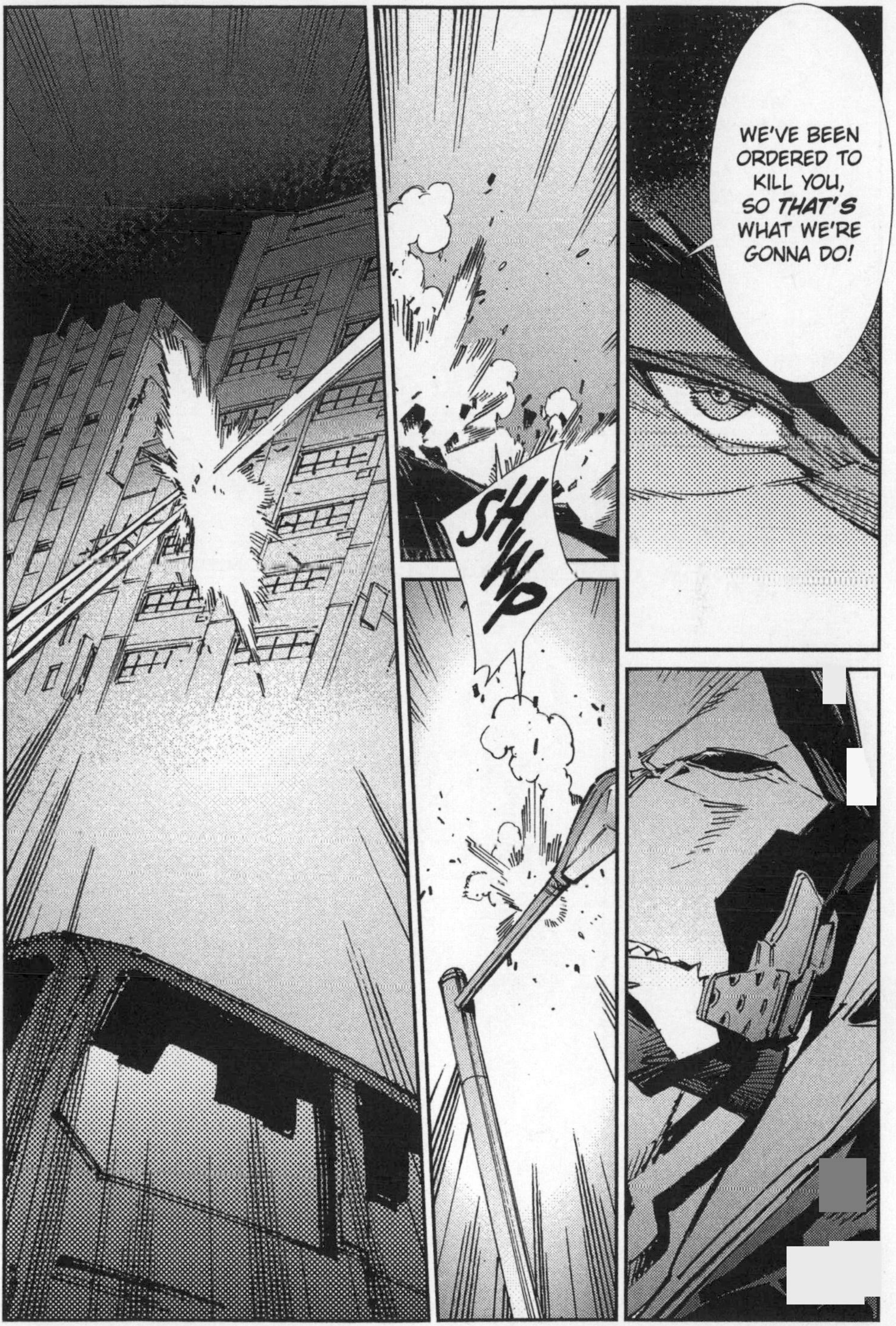
WE'VE BEEN ORDERED TO KILL YOU, SO *THAT'S* WHAT WE'RE GONNA DO!
SHWP

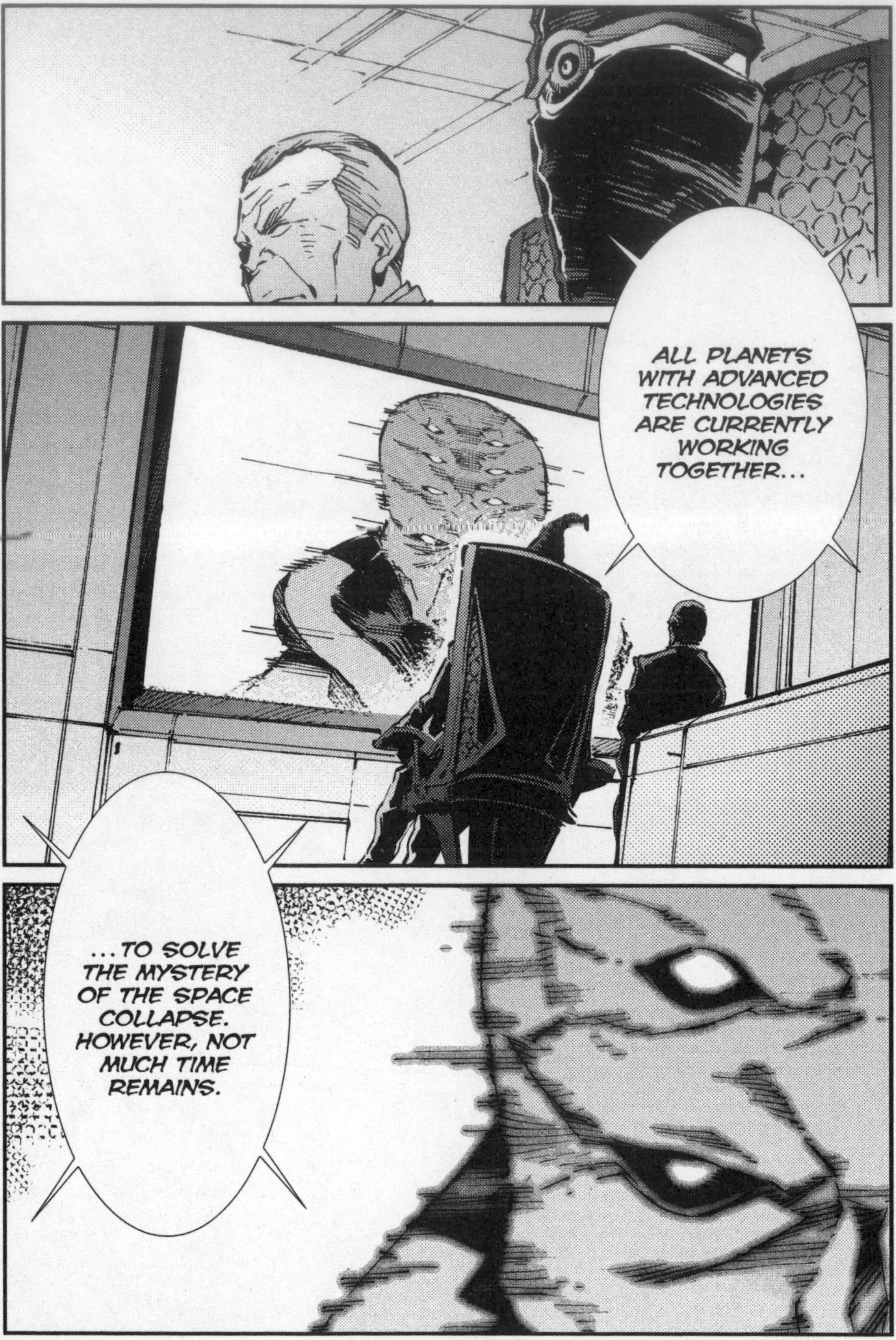
ALL PLANETS WITH ADVANCED TECHNOLOGIES ARE CURRENTLY WORKING TOGETHER...
...TO SOLVE THE MYSTERY OF THE SPACE COLLAPSE. HOWEVER, NOT MUCH TIME REMAINS.

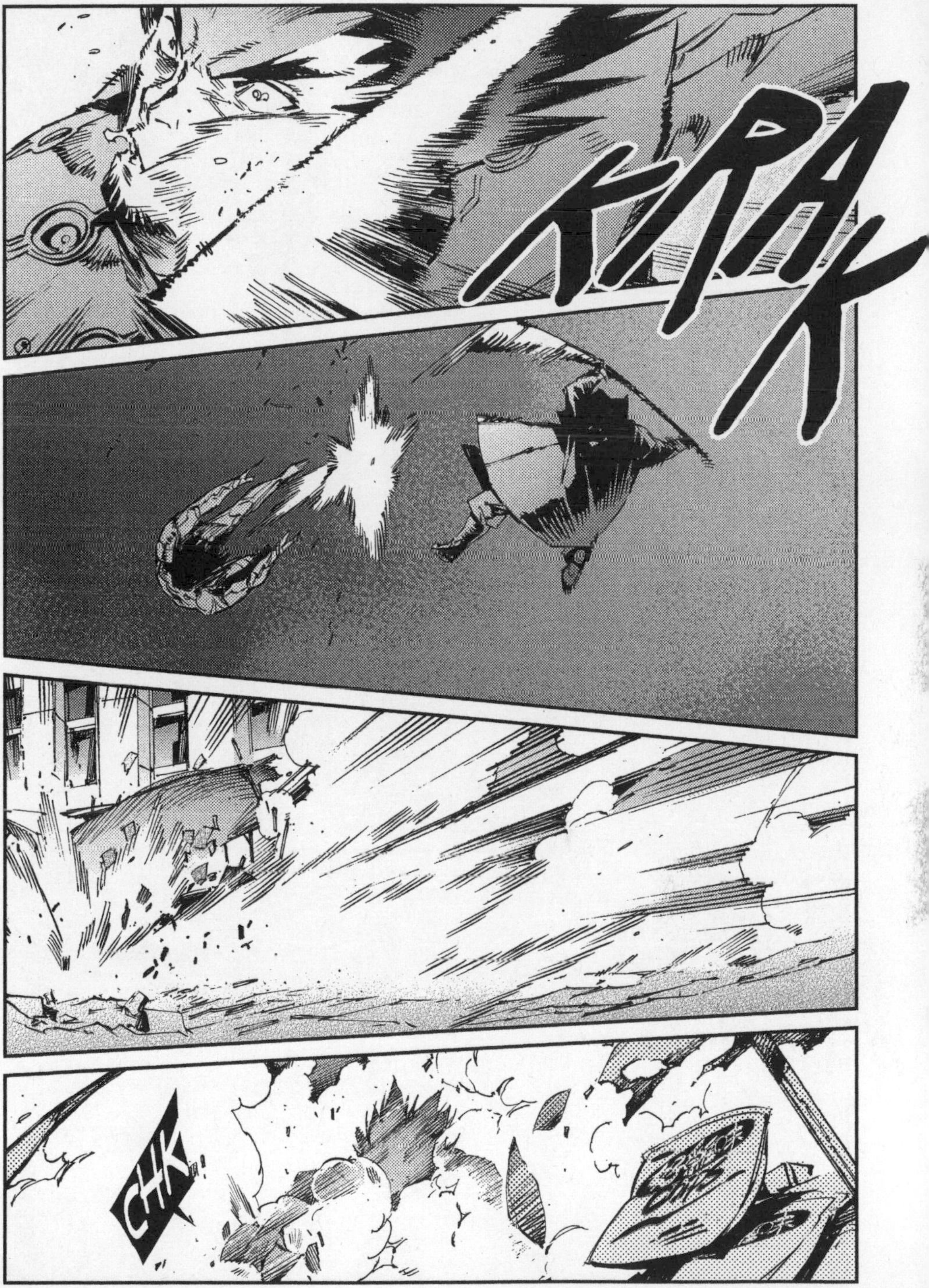
KRAK
CHK

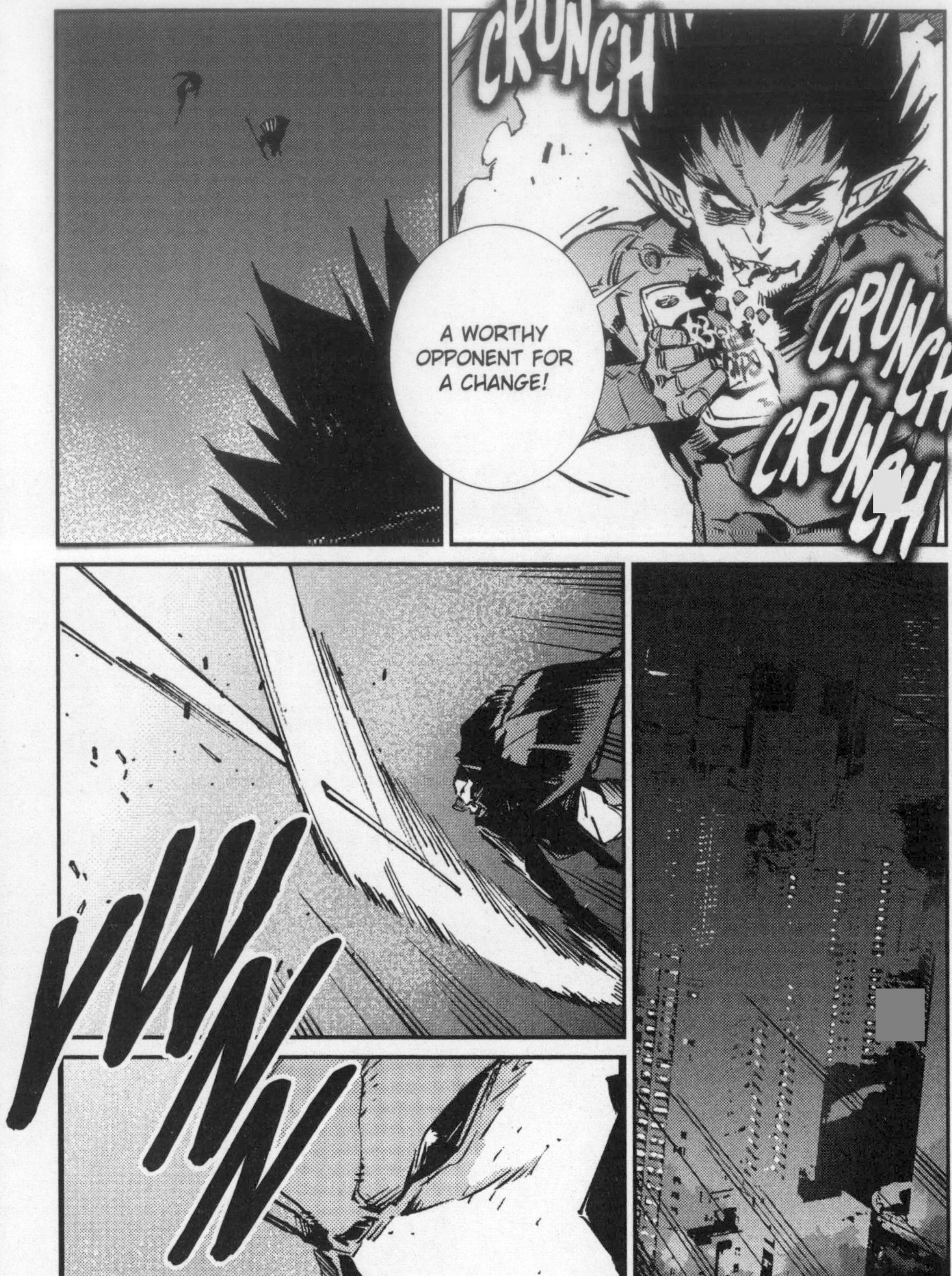
CRUNCH
A WORTHY OPPONENT FOR A CHANGE!
CRUNCH
CRUNCH
VWNNN

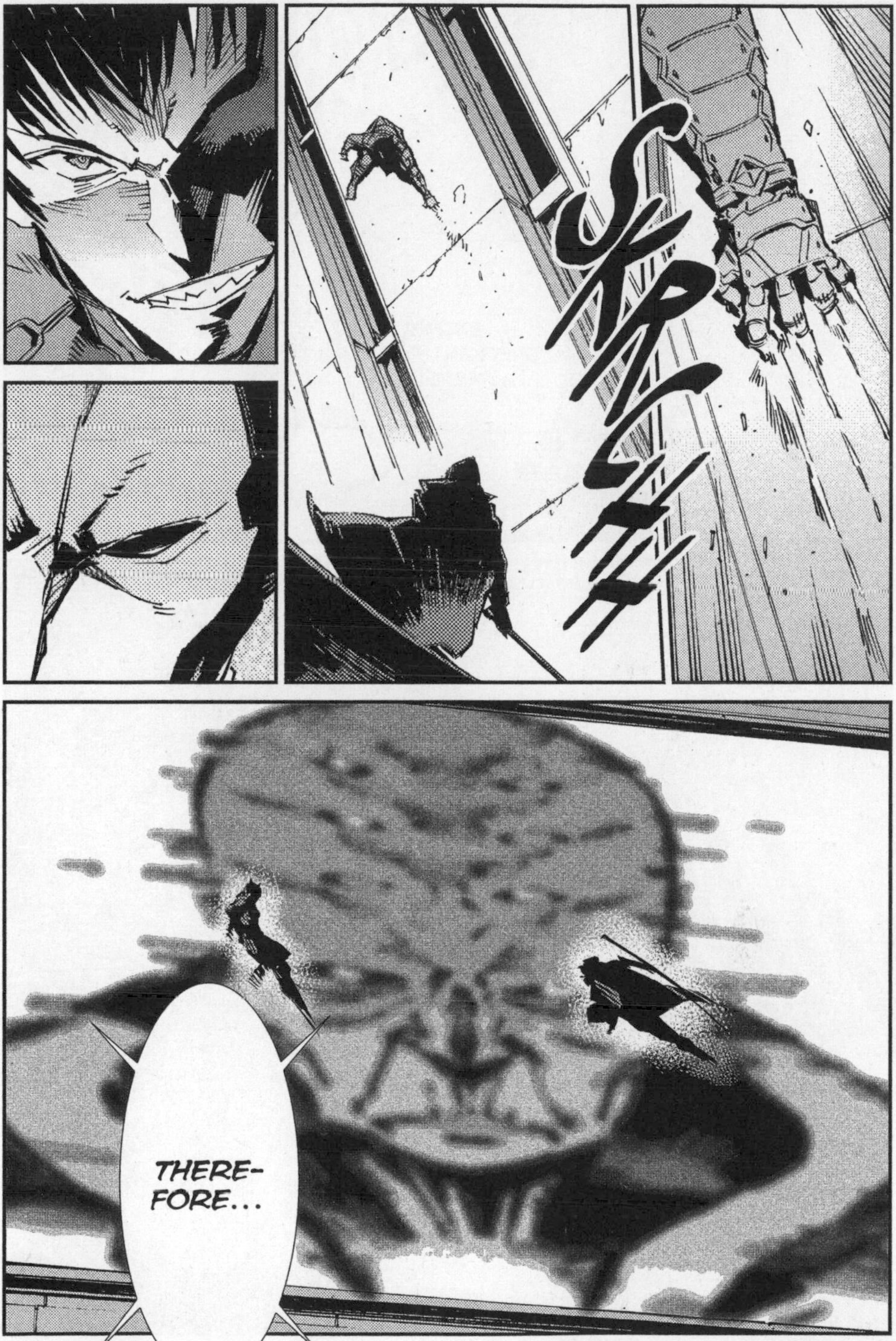
SKRASHHH
THERE-FORE...

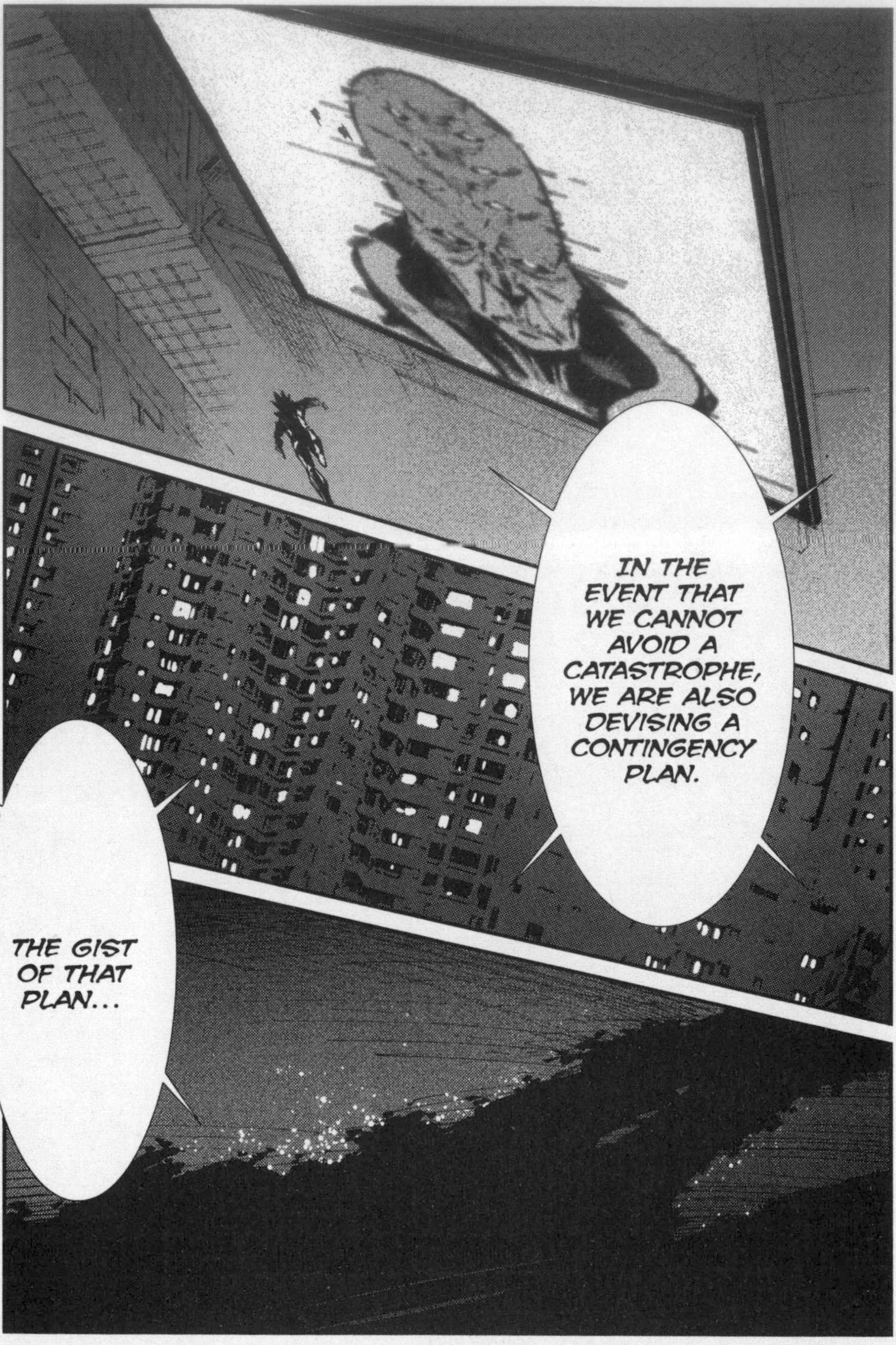
IN THE EVENT THAT WE CANNOT AVOID A CATASTROPHE, WE ARE ALSO DEVISING A CONTINGENCY PLAN.
THE GIST OF THAT PLAN...

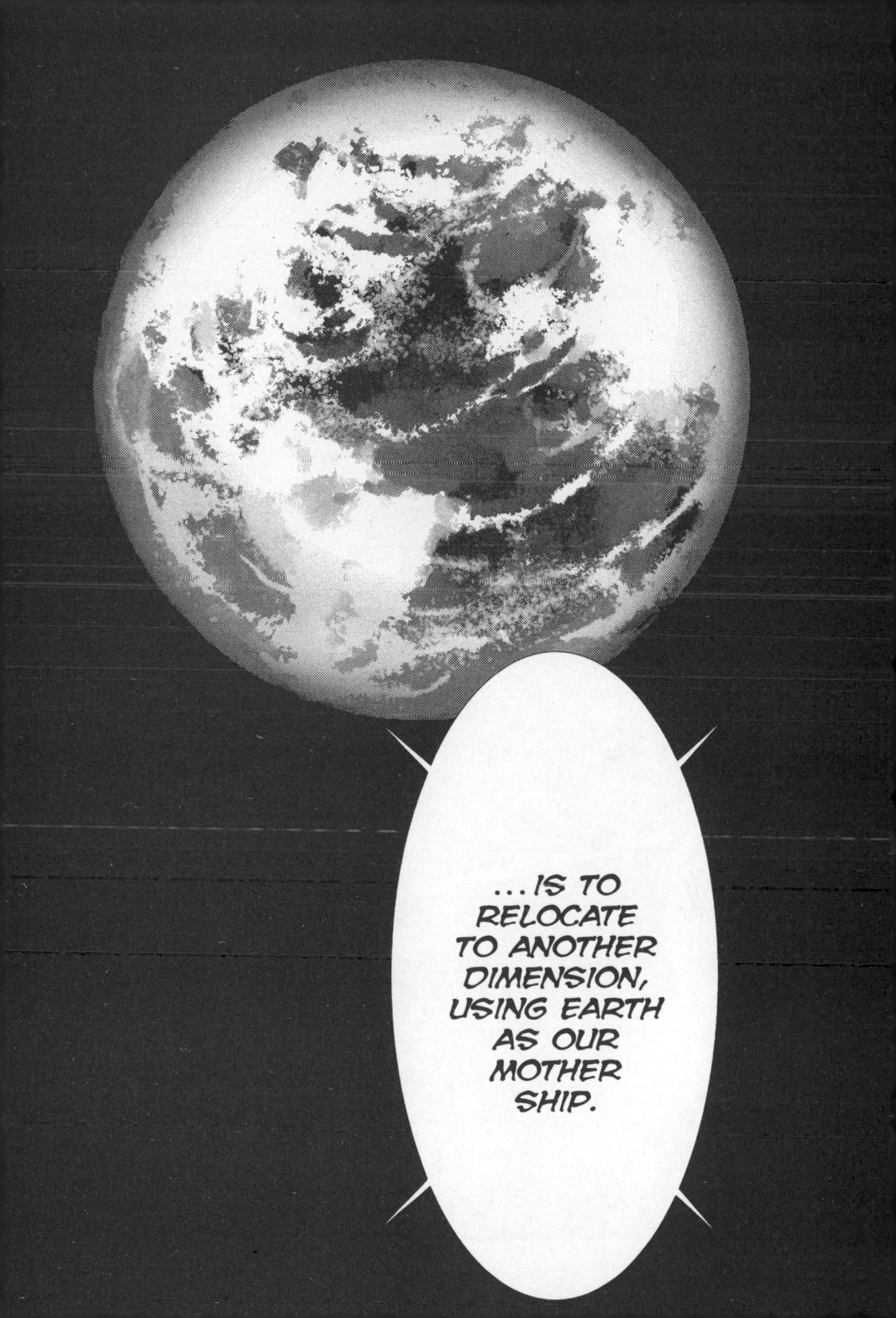
...IS TO RELOCATE TO ANOTHER DIMENSION, USING EARTH AS OUR MOTHER SHIP.

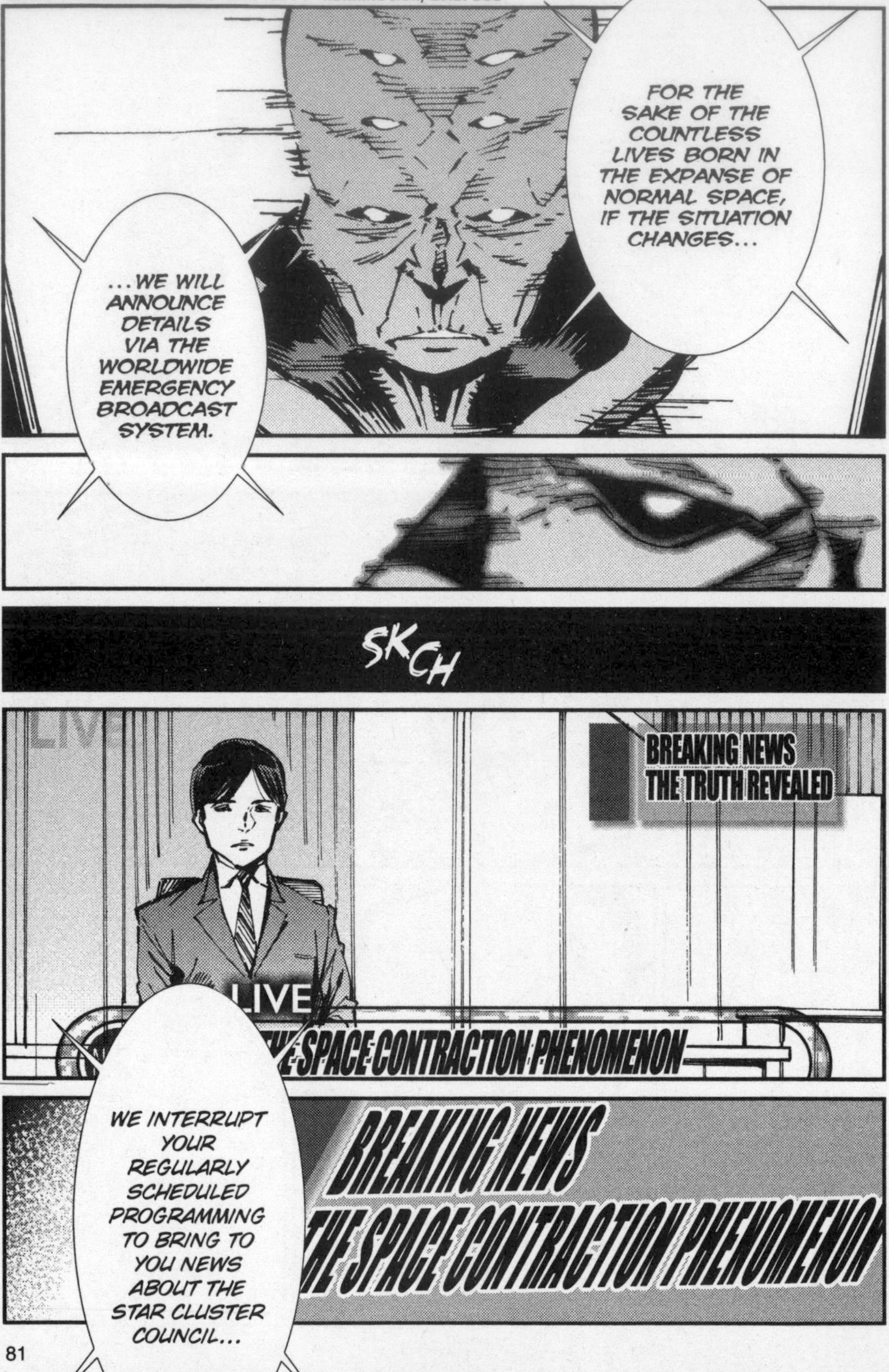
FOR THE SAKE OF THE COUNTLESS LIVES BORN IN THE EXPANSE OF NORMAL SPACE, IF THE SITUATION CHANGES...
...WE WILL ANNOUNCE DETAILS VIA THE WORLDWIDE EMERGENCY BROADCAST SYSTEM.
SKCH
BREAKING NEWS THE TRUTH REVEALED
LIVE
SPACE CONTRACTION PHENOMENON
BREAKING NEWS THE SPACE CONTRACTION PHENOMENON
WE INTERRUPT YOUR REGULARLY SCHEDULED PROGRAMMING TO BRING TO YOU NEWS ABOUT THE STAR CLUSTER COUNCIL...

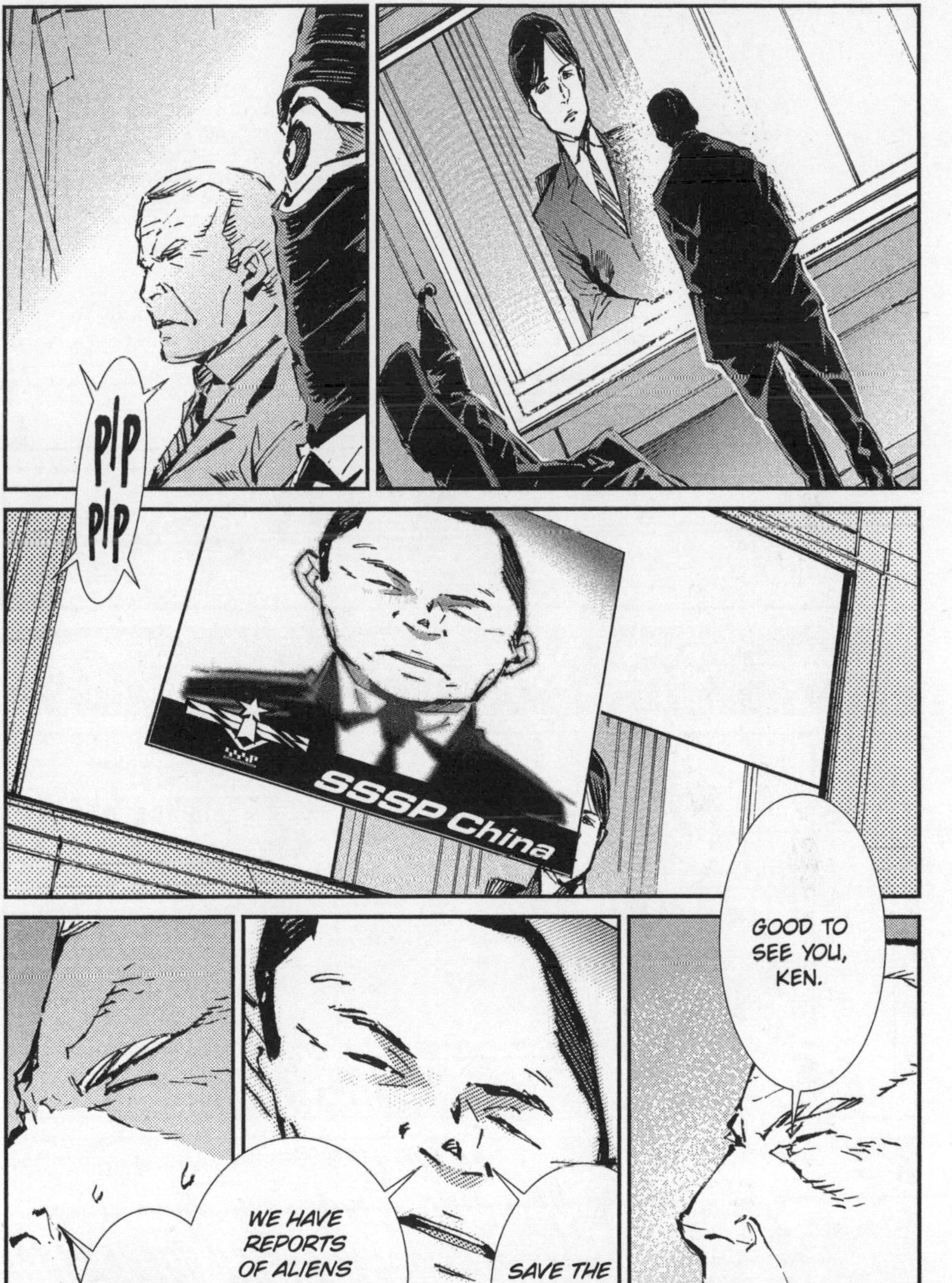
PIP PIP
SSSP China
GOOD TO SEE YOU, KEN.
SAVE THE NICETIES, IDE.
WE HAVE REPORTS OF ALIENS FIGHTING IN HONG KONG.
TAKE A LOOK AT THIS.

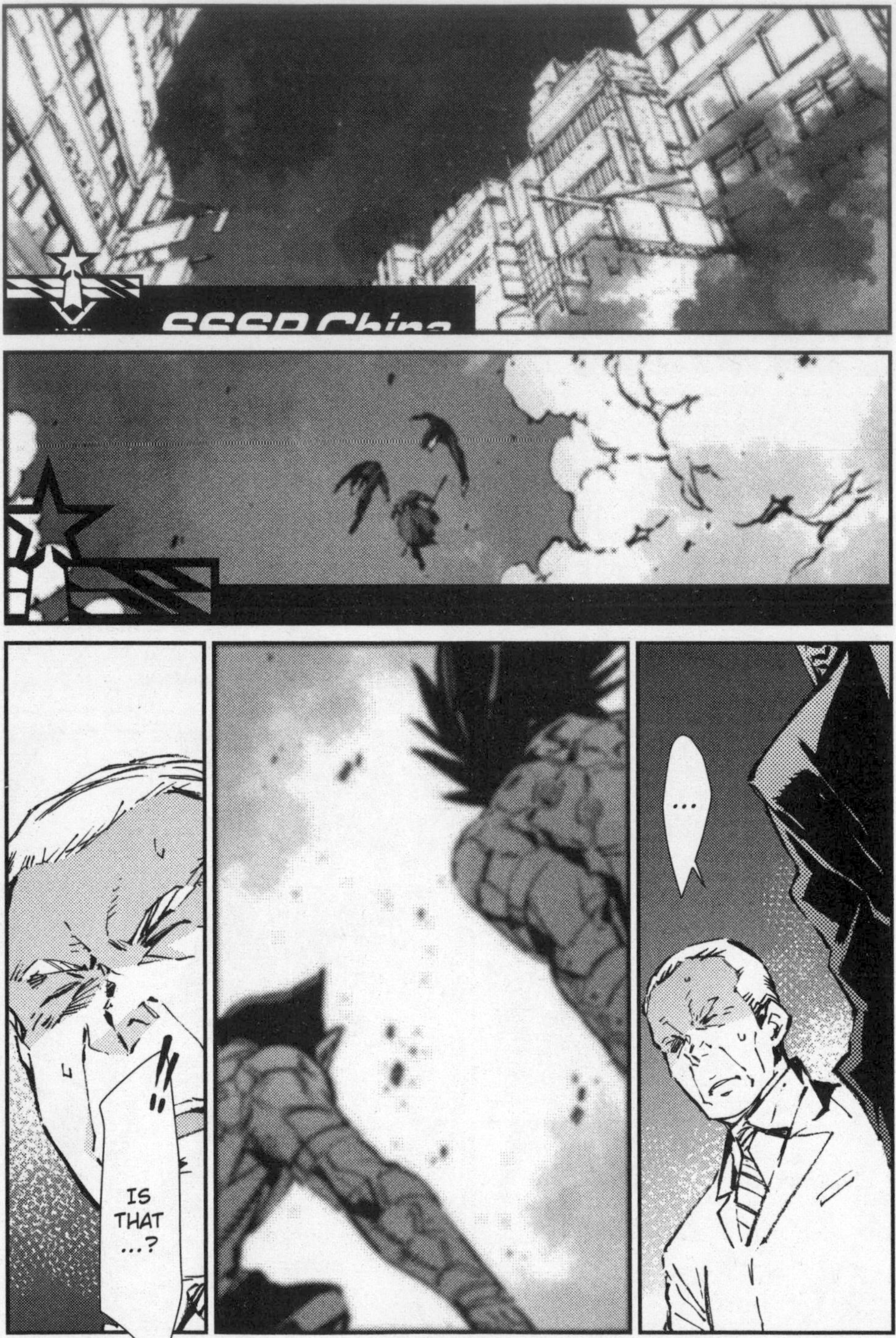
SSSR China
...
IS THAT ...?

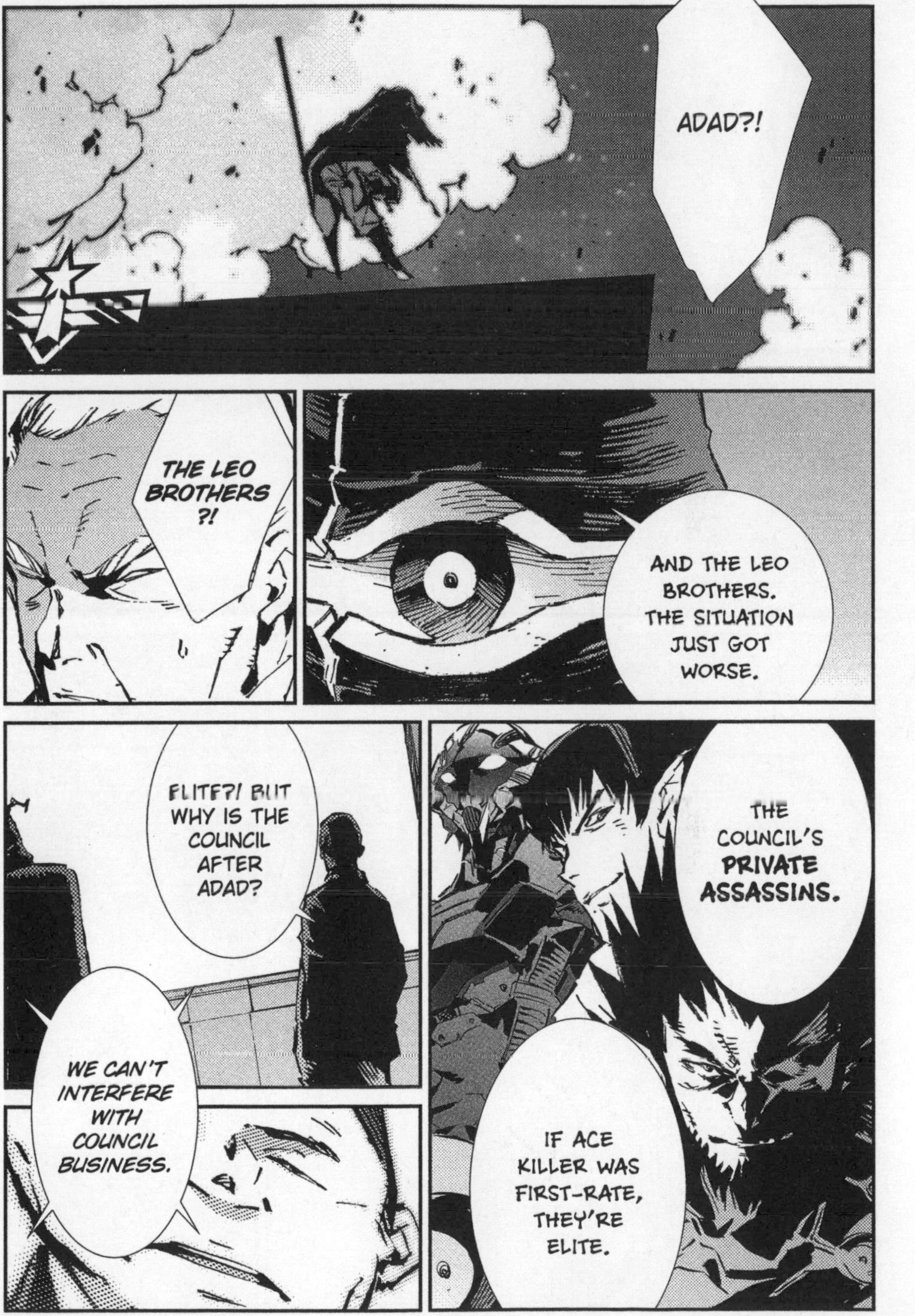
ADAD?!
AND THE LEO BROTHERS. THE SITUATION JUST GOT WORSE.
THE LEO BROTHERS ?!
THE COUNCIL'S PRIVATE ASSASSINS.
IF ACE KILLER WAS FIRST-RATE, THEY'RE ELITE.
ELITE?! BUT WHY IS THE COUNCIL AFTER ADAD?
WE CAN'T INTERFERE WITH COUNCIL BUSINESS.

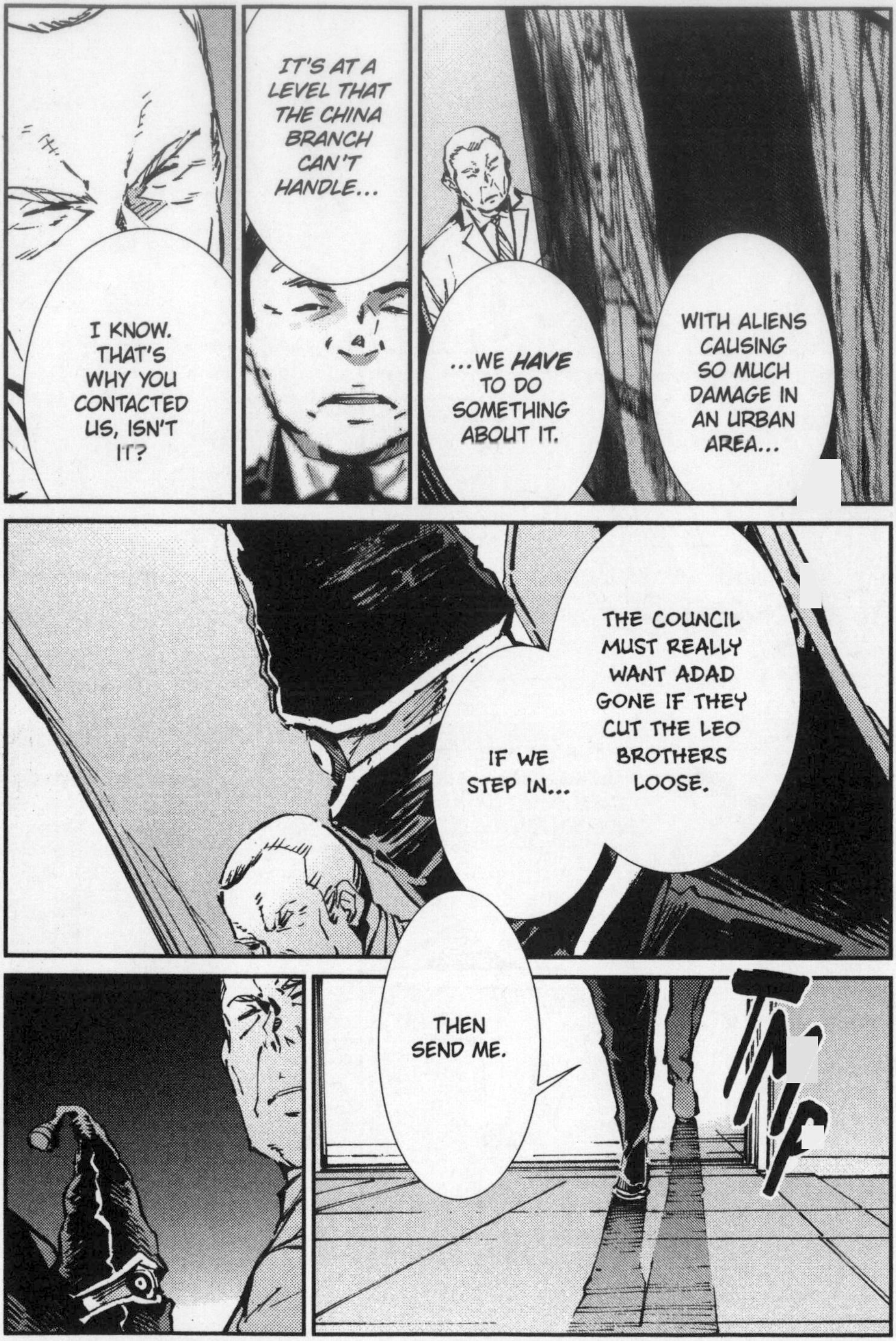
WITH ALIENS CAUSING SO MUCH DAMAGE IN AN URBAN AREA...
...WE *HAVE* TO DO SOMETHING ABOUT IT.
IT'S AT A LEVEL THAT THE CHINA BRANCH CAN'T HANDLE...
I KNOW. THAT'S WHY YOU CONTACTED US, ISN'T IT?
THE COUNCIL MUST REALLY WANT ADAD GONE IF THEY CUT THE LEO BROTHERS LOOSE.
IF WE STEP IN...
THEN SEND ME.

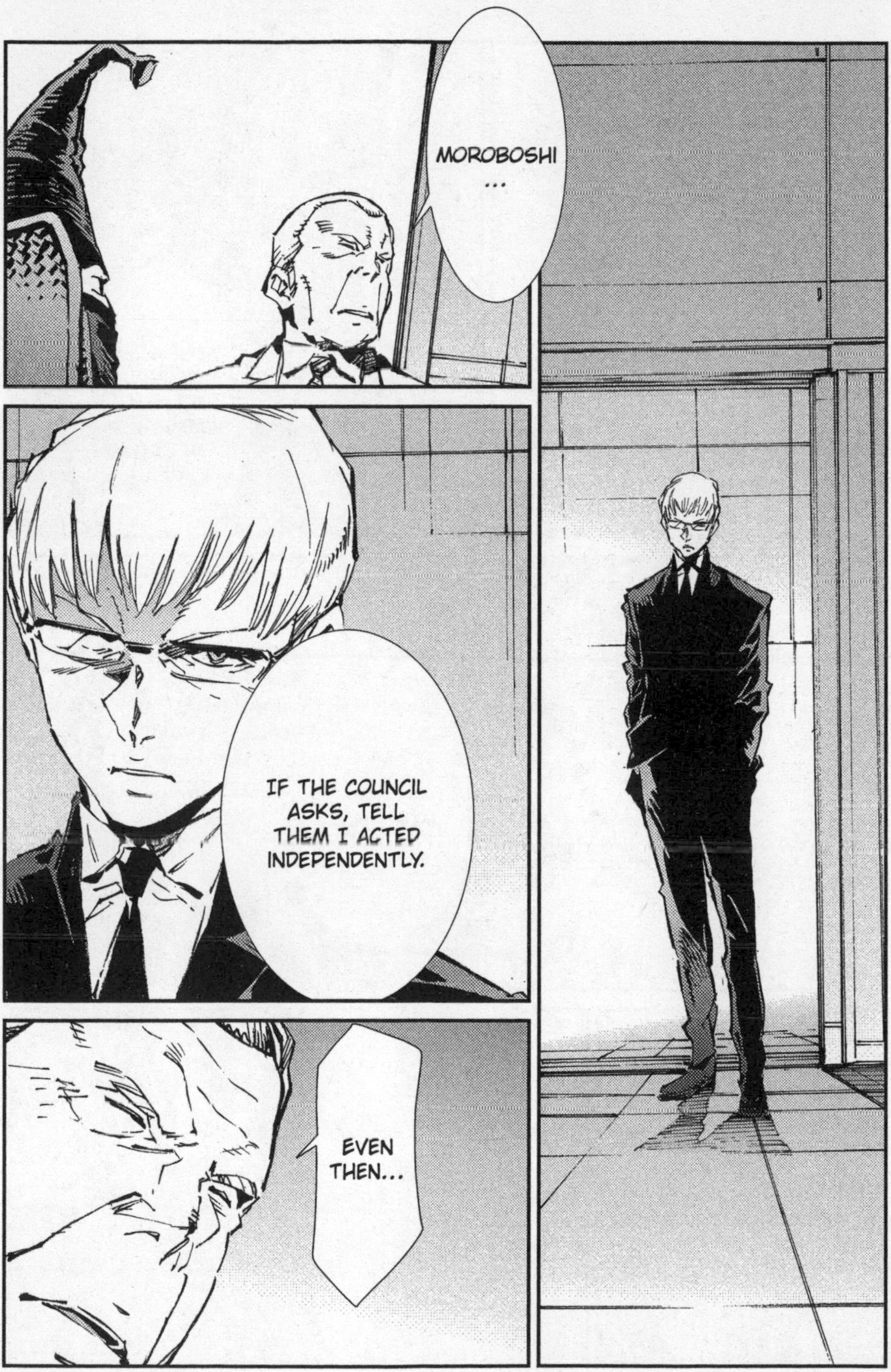
MOROBOSHI ...
IF THE COUNCIL ASKS, TELL THEM I ACTED INDEPENDENTLY.
EVEN THEN...

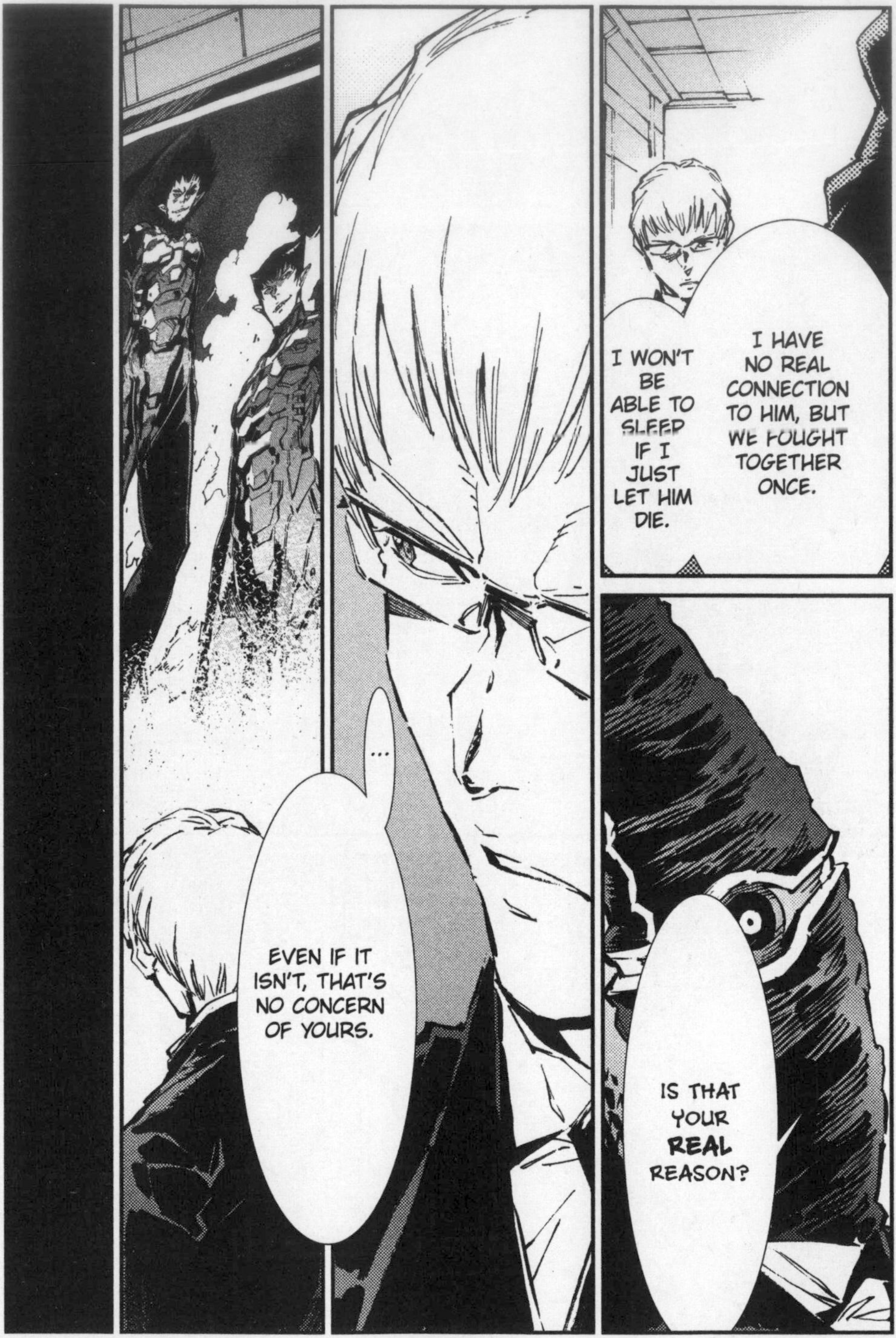
I HAVE NO REAL CONNECTION TO HIM, BUT WE FOUGHT TOGETHER ONCE.
I WON'T BE ABLE TO SLEEP IF I JUST LET HIM DIE.
IS THAT YOUR **REAL** REASON?
...
EVEN IF IT ISN'T, THAT'S NO CONCERN OF YOURS.

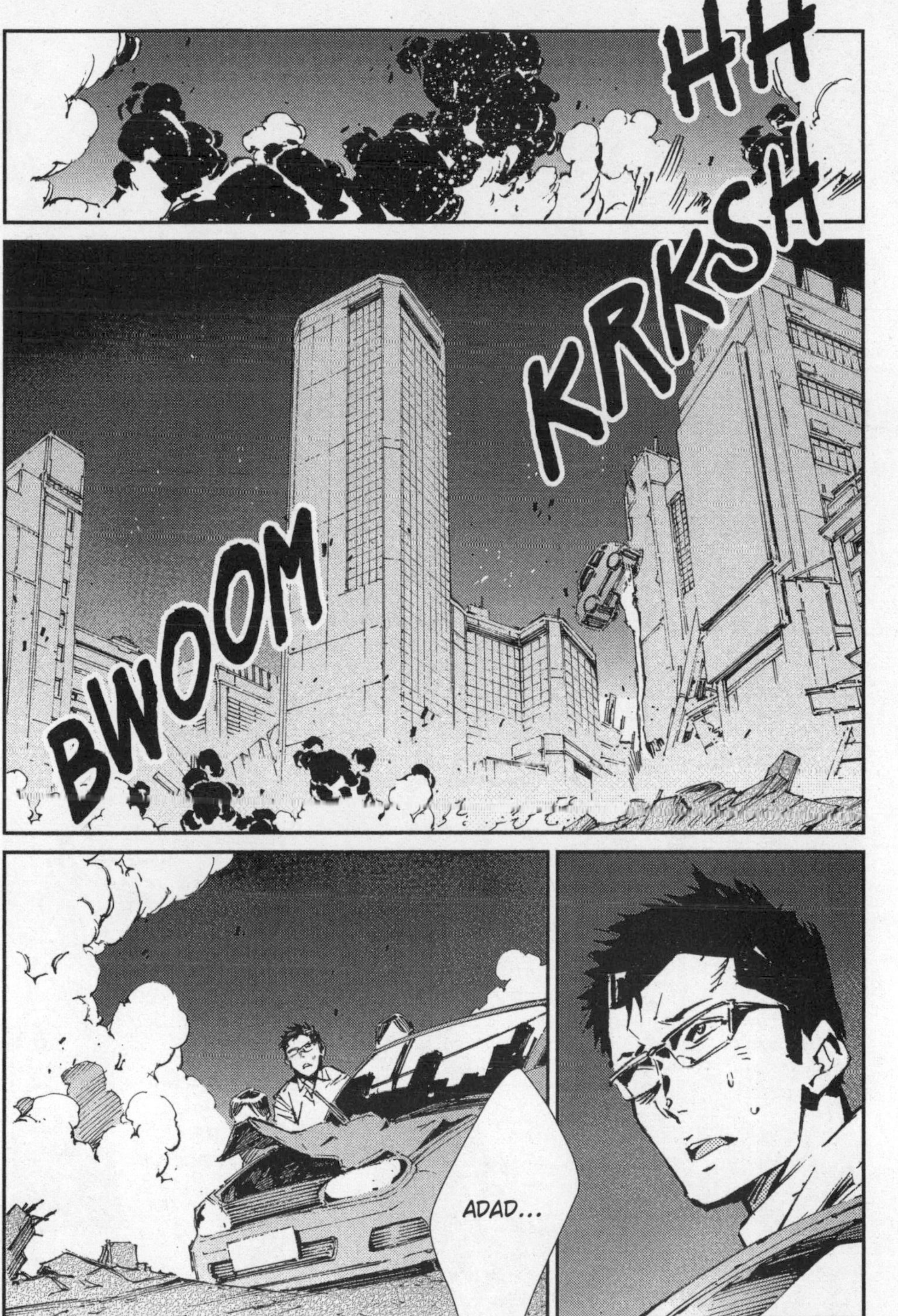
HH
KRKSH
BWOOM
ADAD...

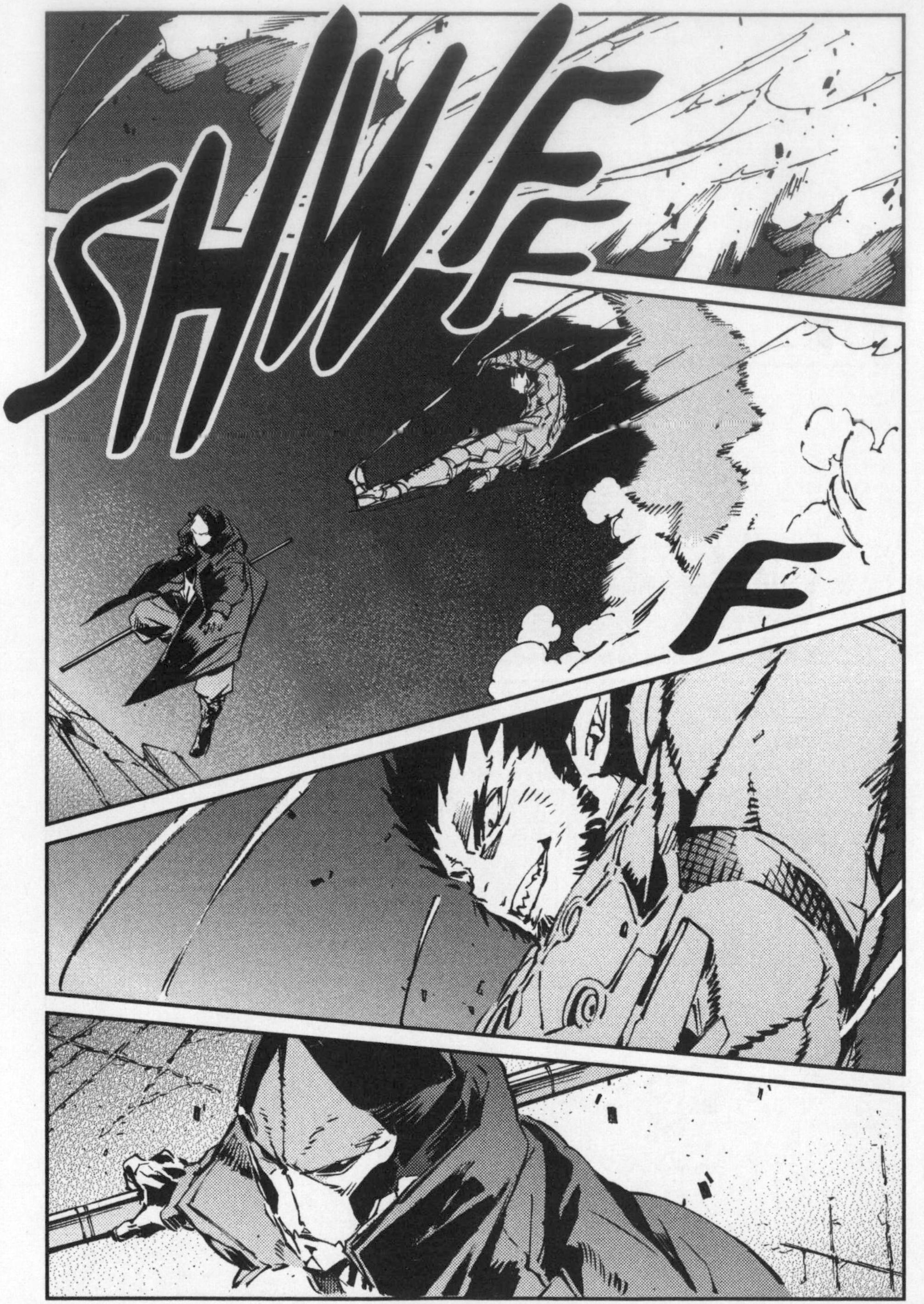
SHWF
F

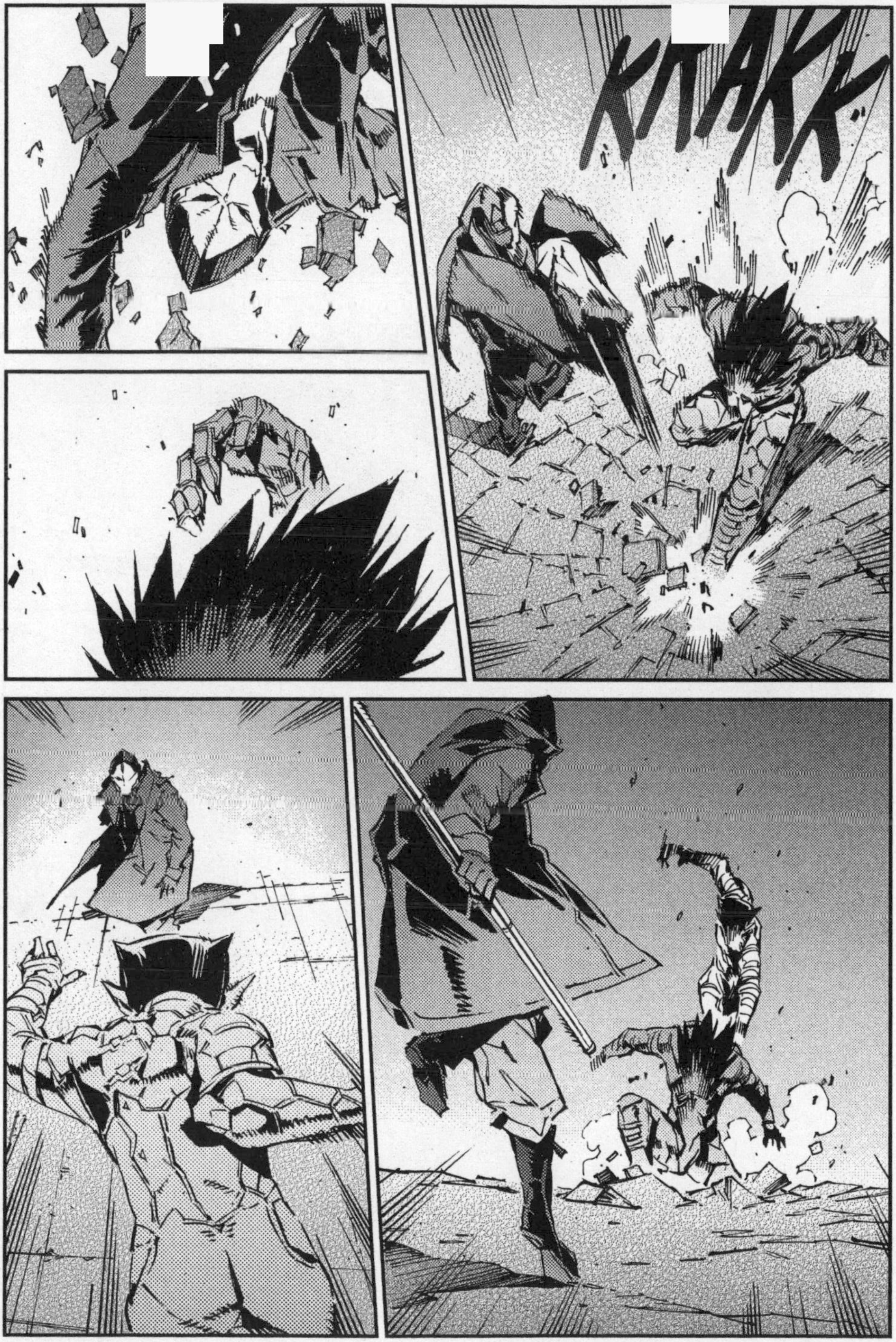
KRAKK

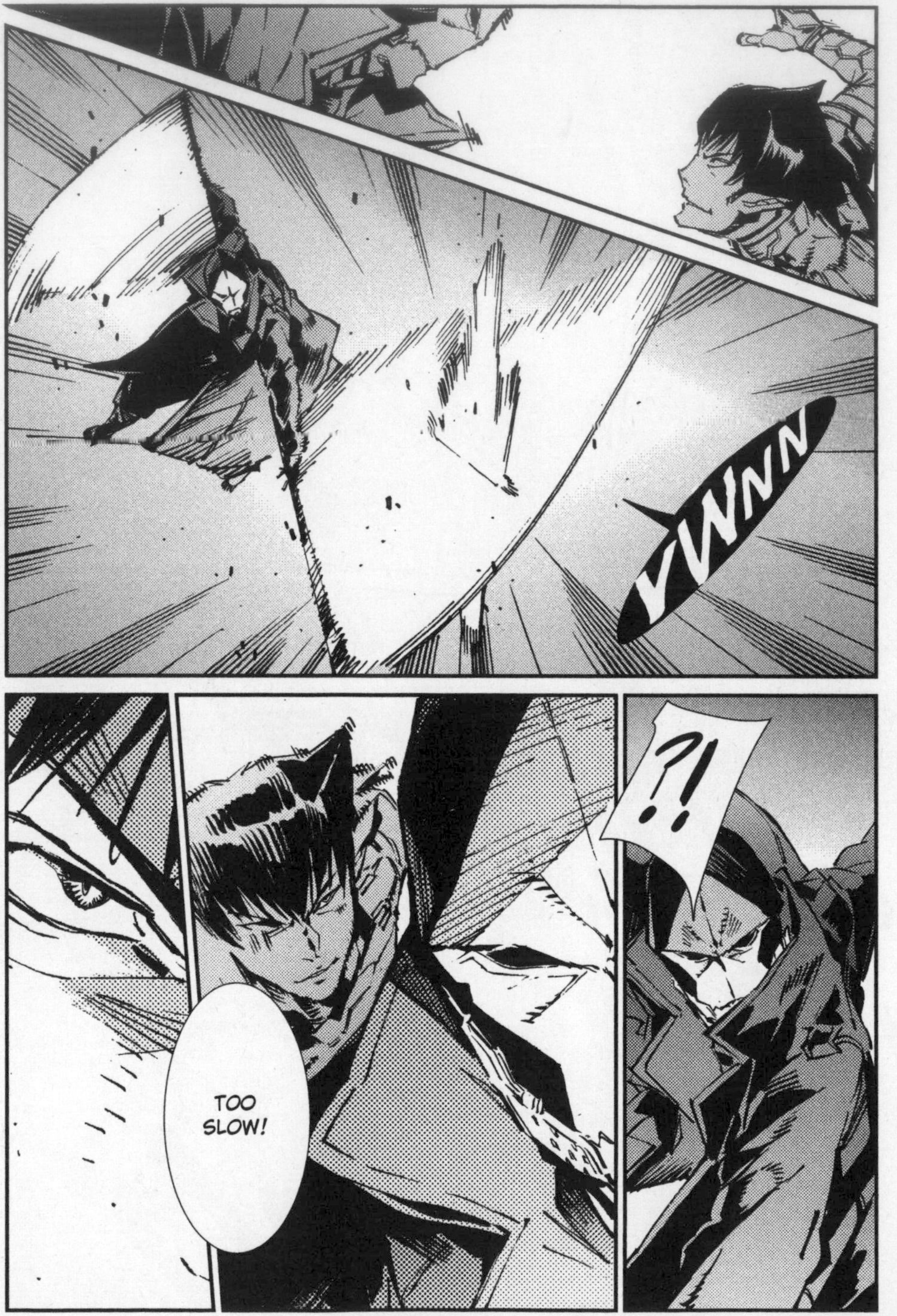
VWNN
?!
TOO SLOW!

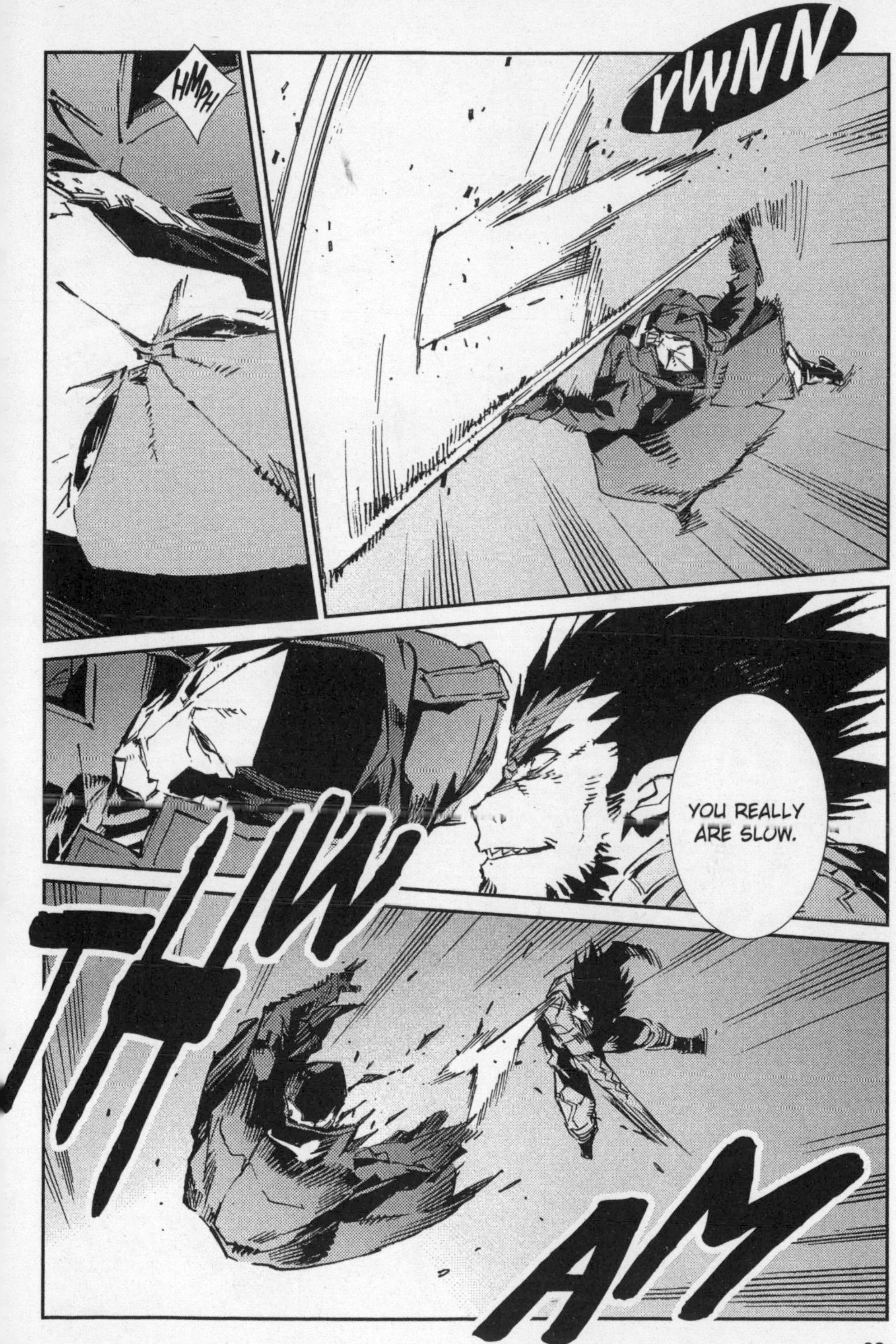
YWNN
HMPH
YOU REALLY ARE SLOW.
THWAM

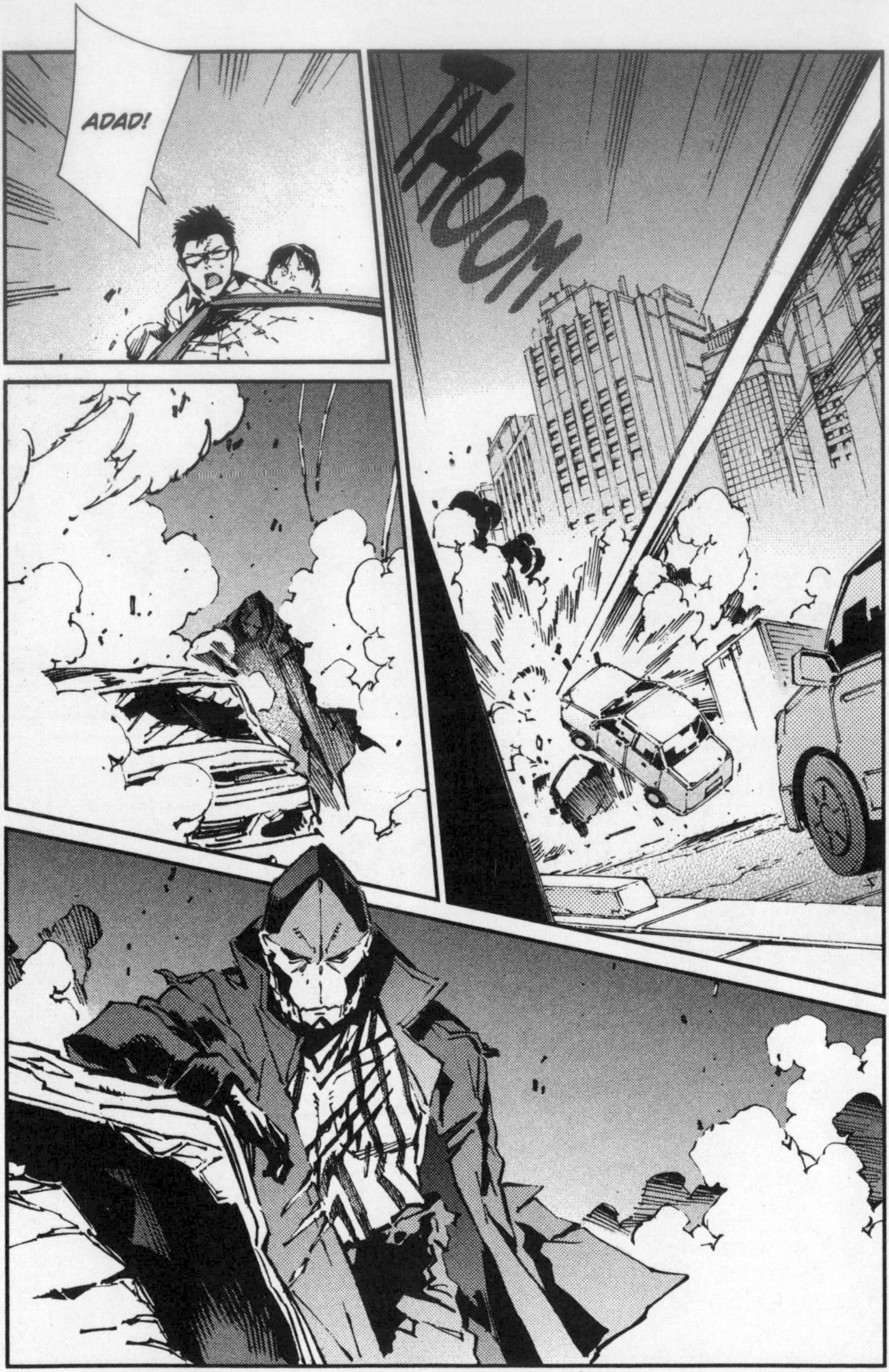
THOOM
ADAD!

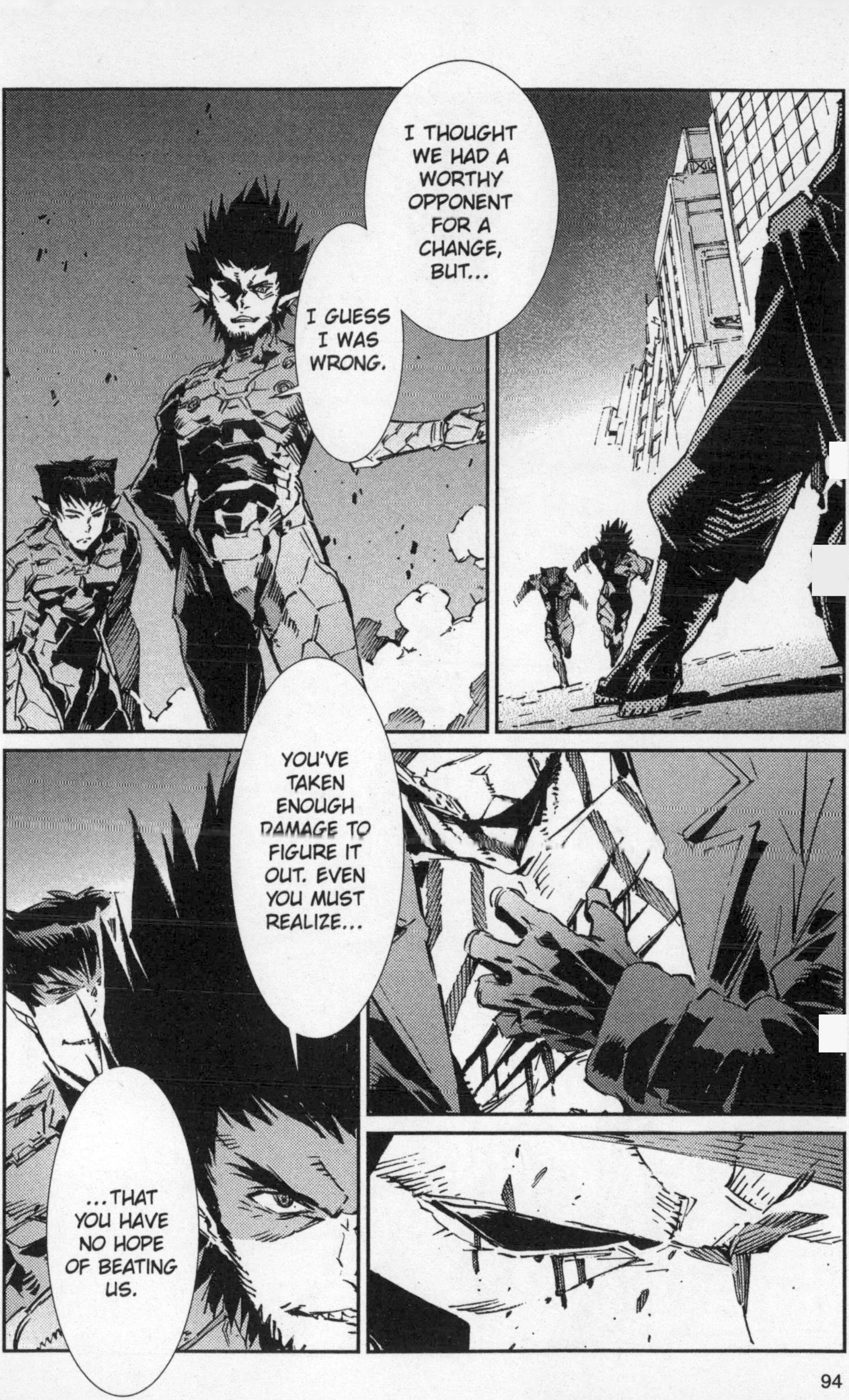
I THOUGHT WE HAD A WORTHY OPPONENT FOR A CHANGE, BUT...
I GUESS I WAS WRONG.
YOU'VE TAKEN ENOUGH DAMAGE TO FIGURE IT OUT. EVEN YOU MUST REALIZE...
...THAT YOU HAVE NO HOPE OF BEATING US.

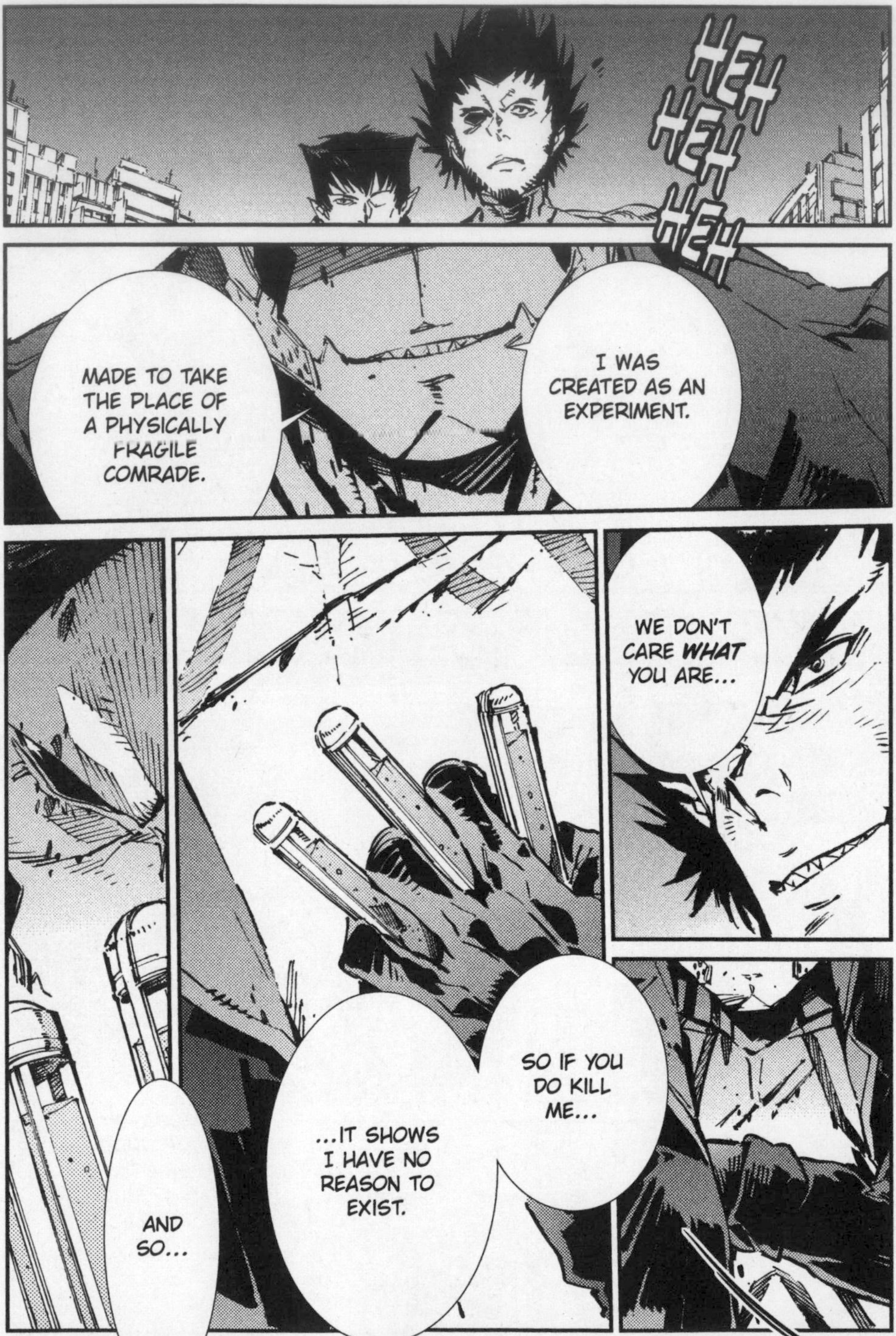
HEH HEH HEH HEH
I WAS CREATED AS AN EXPERIMENT.
MADE TO TAKE THE PLACE OF A PHYSICALLY FRAGILE COMRADE.
WE DON'T CARE ***WHAT*** YOU ARE...
SO IF YOU DO KILL ME...
...IT SHOWS I HAVE NO REASON TO EXIST.
AND SO...

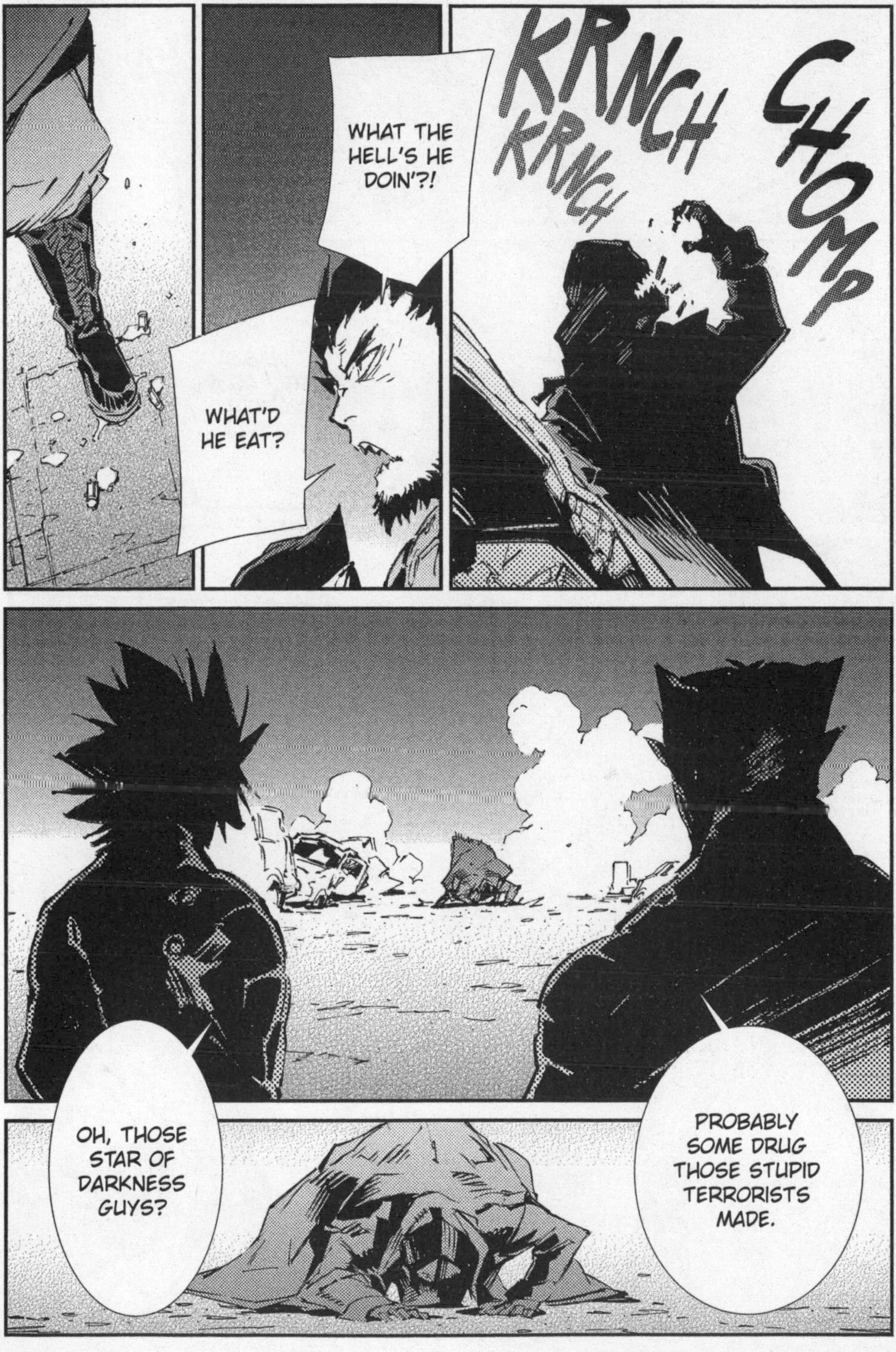
CHOMP
KRNCH
KRNCH
KRNCH
WHAT THE HELL'S HE DOIN'?!
WHAT'D HE EAT?
PROBABLY SOME DRUG THOSE STUPID TERRORISTS MADE.
OH, THOSE STAR OF DARKNESS GUYS?

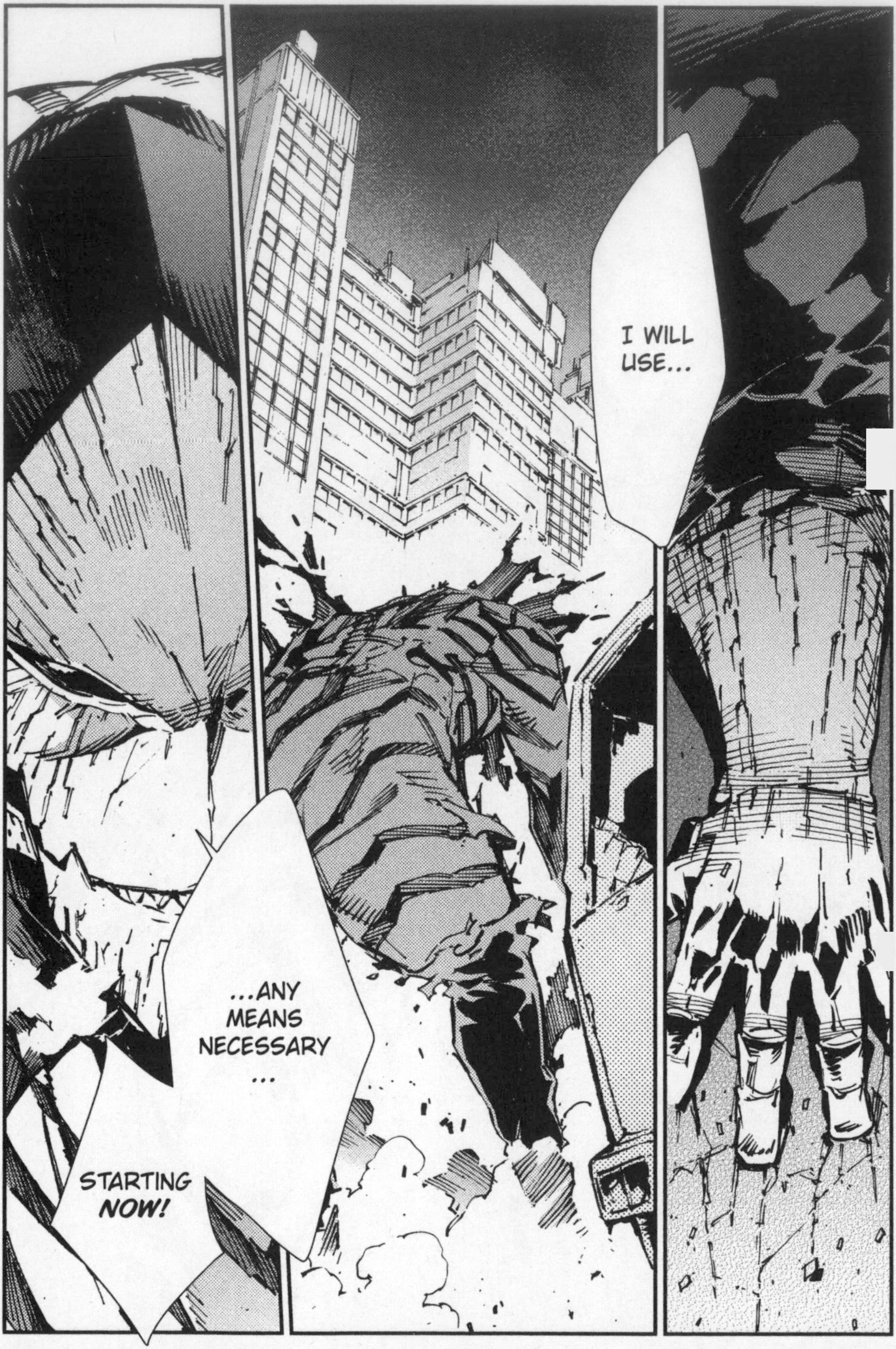
I WILL USE...
...ANY MEANS NECESSARY ...
STARTING NOW!

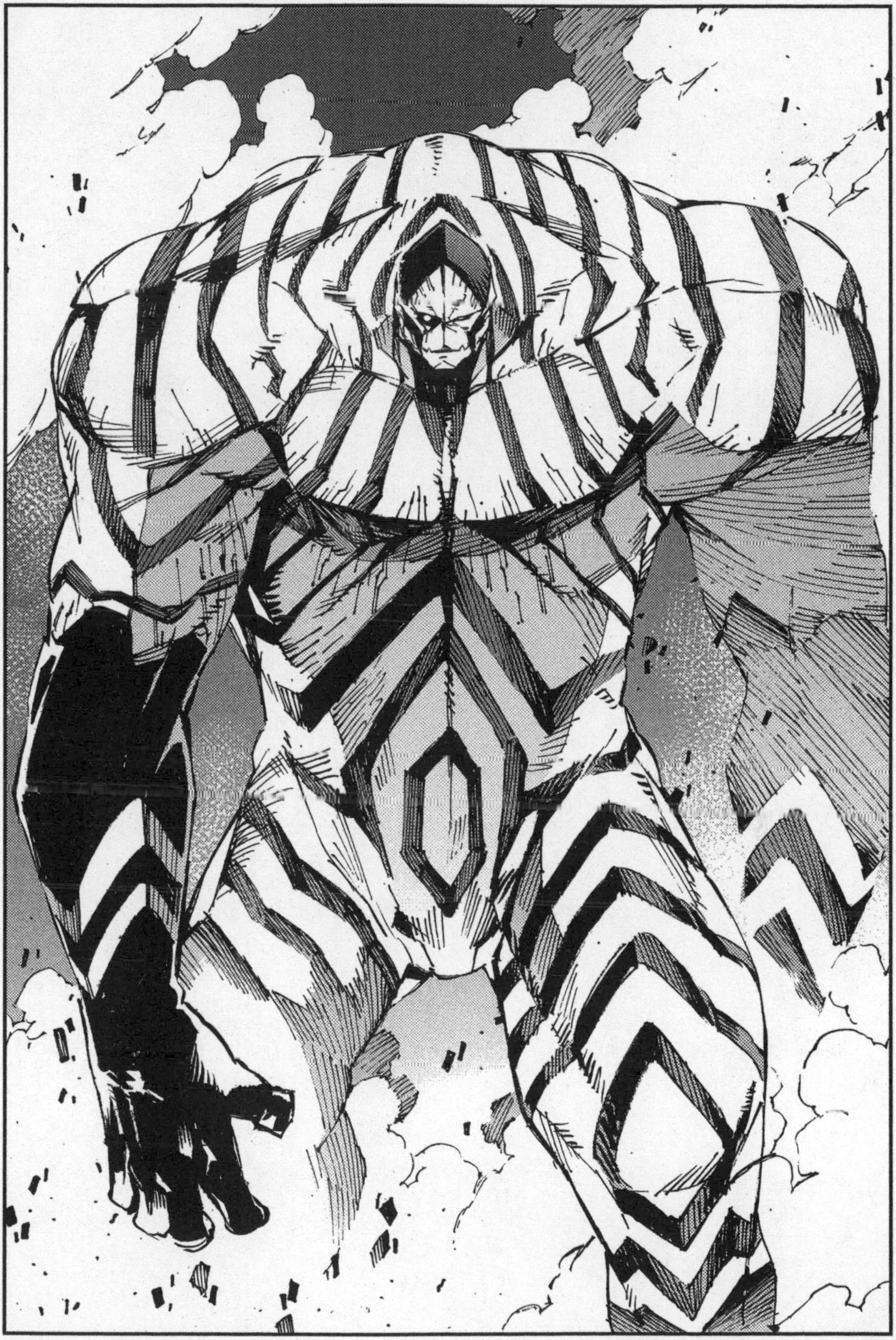

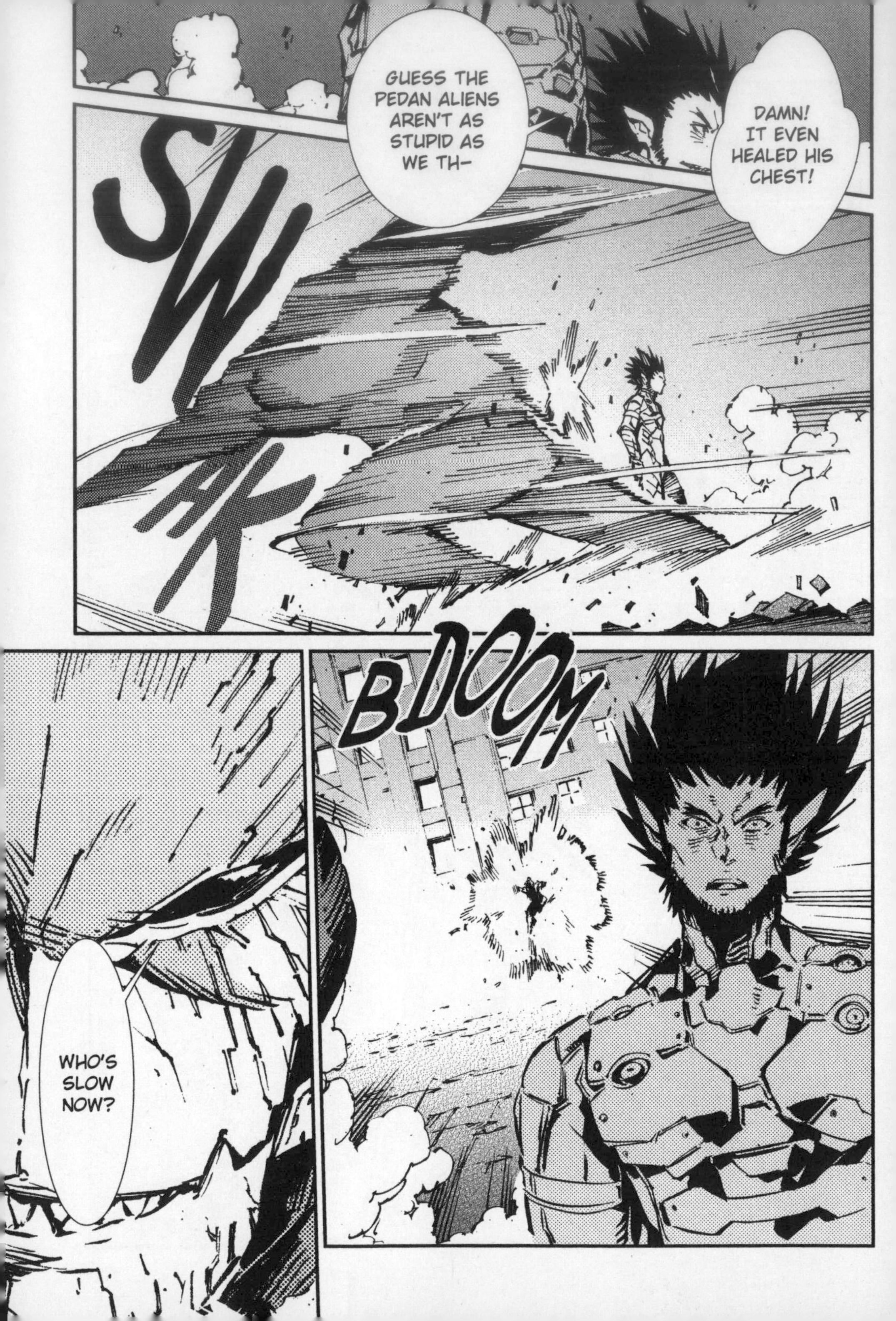
DAMN! IT EVEN HEALED HIS CHEST!
GUESS THE PEDAN ALIENS AREN'T AS STUPID AS WE TH-
SWAK
BDOOM
WHO'S SLOW NOW?

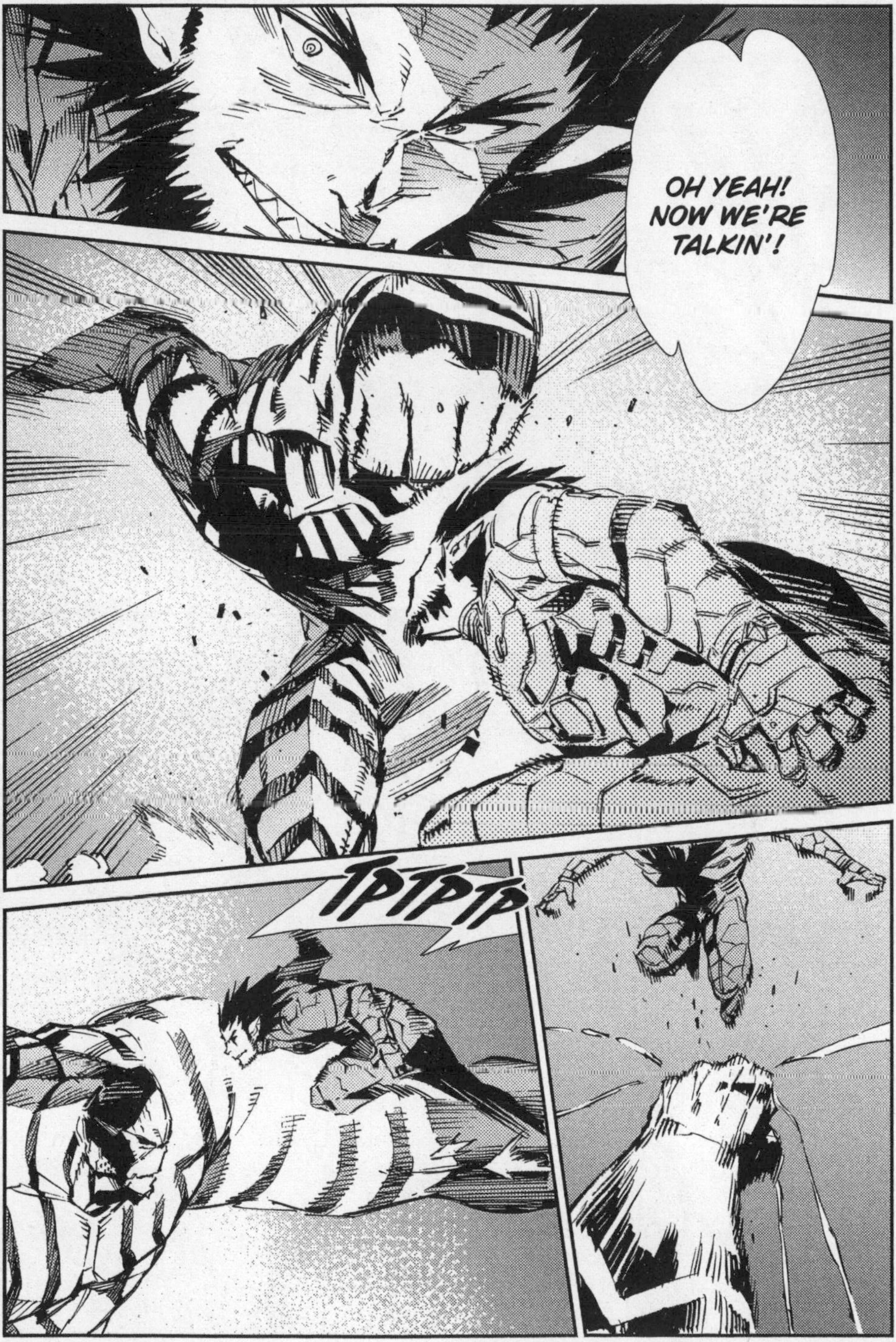
OH YEAH! NOW WE'RE TALKIN'!
TPTPTPTP

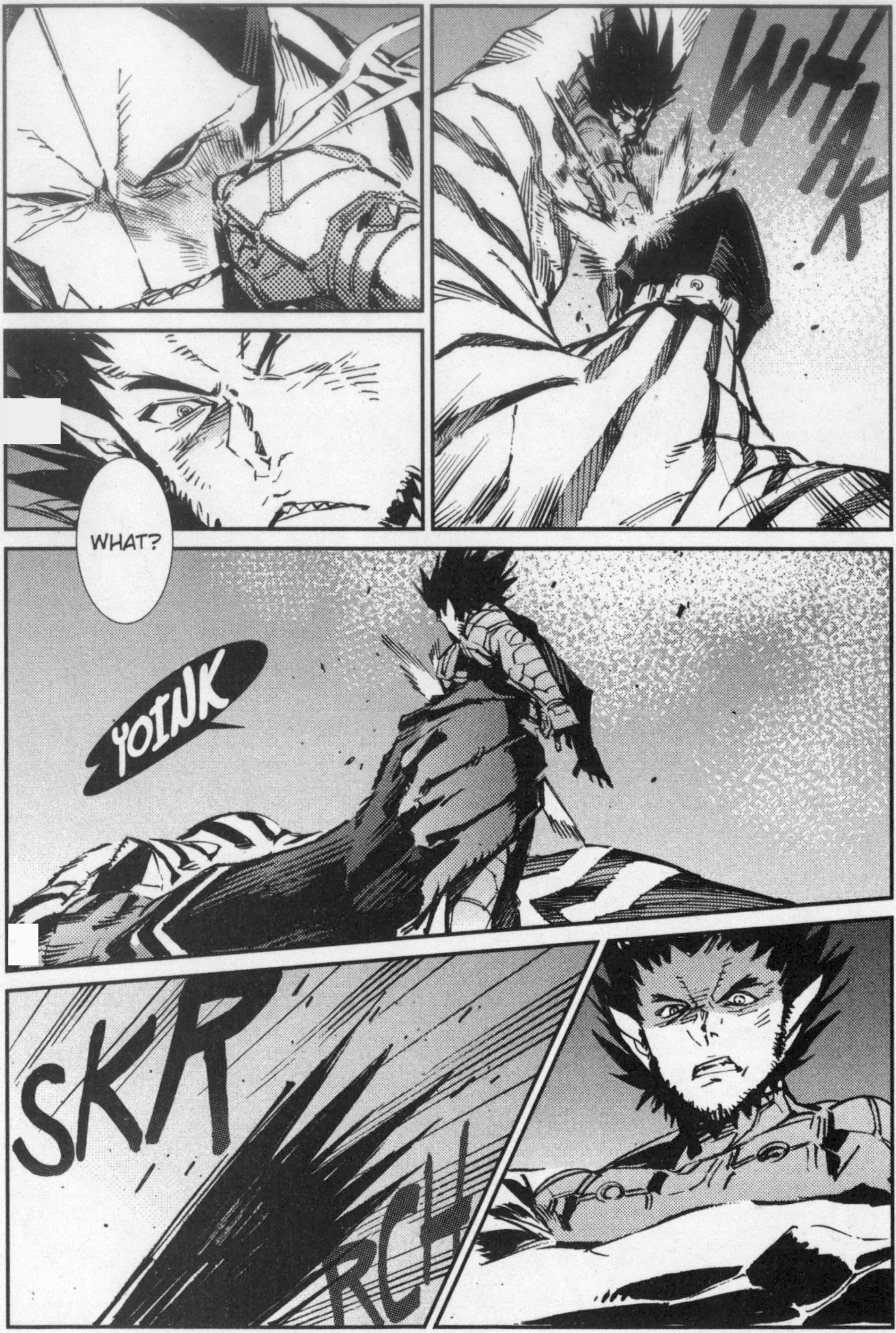
WHAK
WHAT?
YOINK
SKRRCH

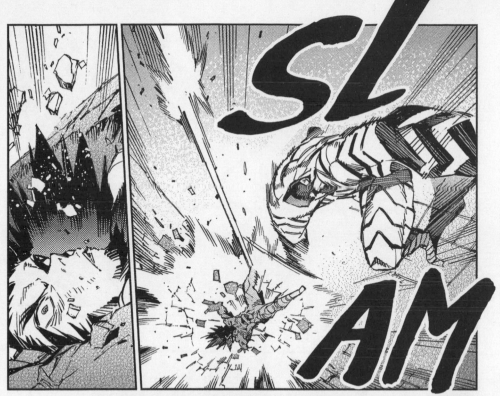

SL

AM

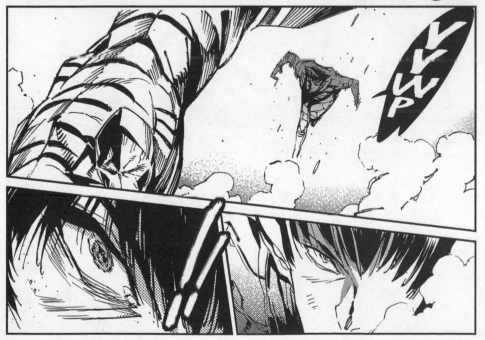

VVWP

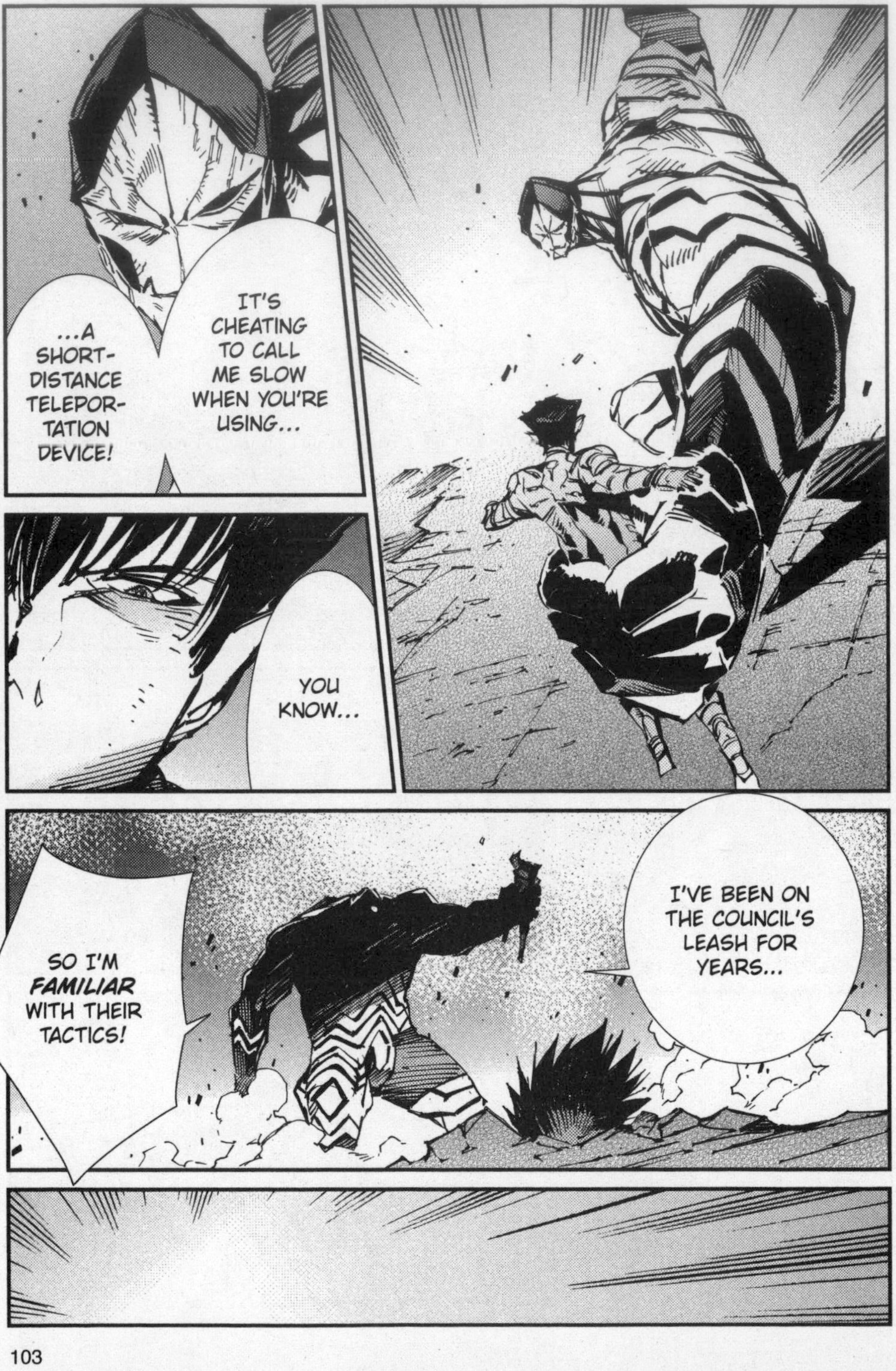
IT'S CHEATING TO CALL ME SLOW WHEN YOU'RE USING...
...A SHORT-DISTANCE TELEPORTATION DEVICE!
YOU KNOW...
I'VE BEEN ON THE COUNCIL'S LEASH FOR YEARS...
SO I'M FAMILIAR WITH THEIR TACTICS!

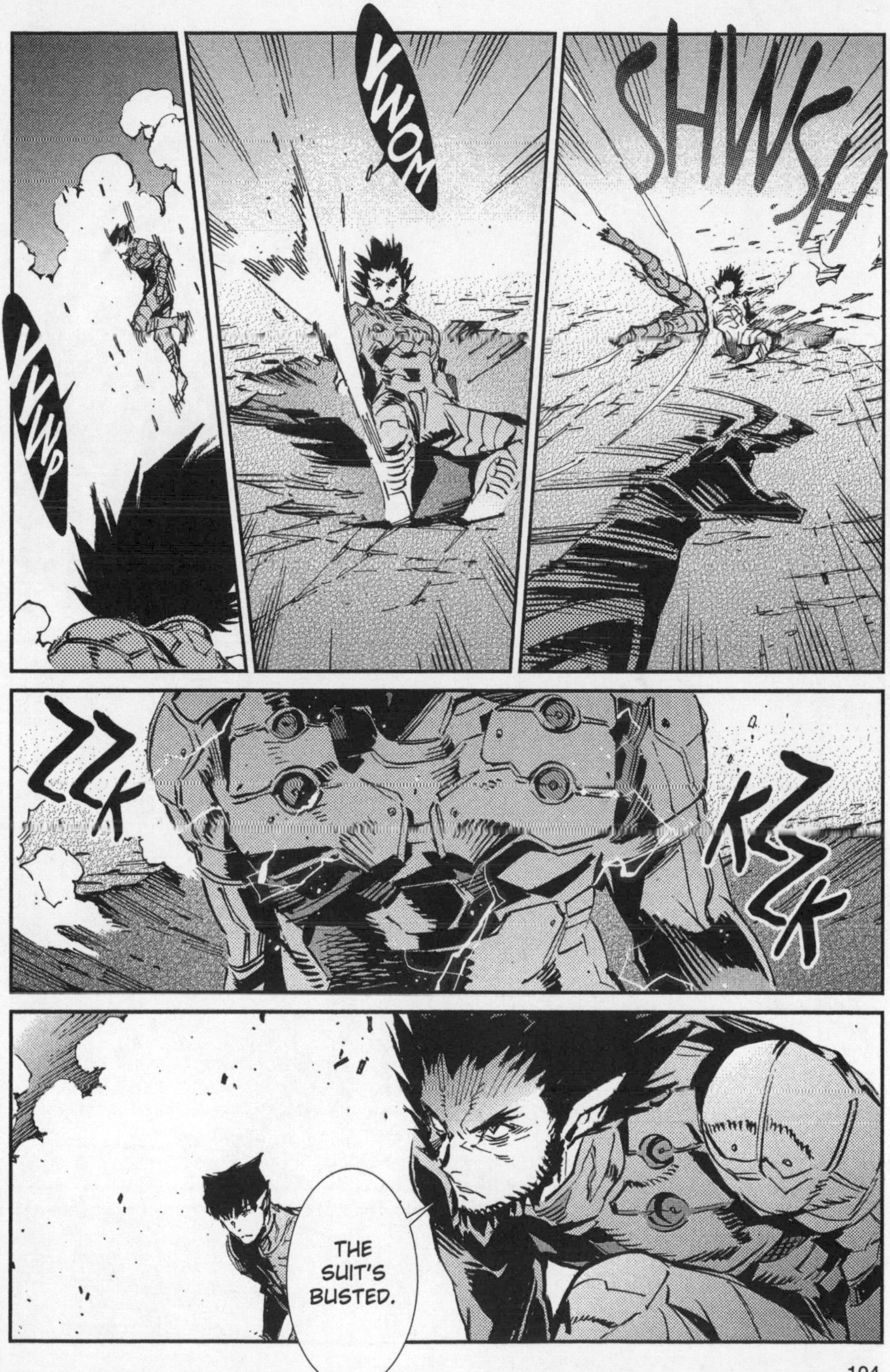
SHWSH
YWOM
KZZK
ZZK
THE SUIT'S BUSTED.

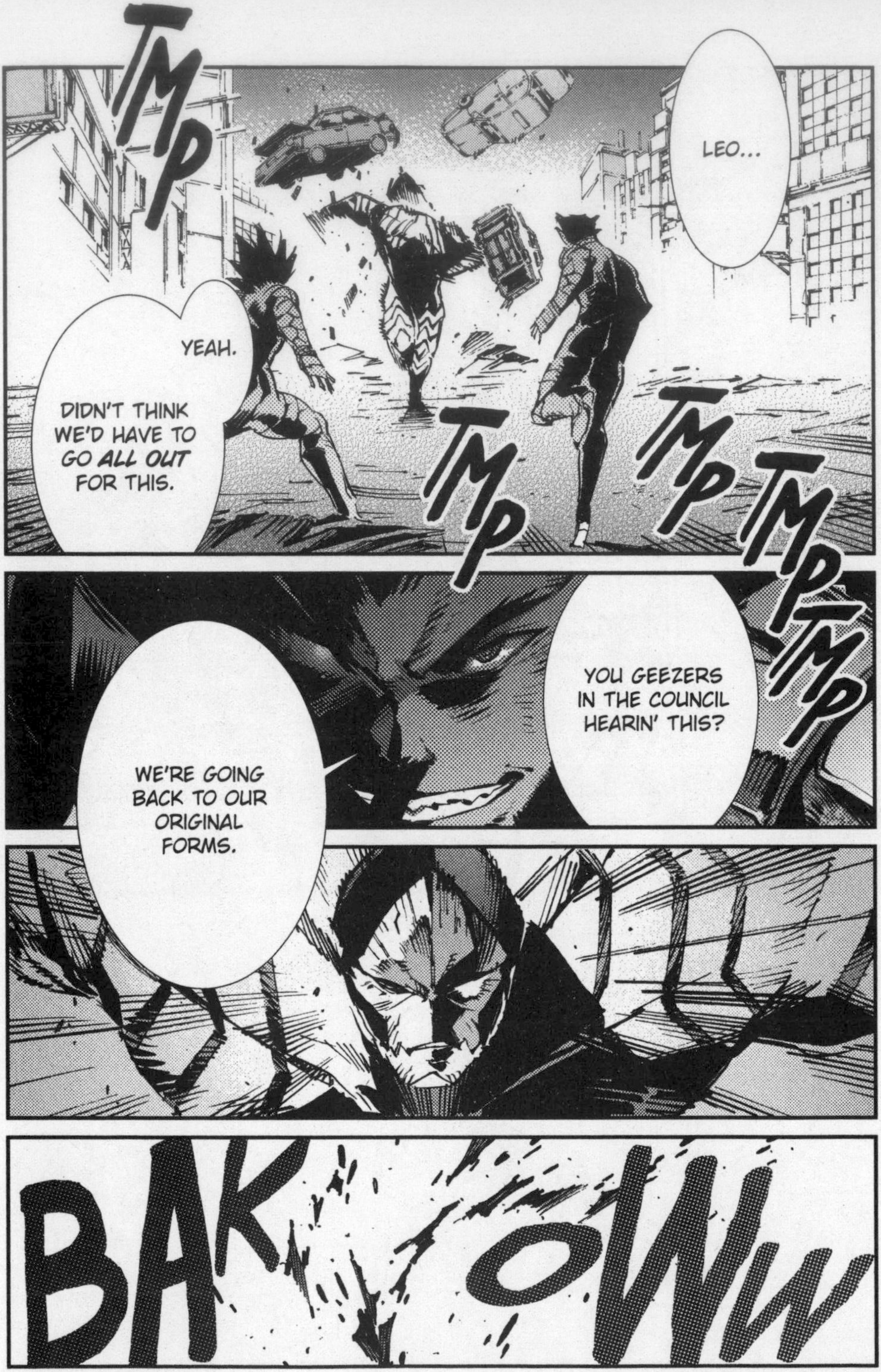
TMP
LEO...
YEAH.
DIDN'T THINK WE'D HAVE TO GO ALL OUT FOR THIS.
TMP TMP TMP
TMP TMP TMP
YOU GEEZERS IN THE COUNCIL HEARIN' THIS?
WE'RE GOING BACK TO OUR ORIGINAL FORMS.
BAK OWW

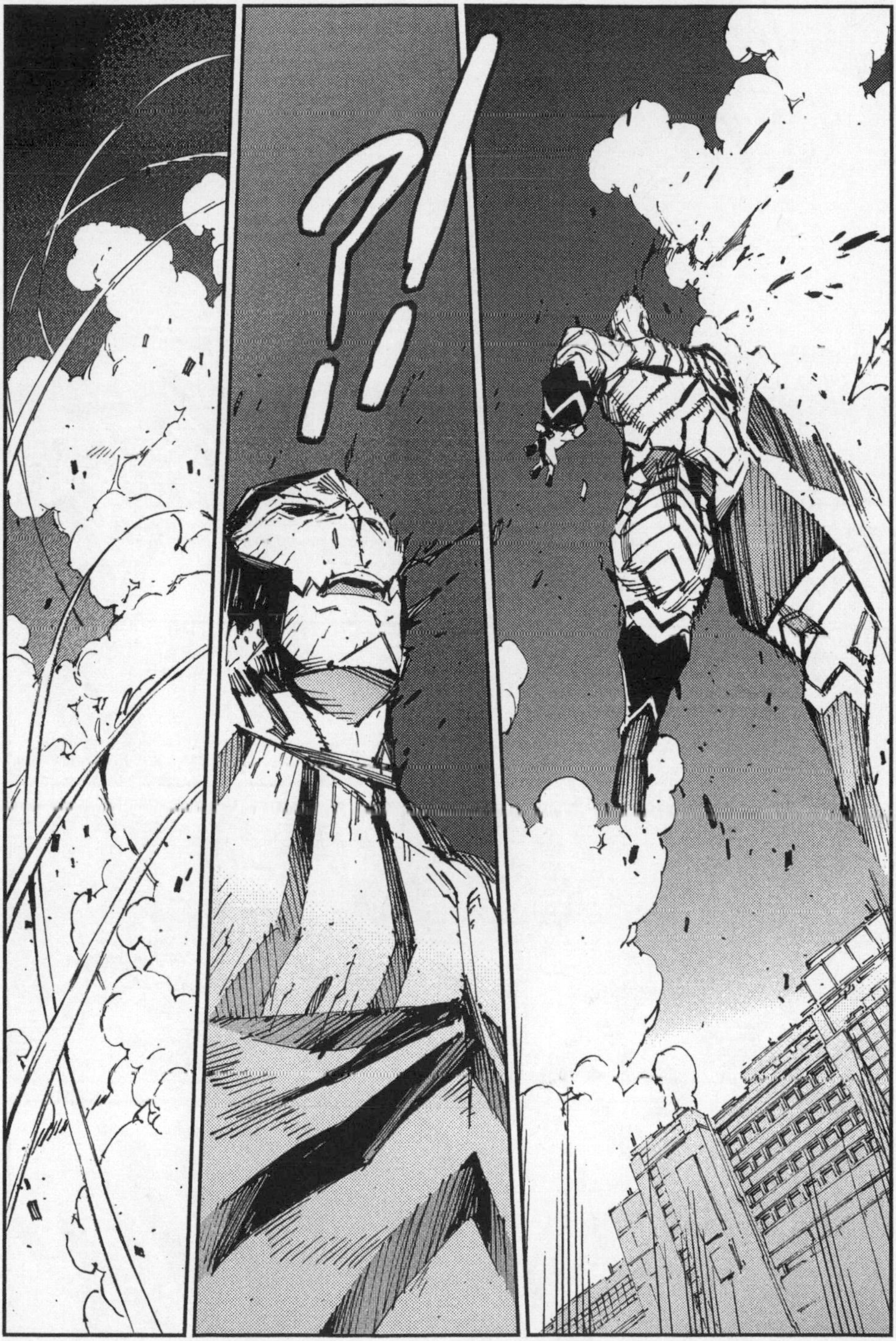
?!

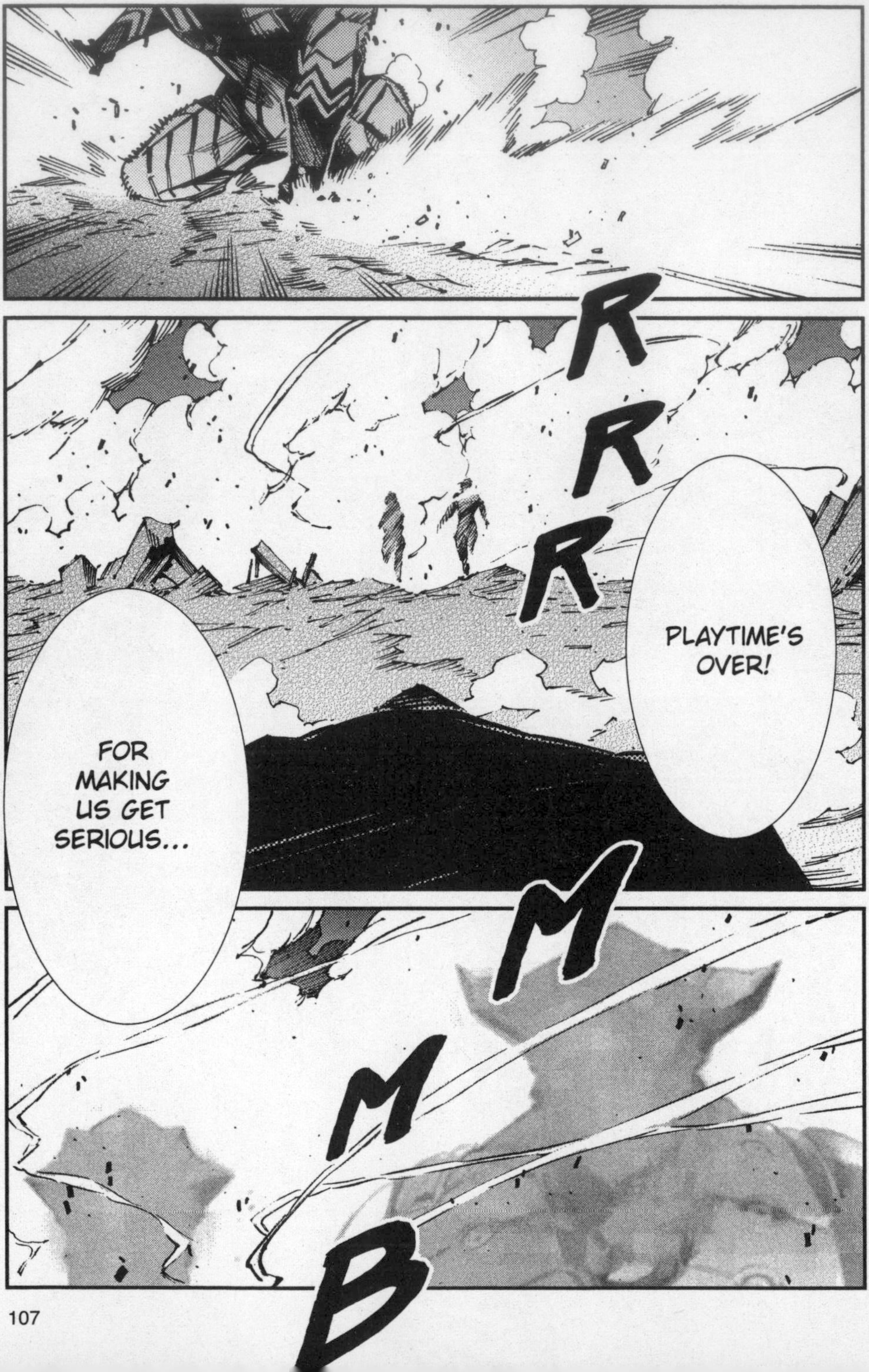
PLAYTIME'S OVER!
FOR MAKING US GET SERIOUS...
RRRMMB

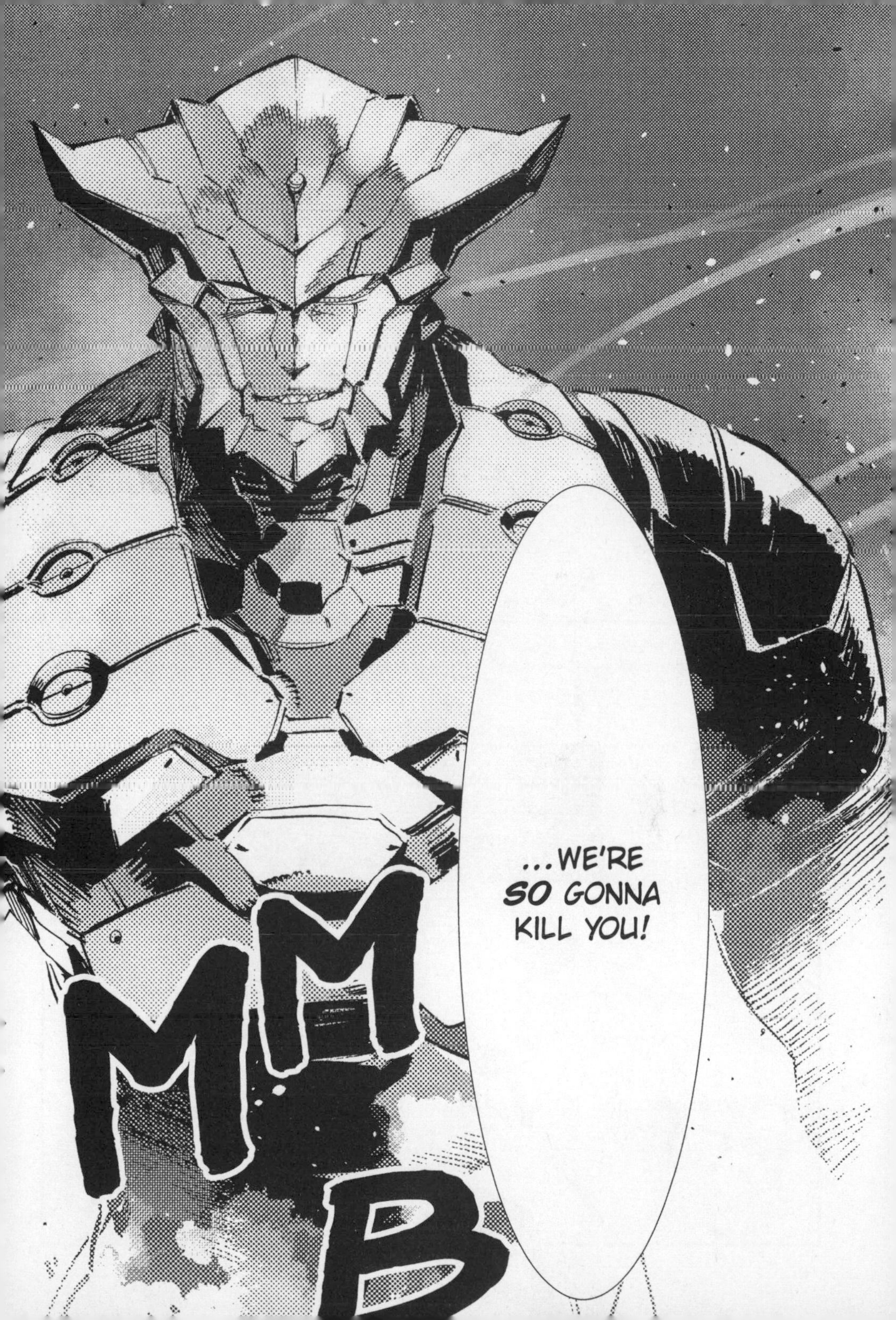
...WE'RE SO GONNA KILL YOU!
MMB

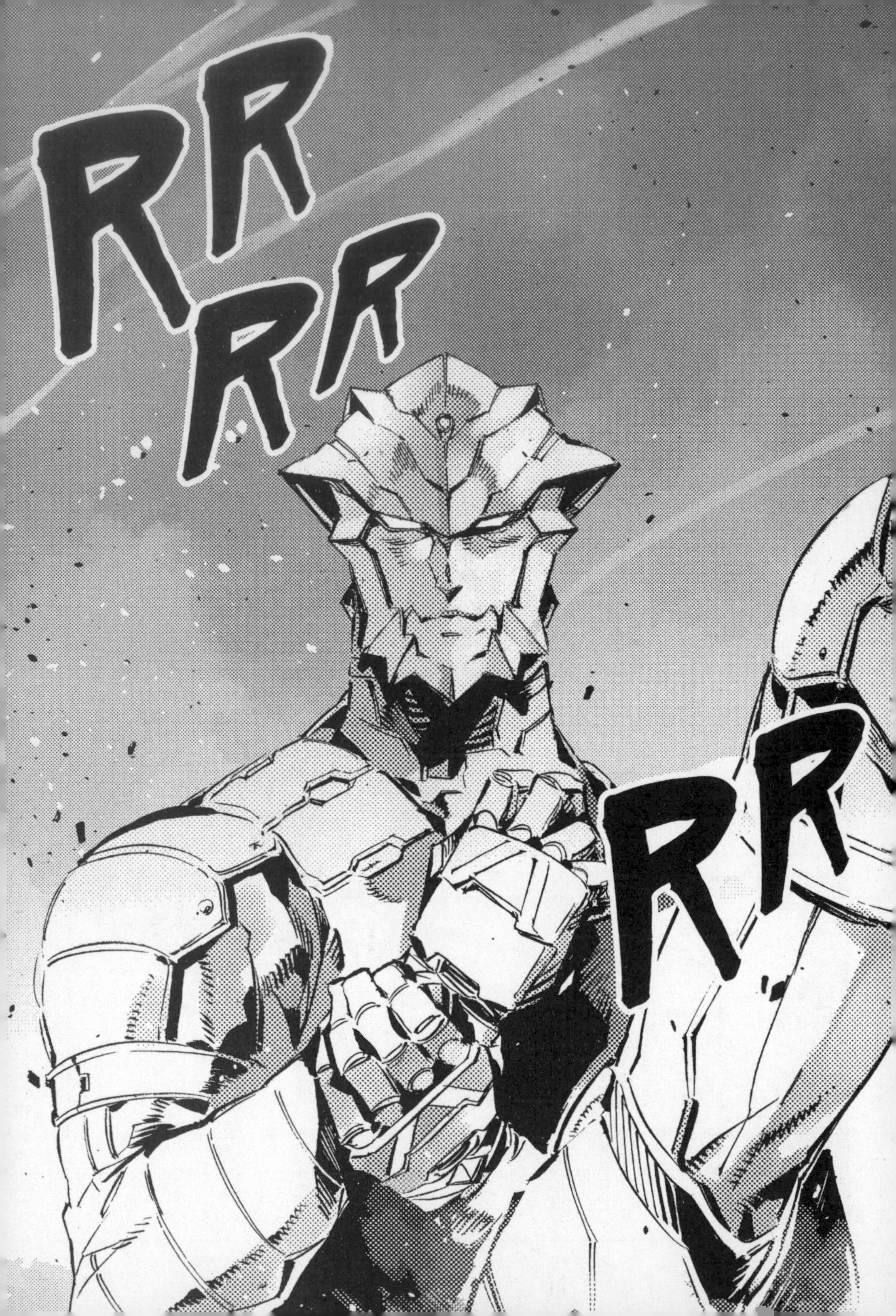
RR
RR
RR

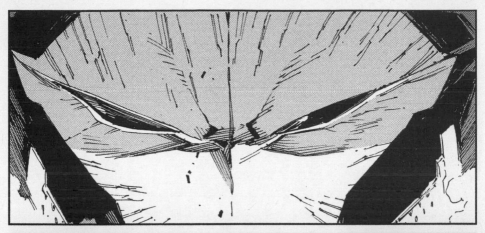

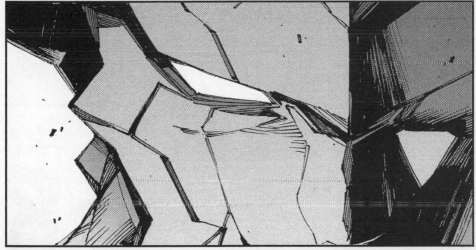

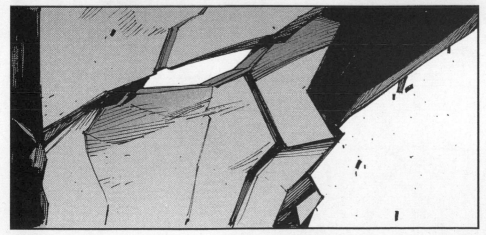

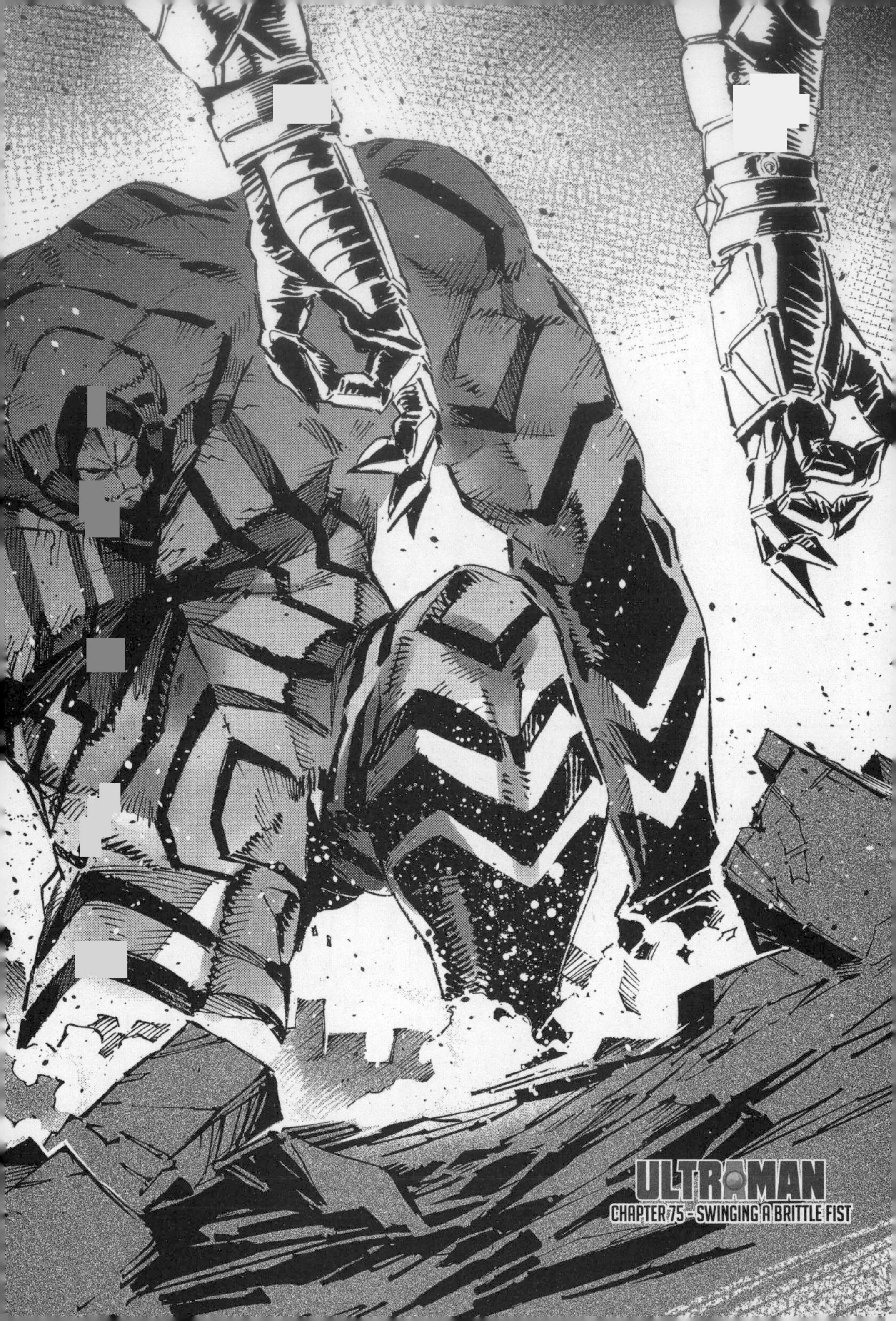
ULTRAMAN
CHAPTER 75 - SWINGING A BRITTLE FIST

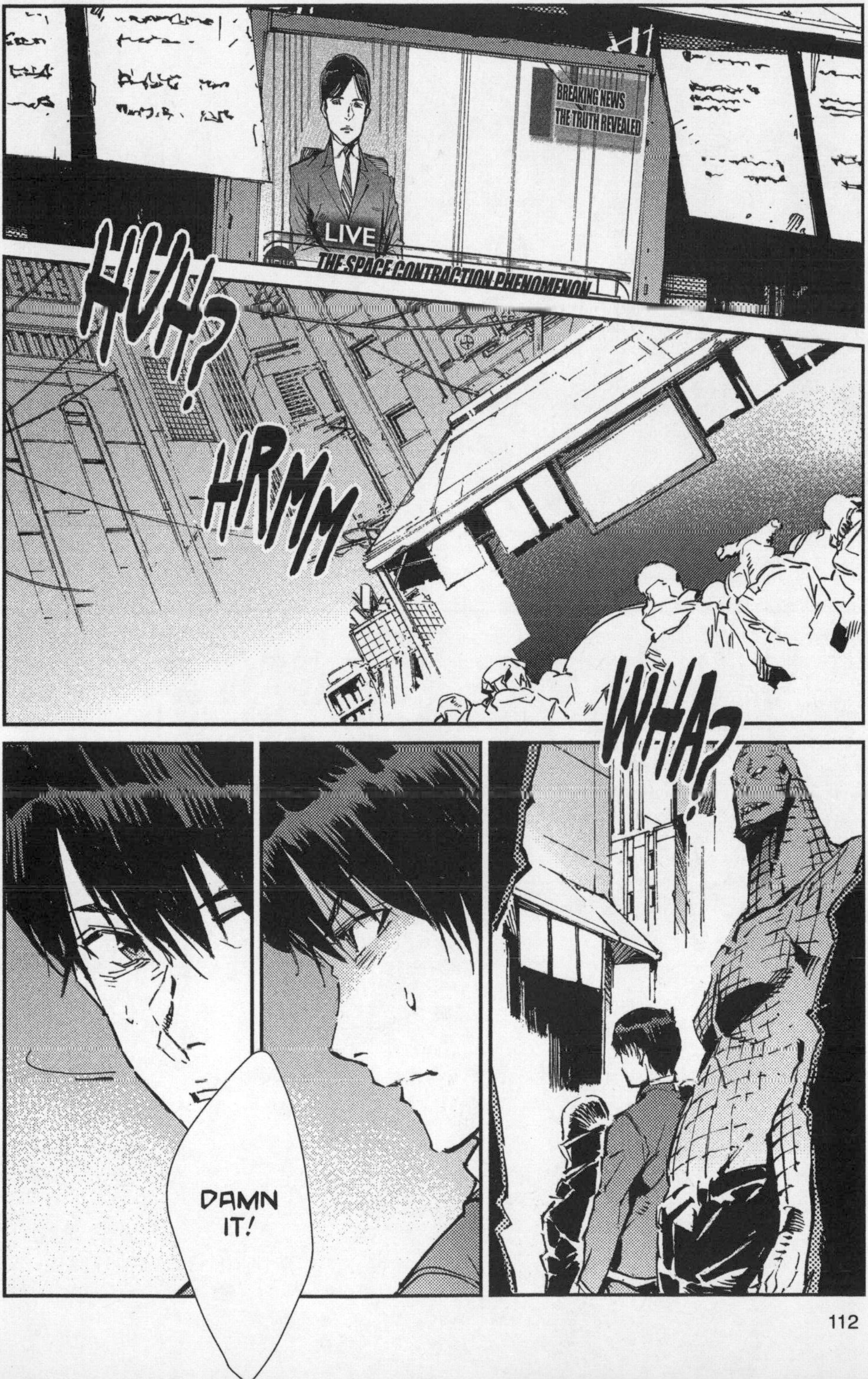
BREAKING NEWS
THE TRUTH REVEALED
LIVE
THE SPACE CONTRACTION PHENOMENON
HUH?
HRMM
WHA?
DAMN IT!

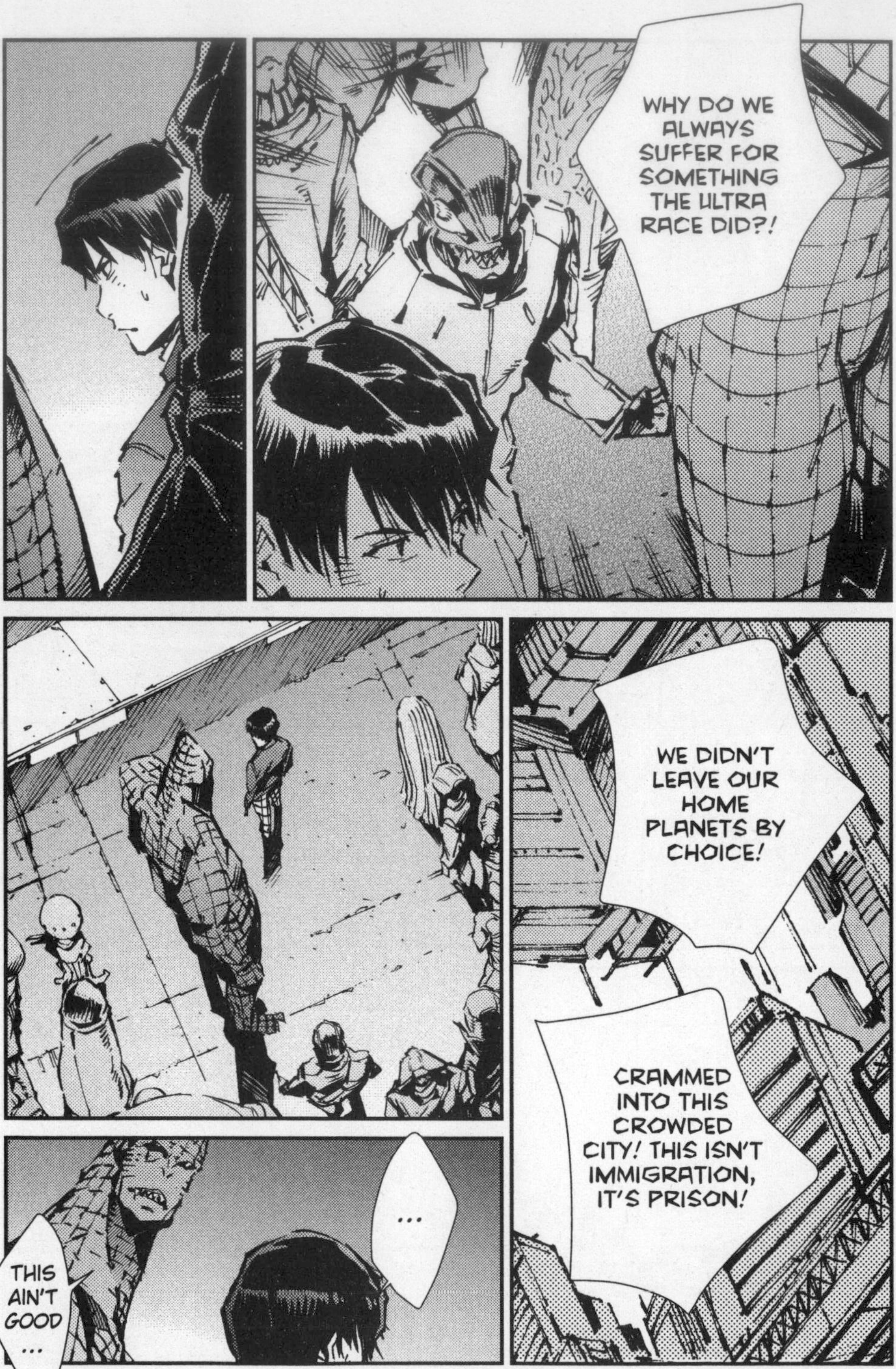

WHY DO WE ALWAYS SUFFER FOR SOMETHING THE ULTRA RACE DID?!
WE DIDN'T LEAVE OUR HOME PLANETS BY CHOICE!
CRAMMED INTO THIS CROWDED CITY! THIS ISN'T IMMIGRATION, IT'S PRISON!
...
THIS AIN'T GOOD ...

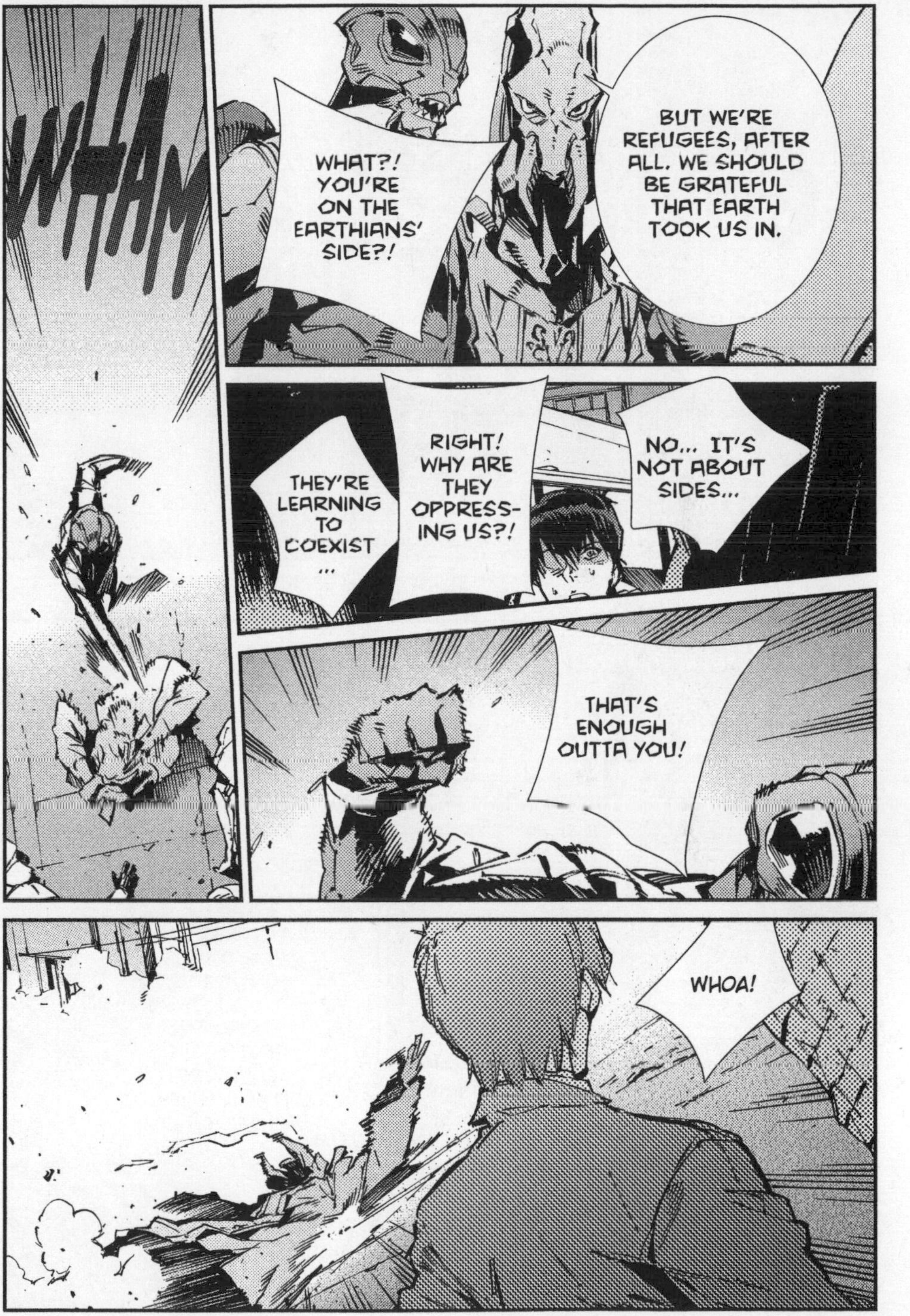
BUT WE'RE REFUGEES, AFTER ALL. WE SHOULD BE GRATEFUL THAT EARTH TOOK US IN.
WHAT?! YOU'RE ON THE EARTHIANS' SIDE?!
NO... IT'S NOT ABOUT SIDES...
RIGHT! WHY ARE THEY OPPRESS-ING US?!
THEY'RE LEARNING TO COEXIST ...
THAT'S ENOUGH OUTTA YOU!
WHAM
WHOA!

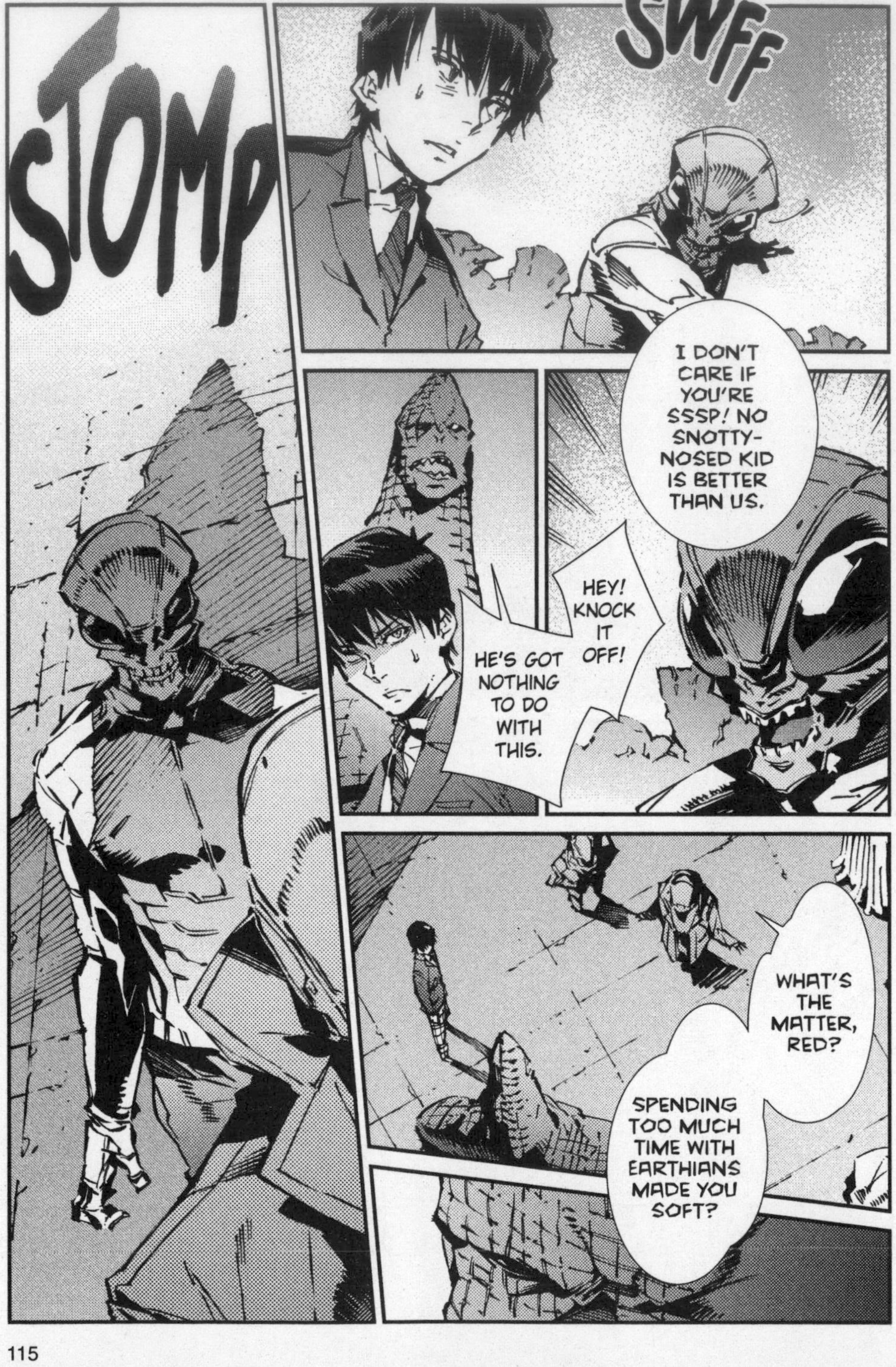
SWFF
I DON'T CARE IF YOU'RE SSSP! NO SNOTTY-NOSED KID IS BETTER THAN US.
HEY! KNOCK IT OFF!
HE'S GOT NOTHING TO DO WITH THIS.
WHAT'S THE MATTER, RED?
SPENDING TOO MUCH TIME WITH EARTHIANS MADE YOU SOFT?
STOMP

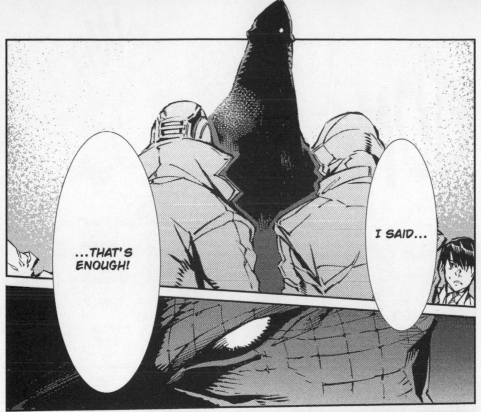

...THAT'S ENOUGH!

I SAID...

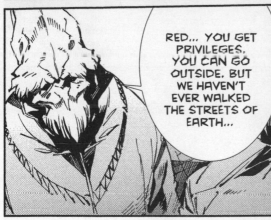

RED... YOU GET PRIVILEGES. YOU CAN GO OUTSIDE. BUT WE HAVEN'T EVER WALKED THE STREETS OF EARTH...

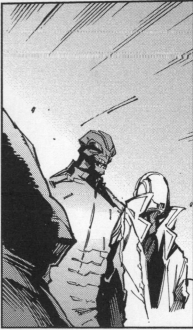

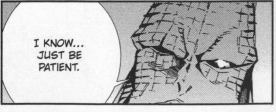

I KNOW... JUST BE PATIENT.

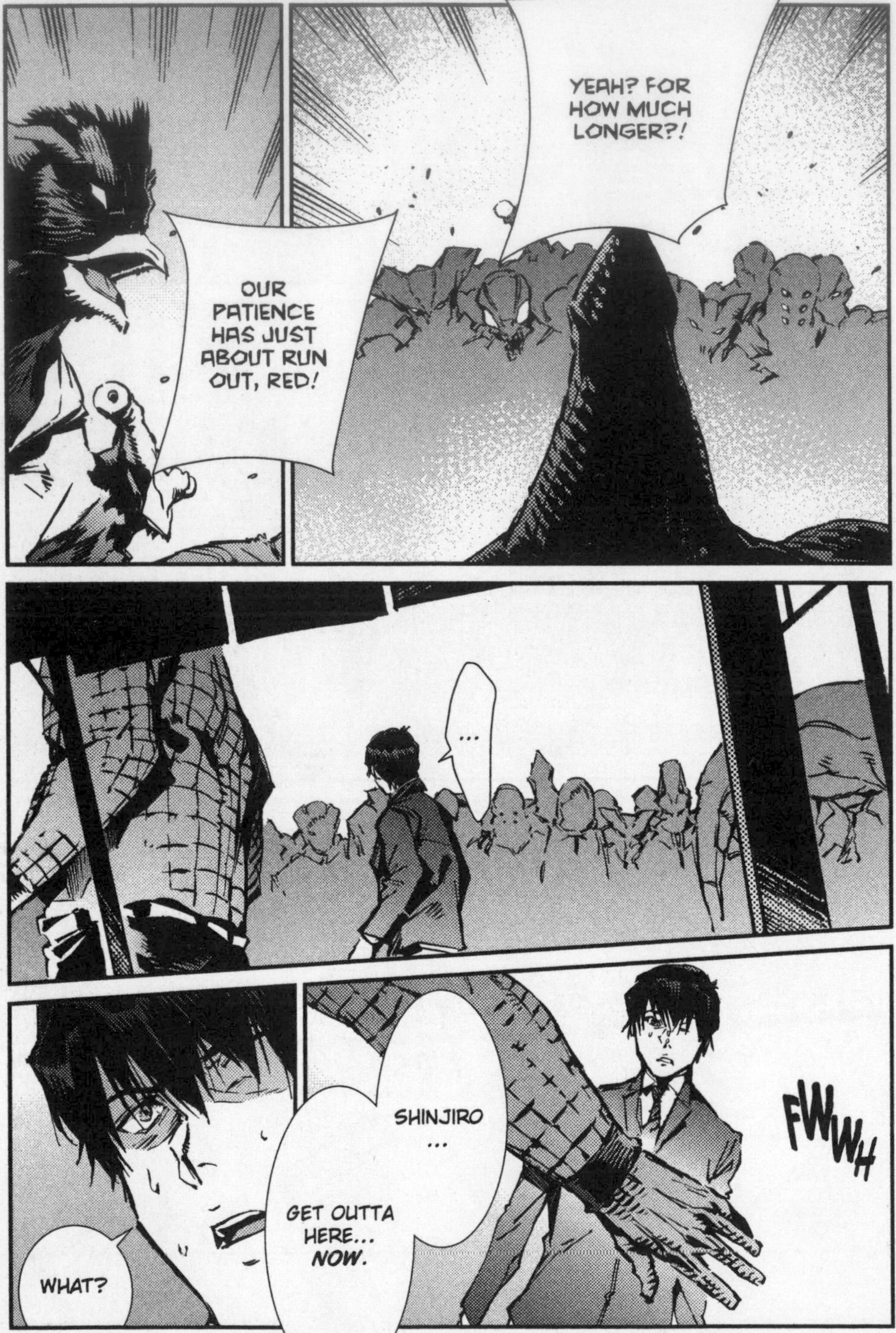
YEAH? FOR HOW MUCH LONGER?!
OUR PATIENCE HAS JUST ABOUT RUN OUT, RED!
...
FWWH
SHINJIRO ...
GET OUTTA HERE... *NOW*.
WHAT?

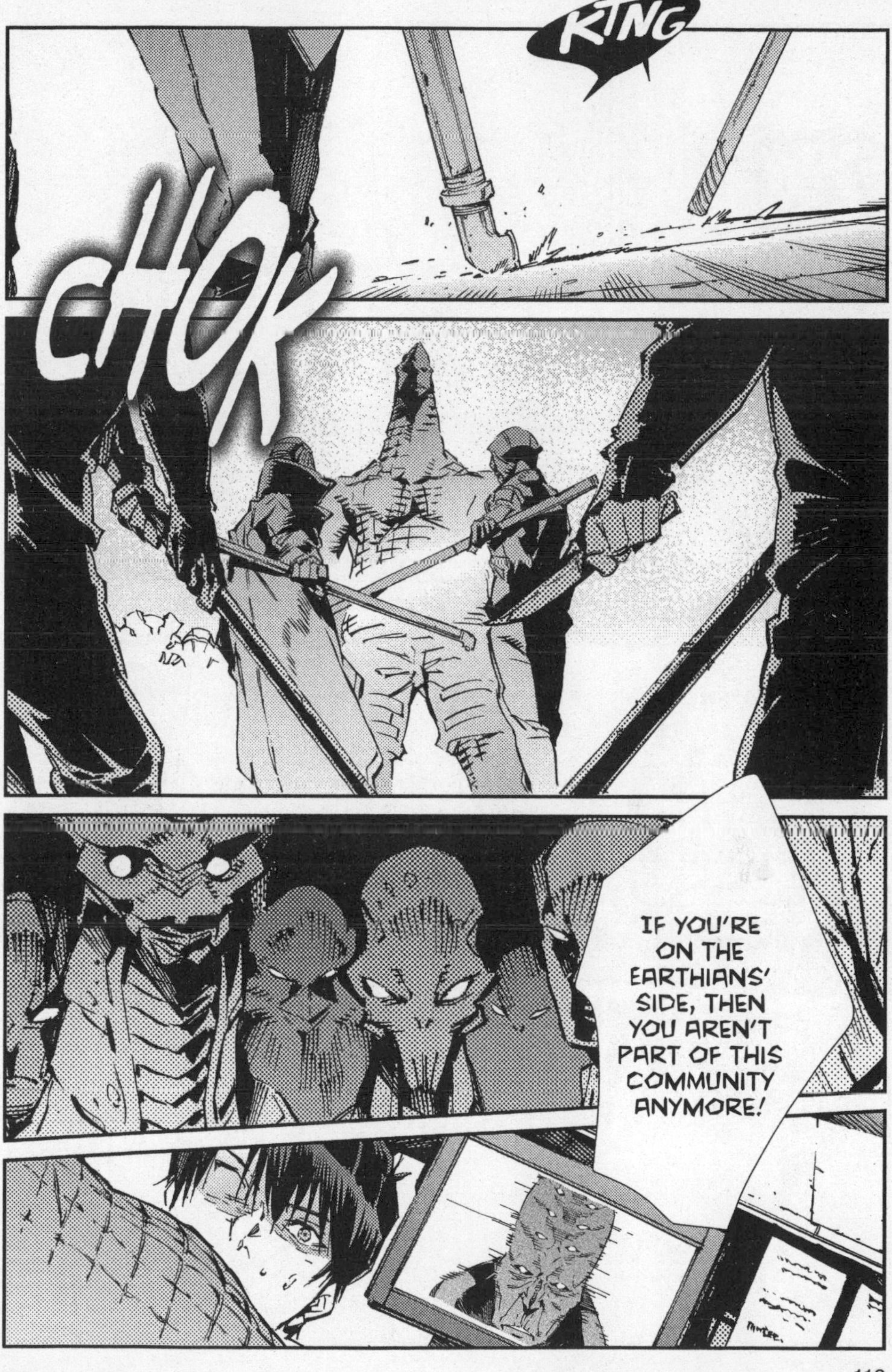
KTNG
CHOK
IF YOU'RE ON THE EARTHIANS' SIDE, THEN YOU AREN'T PART OF THIS COMMUNITY ANYMORE!

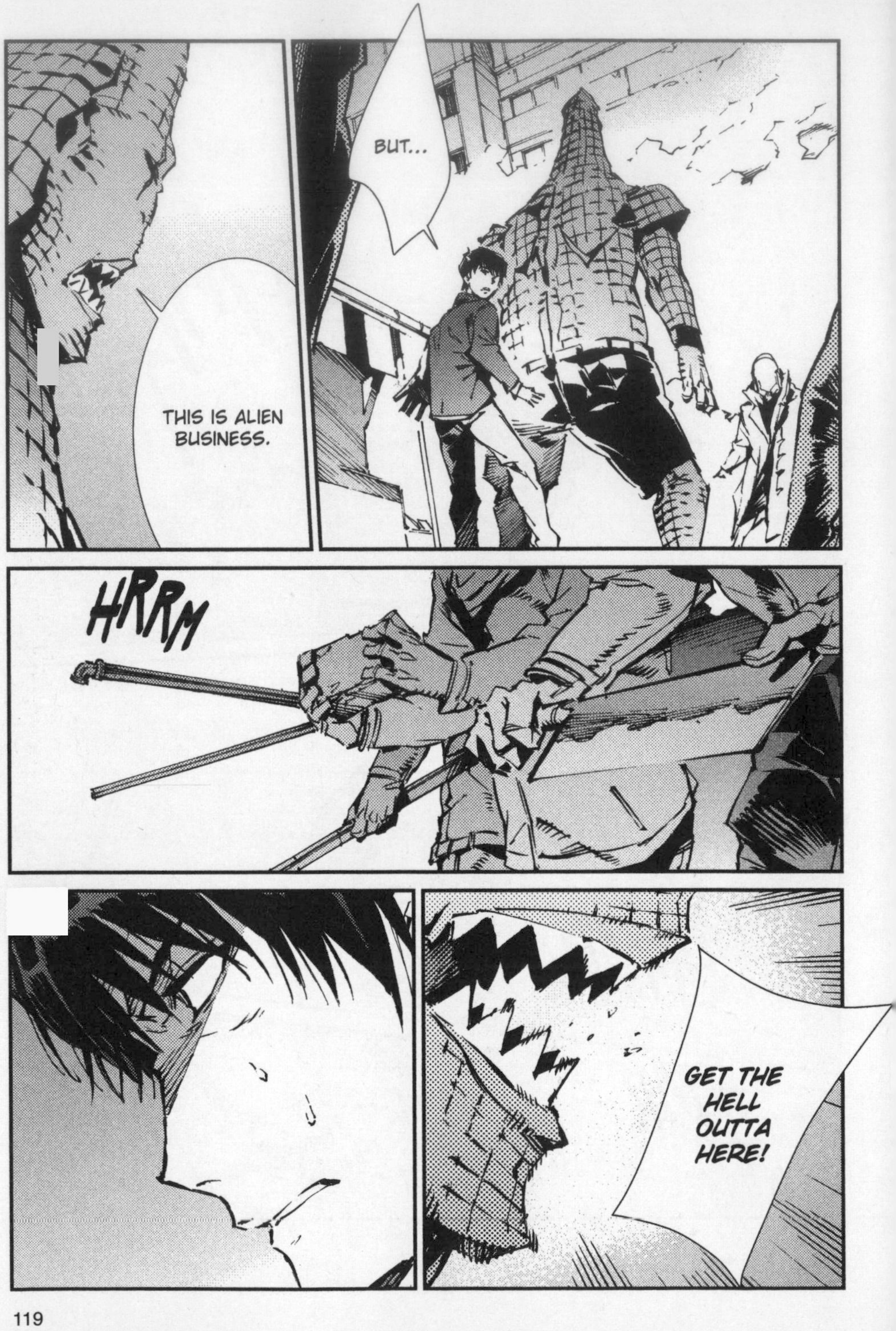
BUT...
THIS IS ALIEN BUSINESS.
HRRM
GET THE HELL OUTTA HERE!

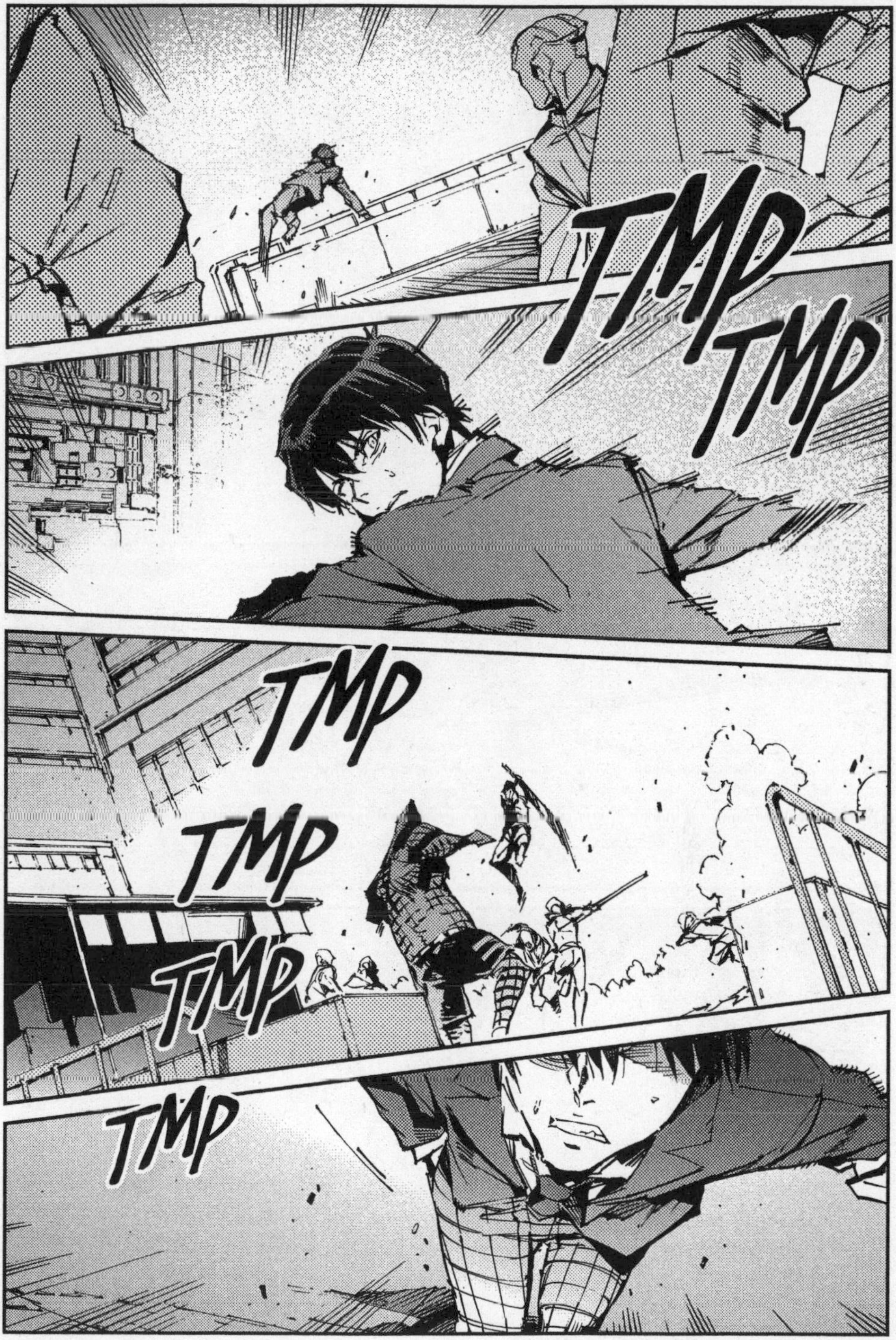
TMP TMP
TMP
TMP
TMP
TMP

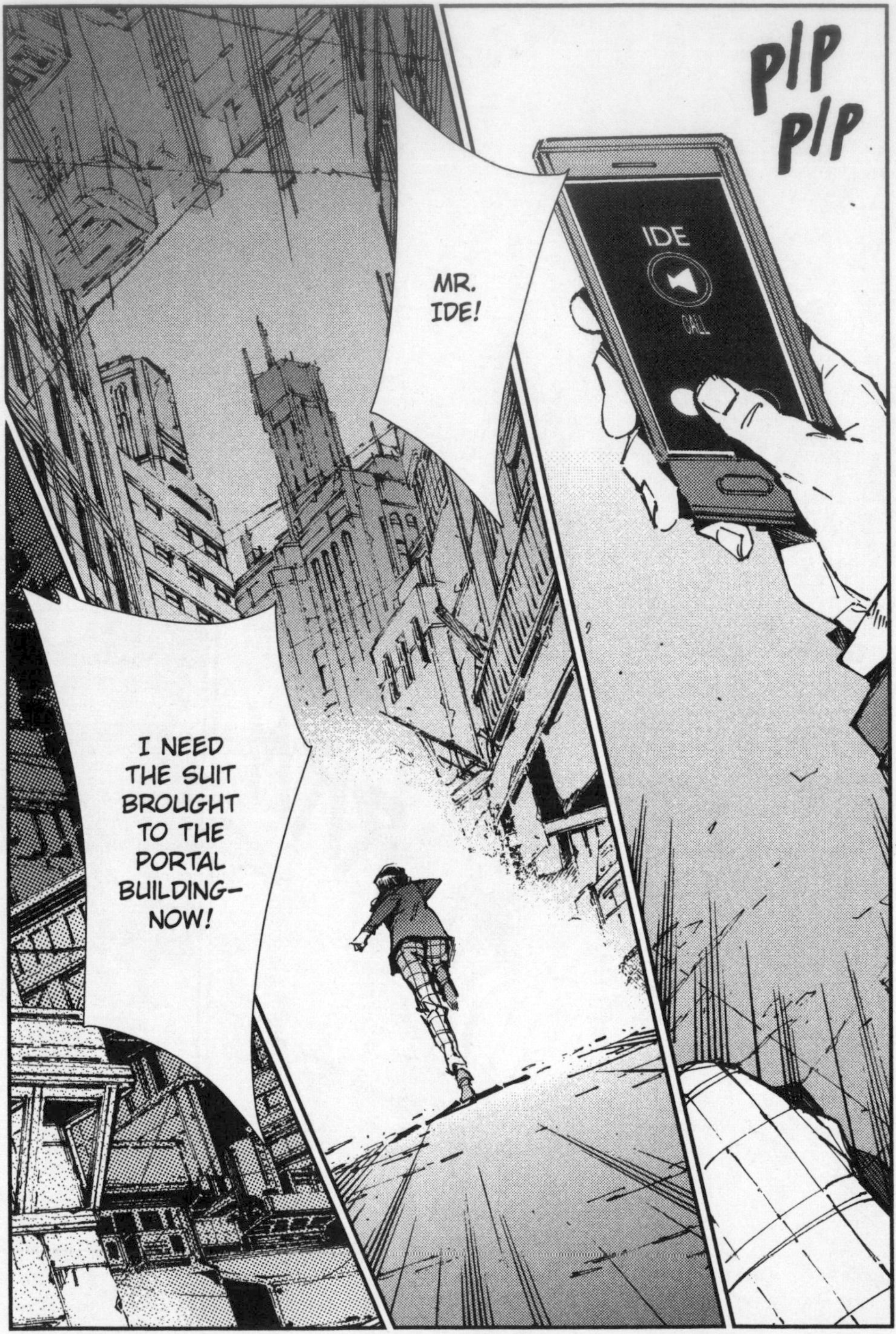
PIP PIP
IDE
CALL
MR. IDE!
I NEED THE SUIT BROUGHT TO THE PORTAL BUILDING—NOW!

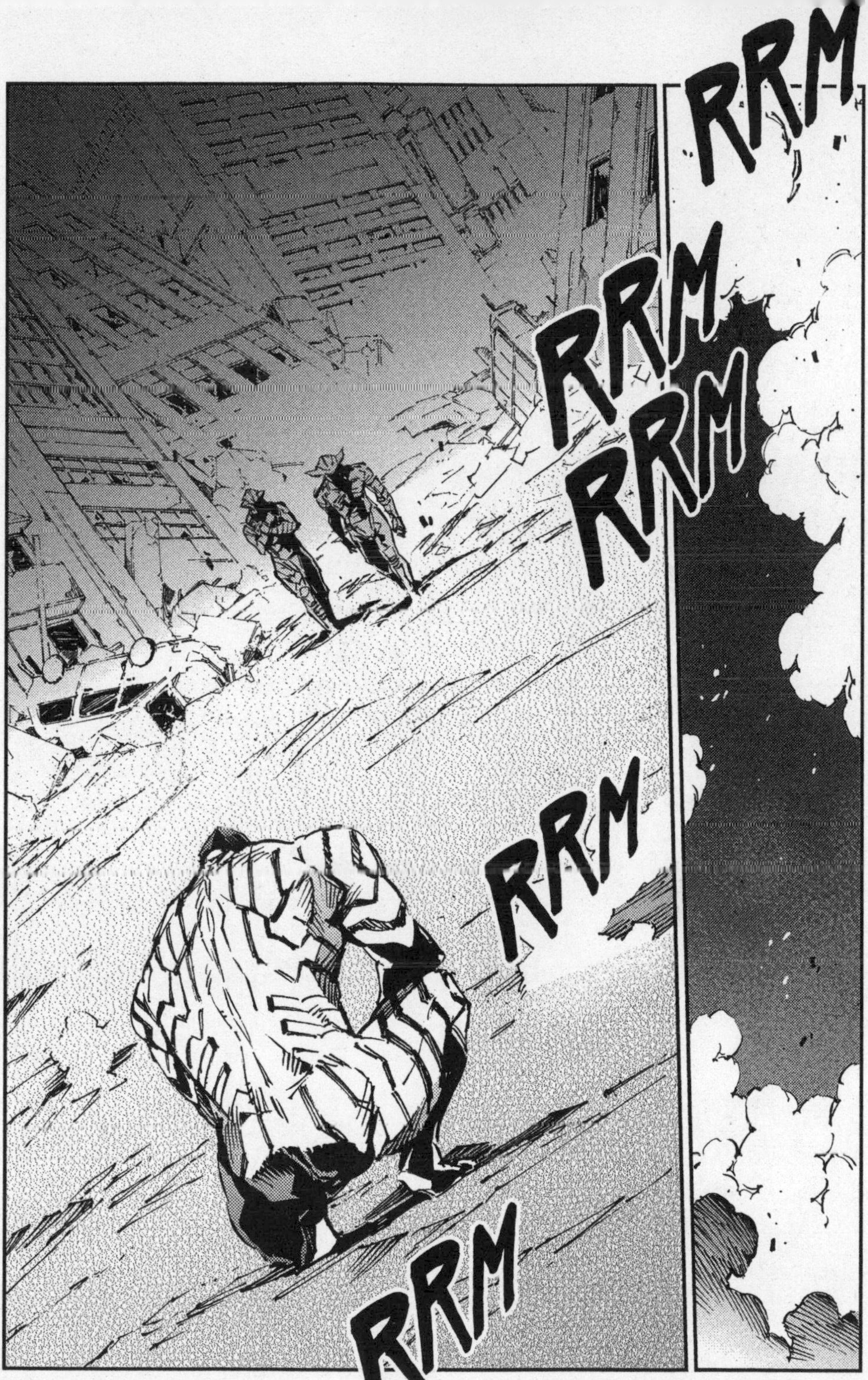
RRM
RRM
RRM
RRM
RRM
RRM

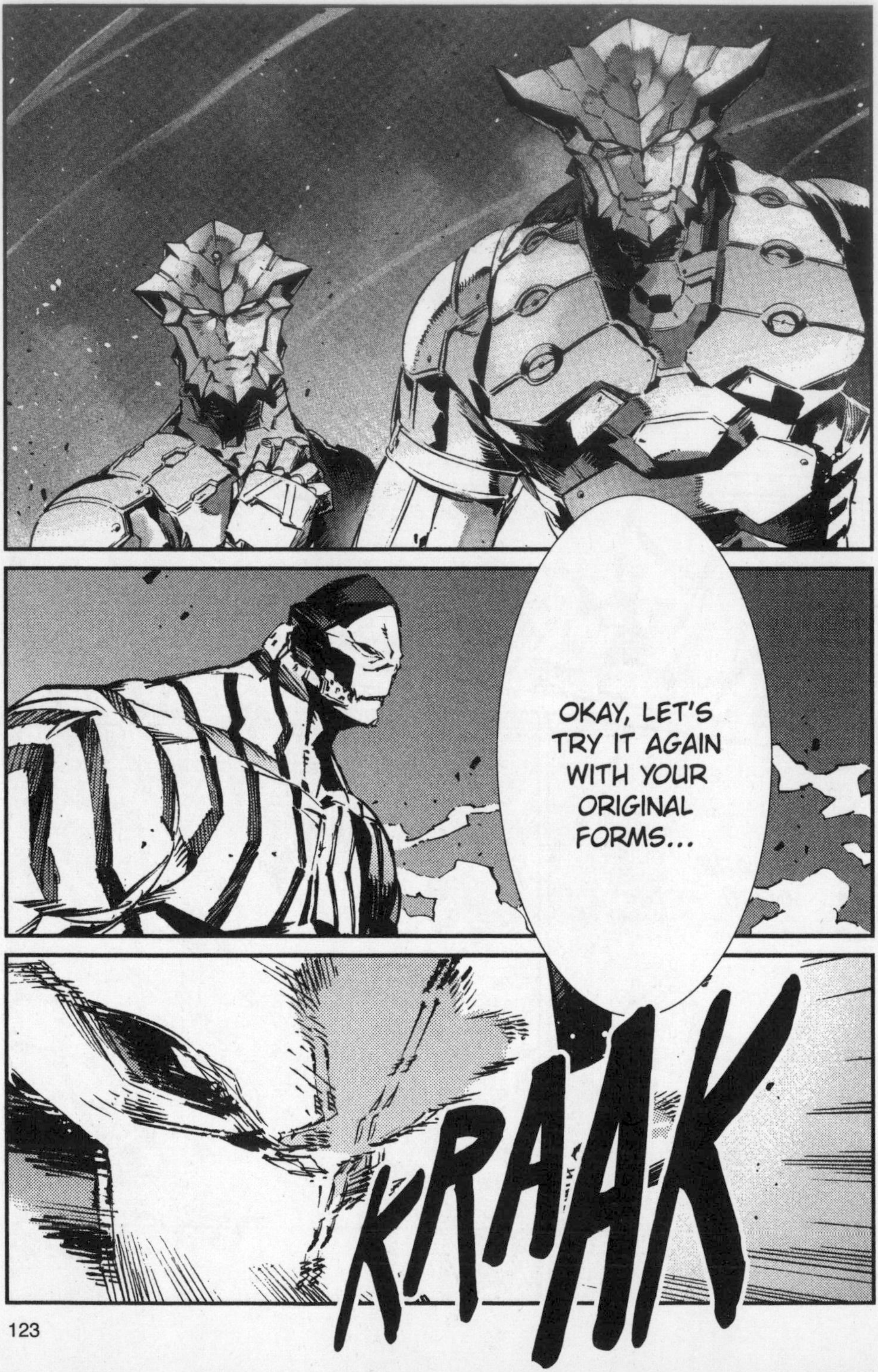
OKAY, LET'S TRY IT AGAIN WITH YOUR ORIGINAL FORMS...
KRAAK

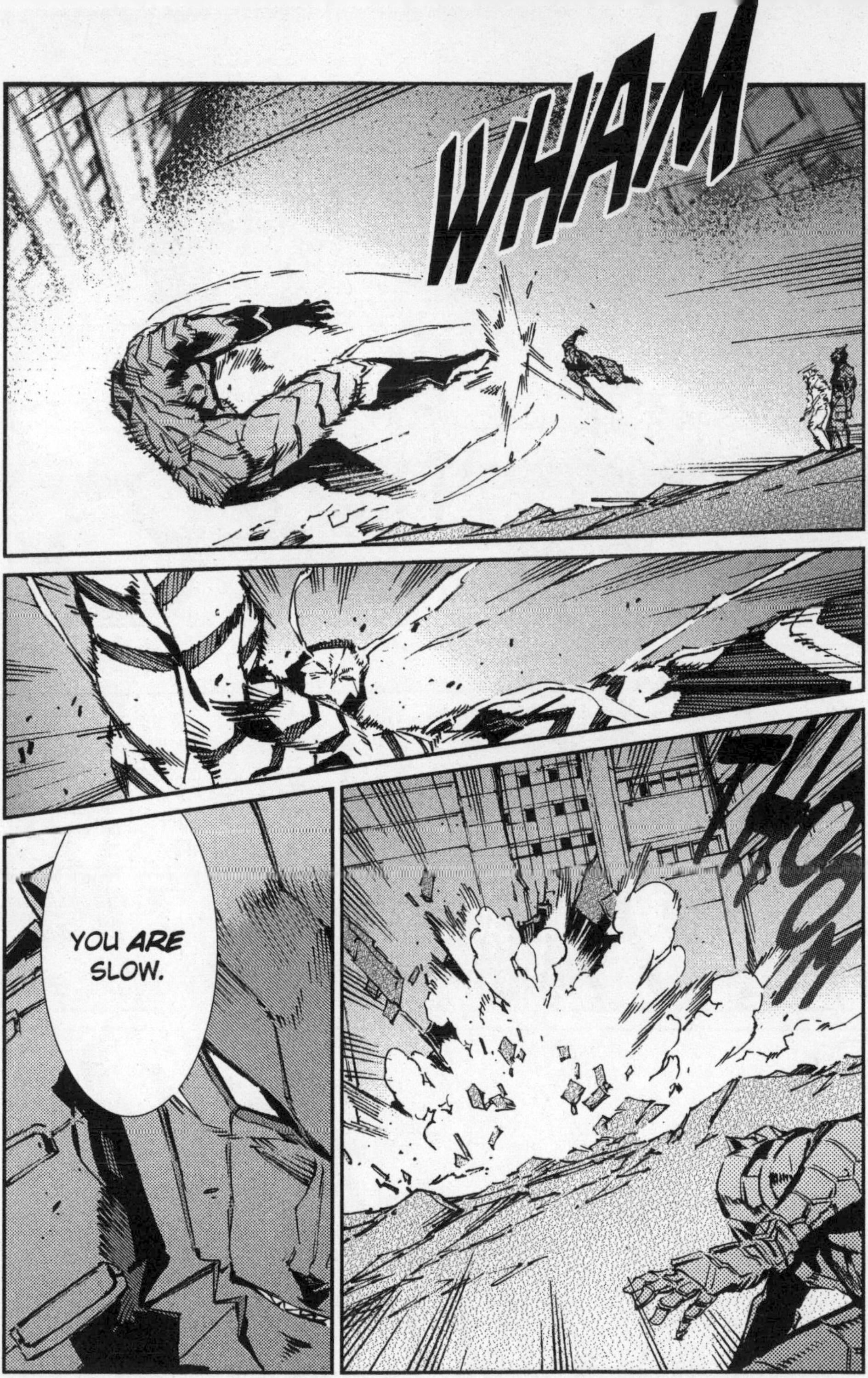
WHAM
THOOM
YOU ARE SLOW.

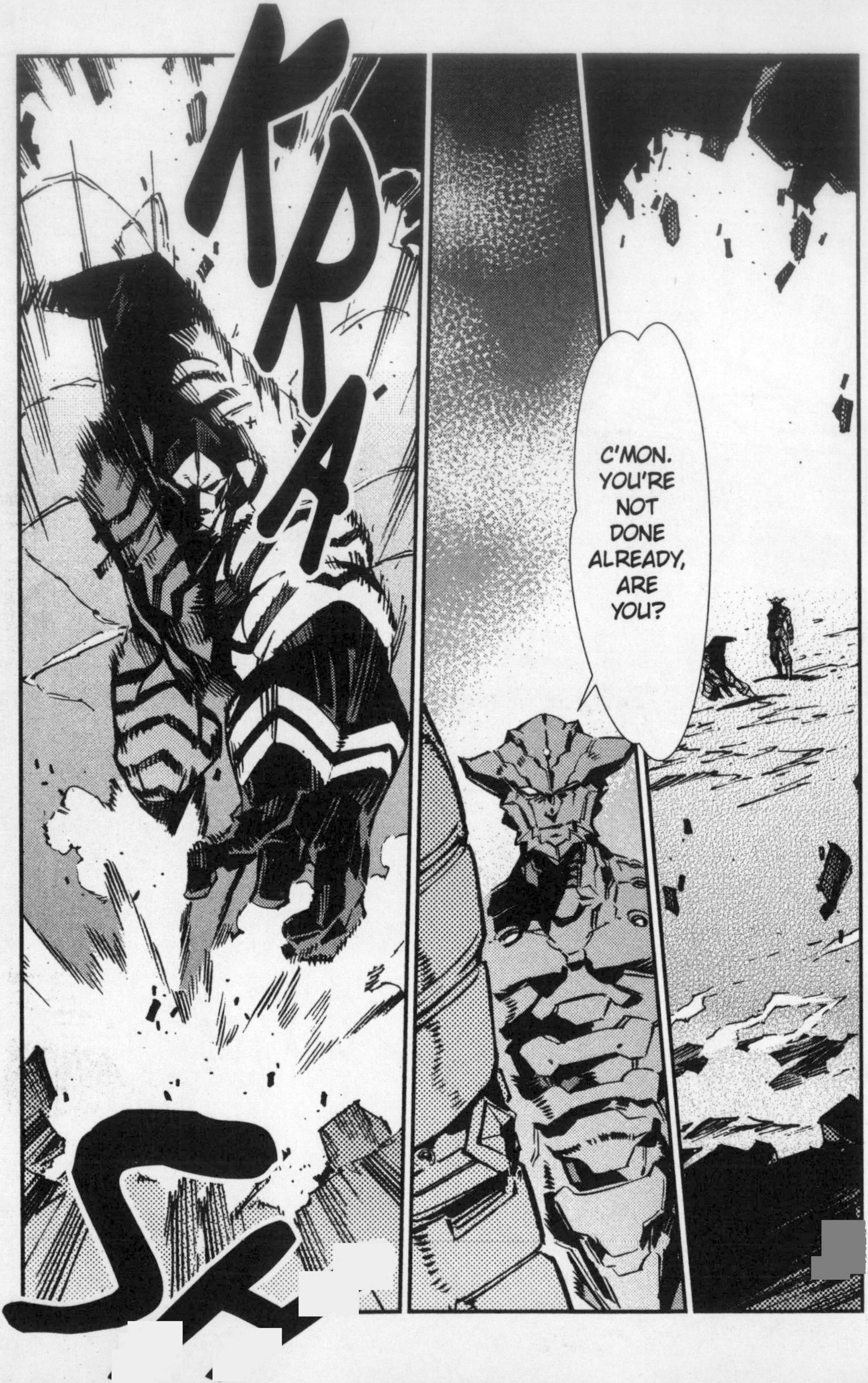
C'MON. YOU'RE NOT DONE ALREADY, ARE YOU?

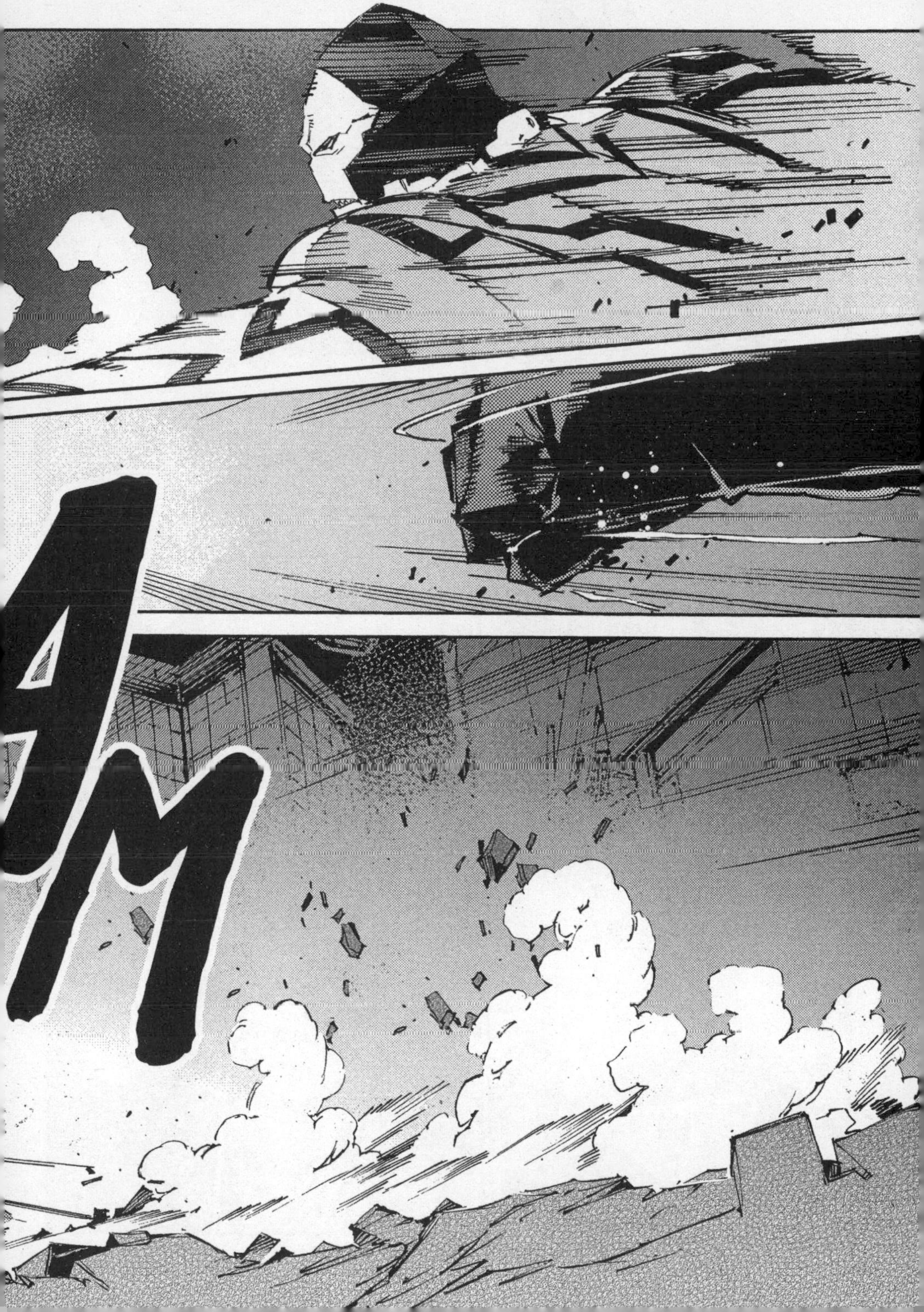
M

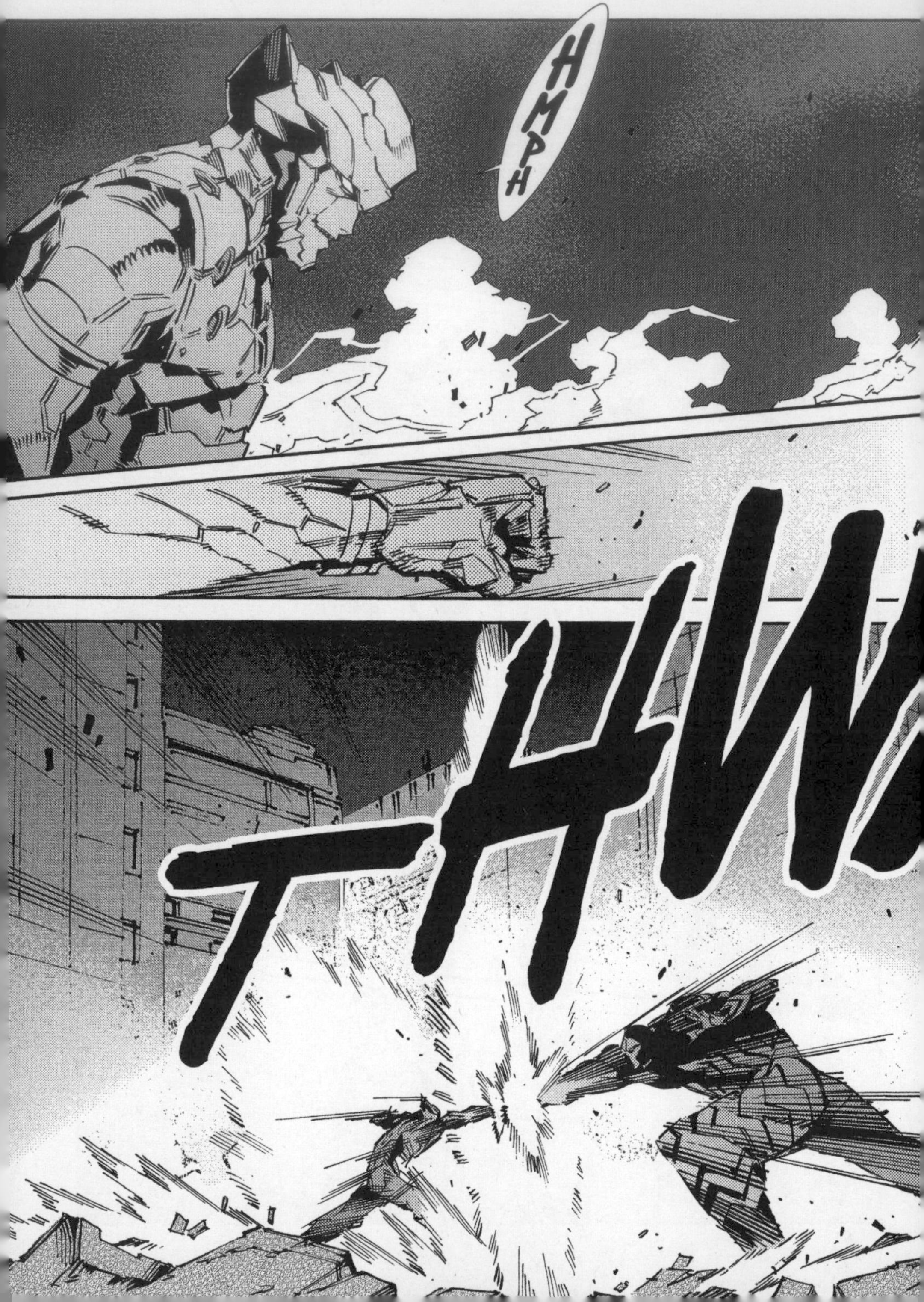
HMMPH
THW

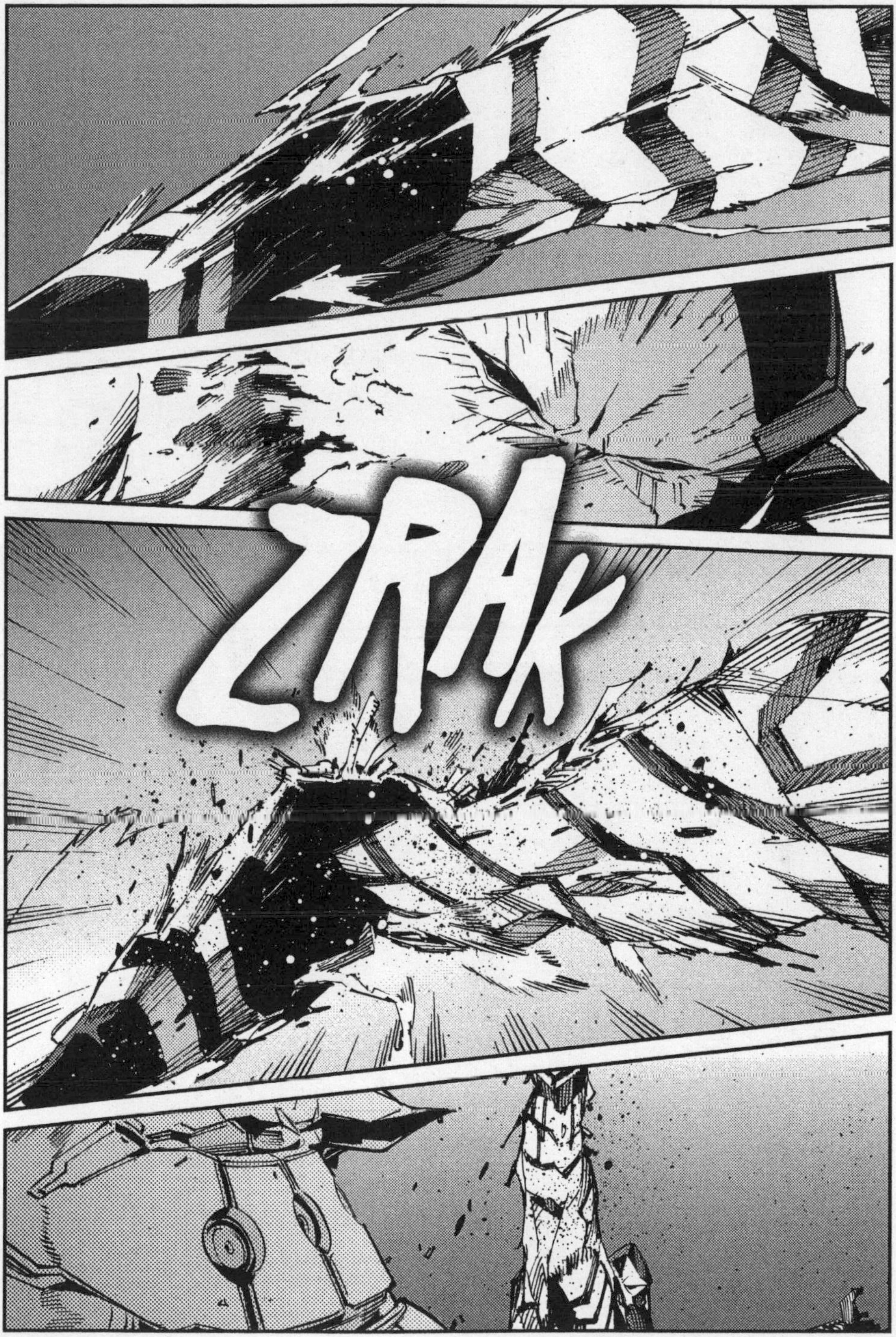
ZRAK

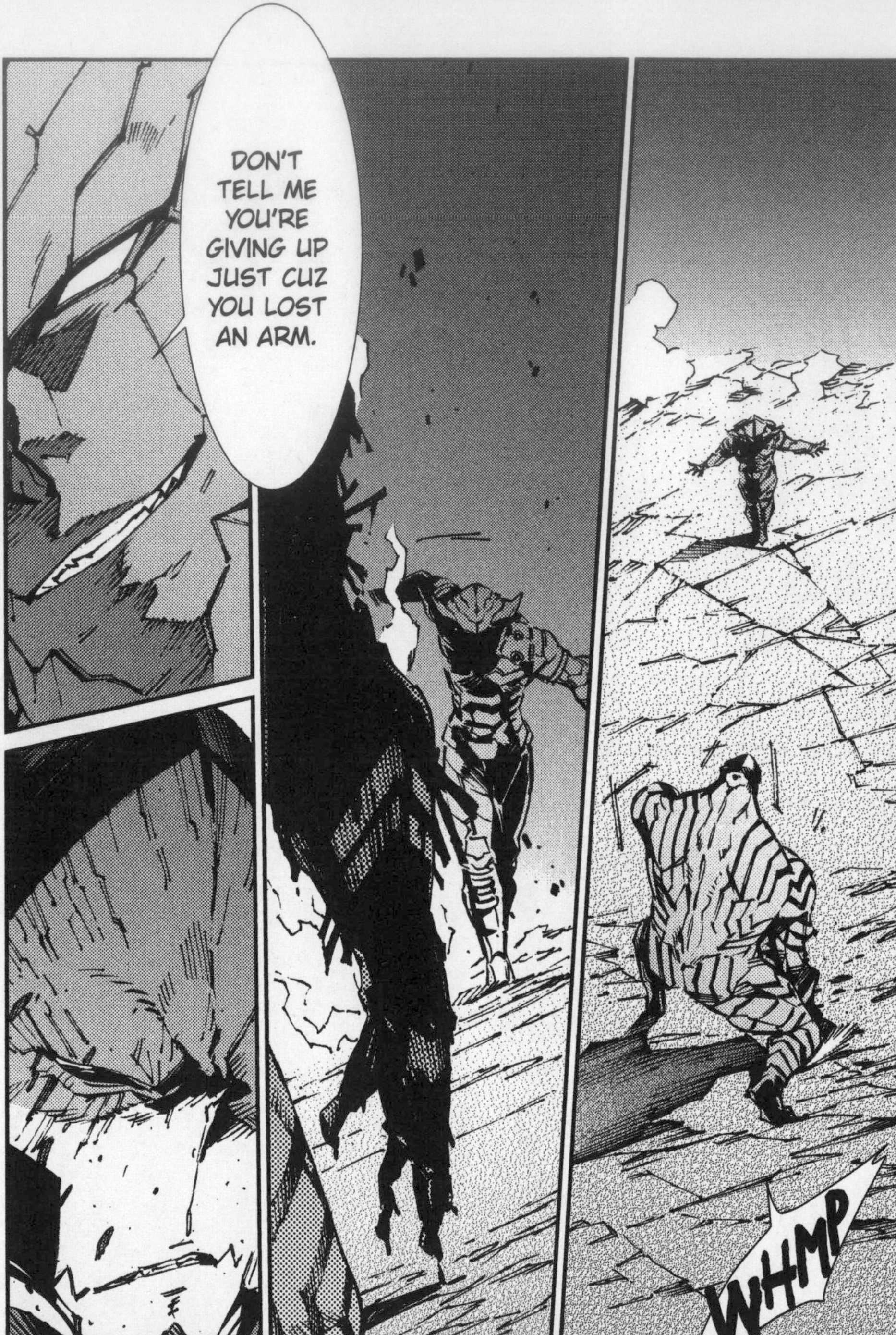
DON'T TELL ME YOU'RE GIVING UP JUST CUZ YOU LOST AN ARM.
WHMP

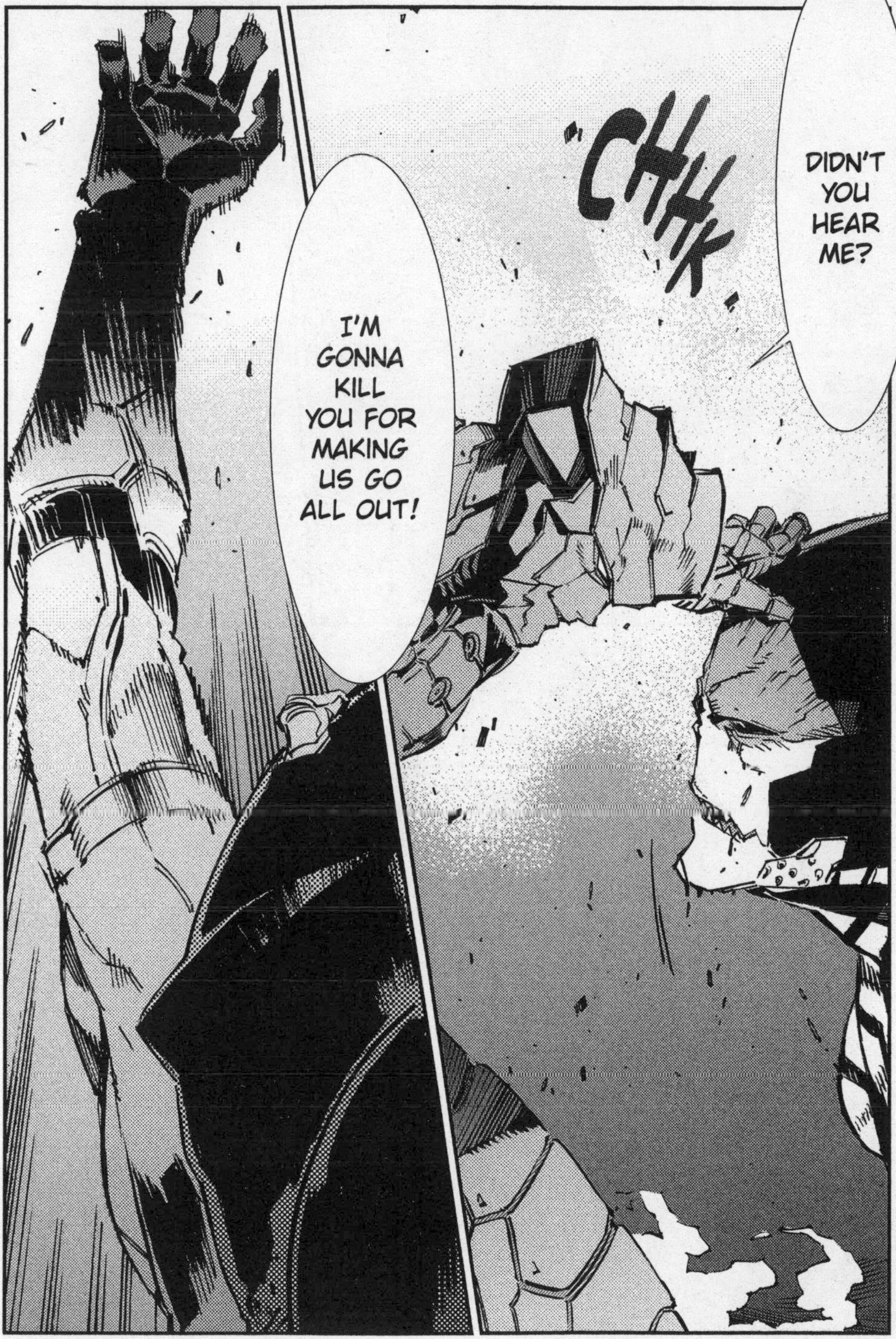
DIDN'T YOU HEAR ME?
CHHK
I'M GONNA KILL YOU FOR MAKING US GO ALL OUT!

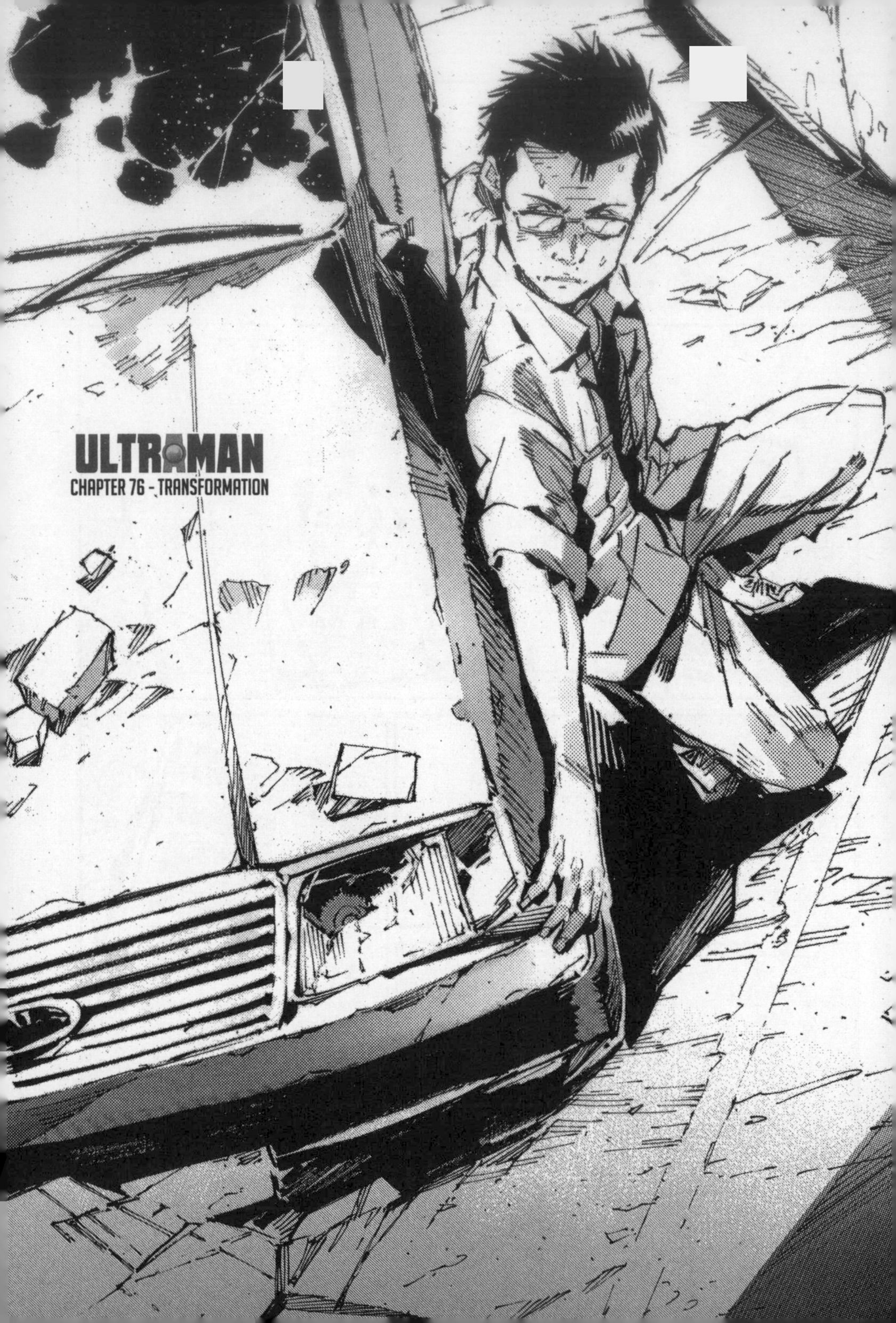
ULTRAMAN
CHAPTER 76 - TRANSFORMATION

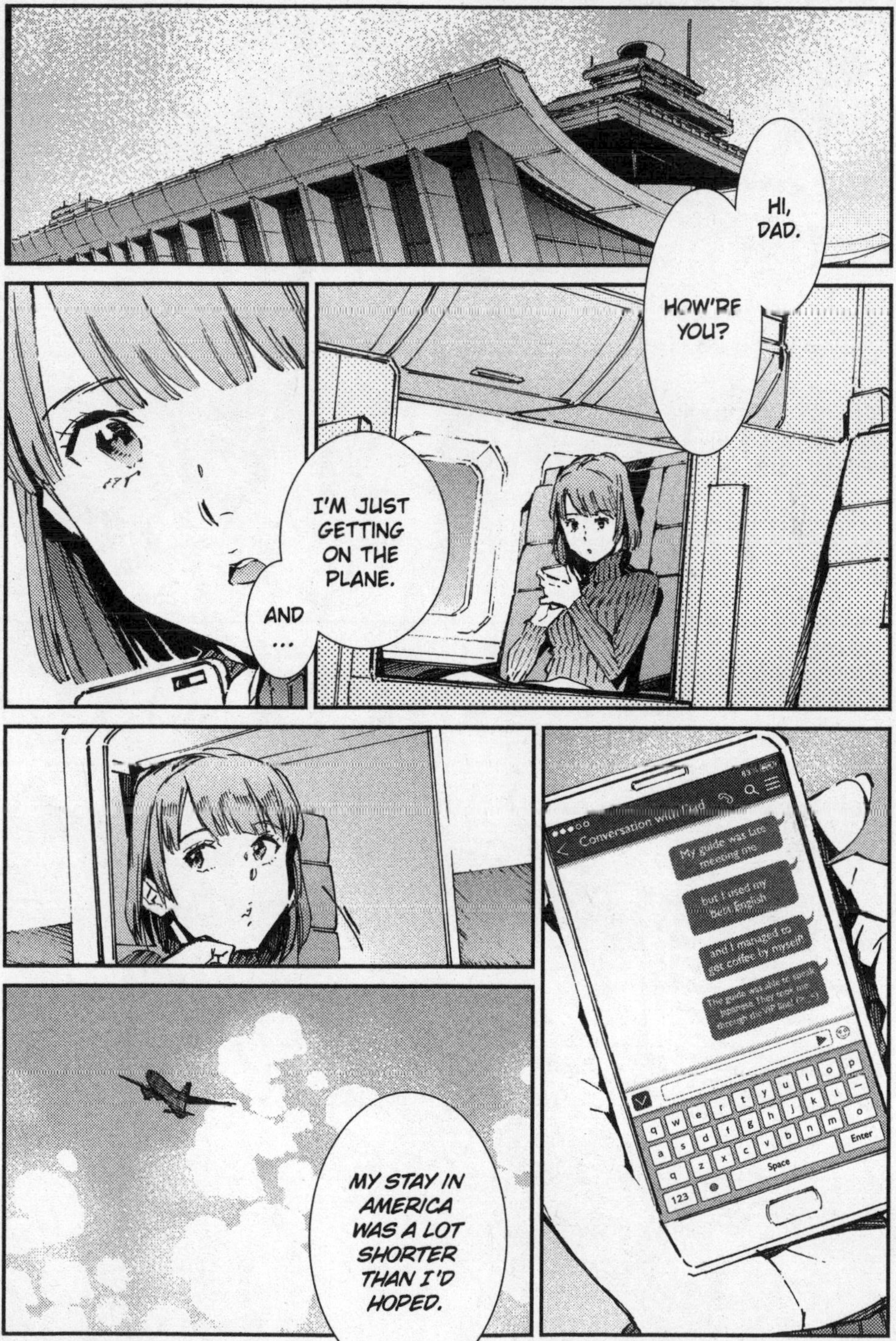
HI, DAD.
HOW'RE YOU?
I'M JUST GETTING ON THE PLANE.
AND ...
My guide was late meeting me
but I used my best English
and I managed to get coffee by myself!
MY STAY IN AMERICA WAS A LOT SHORTER THAN I'D HOPED.

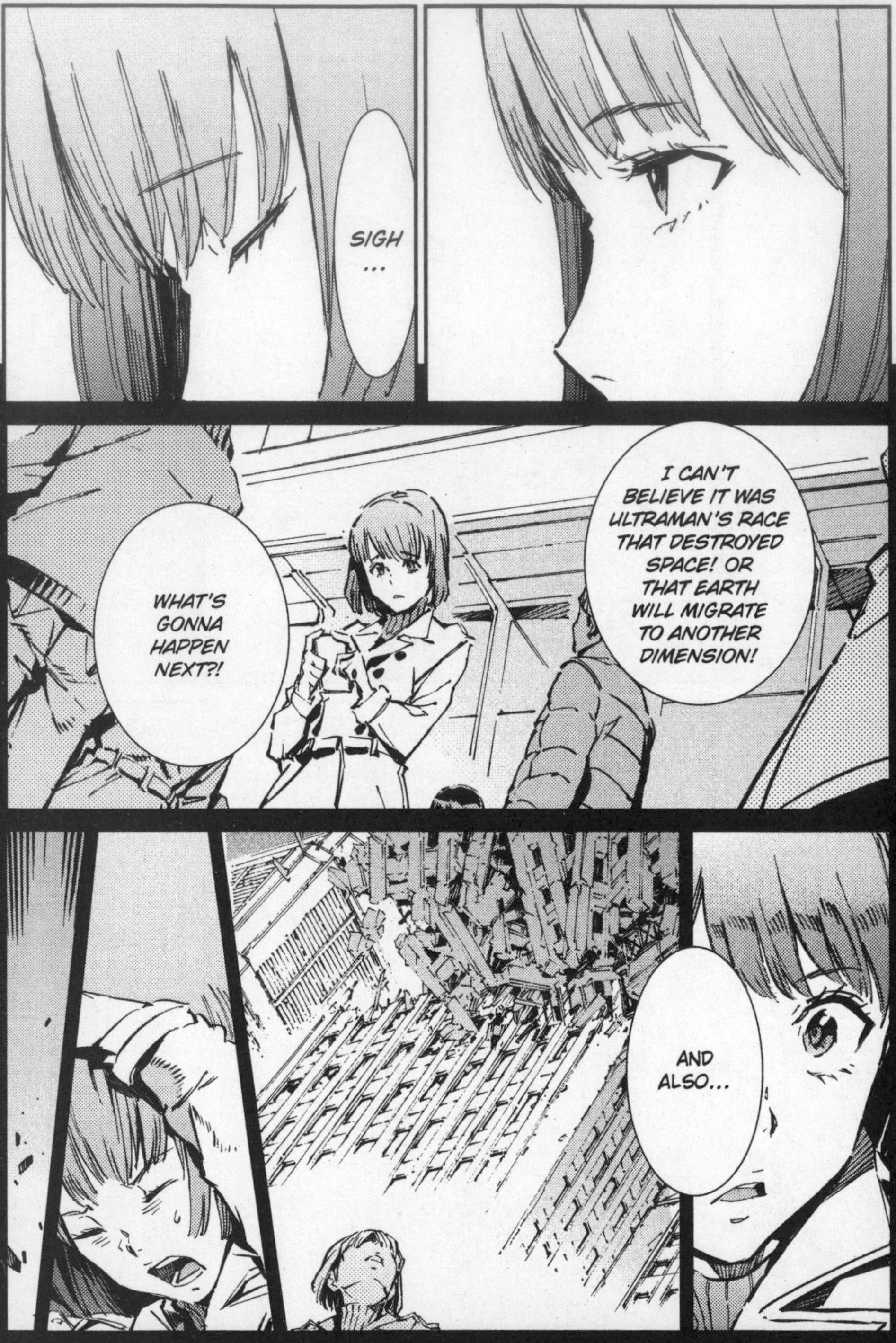
SIGH...
I CAN'T BELIEVE IT WAS ULTRAMAN'S RACE THAT DESTROYED SPACE! OR THAT EARTH WILL MIGRATE TO ANOTHER DIMENSION!
WHAT'S GONNA HAPPEN NEXT?!
AND ALSO...

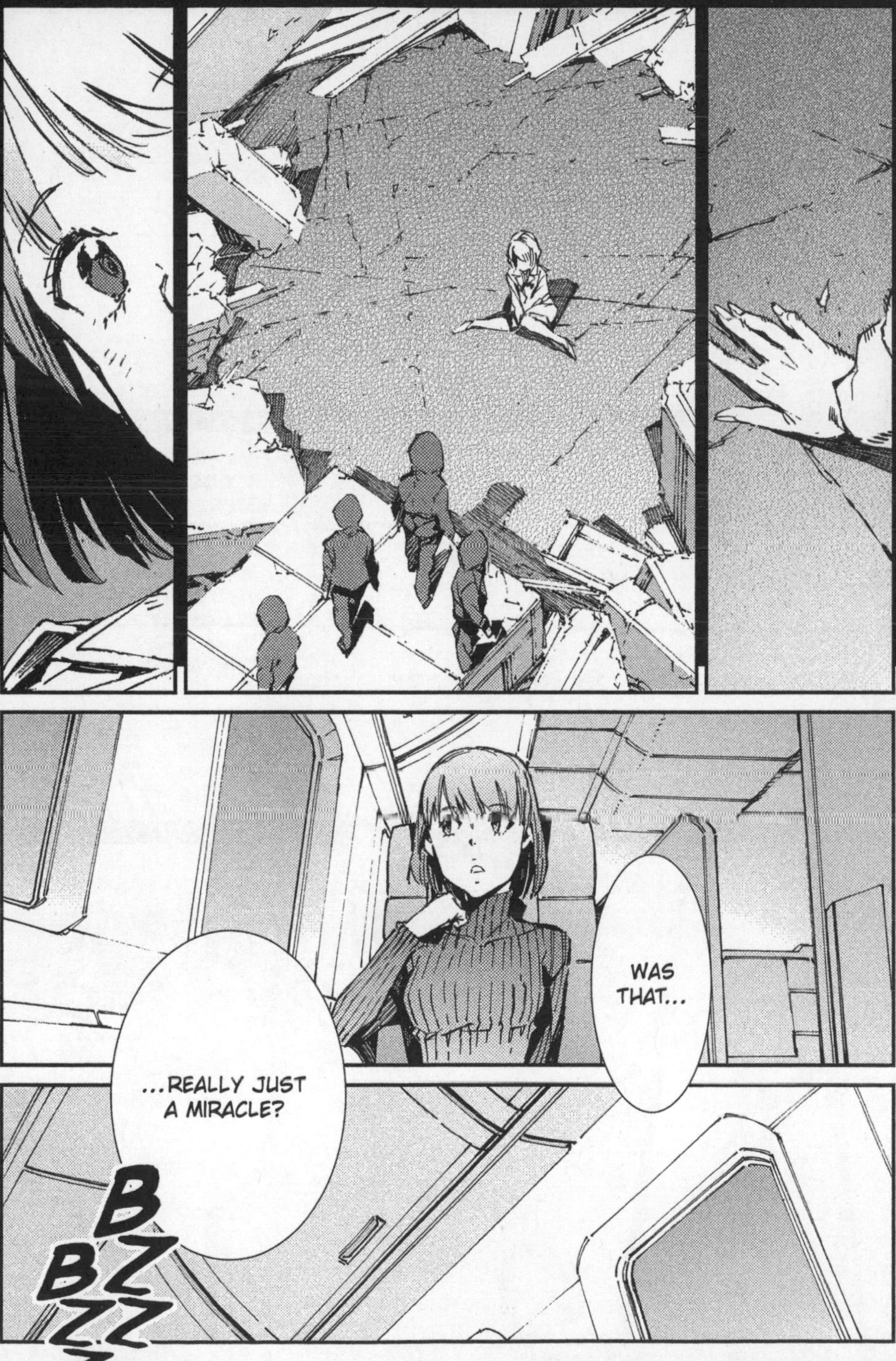
WAS THAT...
...REALLY JUST A MIRACLE?
BZZ
BZZ

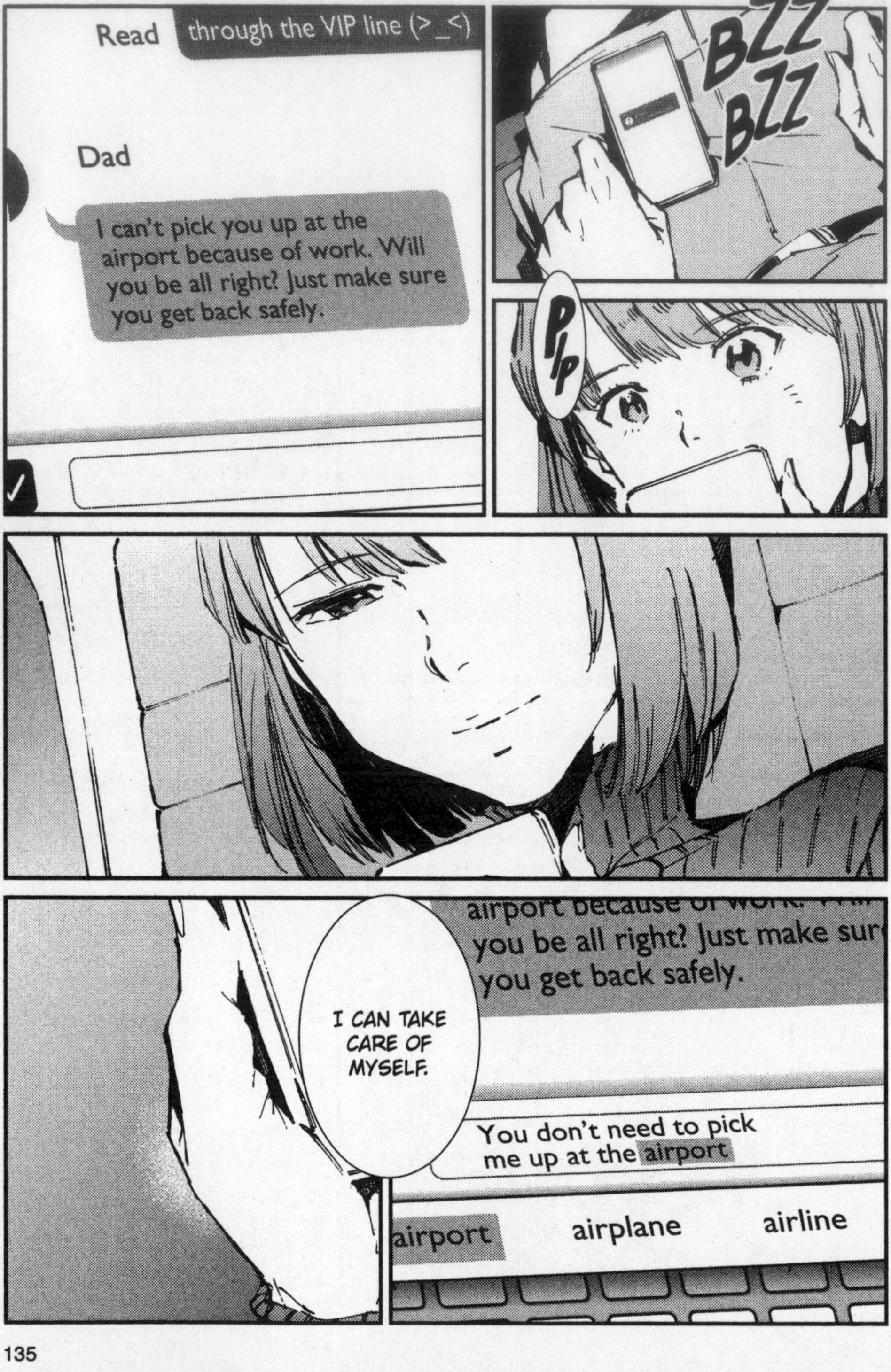
BZZ BZZ
PIP
Read
through the VIP line (>_<)
Dad
I can't pick you up at the airport because of work. Will you be all right? Just make sure you get back safely.
you be all right? Just make sur
you get back safely.
You don't need to pick me up at the airport
airport airplane airline
I CAN TAKE CARE OF MYSELF.

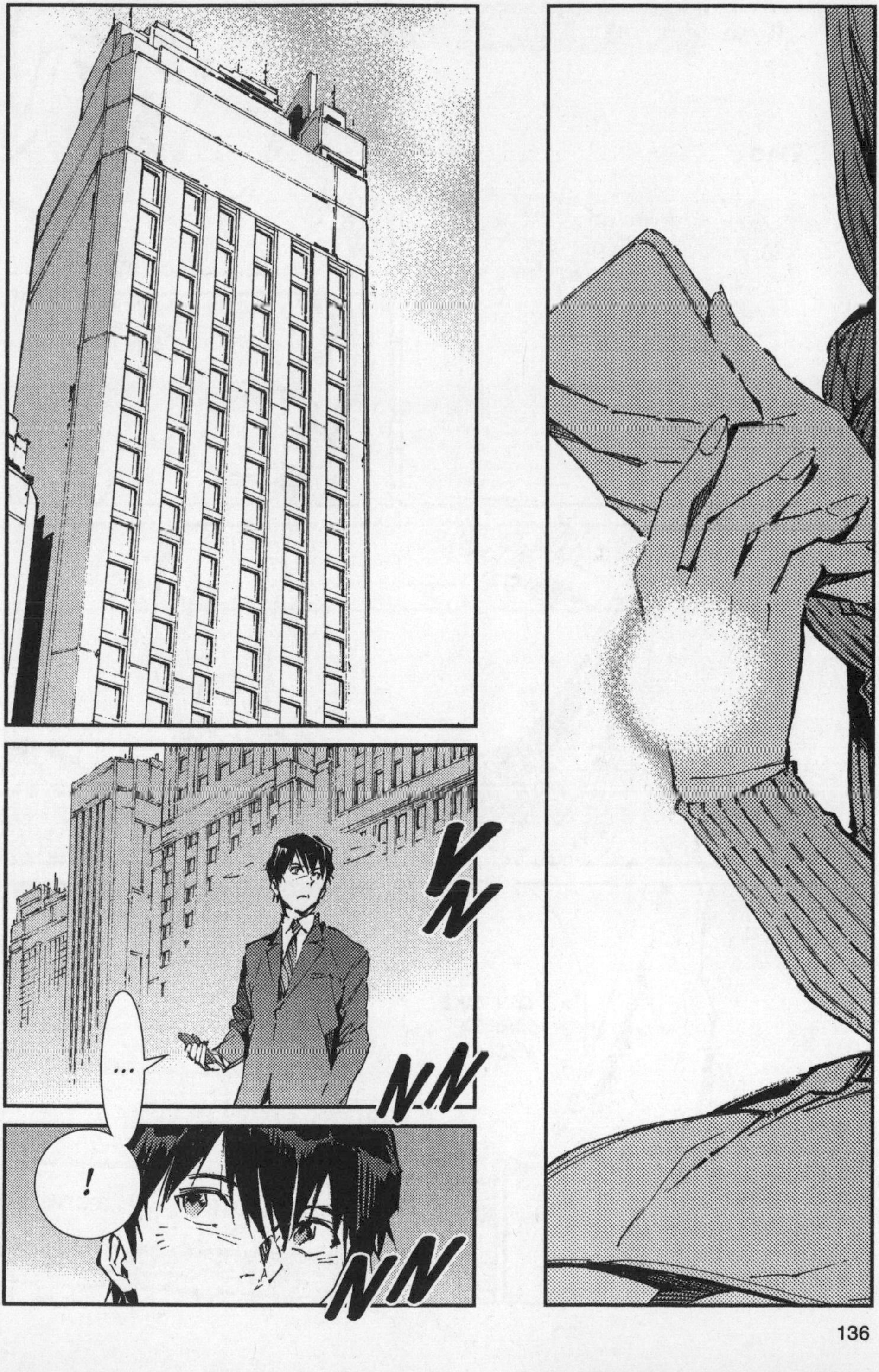
VN
NN
...
!
NN

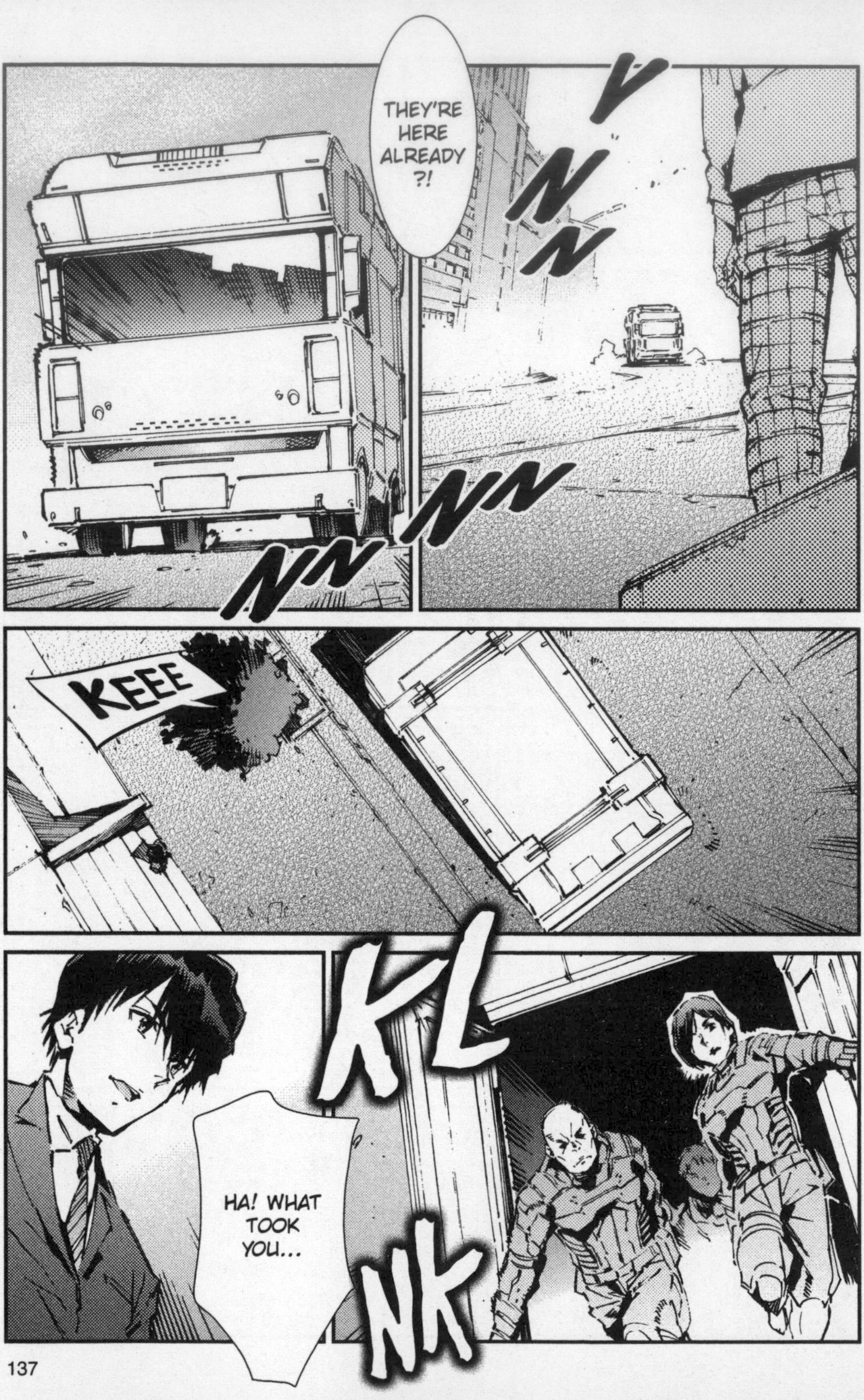
VNNNNNN
THEY'RE HERE ALREADY?!
KEEE
KL
NK
HA! WHAT TOOK YOU...

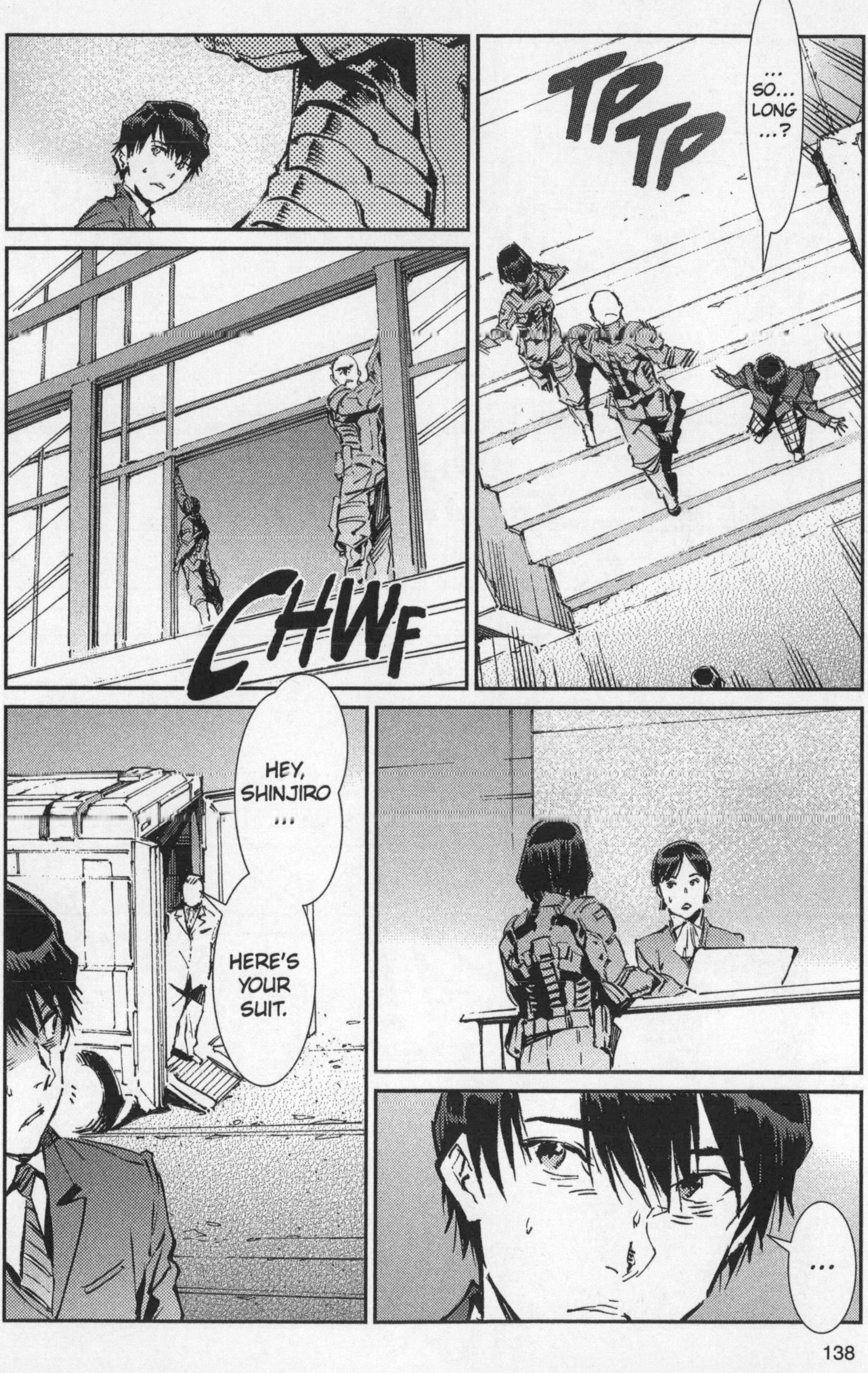
...SO... LONG ...?
TPTP
CHWF
...
HEY, SHINJIRO ...
HERE'S YOUR SUIT.

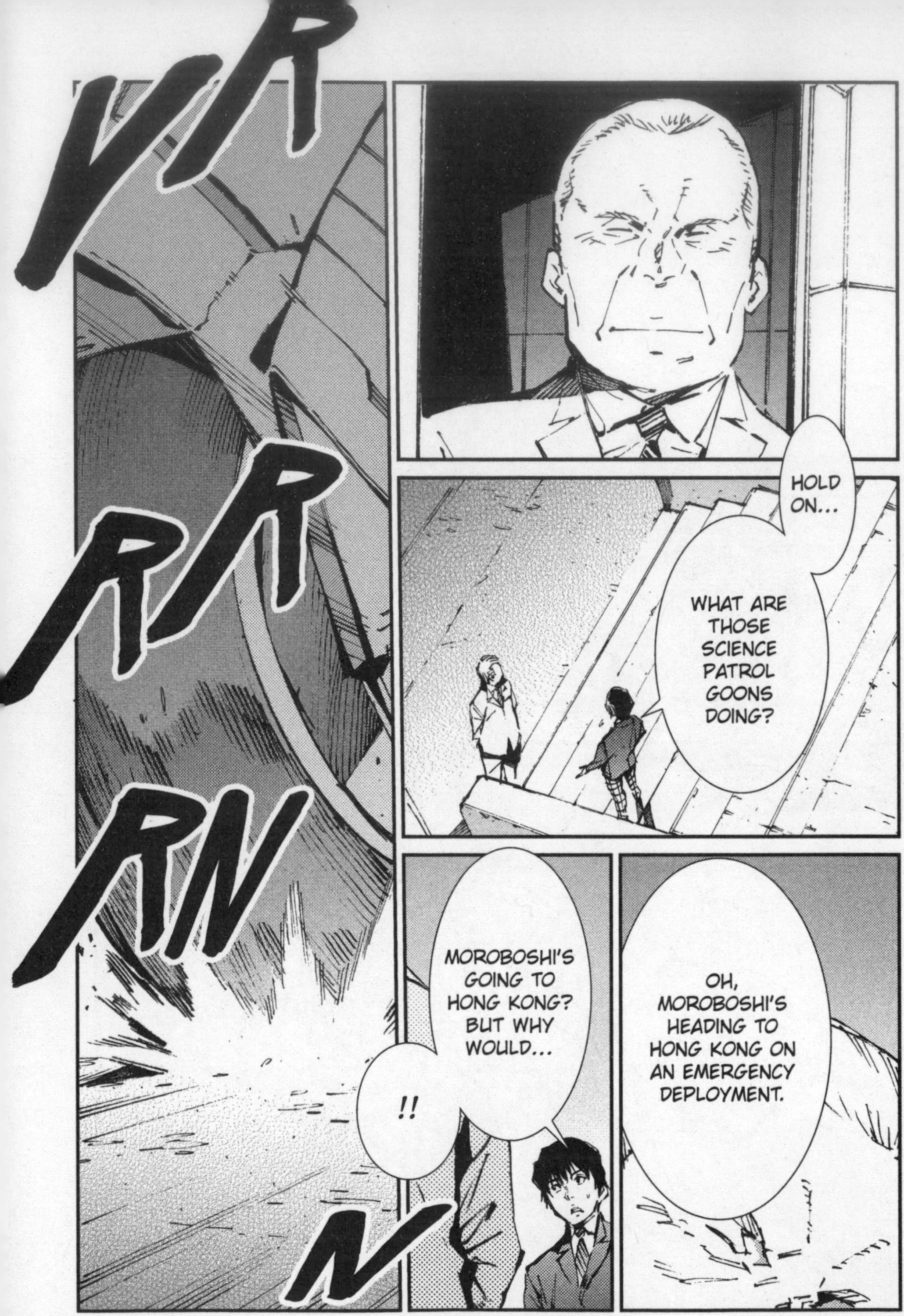
HOLD ON...
WHAT ARE THOSE SCIENCE PATROL GOONS DOING?
OH, MOROBOSHI'S HEADING TO HONG KONG ON AN EMERGENCY DEPLOYMENT.
MOROBOSHI'S GOING TO HONG KONG? BUT WHY WOULD...
!!
VRRRRN

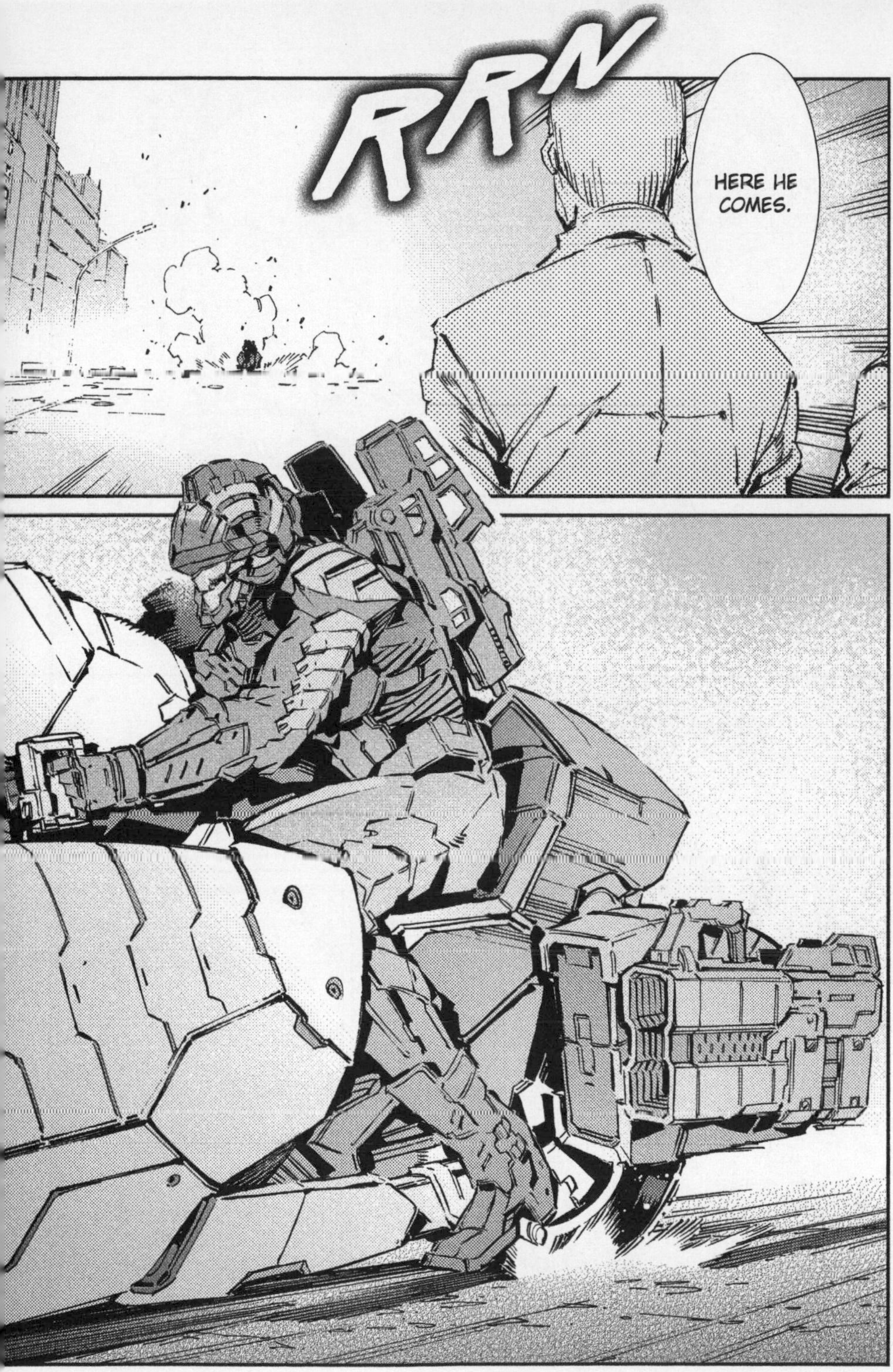
HERE HE COMES.
RRN

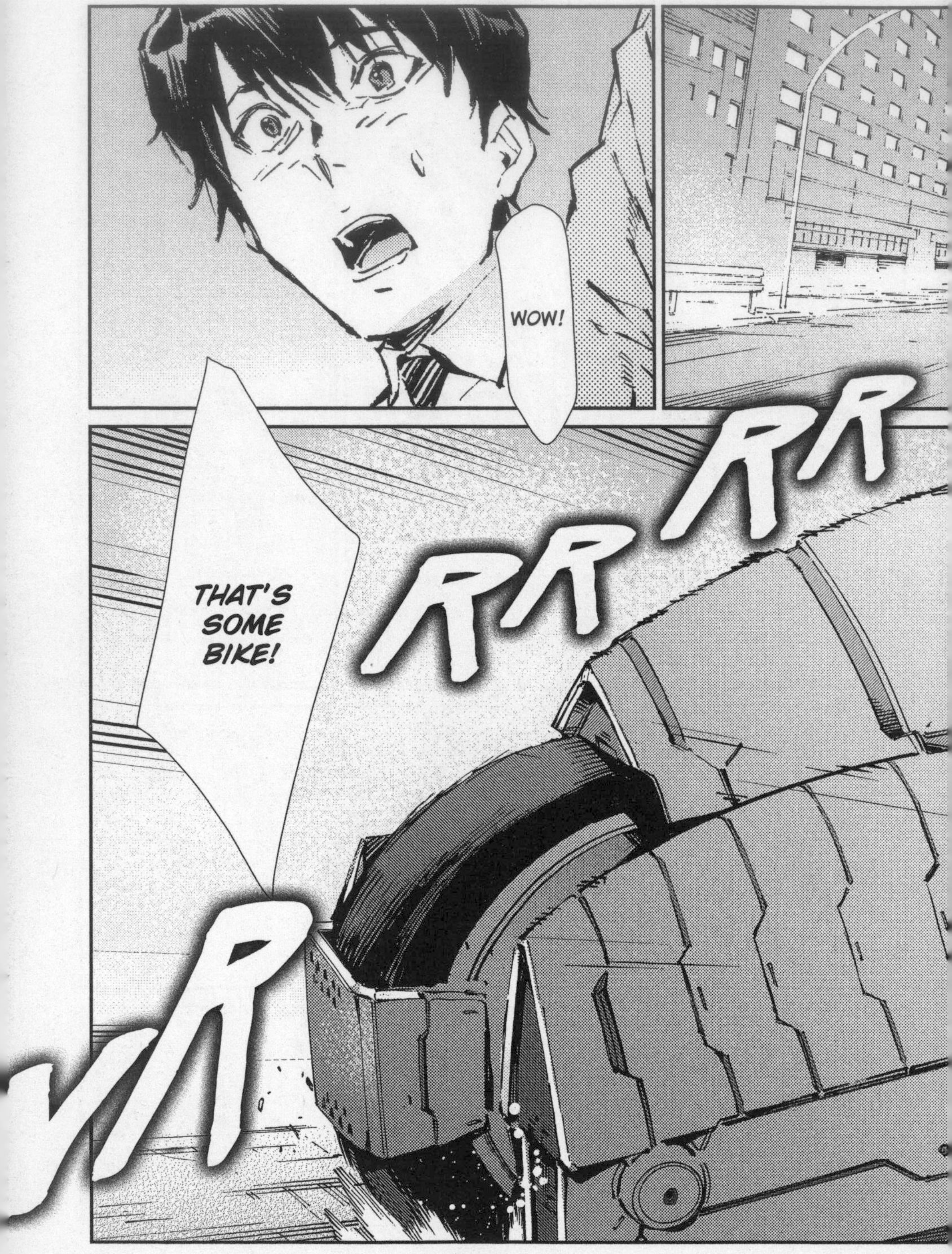
WOW!
THAT'S SOME BIKE!
VRRRRR

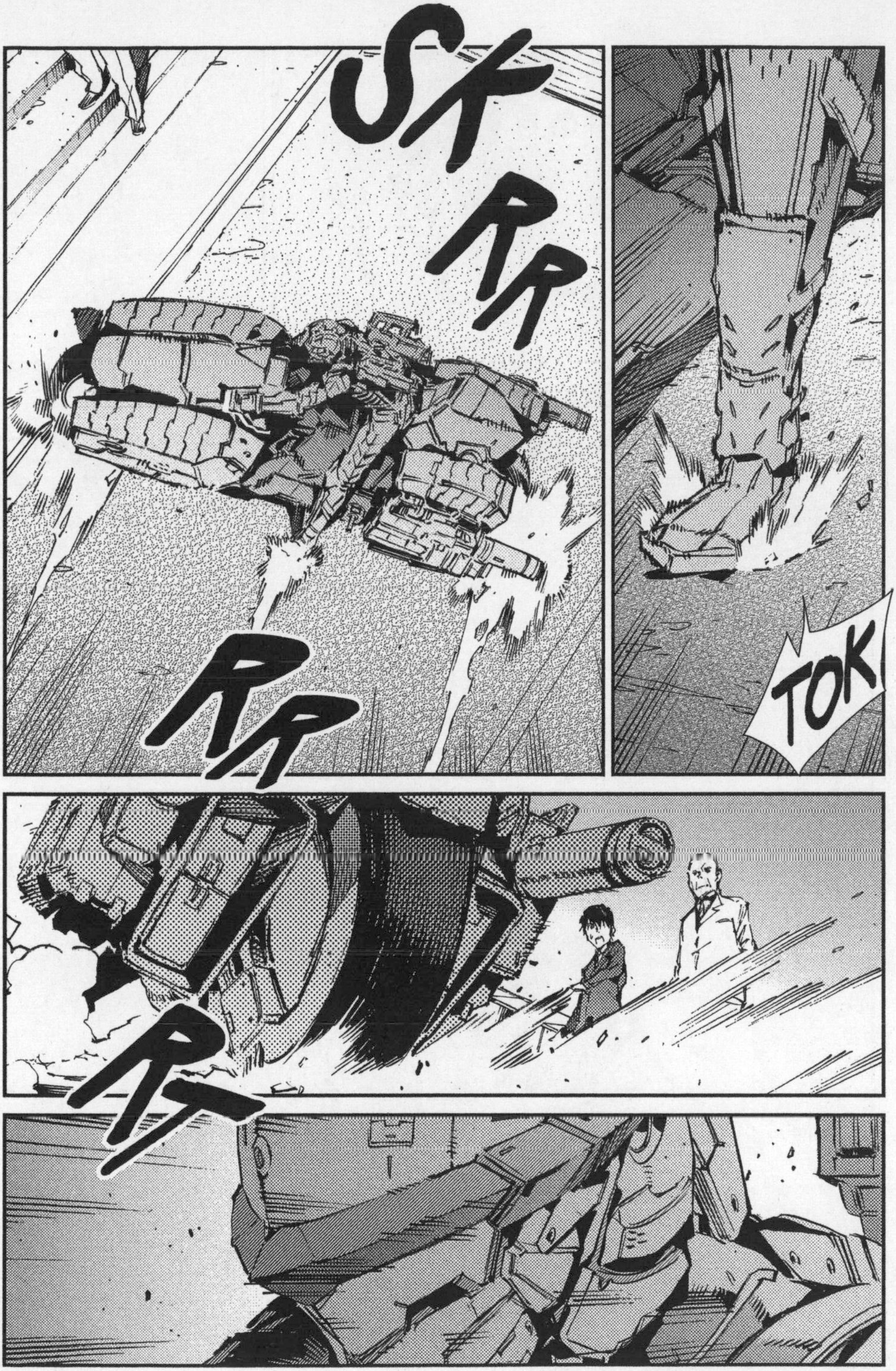
TOK
SKRR
RRRT

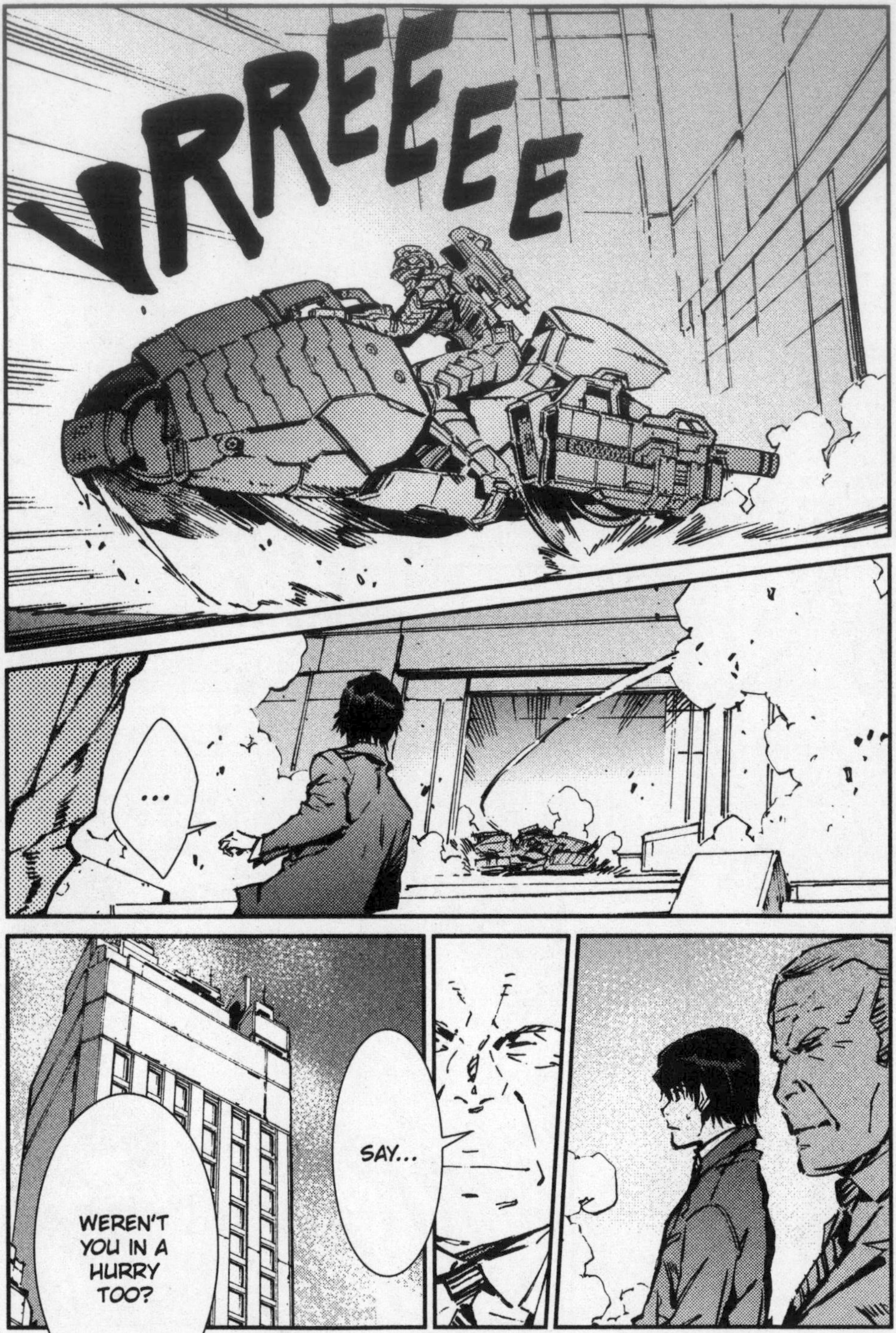
VRREEEE
...
SAY...
WEREN'T YOU IN A HURRY TOO?

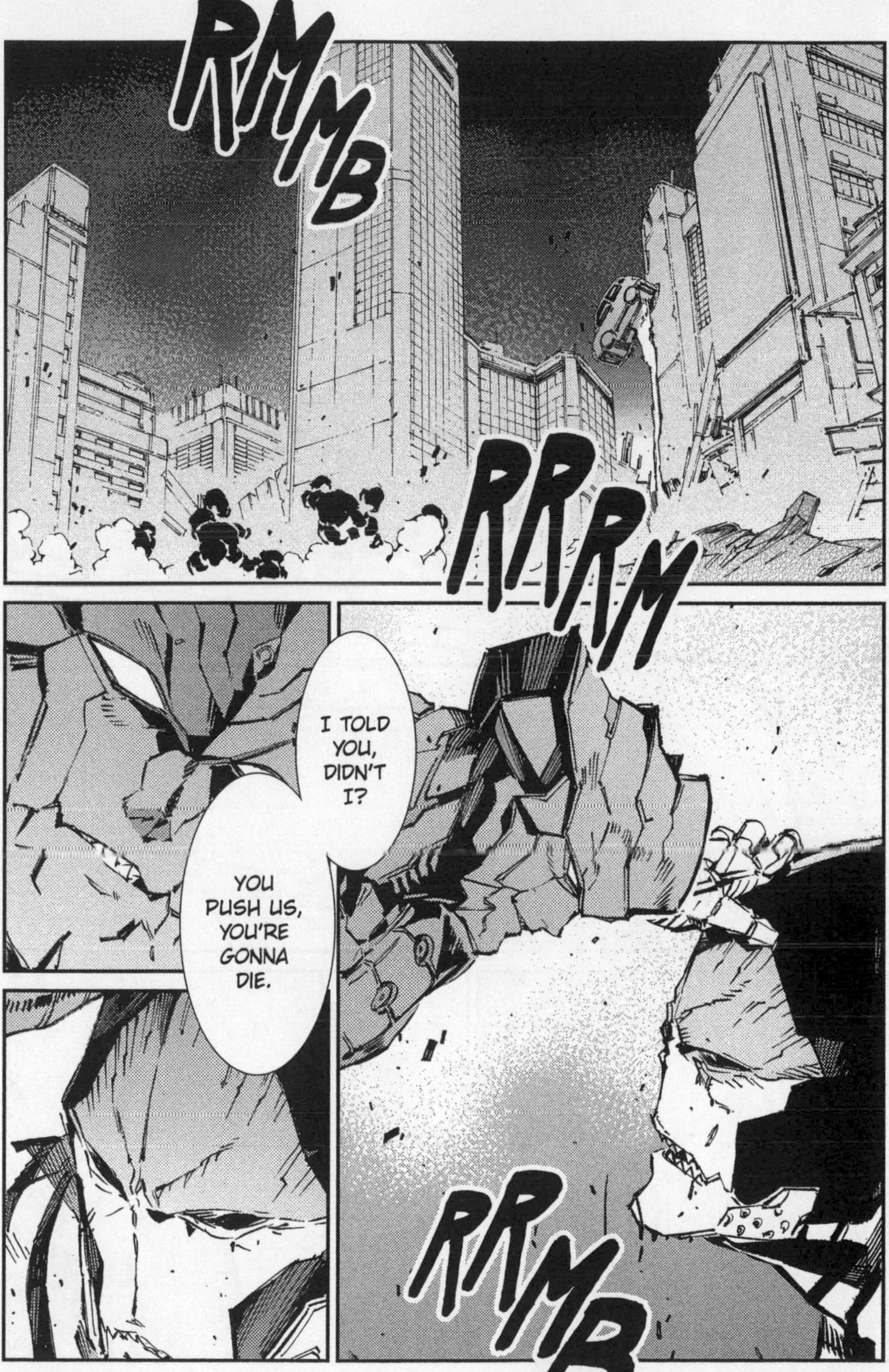
RMMB
RRRM
I TOLD YOU, DIDN'T I?
YOU PUSH US, YOU'RE GONNA DIE.
RRRMB

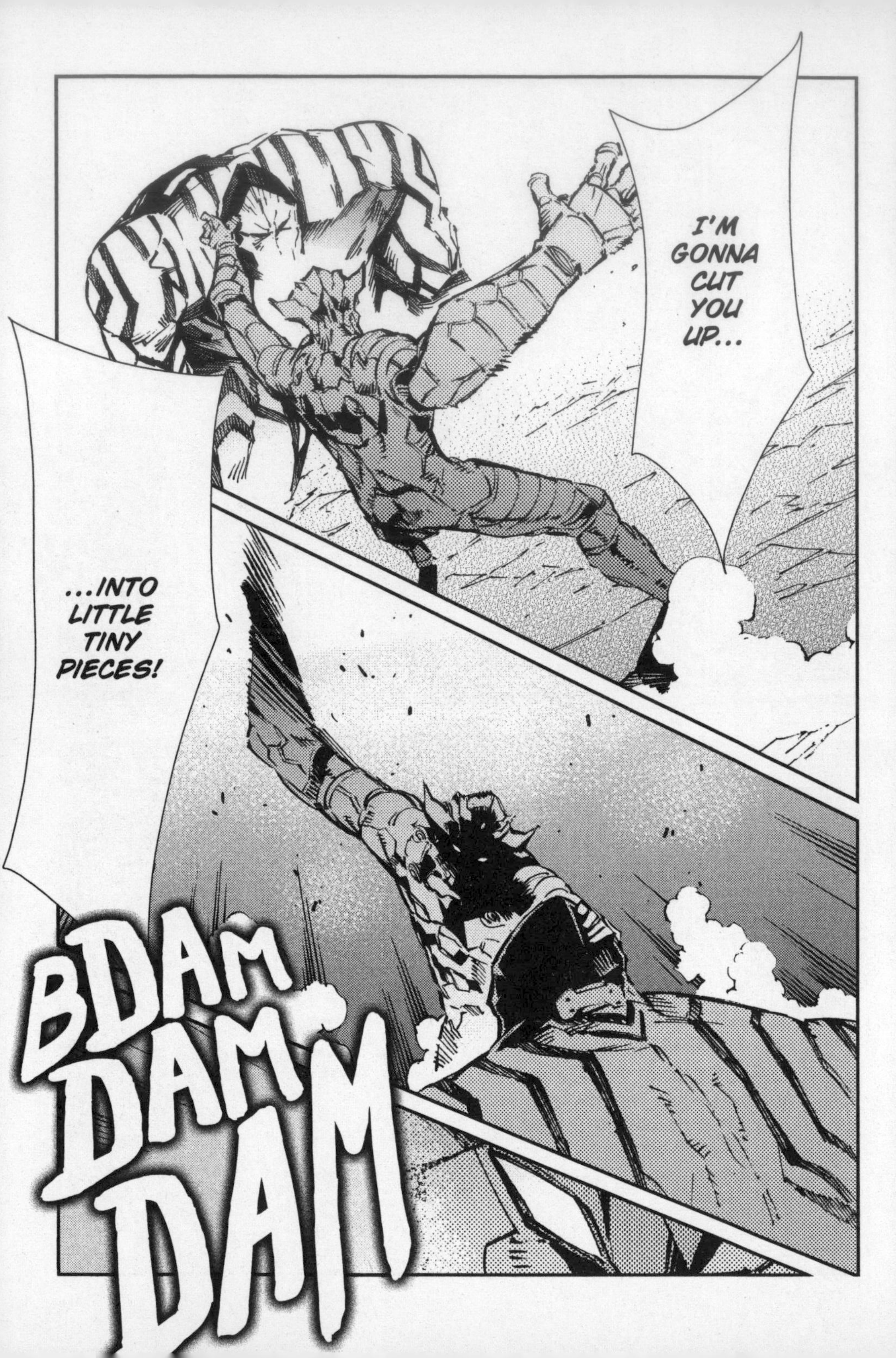
I'M GONNA CUT YOU UP...
...INTO LITTLE TINY PIECES!
BDAM DAM DAM

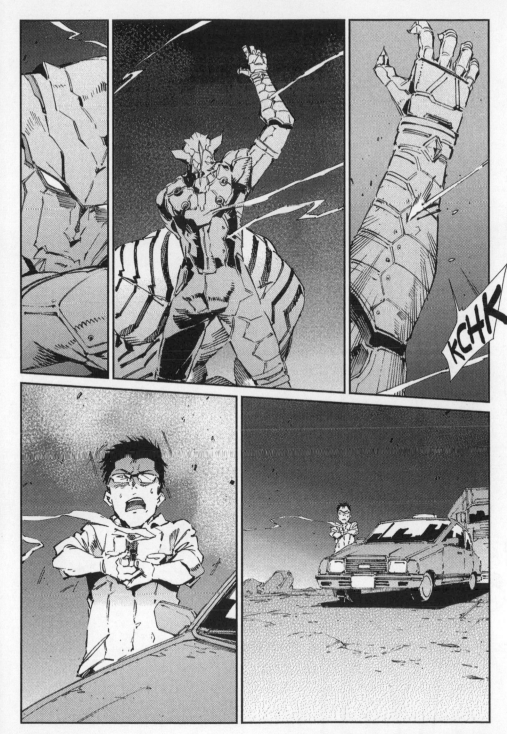

KCHK

146

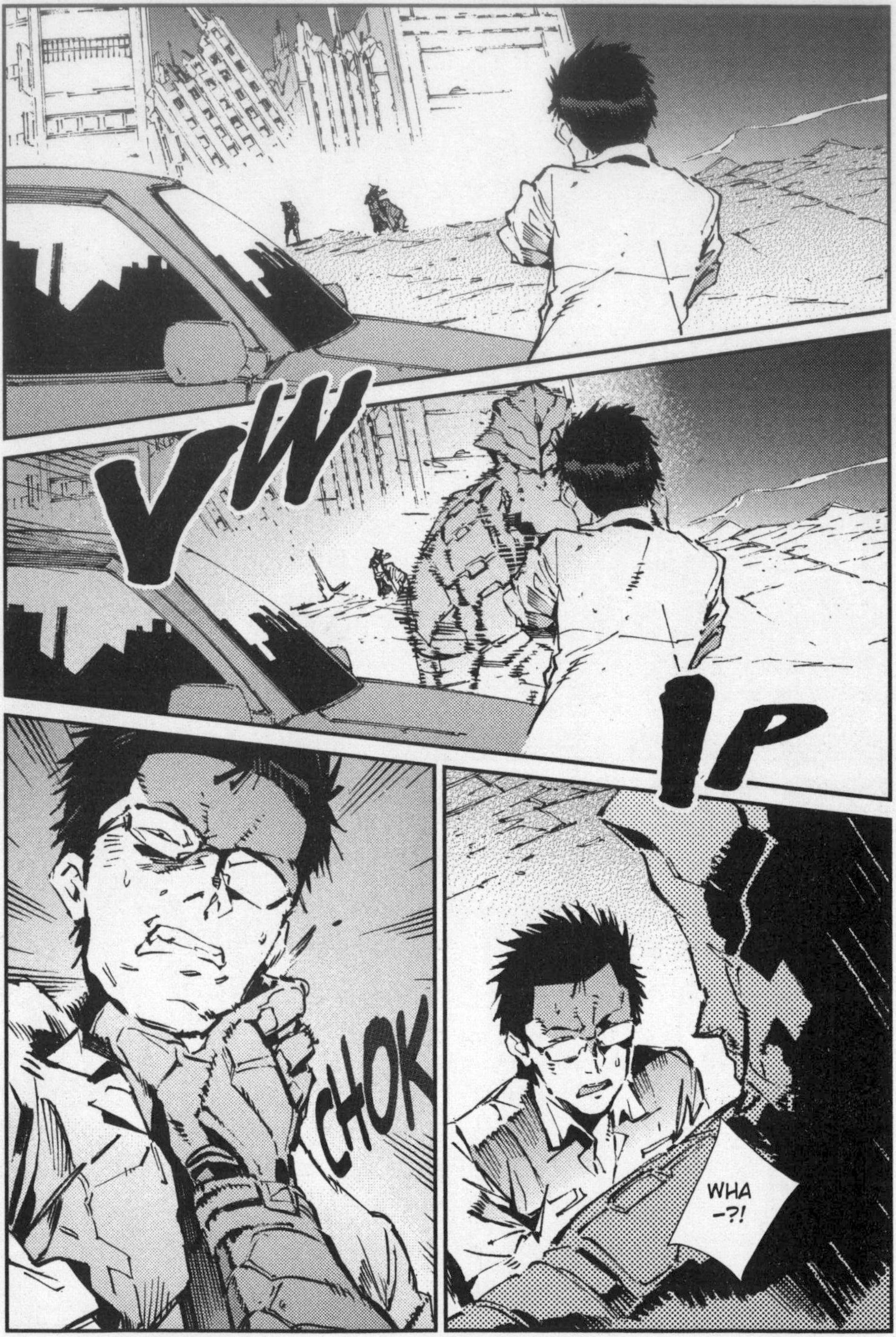
VW
IP
WHA
-?!
CHOK

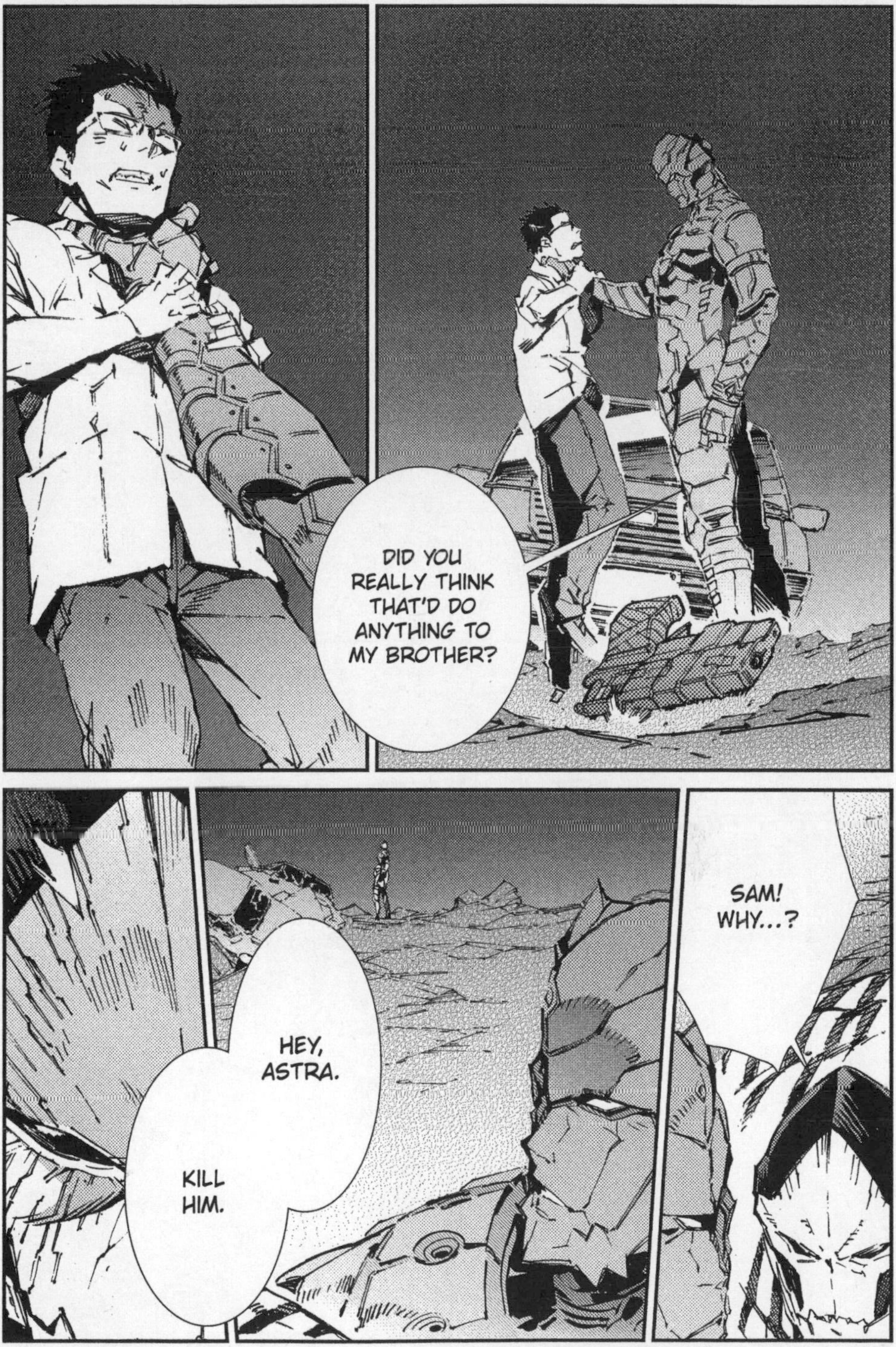
DID YOU REALLY THINK THAT'D DO ANYTHING TO MY BROTHER?
SAM! WHY...?
HEY, ASTRA.
KILL HIM.

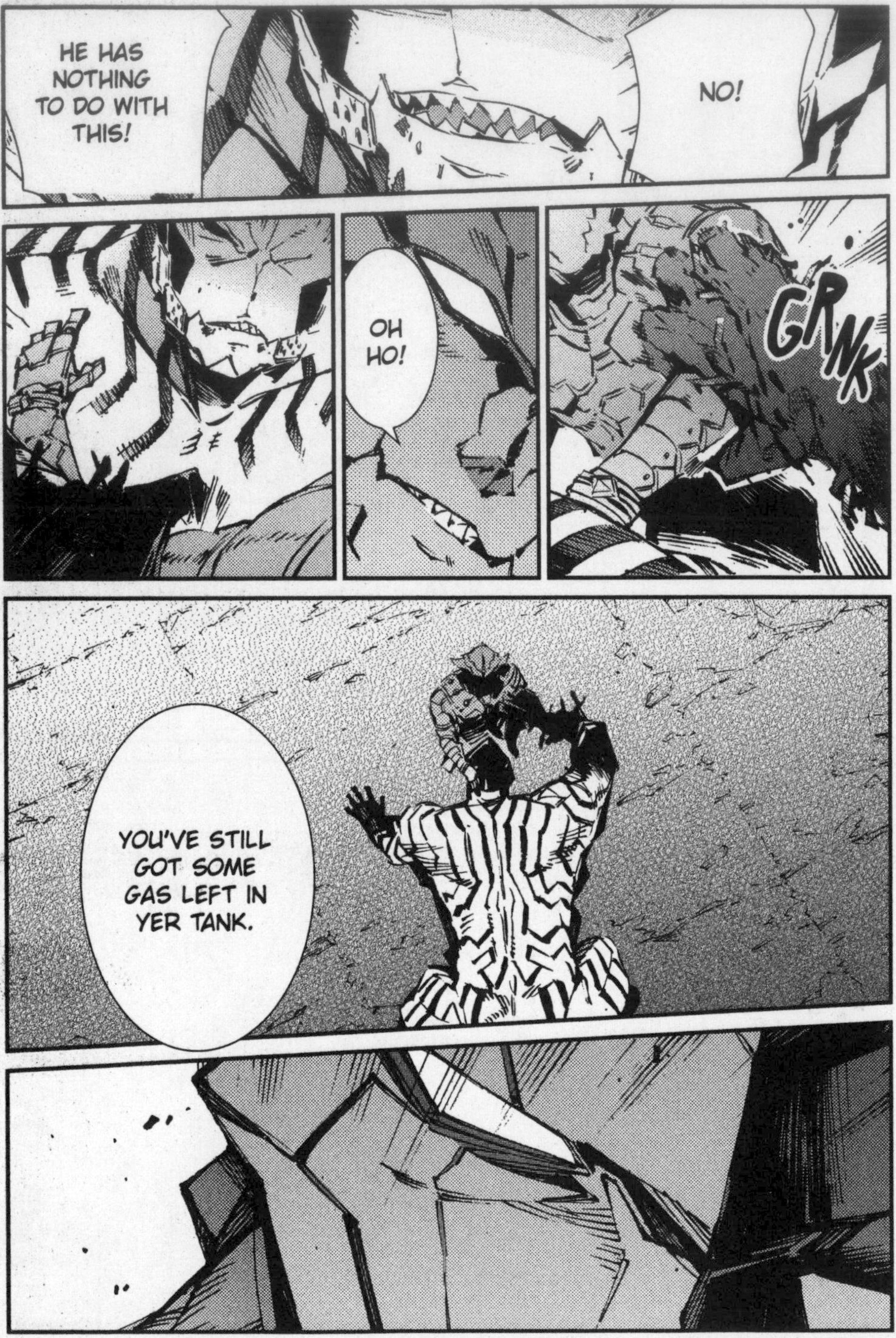
NO!
HE HAS NOTHING TO DO WITH THIS!
GRNK
OH HO!
YOU'VE STILL GOT SOME GAS LEFT IN YER TANK.

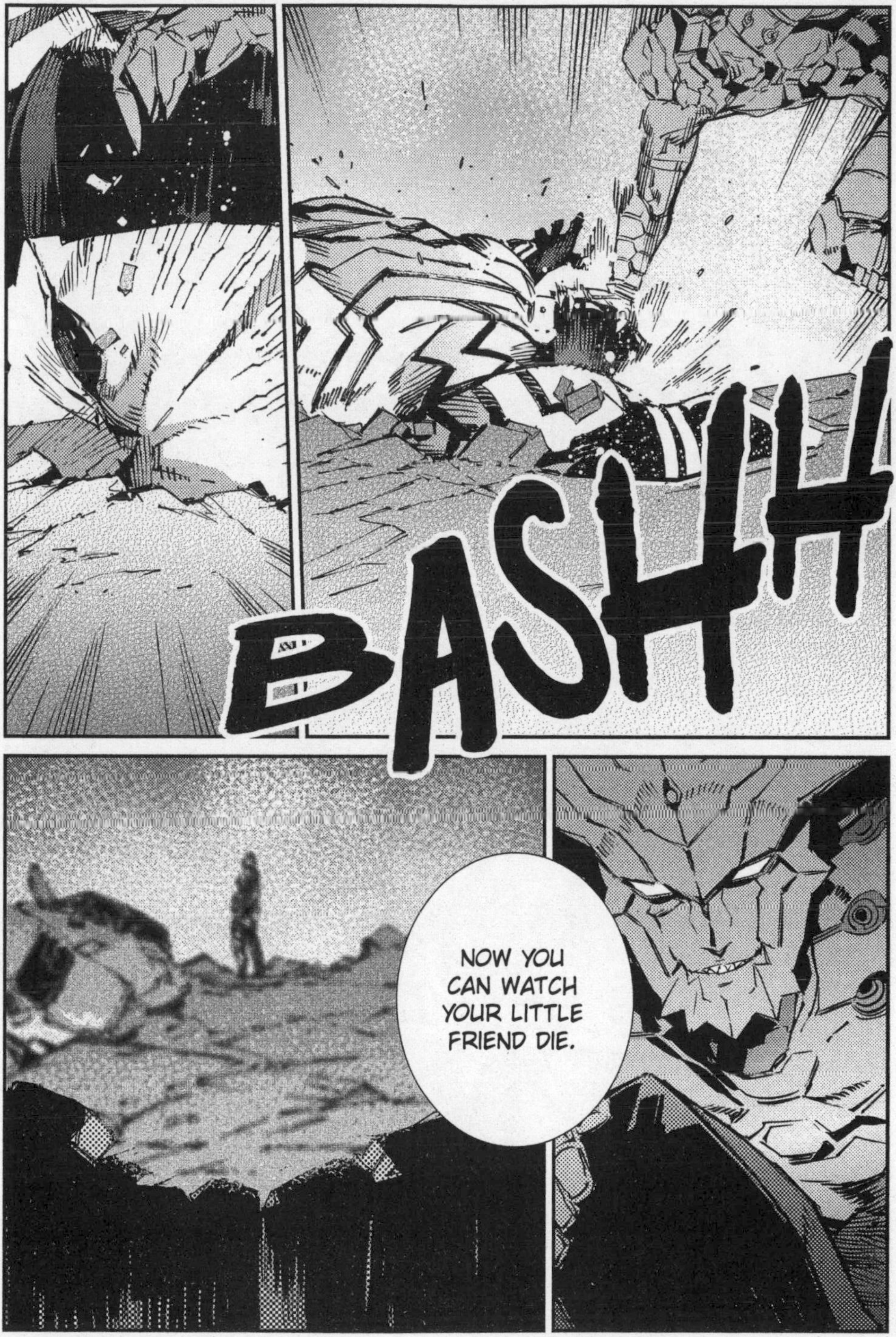
BASHH
NOW YOU CAN WATCH YOUR LITTLE FRIEND DIE.

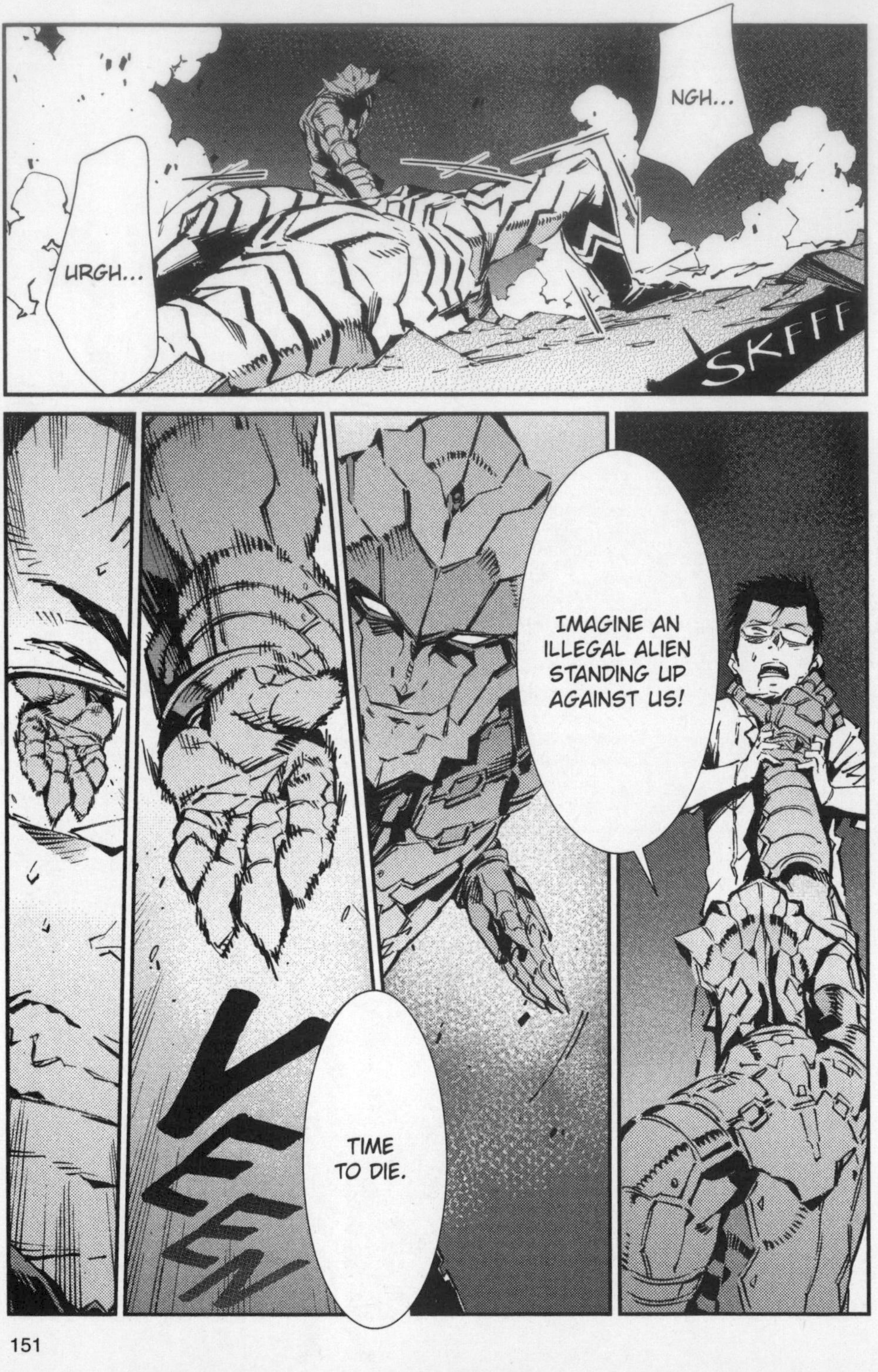
NGH...
URGH...
SKFFF
IMAGINE AN ILLEGAL ALIEN STANDING UP AGAINST US!
TIME TO DIE.

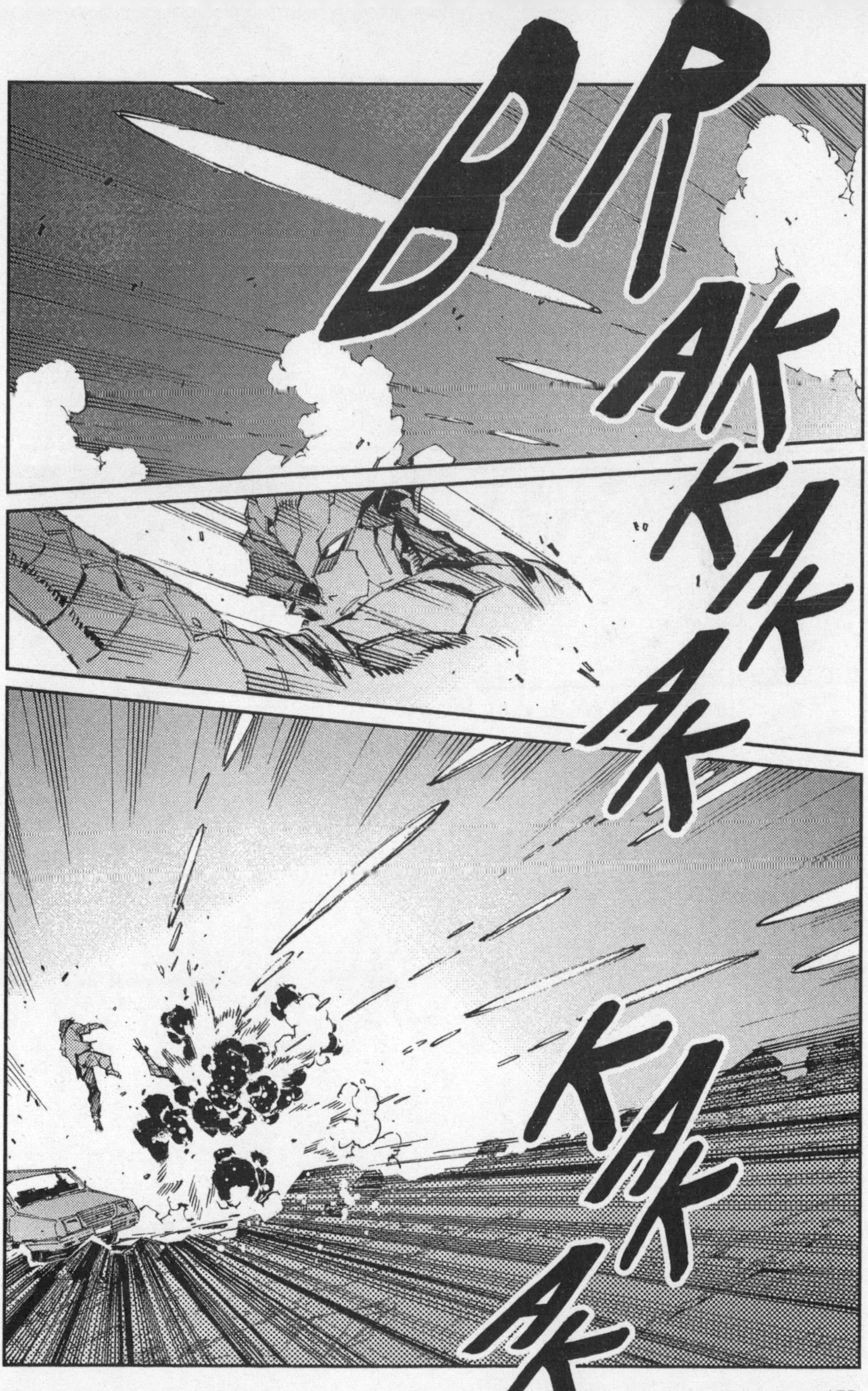
BRAKAKAKAKAK
KAKAKAK

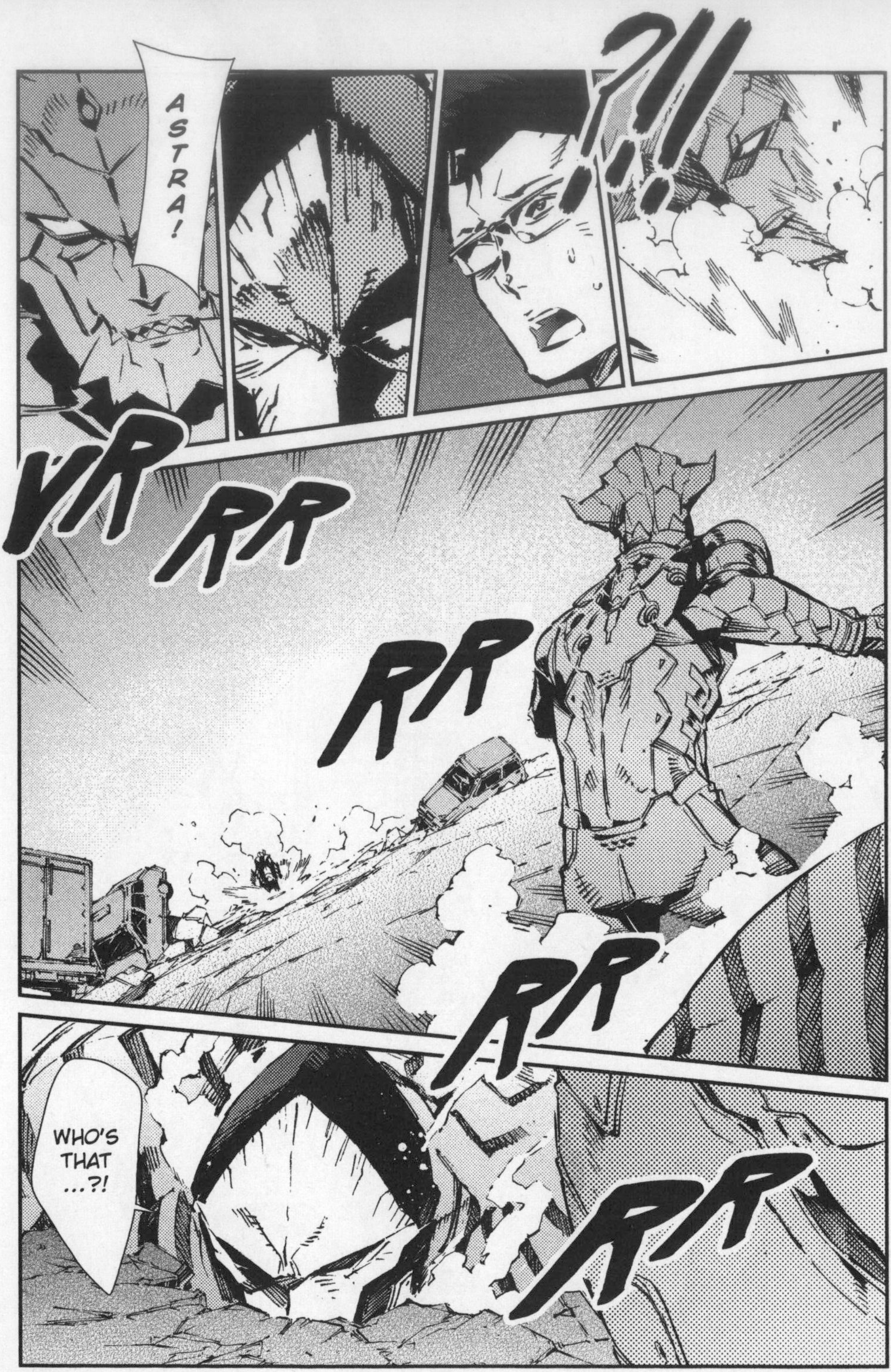
?!!
ASTRA!
VR
RR
RR
RR
WHO'S THAT ...?!
RR

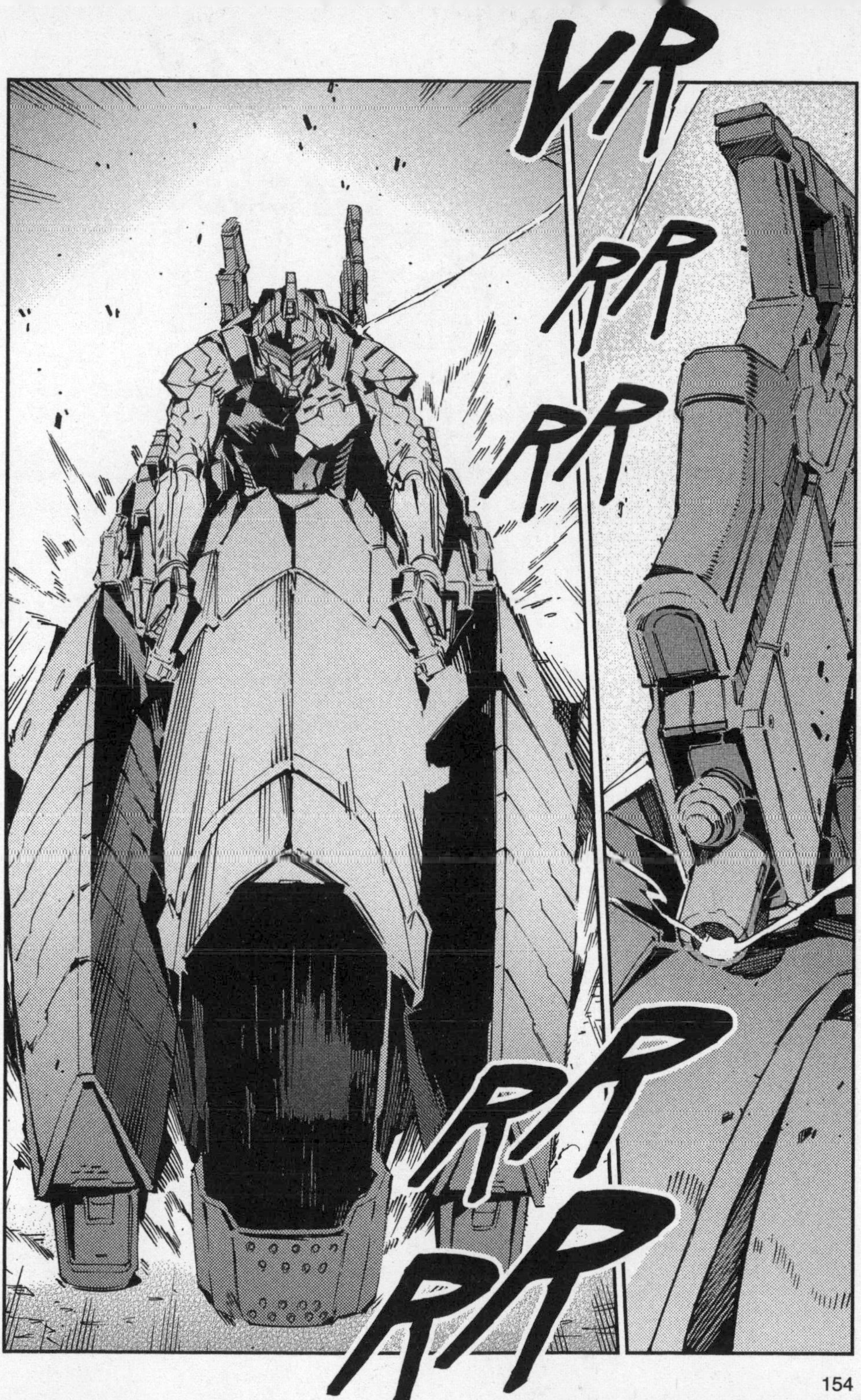
VRRRRR
RRRR

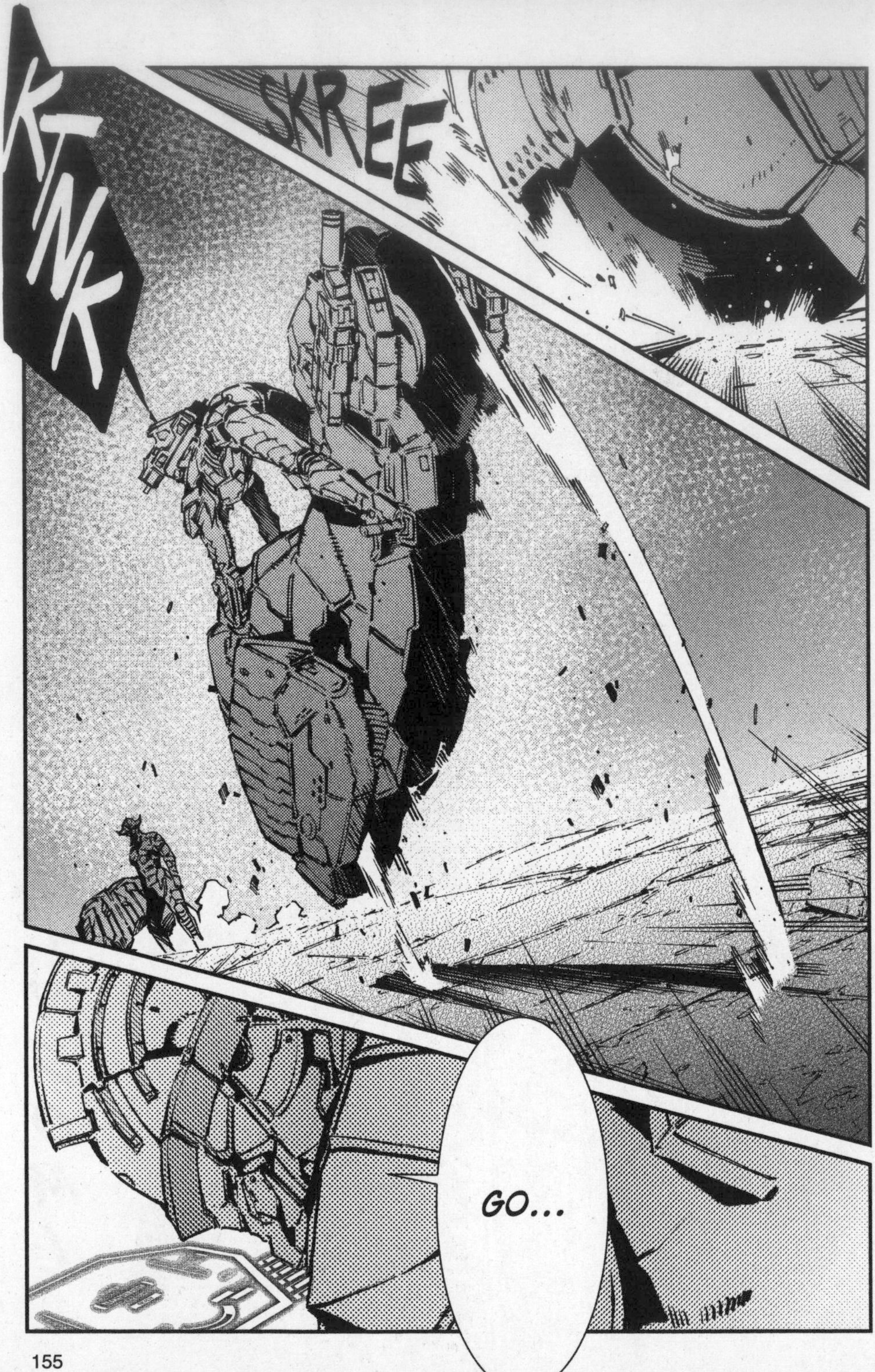
SKREE
KTINK
GO...

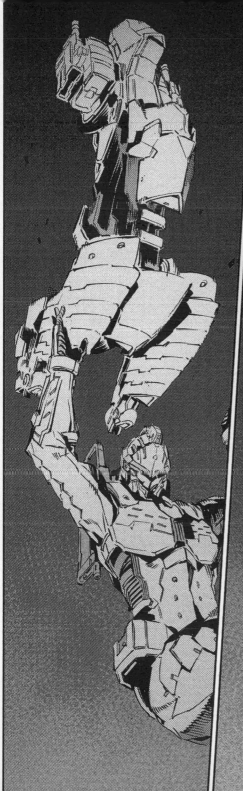
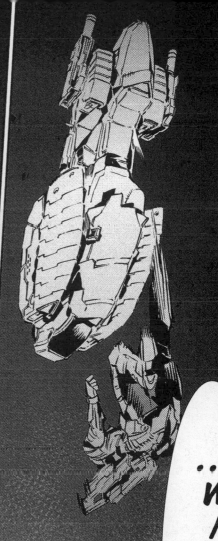

...WINDOM!

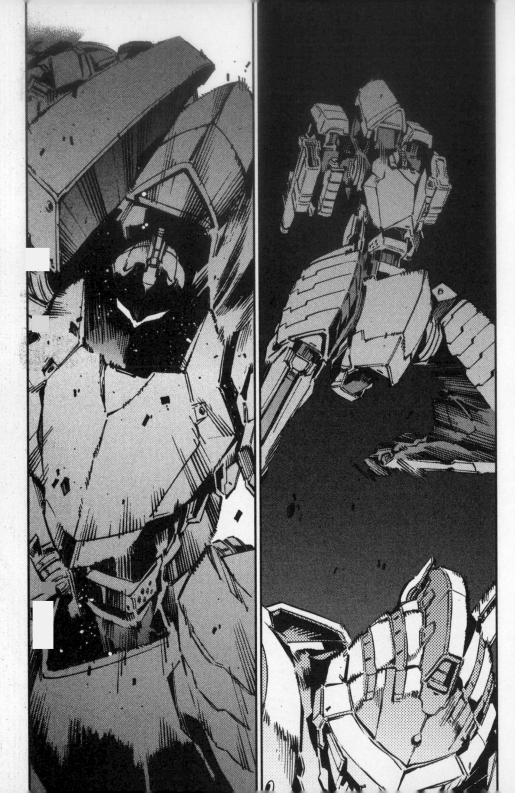

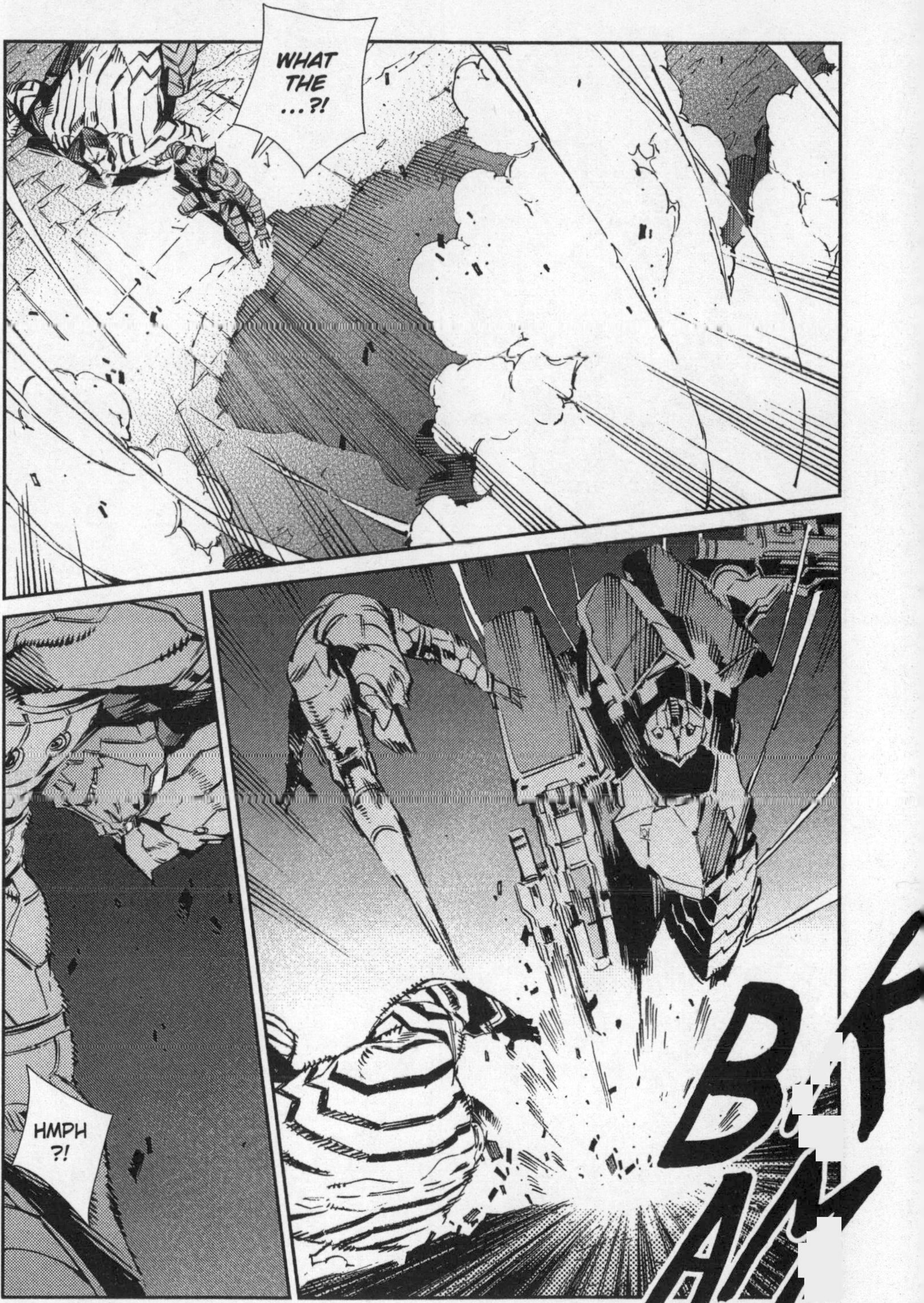
WHAT THE ...?!
HMPH ?!

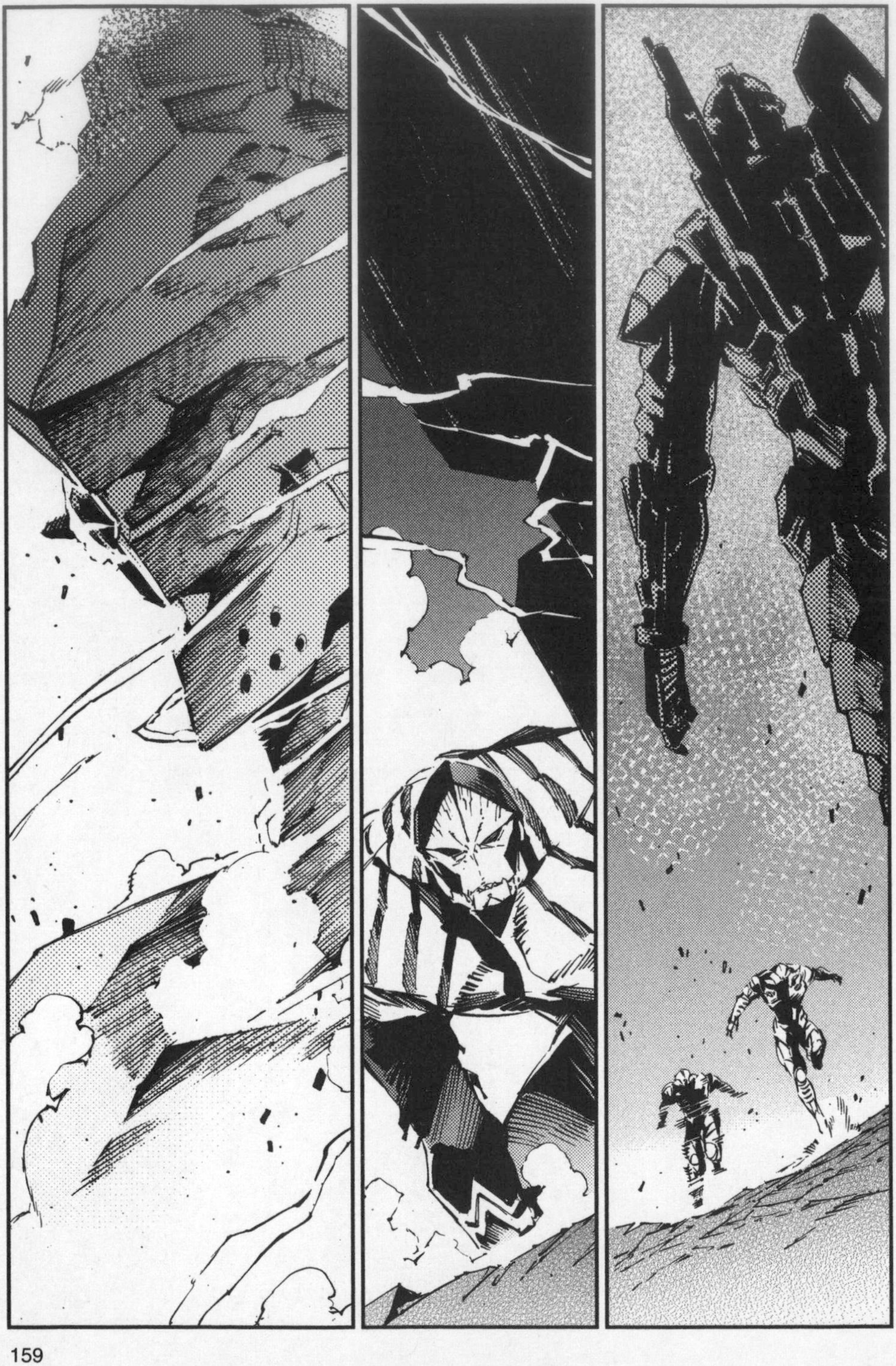

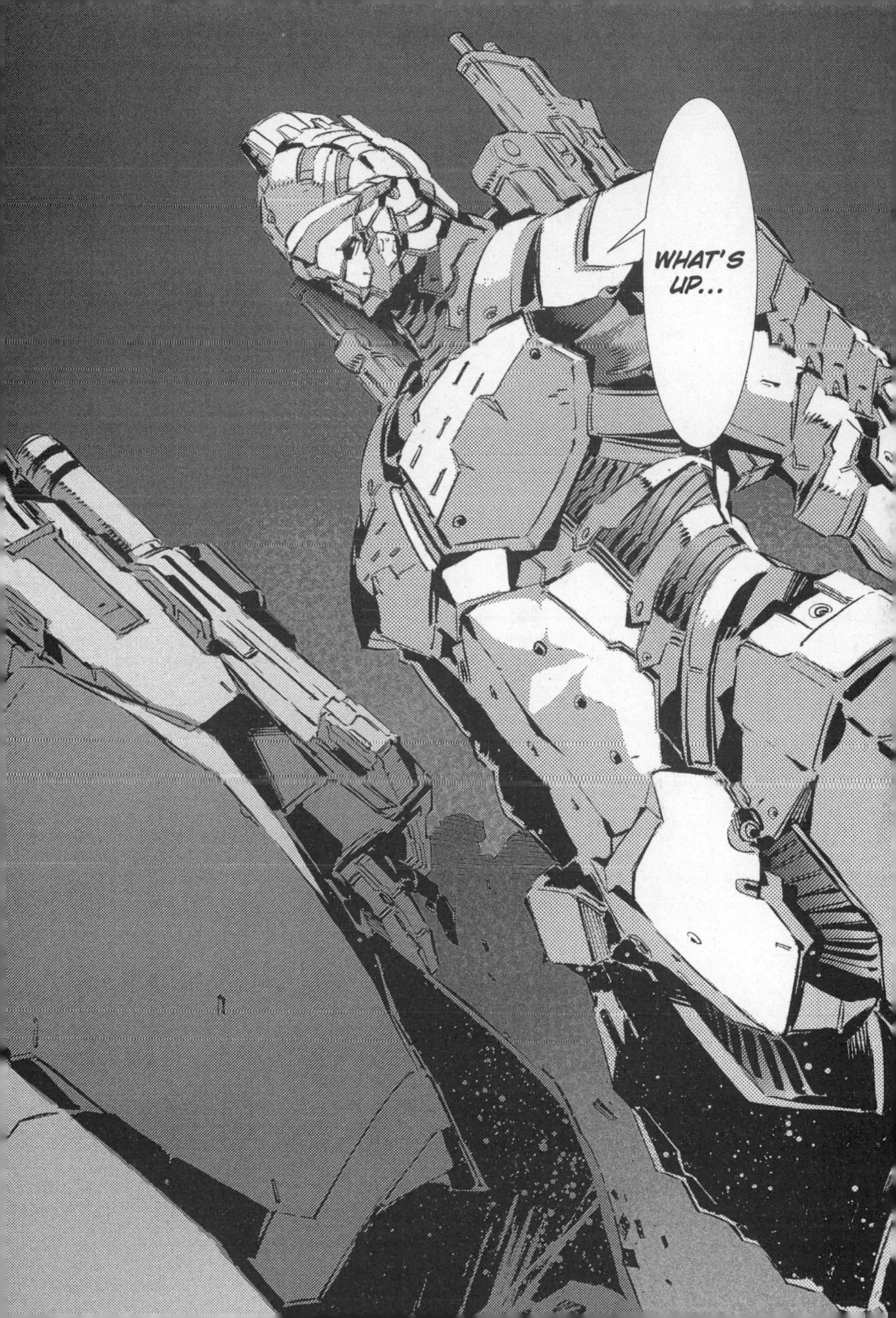
WHAT'S UP...

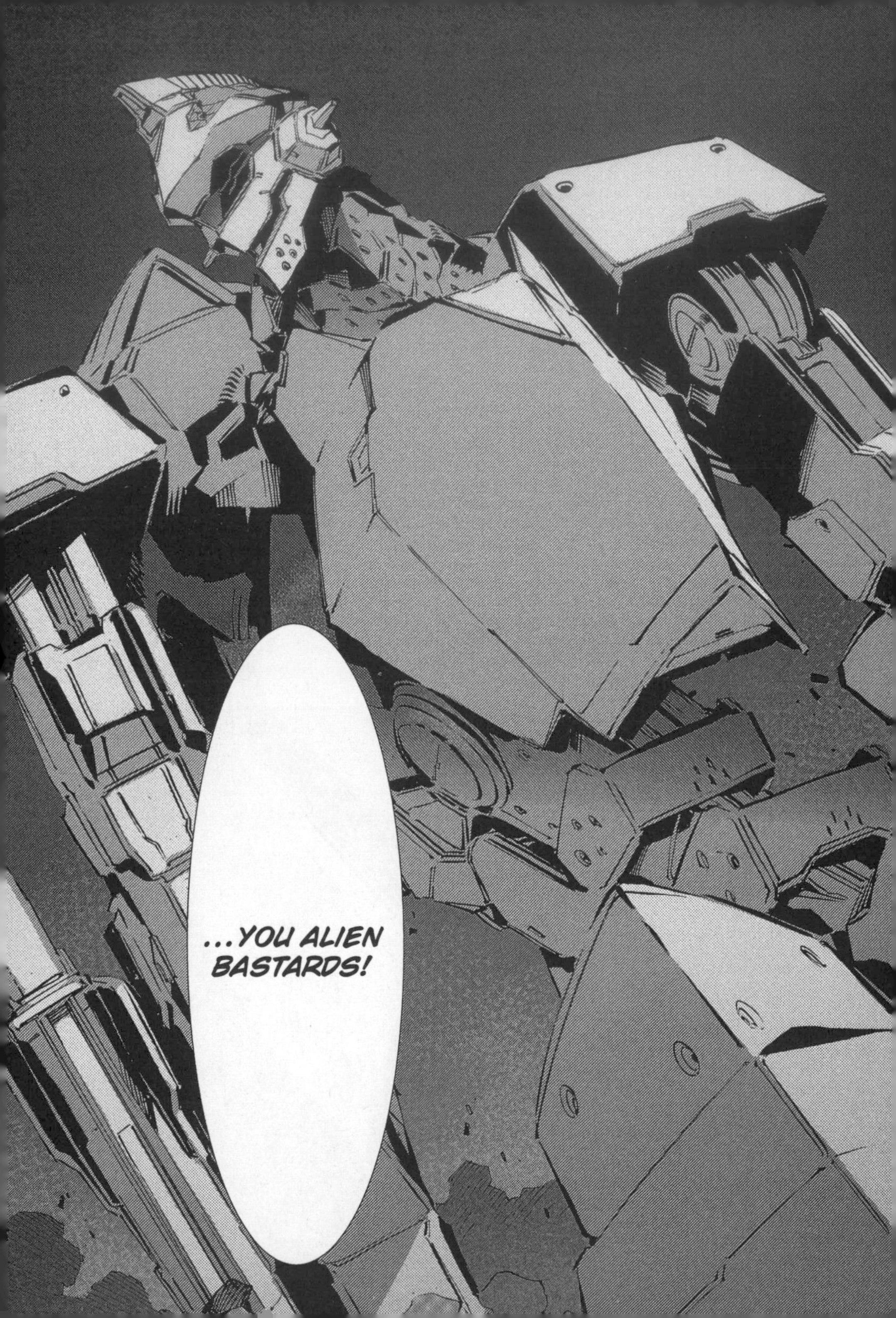
...YOU ALIEN BASTARDS!

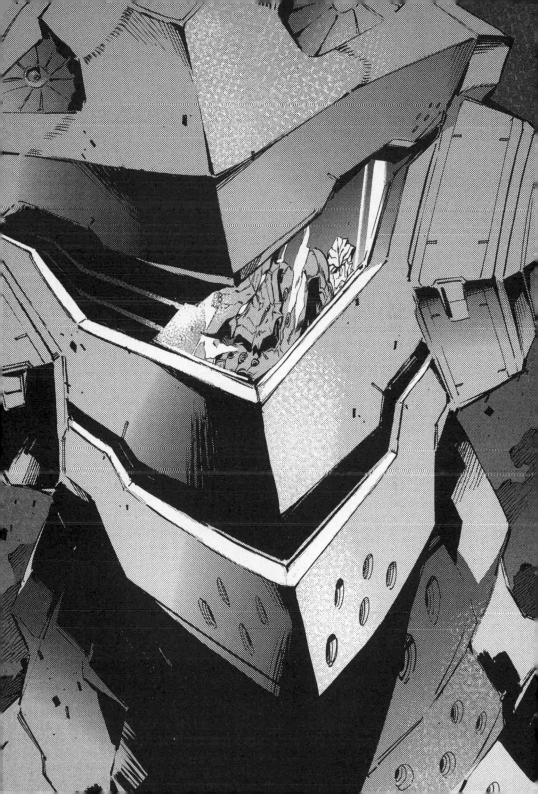

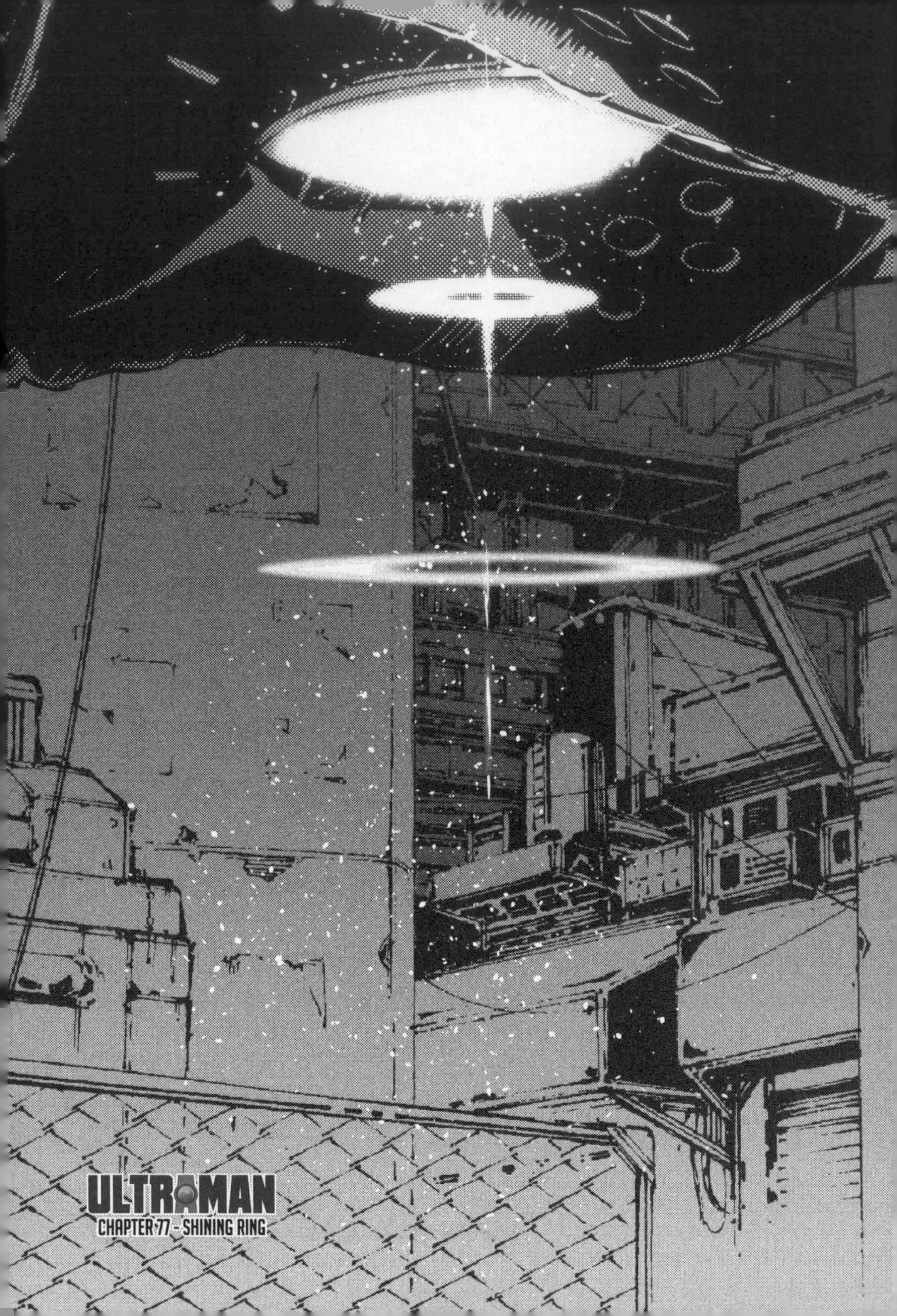
ULTRAMAN
CHAPTER 77 - SHINING RING

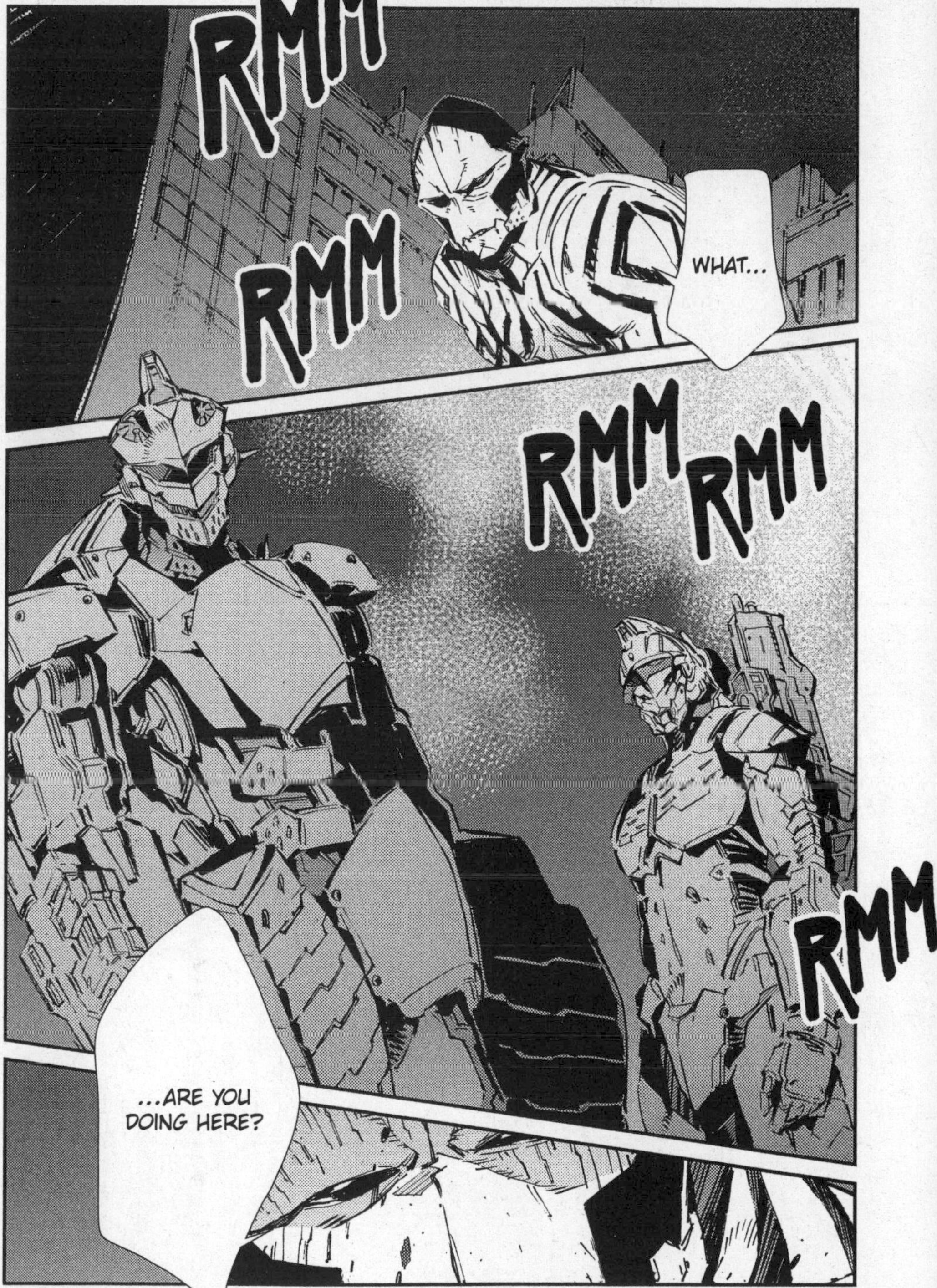
RMM
RMM
WHAT...
RMM
RMM
RMM
...ARE YOU DOING HERE?

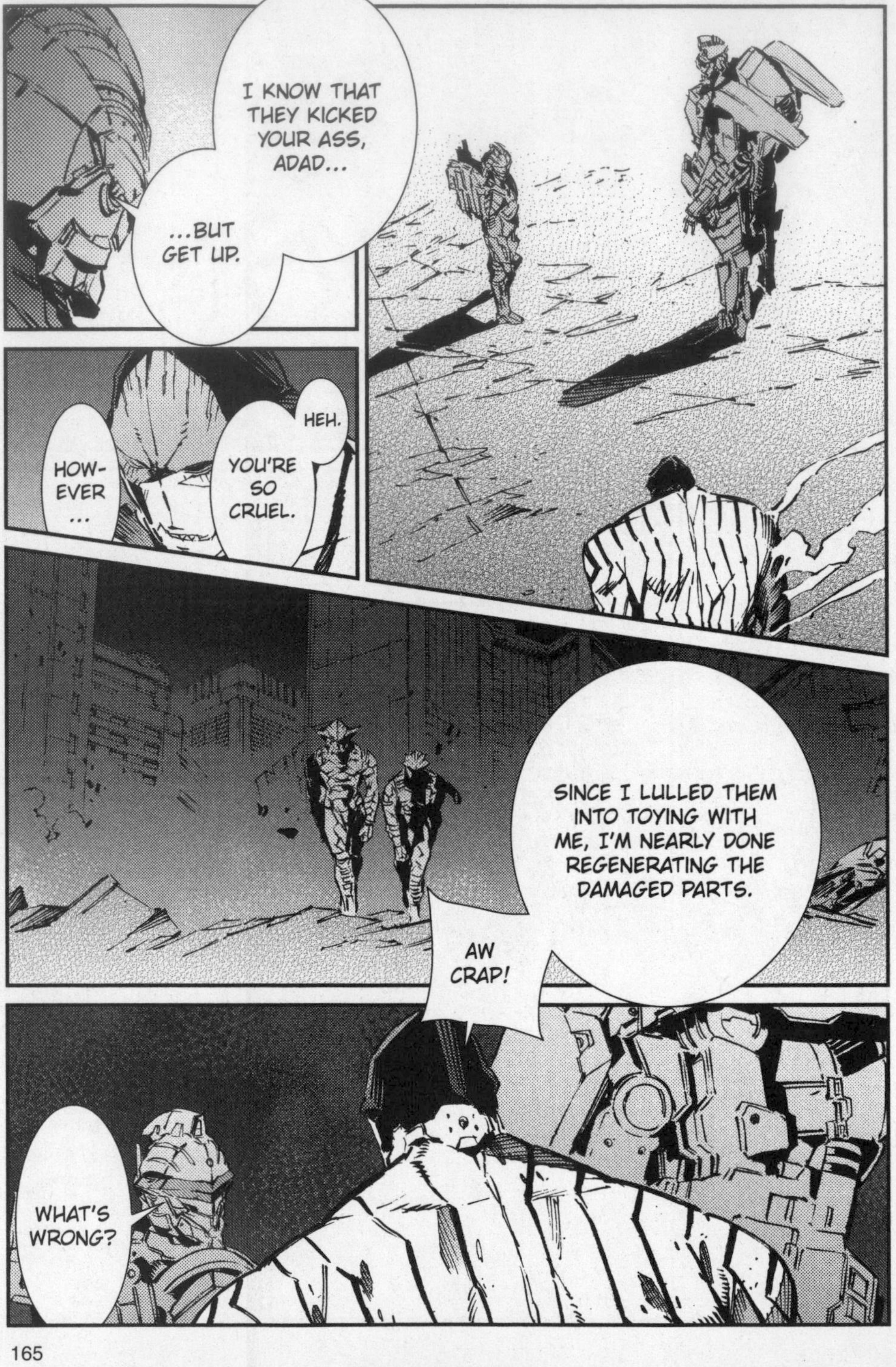
I KNOW THAT THEY KICKED YOUR ASS, ADAD...
...BUT GET UP.
HEH.
YOU'RE SO CRUEL.
HOW-EVER ...
SINCE I LULLED THEM INTO TOYING WITH ME, I'M NEARLY DONE REGENERATING THE DAMAGED PARTS.
AW CRAP!
WHAT'S WRONG?

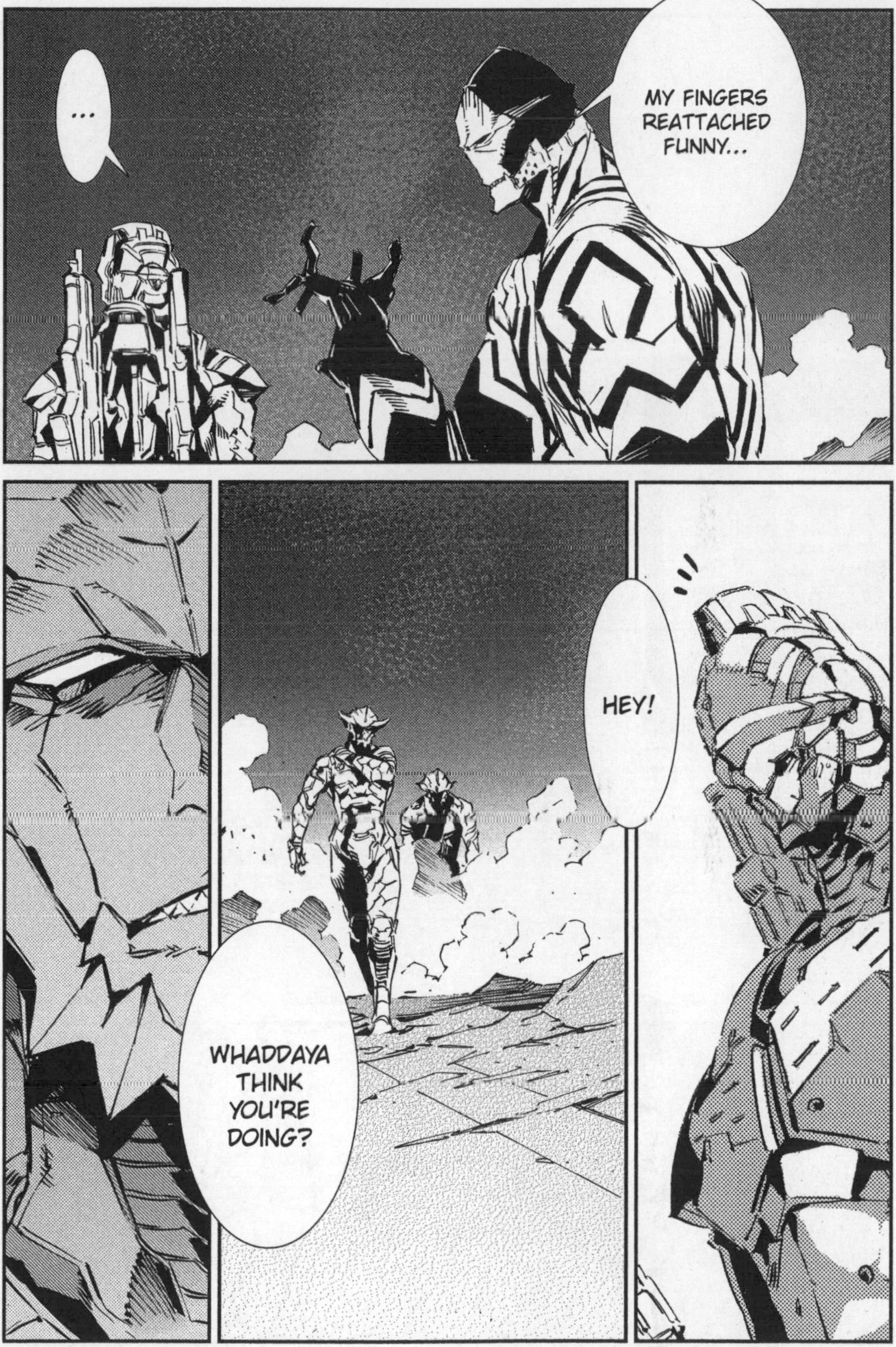
MY FINGERS REATTACHED FUNNY...
...
HEY!
WHADDAYA THINK YOU'RE DOING?

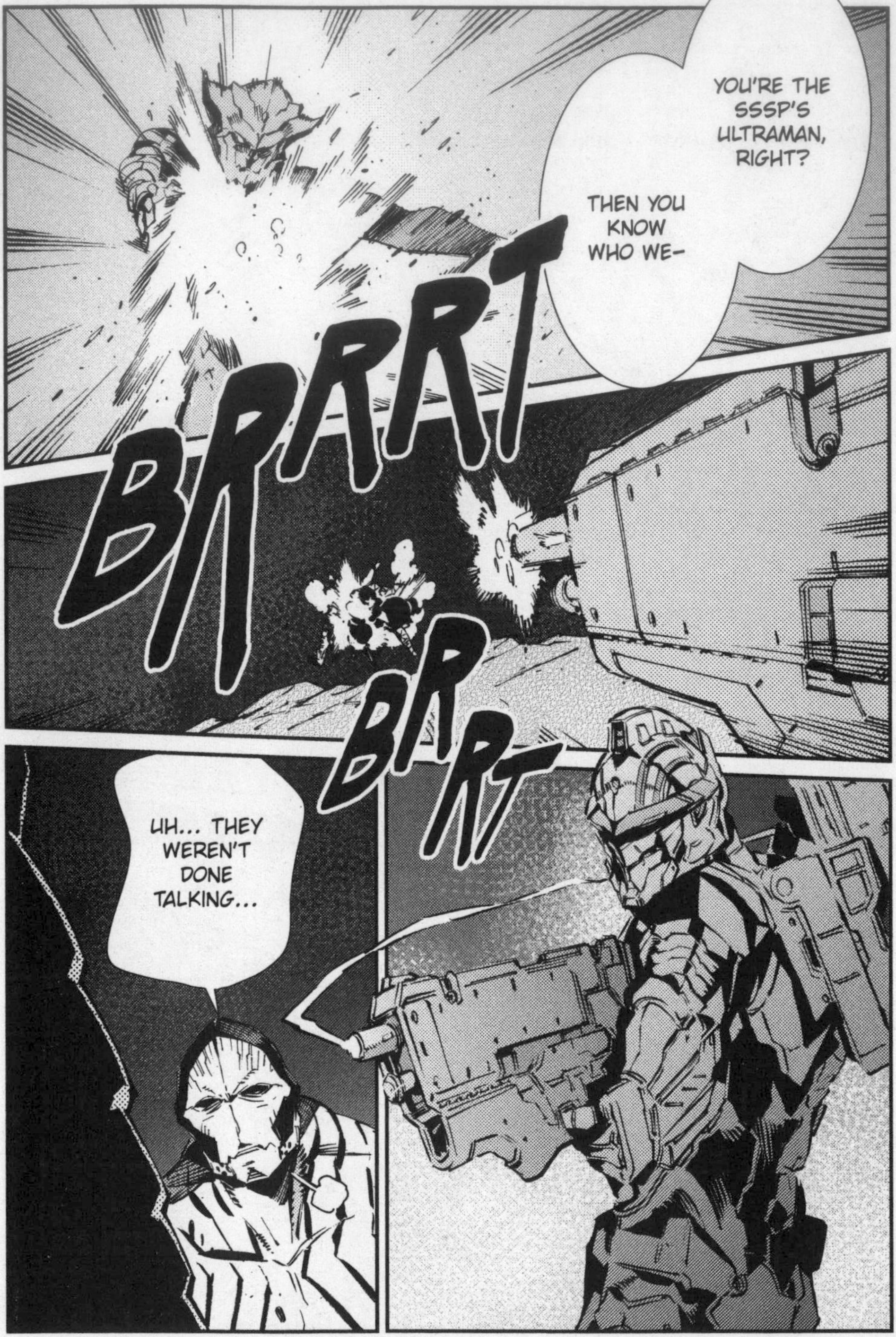
YOU'RE THE SSSP'S ULTRAMAN, RIGHT?
THEN YOU KNOW WHO WE-
BRRRT
BRRT
UH... THEY WEREN'T DONE TALKING...

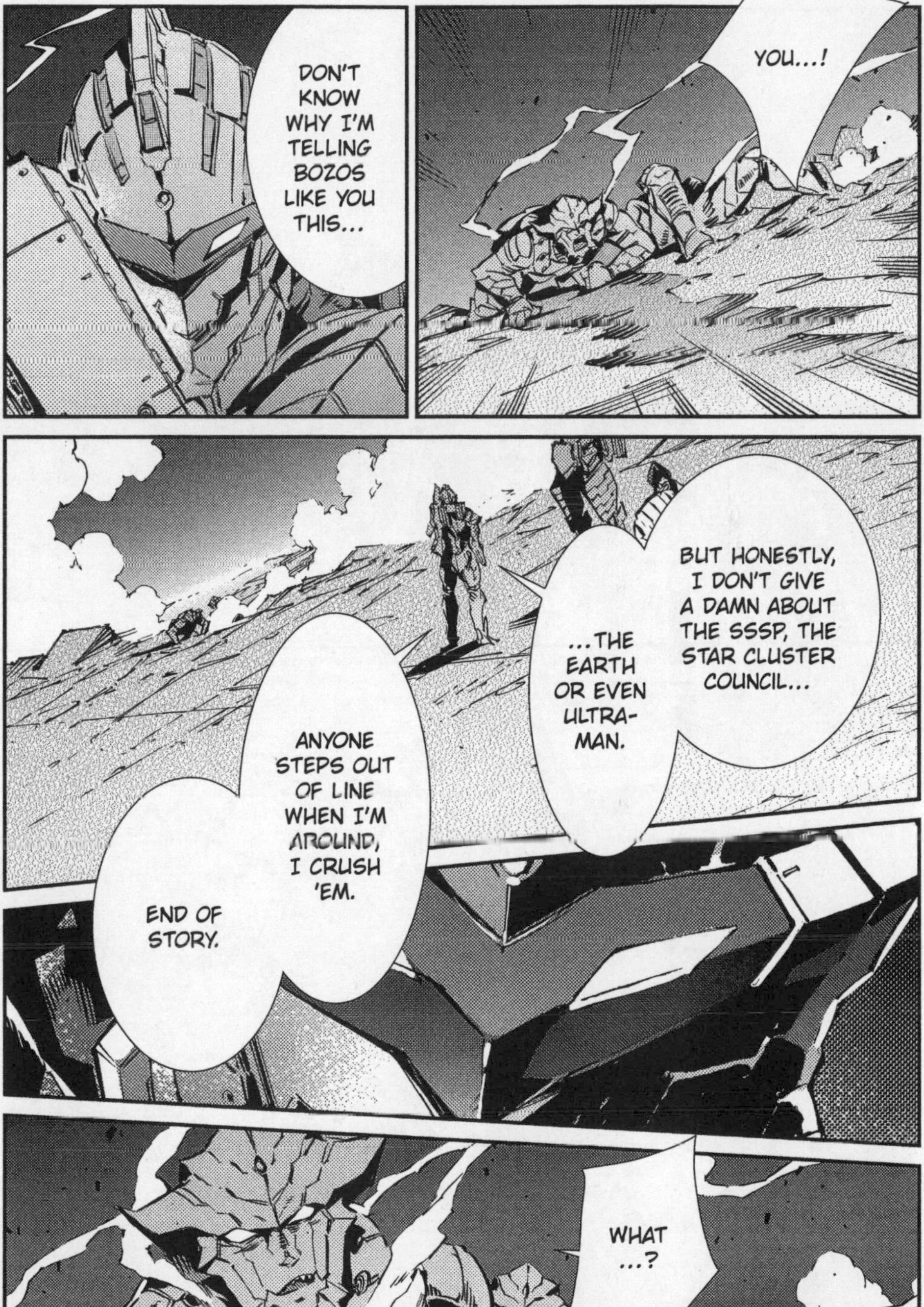
YOU...!
DON'T KNOW WHY I'M TELLING BOZOS LIKE YOU THIS...
BUT HONESTLY, I DON'T GIVE A DAMN ABOUT THE SSSP, THE STAR CLUSTER COUNCIL...
...THE EARTH OR EVEN ULTRA-MAN.
ANYONE STEPS OUT OF LINE WHEN I'M AROUND, I CRUSH 'EM.
END OF STORY.
WHAT ...?

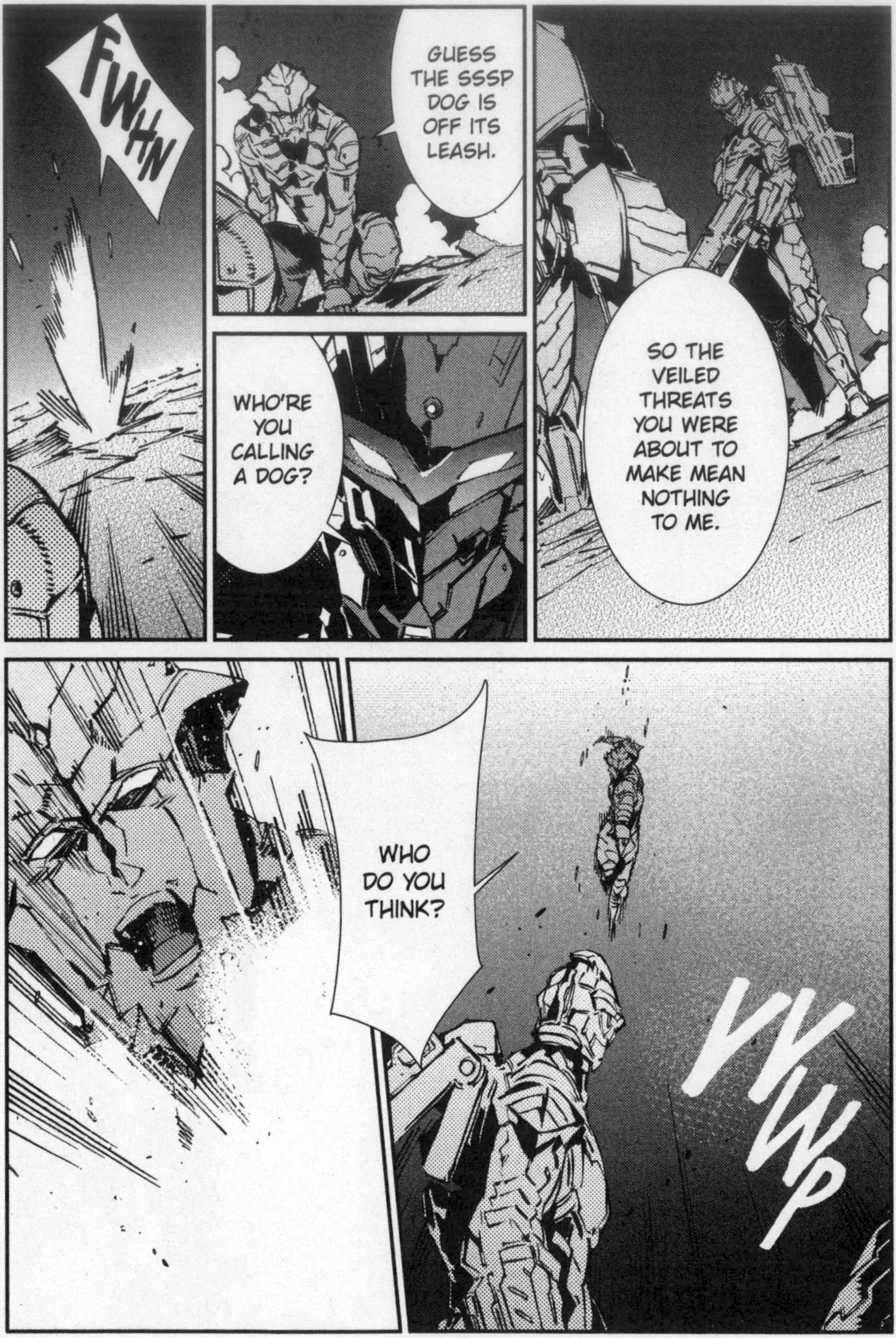
SO THE VEILED THREATS YOU WERE ABOUT TO MAKE MEAN NOTHING TO ME.
GUESS THE SSSP DOG IS OFF ITS LEASH.
WHO'RE YOU CALLING A DOG?
FWHN
WHO DO YOU THINK?
VWWP

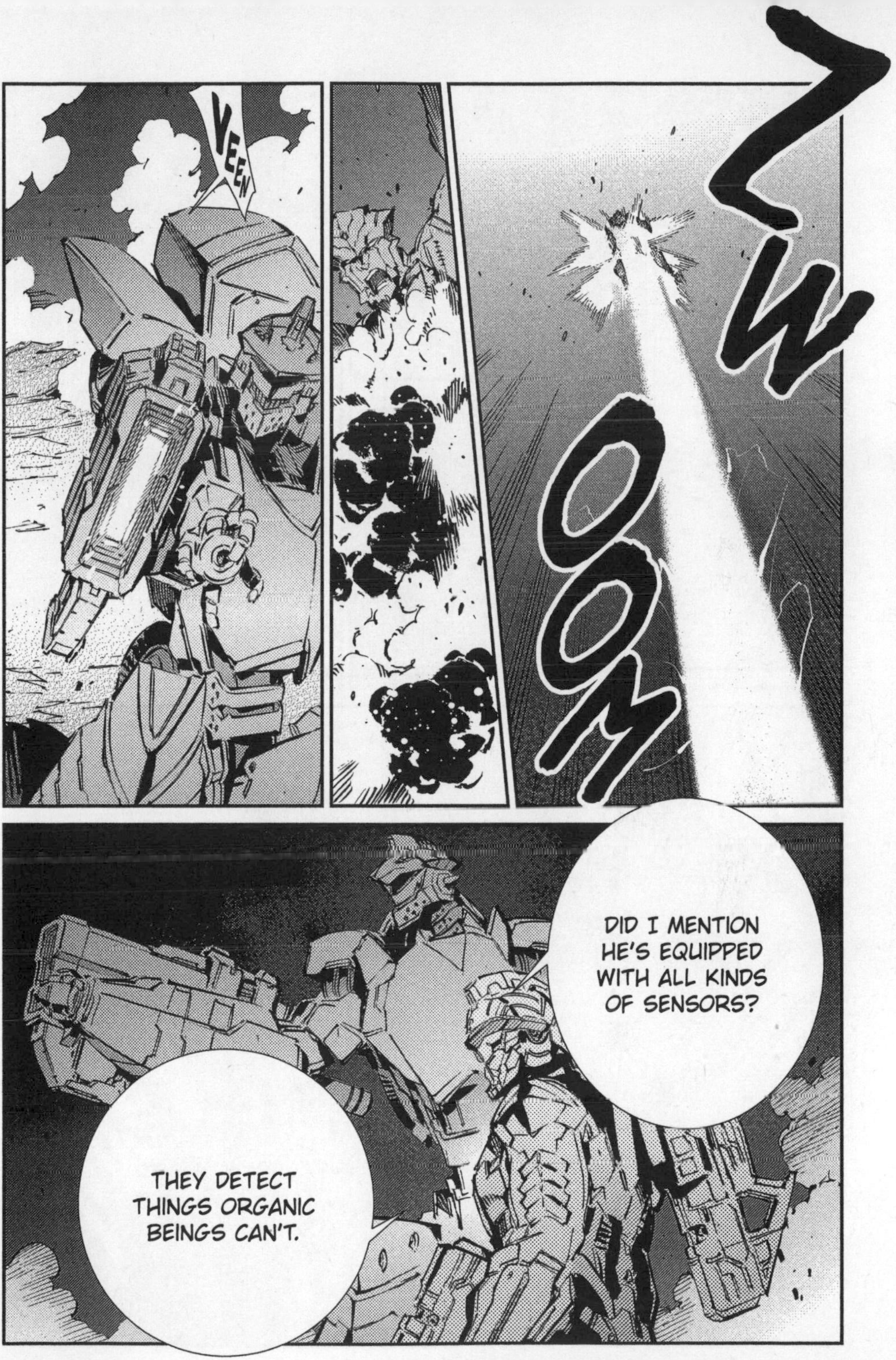
VWOOM
VEEN
DID I MENTION HE'S EQUIPPED WITH ALL KINDS OF SENSORS?
THEY DETECT THINGS ORGANIC BEINGS CAN'T.

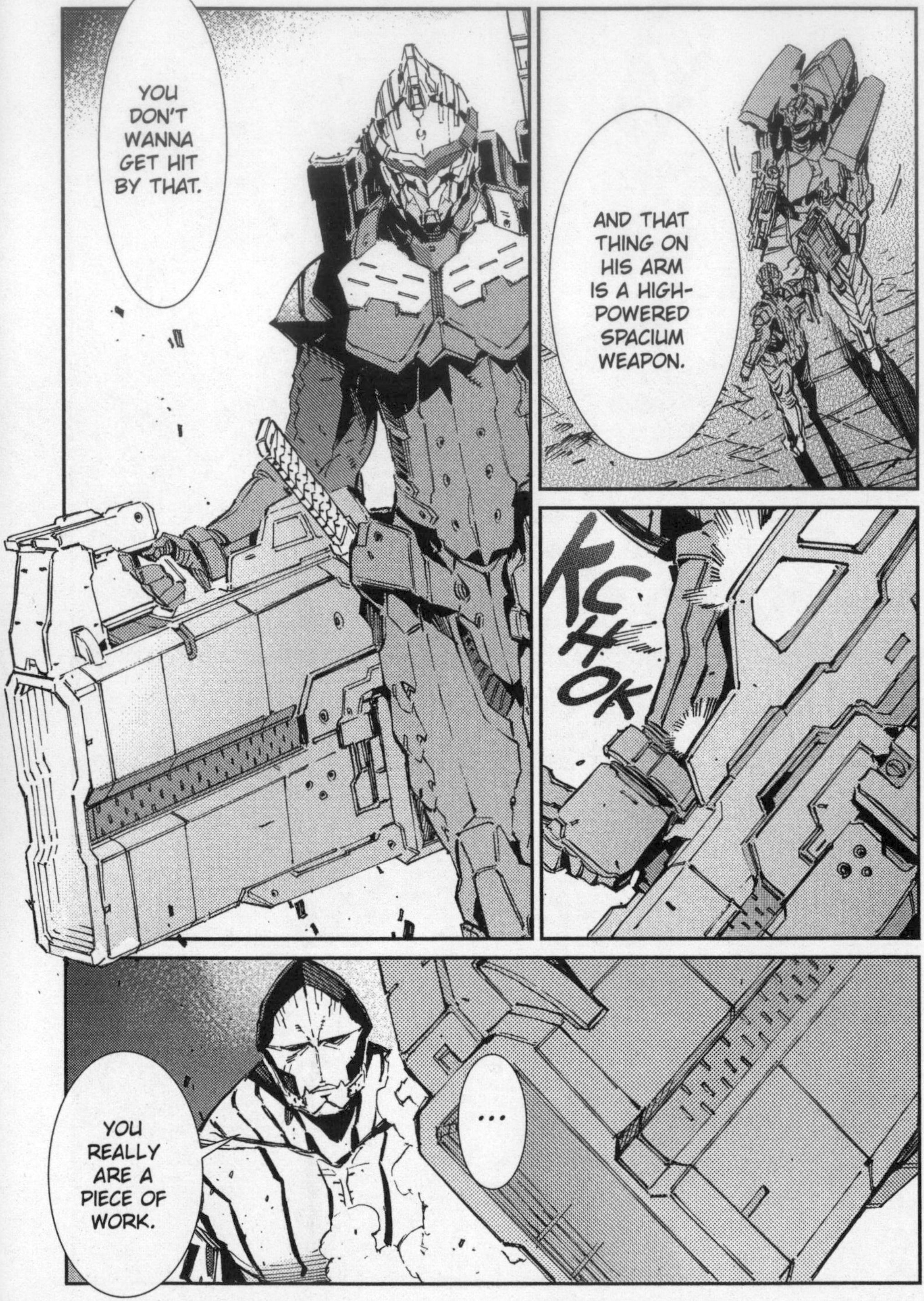
AND THAT THING ON HIS ARM IS A HIGH-POWERED SPACIUM WEAPON.
KCHOK
YOU DON'T WANNA GET HIT BY THAT.
...
YOU REALLY ARE A PIECE OF WORK.

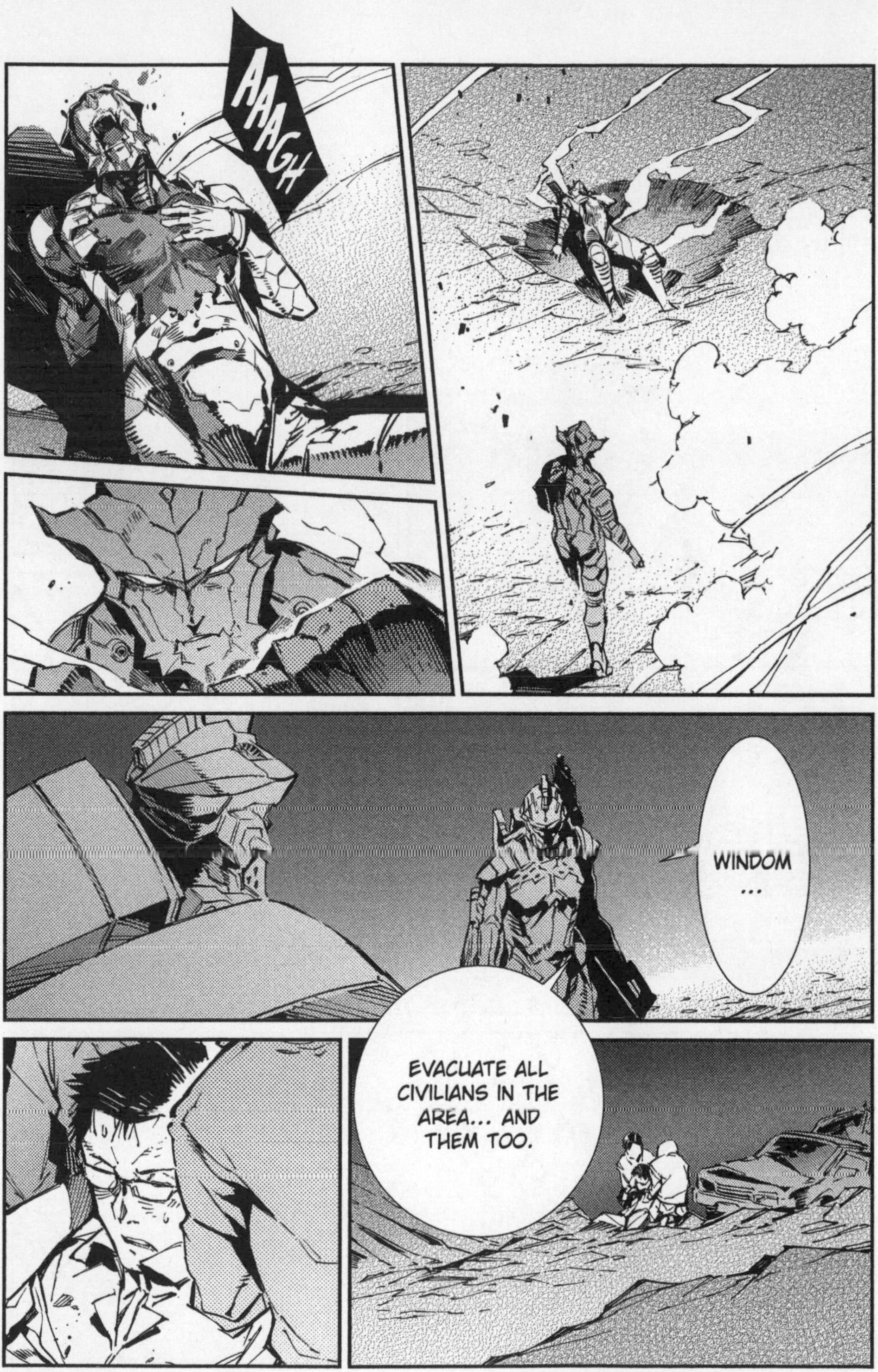
AAAGH
WINDOM ...
EVACUATE ALL CIVILIANS IN THE AREA... AND THEM TOO.

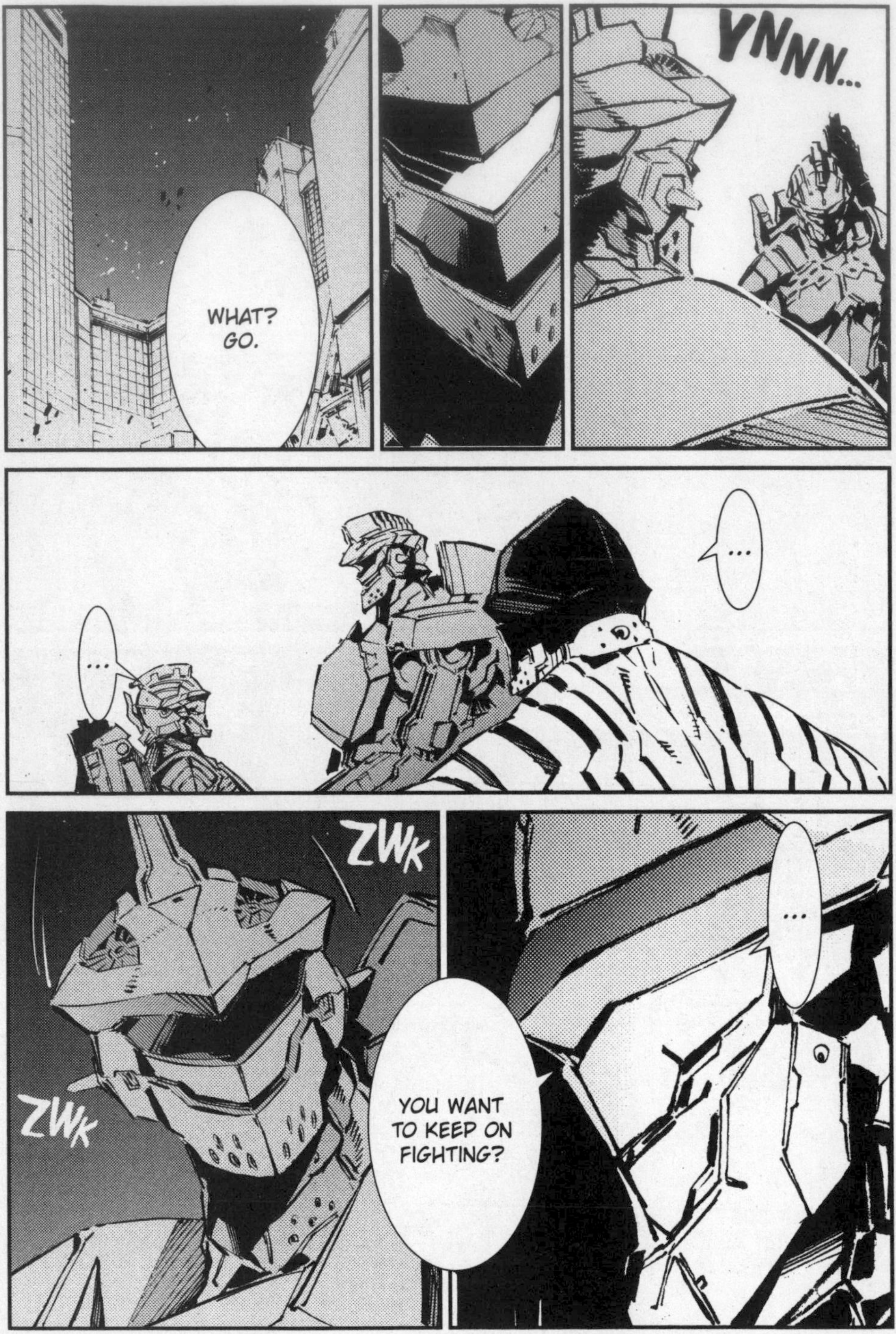
YNNN...
WHAT? GO.
...
...
...
YOU WANT TO KEEP ON FIGHTING?
ZWK
ZWK

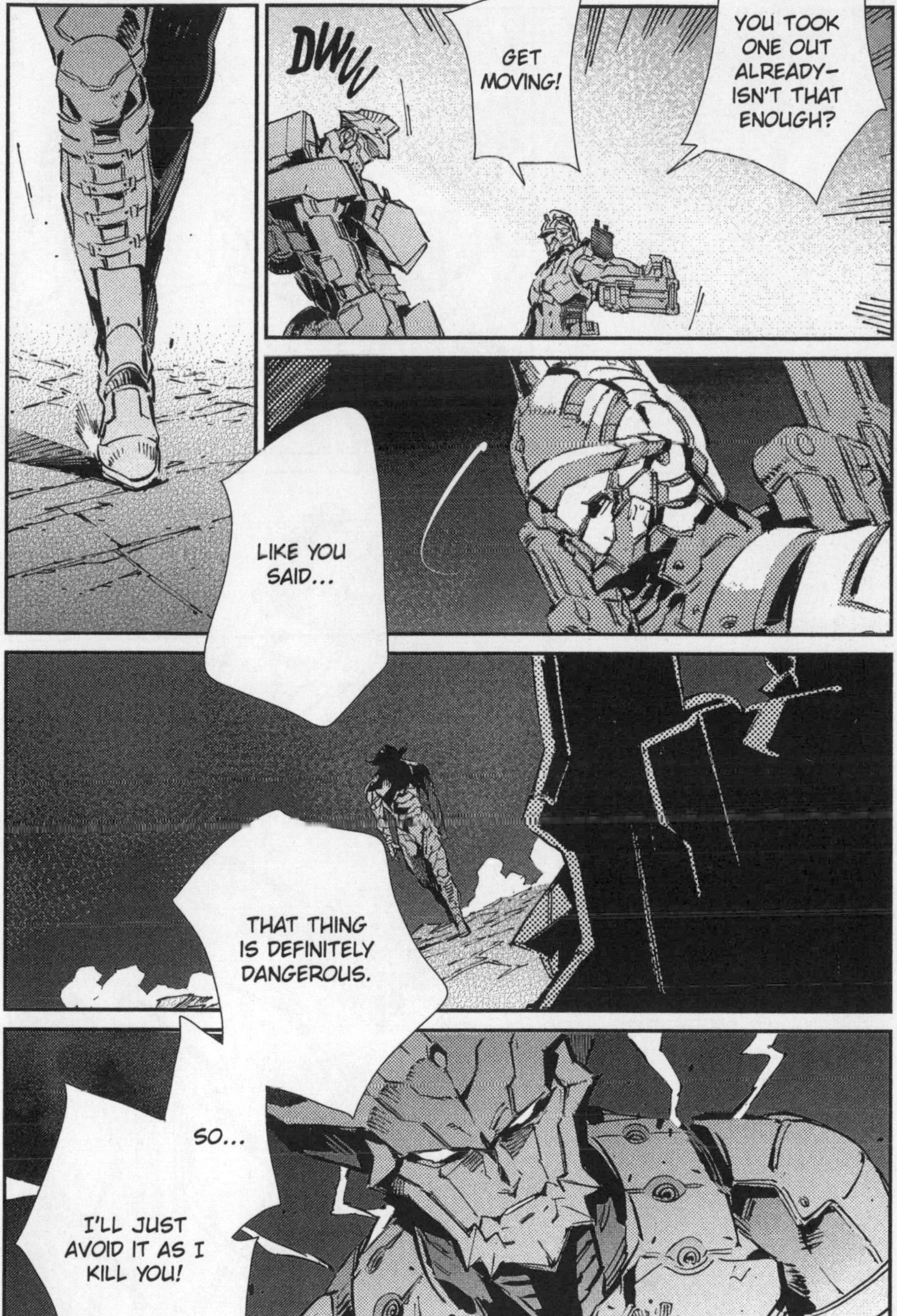
YOU TOOK ONE OUT ALREADY–ISN'T THAT ENOUGH?
GET MOVING!
DWW
LIKE YOU SAID...
THAT THING IS DEFINITELY DANGEROUS.
SO...
I'LL JUST AVOID IT AS I KILL YOU!

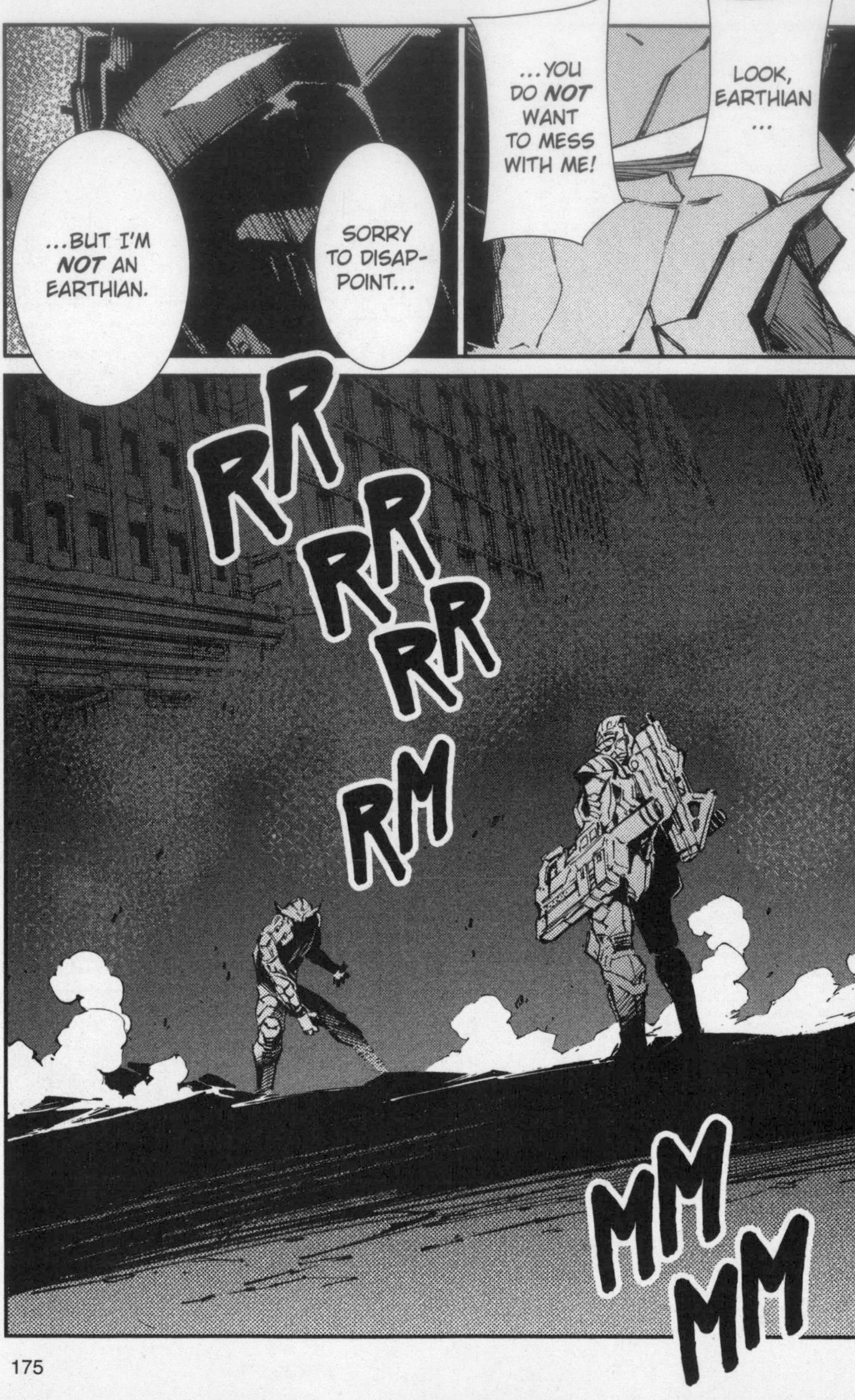
LOOK, EARTHIAN ...
...YOU DO NOT WANT TO MESS WITH ME!
SORRY TO DISAP-POINT...
...BUT I'M NOT AN EARTHIAN.
RRRRRRRM
MMMMMM

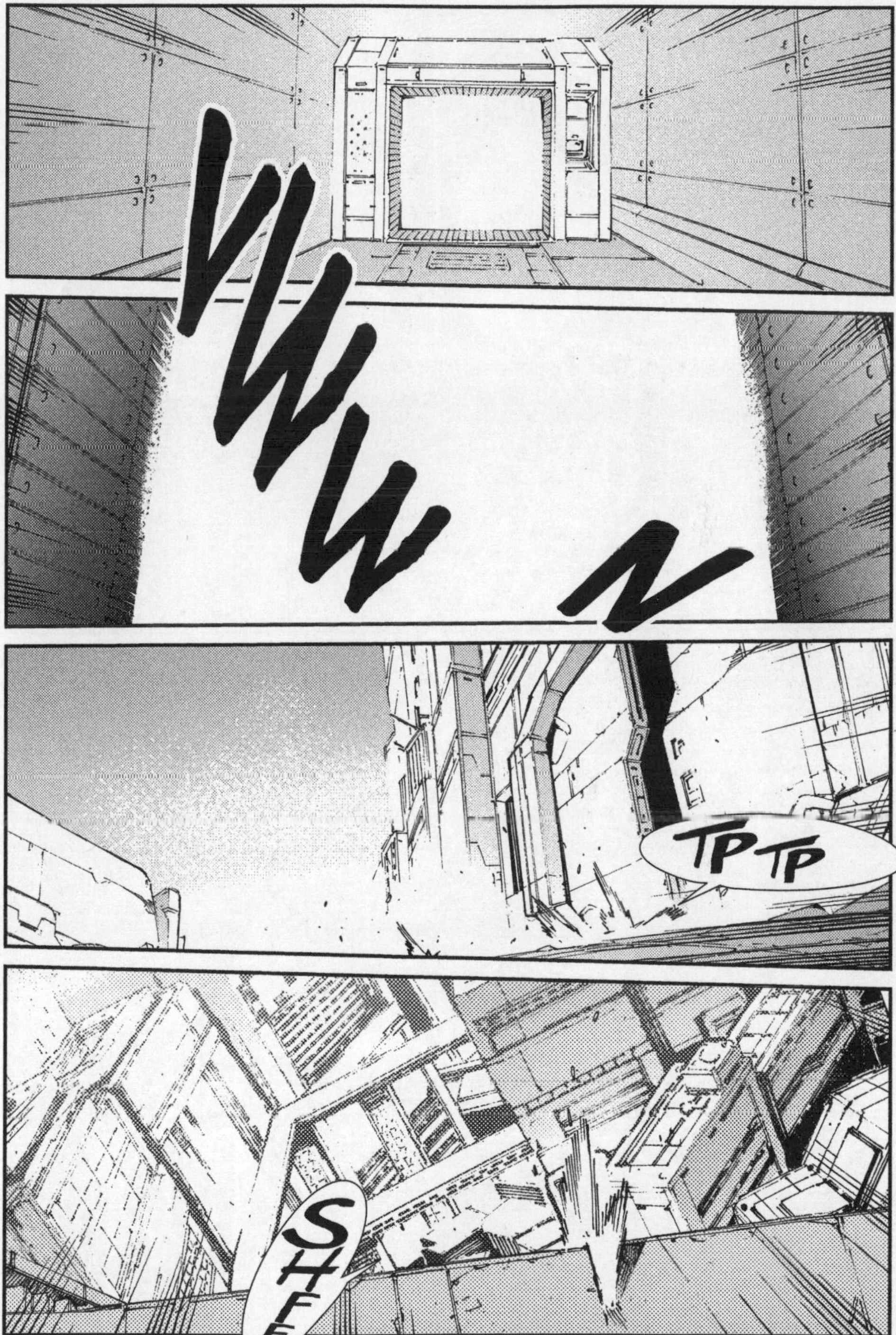
VVVWWWN
TP TP
SHFF

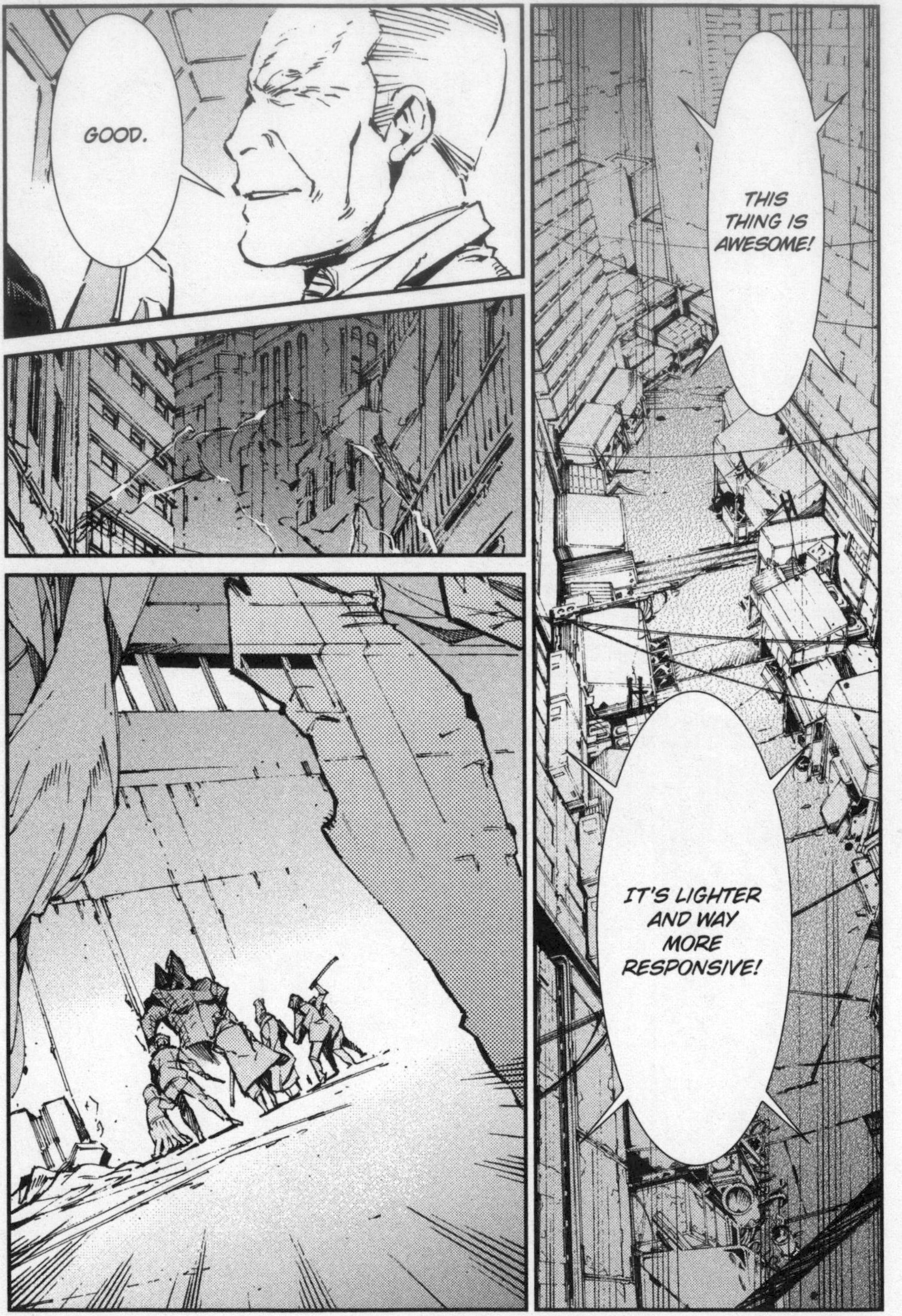
THIS THING IS AWESOME!
IT'S LIGHTER AND WAY MORE RESPONSIVE!
GOOD.

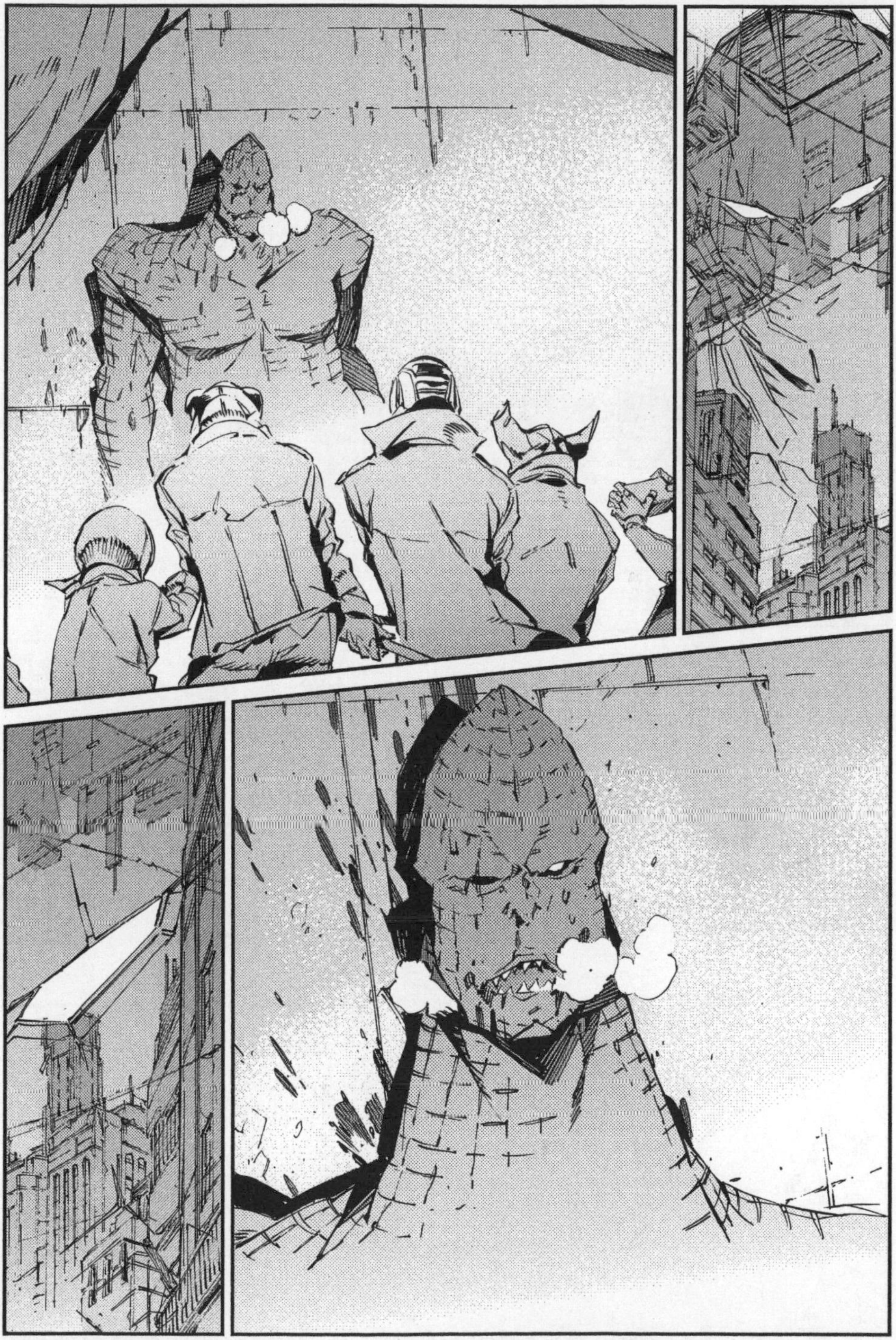

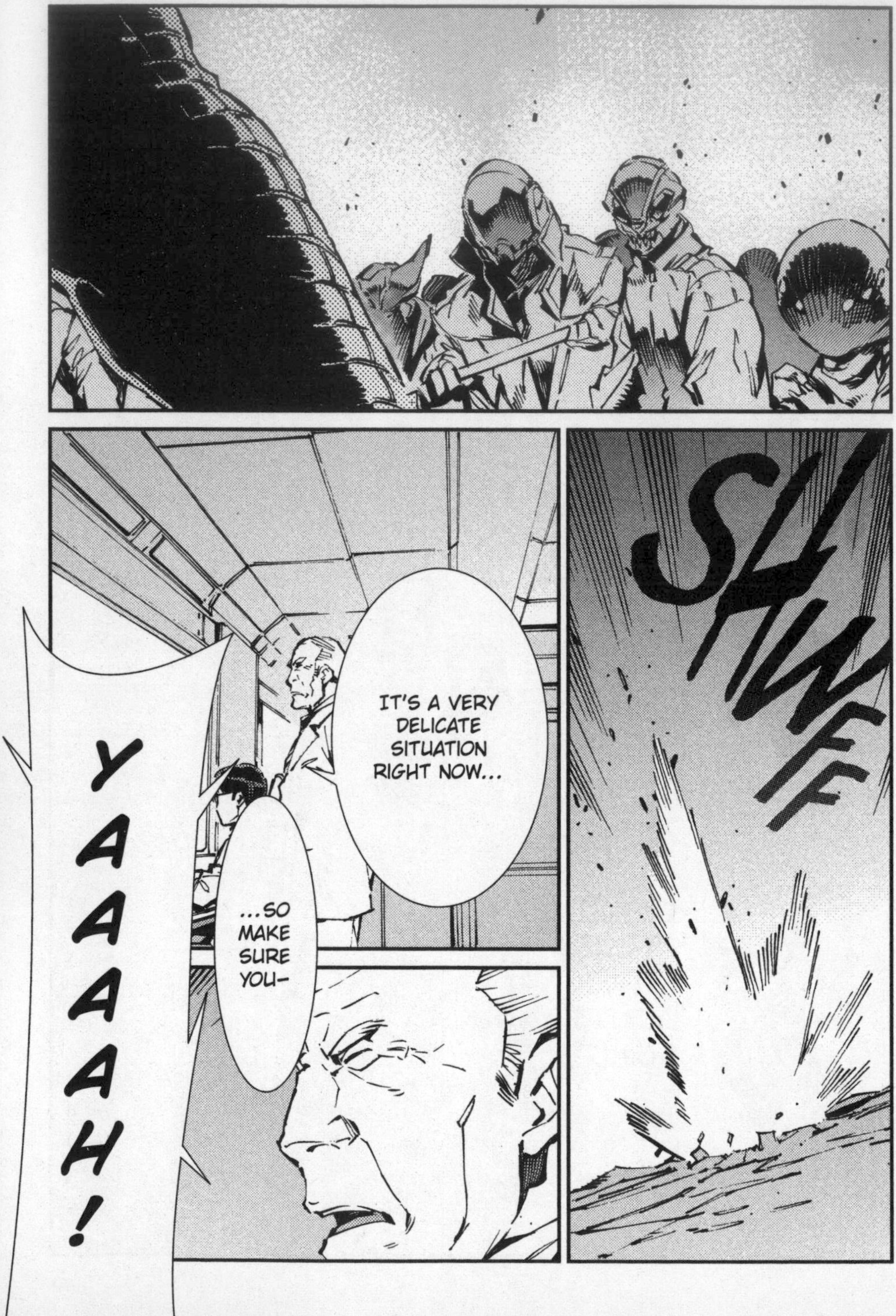
SHWFF
IT'S A VERY DELICATE SITUATION RIGHT NOW...
...SO MAKE SURE YOU-
YAAAAH!

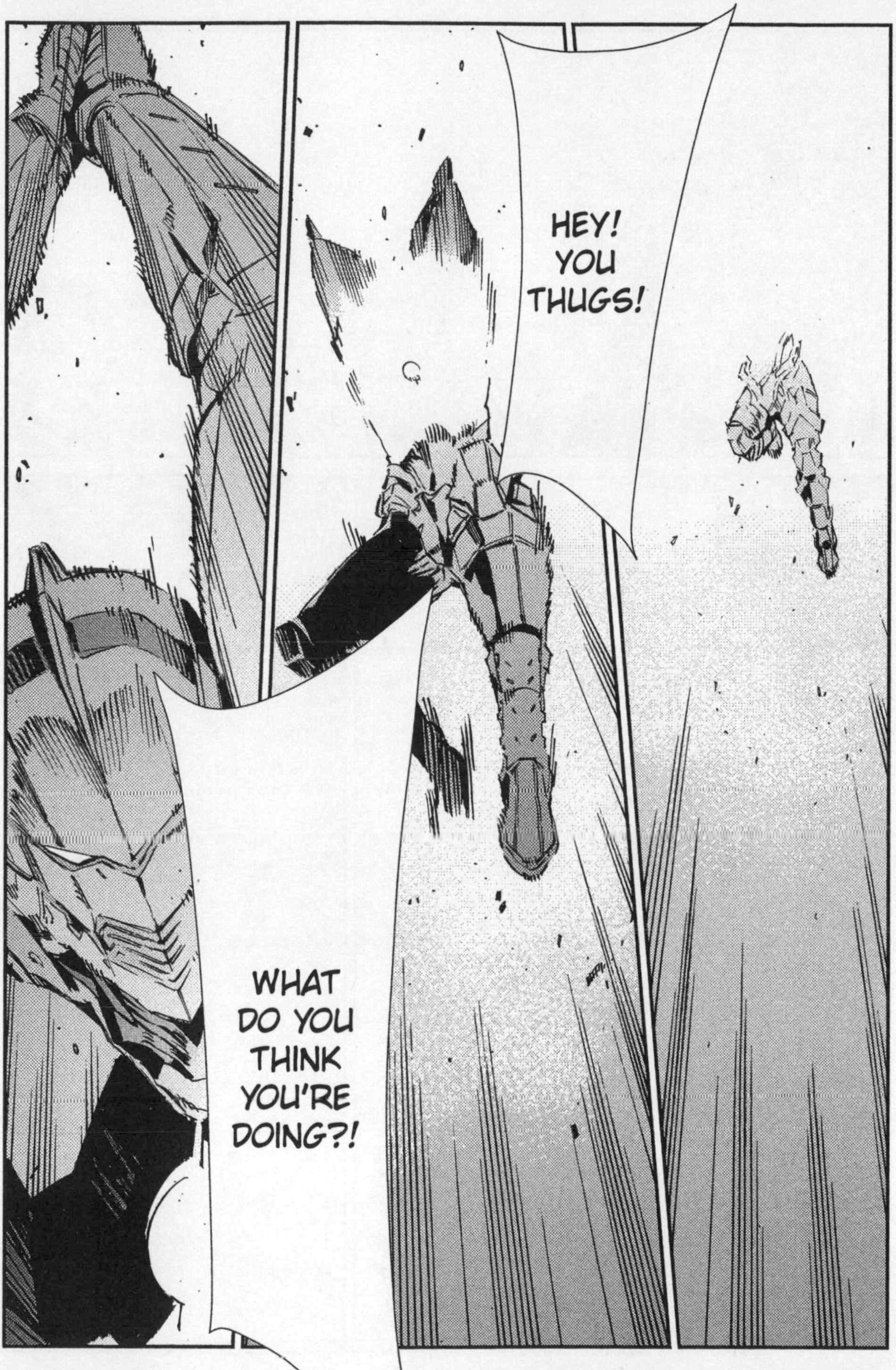
HEY! YOU THUGS!
WHAT DO YOU THINK YOU'RE DOING?!

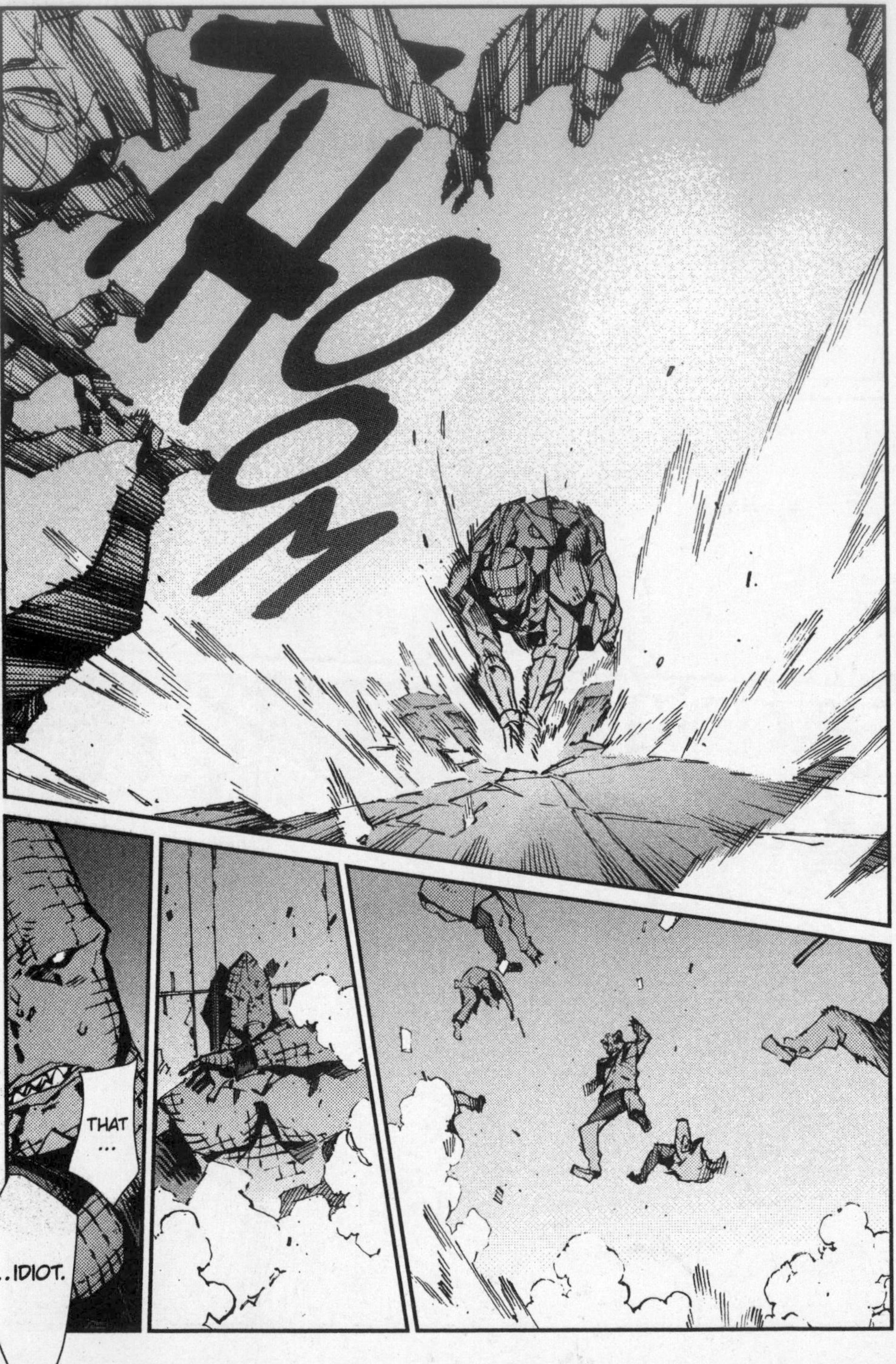
THOOM
THAT ...
...IDIOT.

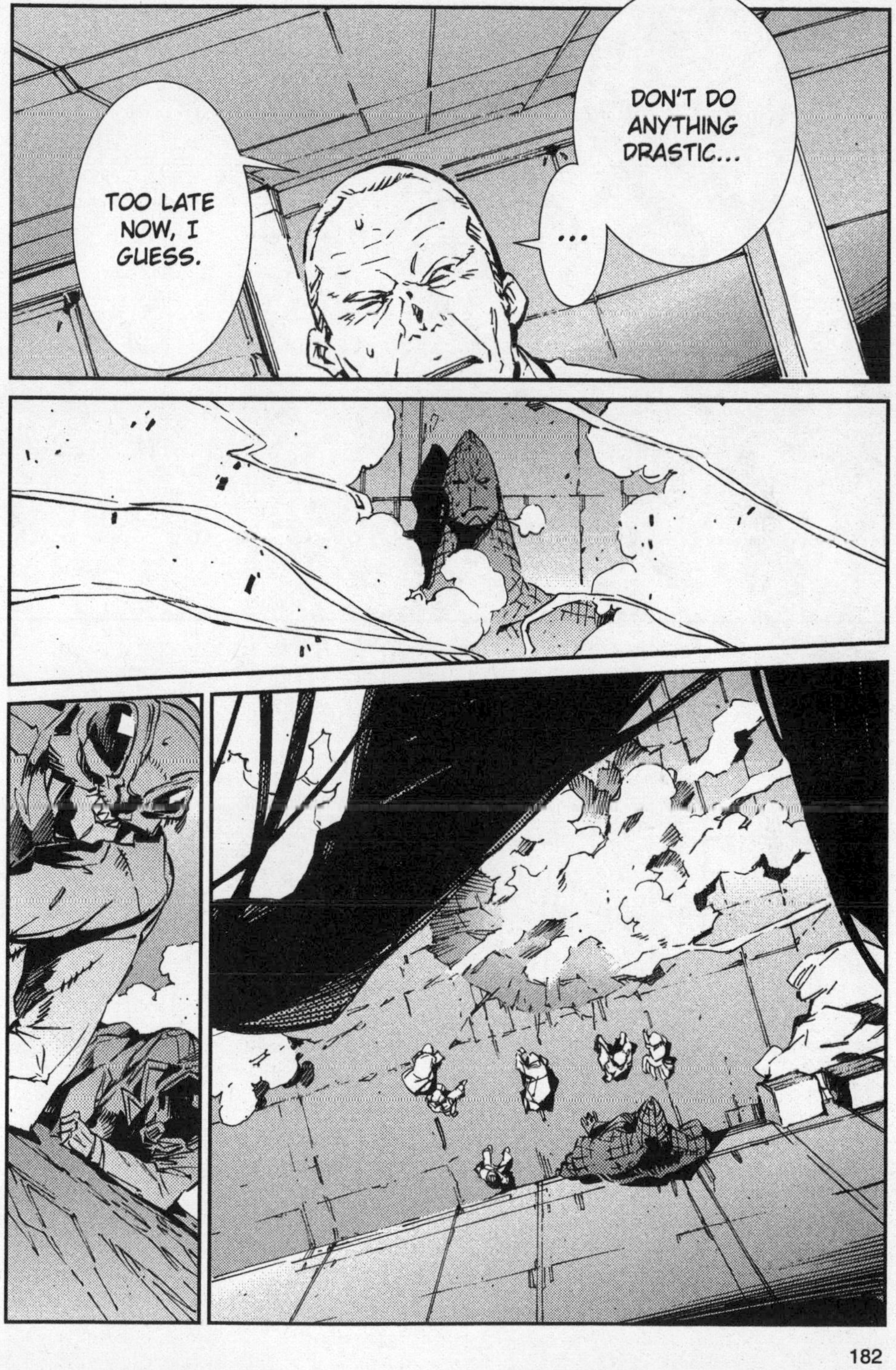
DON'T DO ANYTHING DRASTIC...
...
TOO LATE NOW, I GUESS.

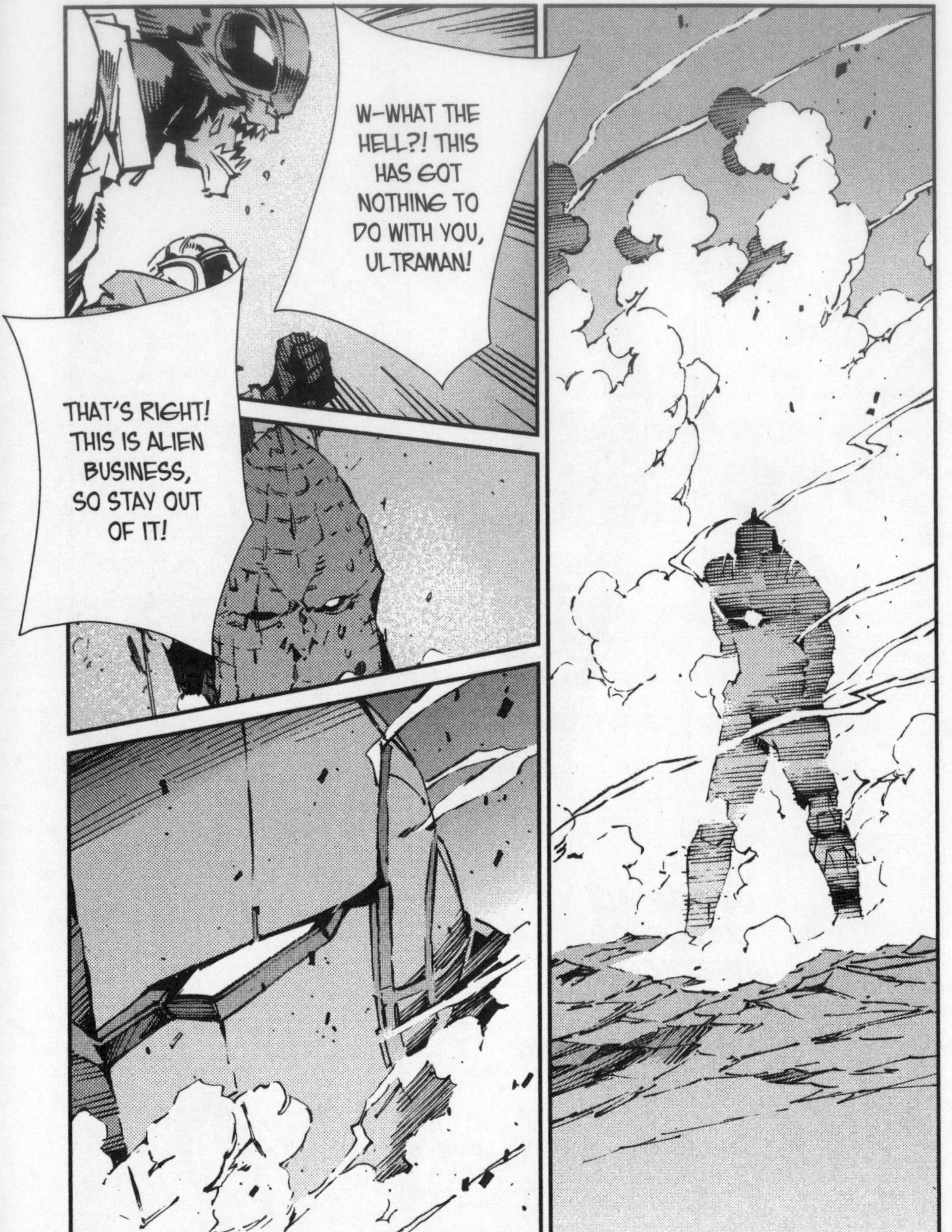
W-WHAT THE HELL?! THIS HAS GOT NOTHING TO DO WITH YOU, ULTRAMAN!
THAT'S RIGHT! THIS IS ALIEN BUSINESS, SO STAY OUT OF IT!

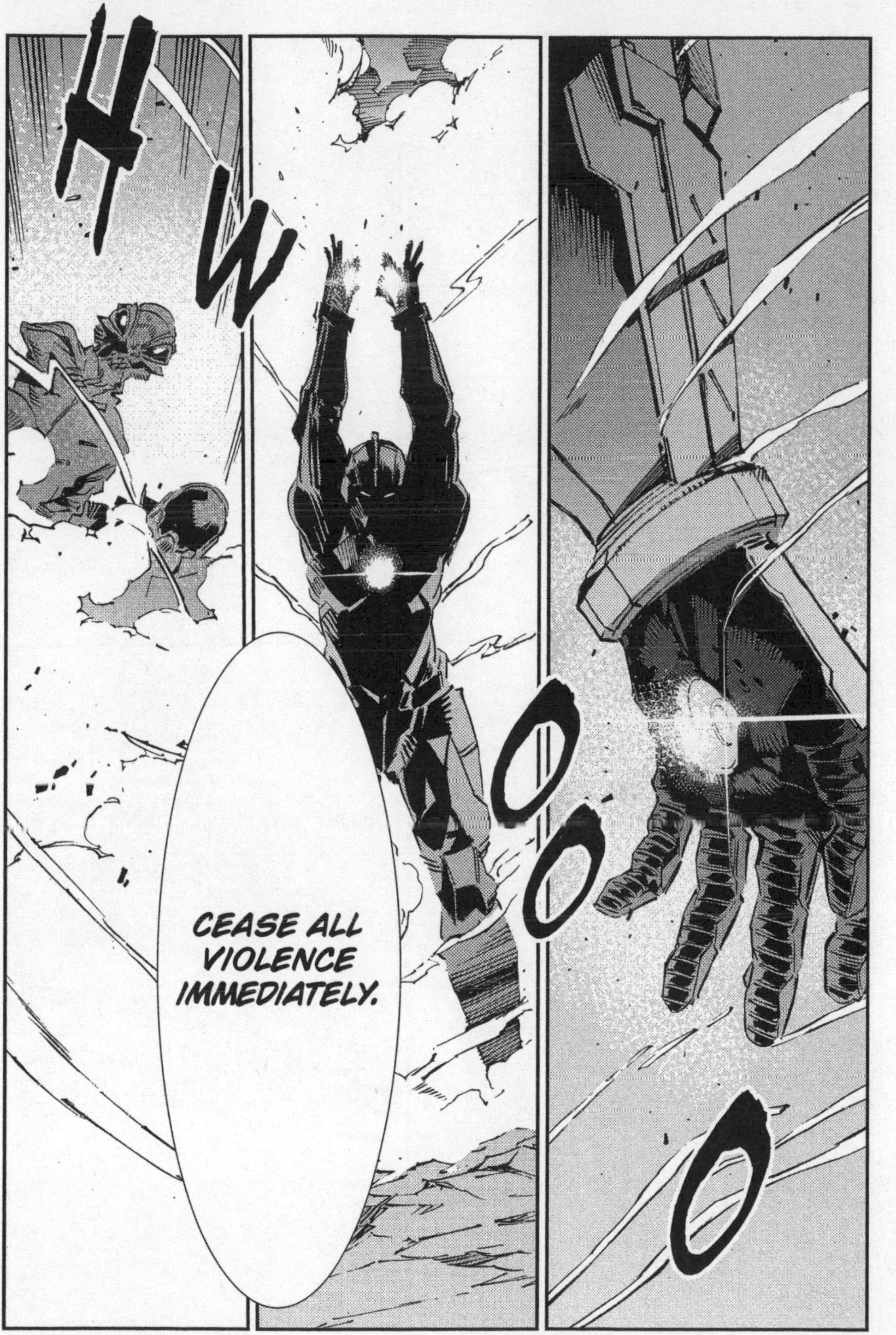
HWOOOO
CEASE ALL VIOLENCE IMMEDIATELY.

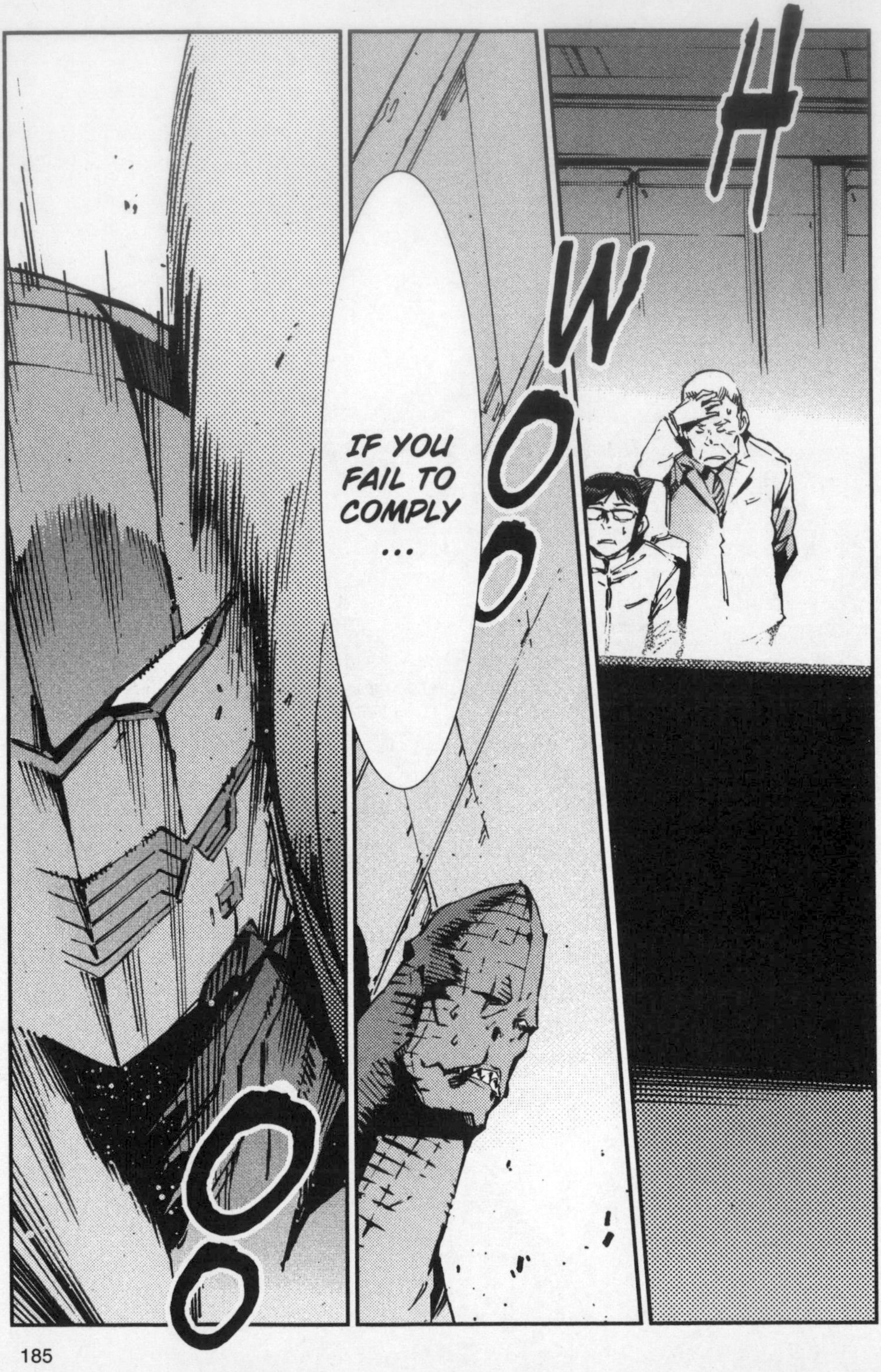
HWOOOO
IF YOU FAIL TO COMPLY ...

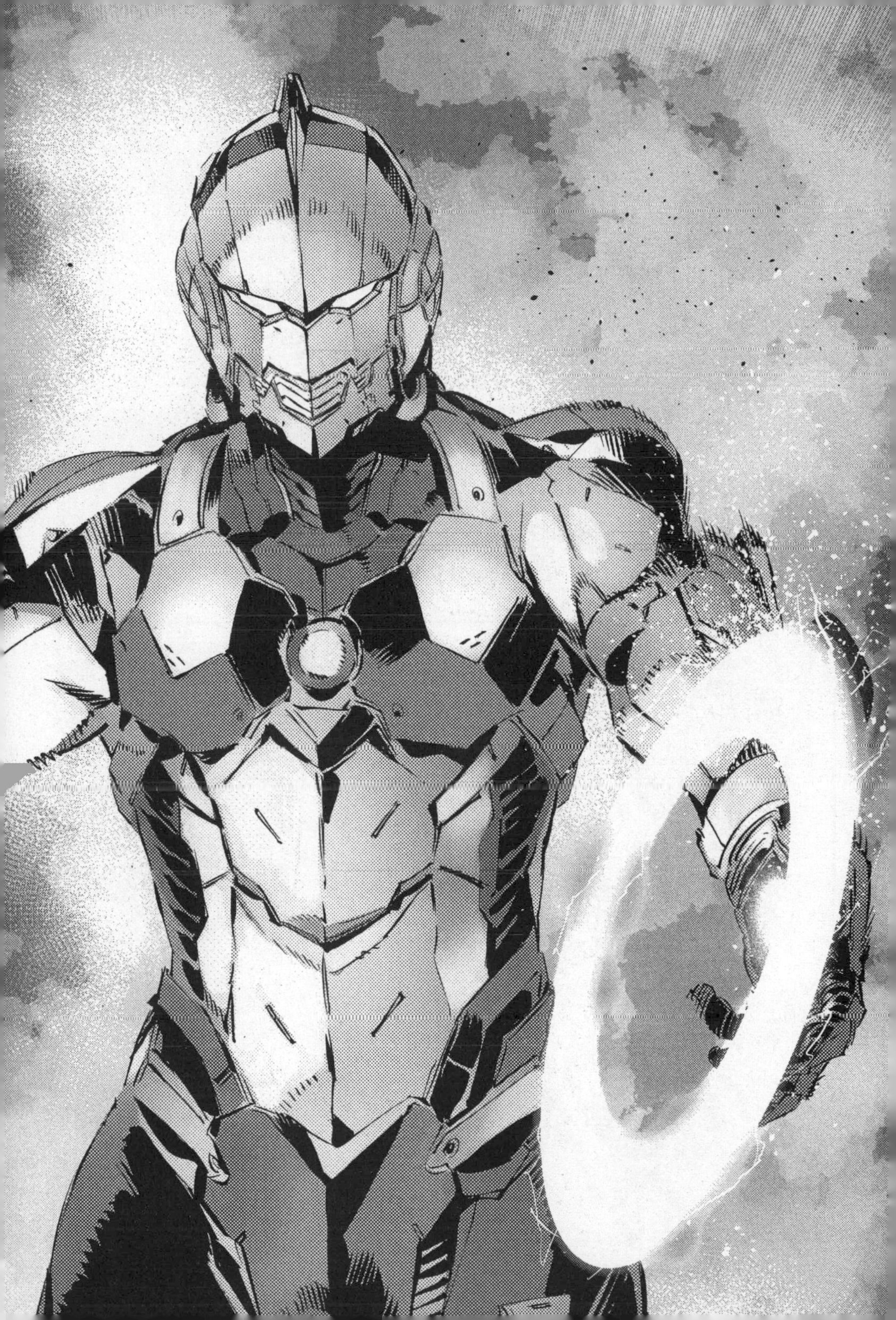

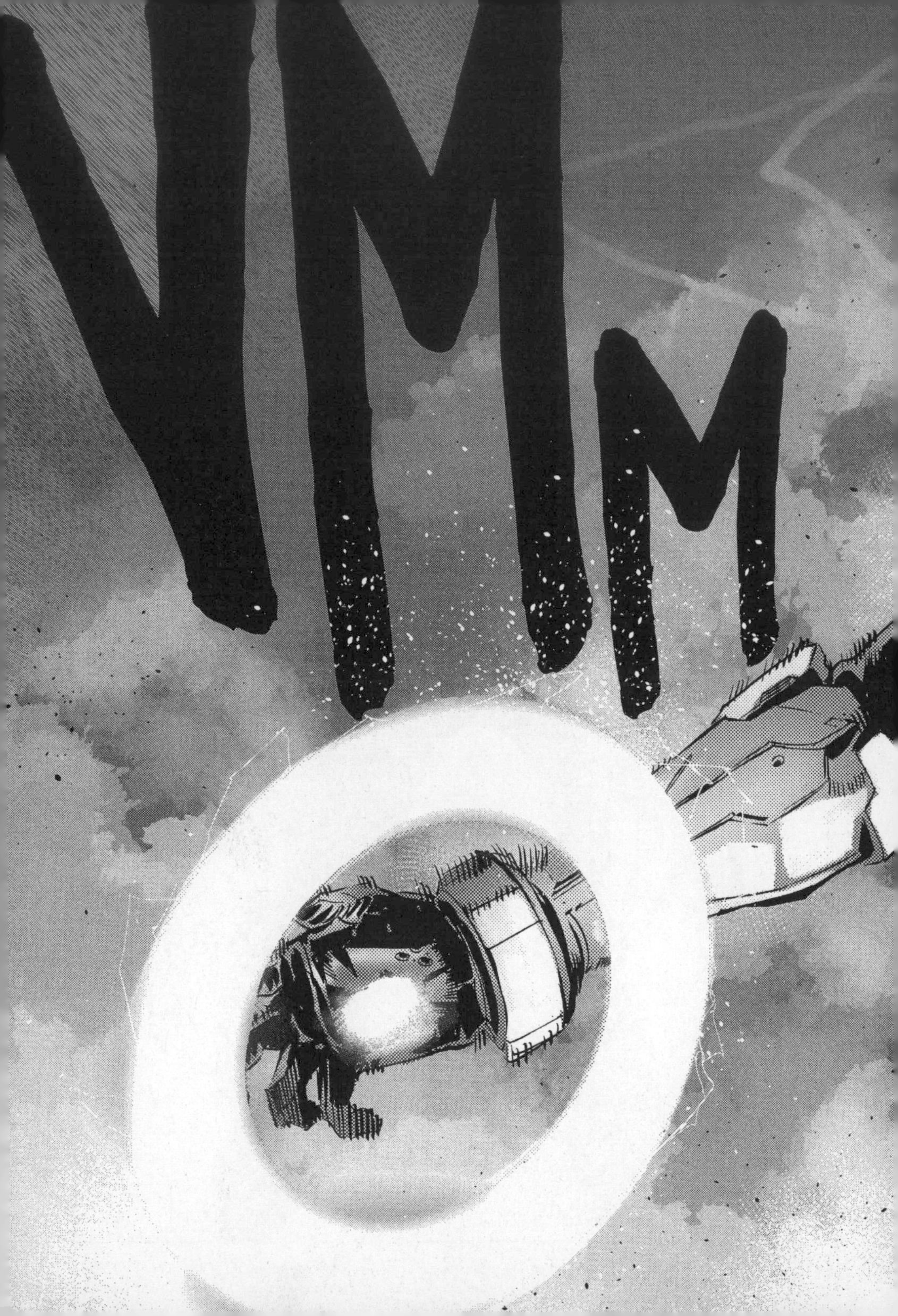
VMM

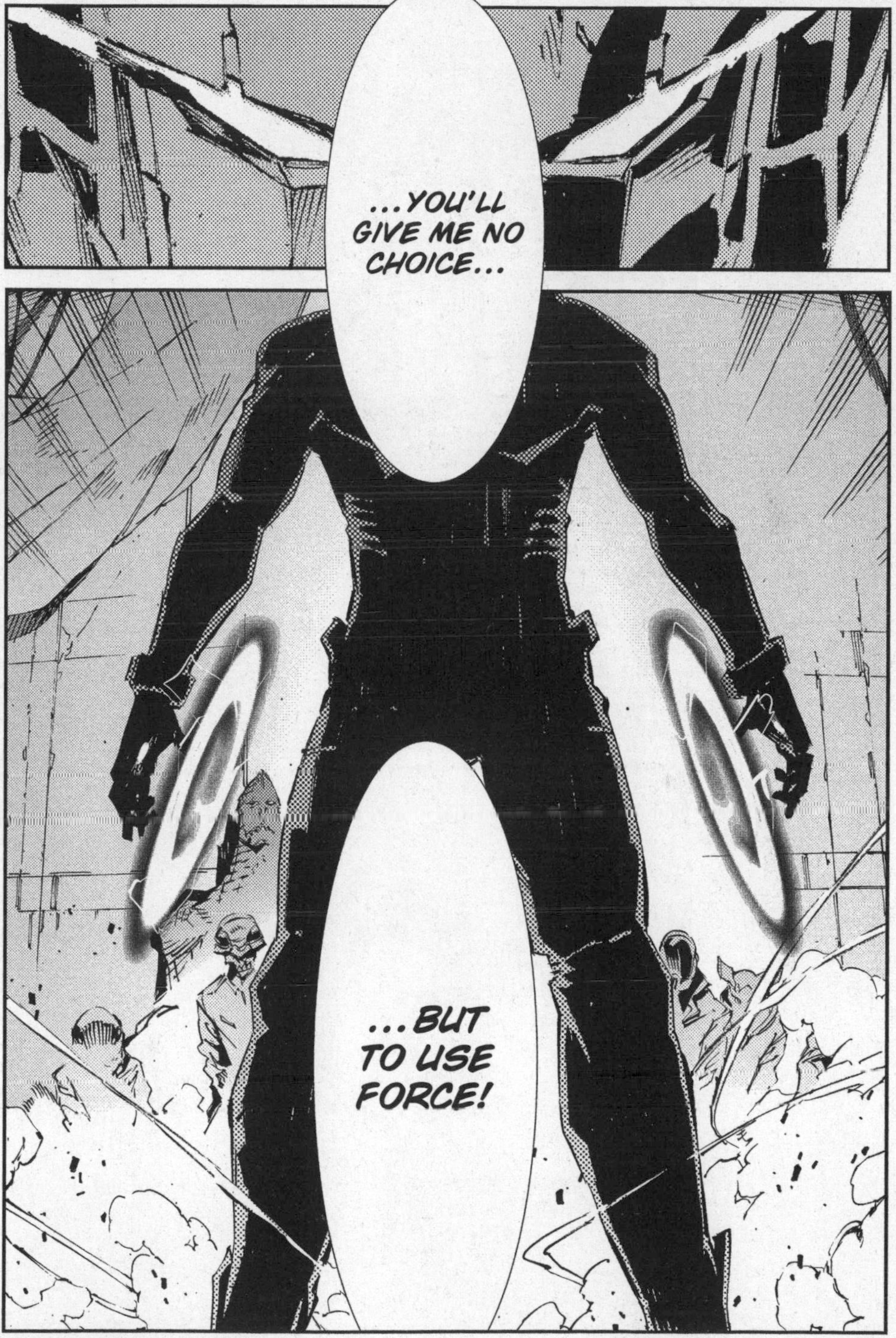
...YOU'LL GIVE ME NO CHOICE...
...BUT TO USE FORCE!

ULTRAMAN 12 - END

THIS IS THE BEGINNING OF A NEW AGE

ULTRAMAN SUIT TYPE B

■ A new Ultraman suit built specifically for Shinjiro. This suit is called Type B to differentiate it from its predecessor (the previous suit is now referred to as Type A).

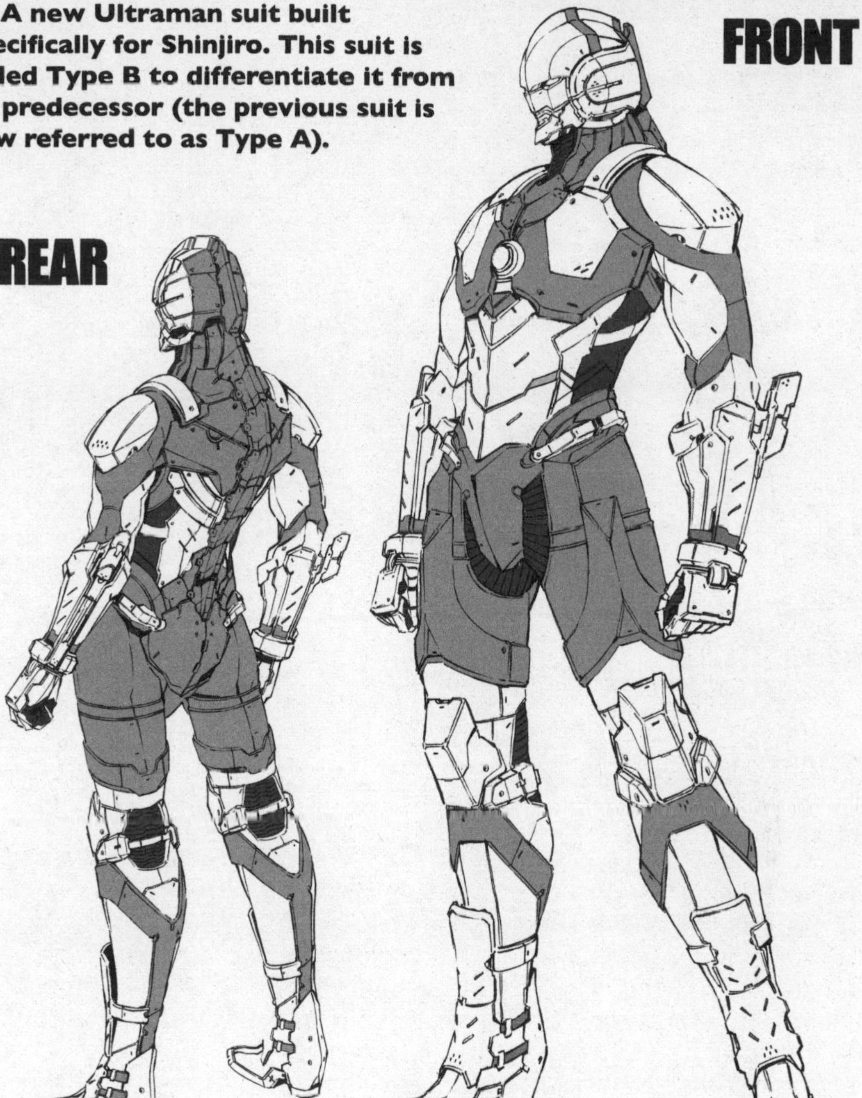
FRONT
REAR

■ As Shinjiro's physical abilities improved due to the Ultraman Factor, the previous suit's mobility and features began to hinder him. Realizing the suit—which was intended to assist and amplify Shinjiro's abilities and defenses—was now restricting him, Ide began development of a new, improved suit. Upgrades were made to three areas: the weight, servos and ancillary equipment.

■ Taking notice of the Ace suit's far-superior functionality in these three areas, Ide worked with Yapool to develop the new suit on an aggressive schedule. The auxiliary motor now uses the nano motor designed for the Ace suit. Ide is currently developing a way for the suit to be wearable during teleportation, like the Ace and Jack suits. Coloring changes were made to suit Ide's taste.

ARM

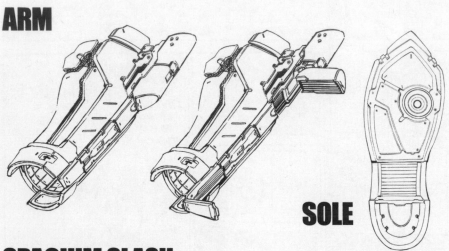

SOLE

SPACIUM SLASH

■ In addition to a Cloaking device (providing invisibility) and image-simulation abilities, the Type B suit is equipped with a new Spacium weapon in both palms (the Cloaking feature had previously been implemented on the Seven suit). The generators in the palm create Spacium energy rings that can be used to fire projectiles. After some initial debate over what to call the new weapon (including some rather unsettling and inappropriate suggestions), Ide decided to simply refer to it as the Spacium Slash. Design is currently underway for exterior weapons that conserve energy while the Spacium weapons are in use. They are being developed specifically for Shinjiro.

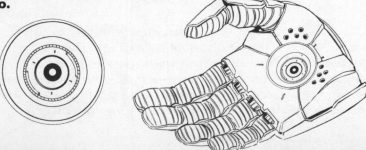

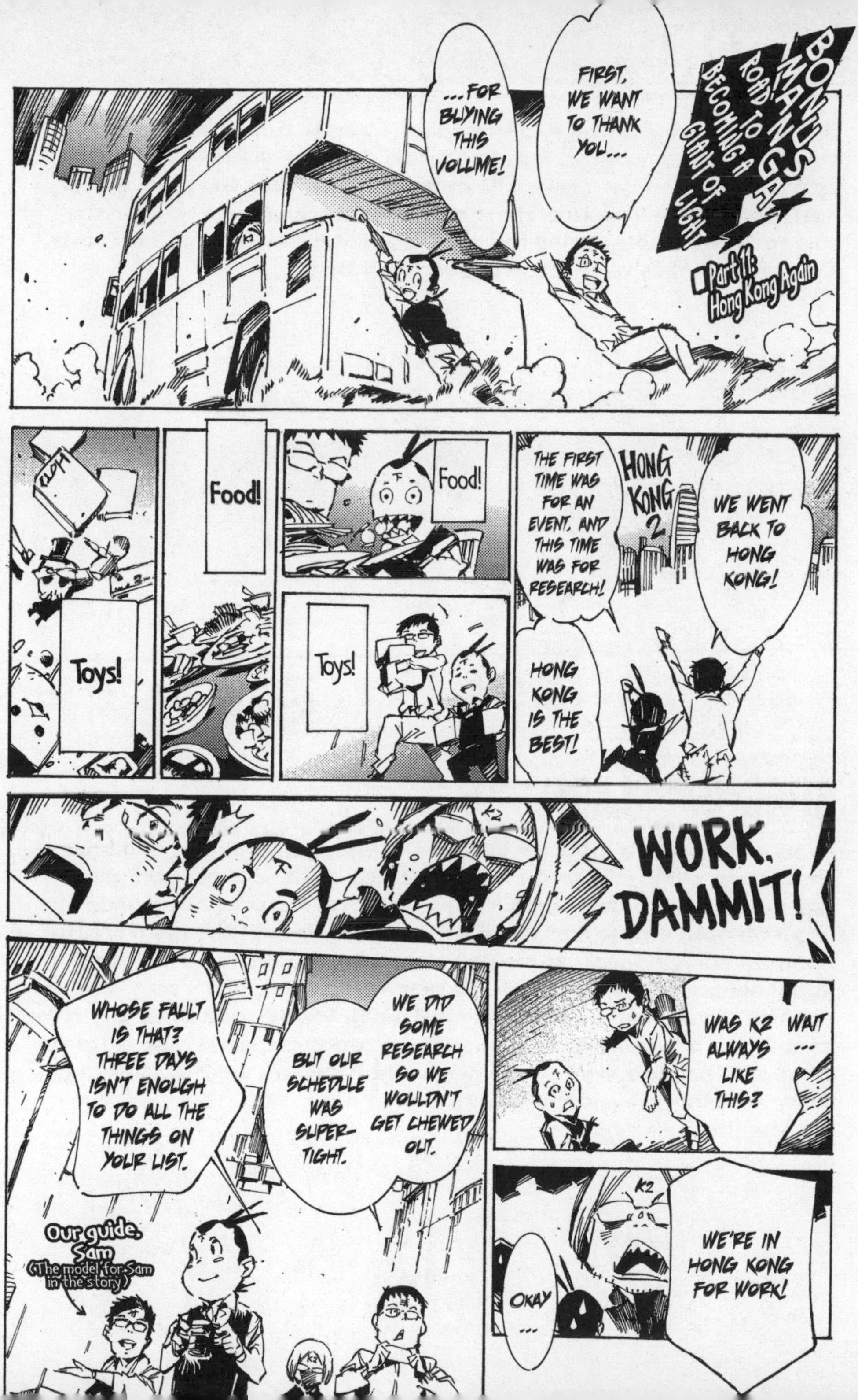
BONUS MANGA: ROAD TO BECOMING A GIANT OF LIGHT
Part 11: Hong Kong Again
FIRST, WE WANT TO THANK YOU...
...FOR BUYING THIS VOLUME!
WE WENT BACK TO HONG KONG!
THE FIRST TIME WAS FOR AN EVENT, AND THIS TIME WAS FOR RESEARCH!
HONG KONG 2
HONG KONG IS THE BEST!
Food!
Toys!
Food!
Toys!
WORK, DAMMIT!
WAIT...
WAS K2 ALWAYS LIKE THIS?
WE'RE IN HONG KONG FOR WORK!
OKAY...
WE DID SOME RESEARCH SO WE WOULDN'T GET CHEWED OUT.
BUT OUR SCHEDULE WAS SUPER-TIGHT.
WHOSE FAULT IS THAT? THREE DAYS ISN'T ENOUGH TO DO ALL THE THINGS ON YOUR LIST.
Our guide, Sam
(The model for Sam in the story)

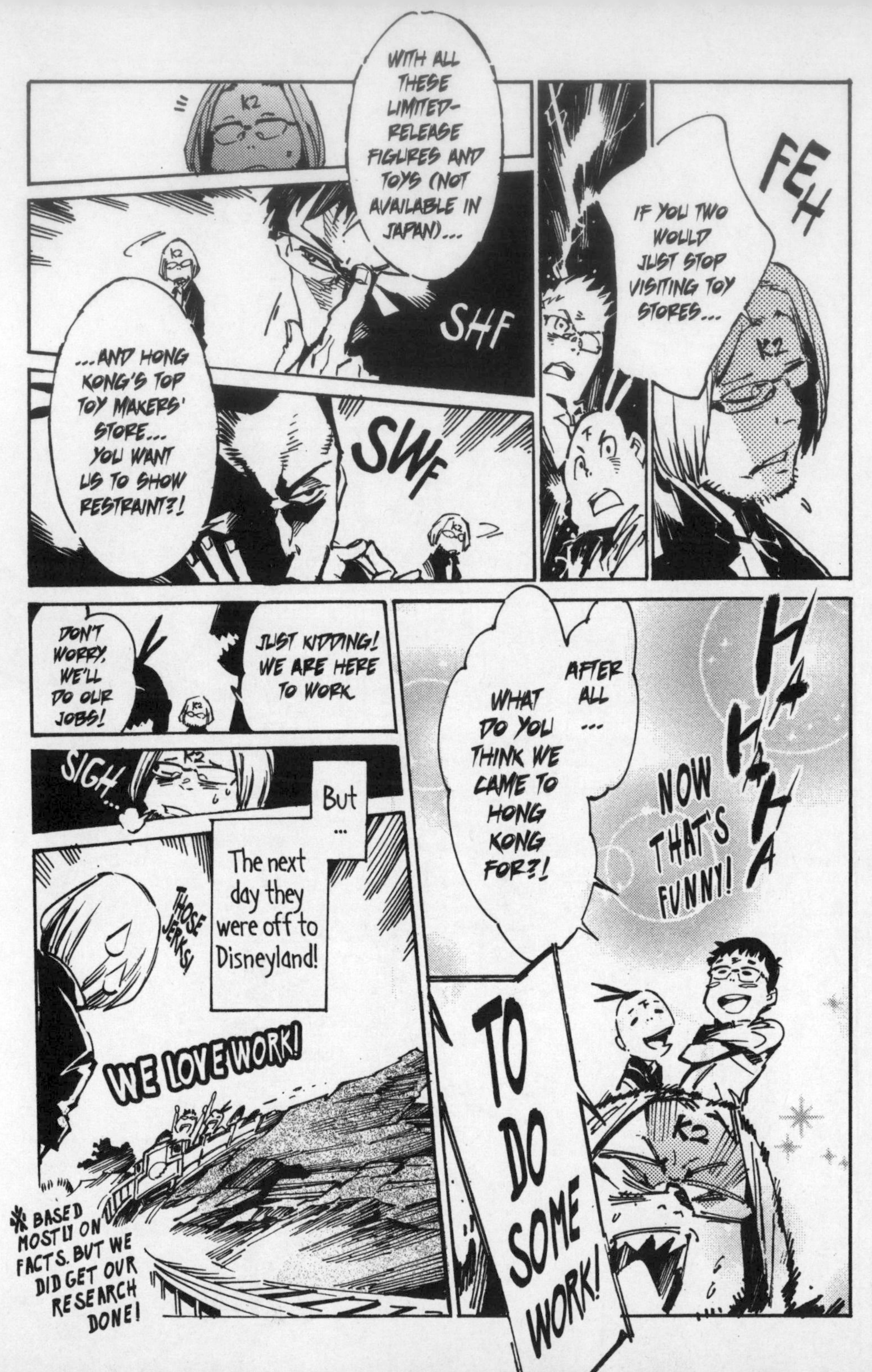
FEH
IF YOU TWO WOULD JUST STOP VISITING TOY STORES...
WITH ALL THESE LIMITED-RELEASE FIGURES AND TOYS (NOT AVAILABLE IN JAPAN)...
SHF
...AND HONG KONG'S TOP TOY MAKERS' STORE... YOU WANT US TO SHOW RESTRAINT?!
SWF
AFTER ALL...
WHAT DO YOU THINK WE CAME TO HONG KONG FOR?!
HA HA HA HA
NOW THAT'S FUNNY!
TO DO SOME WORK!
JUST KIDDING! WE ARE HERE TO WORK.
DON'T WORRY, WE'LL DO OUR JOBS!
SIGH...
But...
The next day they were off to Disneyland!
THOSE JERKS!
WE LOVE WORK!
※BASED MOSTLY ON FACTS. BUT WE DID GET OUR RESEARCH DONE!

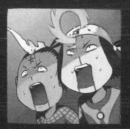

EIICHI SHIMIZU × TOMOHIRO SHIMOGUCHI

We went on a research trip to Hong Kong for this volume.
We fell in love right away. The people were friendly,
everything we ate was delicious, and most importantly,
there are a ton of toy stores!! That part is important,
so let me say it again. There are a ton of toy stores!!!
To illustrate how amazing it is, an action figure that
was sold-out everywhere I looked was for sale at the
airport!! In other words, there are stores that sell
high-end toys even at the airport.
Banzai Hong Kong!

ULTRAMAN

VOLUME 12
VIZ SIGNATURE EDITION

STORY/ART BY **EIICHI SHIMIZU** AND **TOMOHIRO SHIMOGUCHI**

©2018 Eiichi Shimizu and Tomohiro Shimoguchi / TSUBURAYA PROD.
Originally published by HERO'S INC.

TRANSLATION **JOE YAMAZAKI**
ENGLISH ADAPTATION **STAN!**
TOUCH-UP ART & LETTERING **EVAN WALDINGER**
DESIGN **KAM LI**
EDITOR **MIKE MONTESA**

Printed in the U.S.A.

Published by VIZ Media, LLC
P.O. Box 77010
San Francisco, CA 94107

10 9 8 7 6 5 4 3 2 1
First printing, June 2019

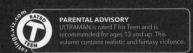

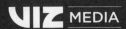

viz.com   vizsignature.com

HEY! YOU'RE READING IN THE WRONG DIRECTION!

This is the END of the graphic novel

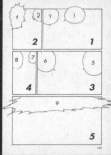

Follow the action this way.

To properly enjoy this VIZ graphic novel, please turn it around and begin reading from RIGHT TO LEFT. Unlike English, Japanese is read right to left, so Japanese comics are read in reverse order from the way English comics are typically read.

This book has been printed in the original Japanese format in order to preserve the orientation of the original artwork.

HAVE FUN WITH IT!